Shabbat
Connections

KABBALAH
CENTRE
PUBLISHING

© 2004, 2016 Kabbalah Centre International, Inc. All rights reserved.

No part of this publication may be reproduced or transmitted in any form or by any means, electronic or mechanical, including photocopying, recording, or by any information storage and retrieval system, without permission in writing from the publisher, except by a reviewer who wishes to quote brief passages in connection with a review written for inclusion in a magazine, newspaper, or broadcast.

Kabbalah Centre Publishing is a registered DBA of
Kabbalah Centre International, Inc.

For further information:

The Kabbalah Centre
155 E. 48th St., New York, NY 10017
1062 S. Robertson Blvd., Los Angeles, CA 90035

1.800.Kabbalah   www.kabbalah.com

Printed in China, **July** 2018

ISBN: 978-1-57189-946-0

Design: HL Design (Hyun Min Lee)   www.hldesignco.com

Table of Contents

Introduction
- Rav Berg on the Nature of Shabbat ... 1
- Shabbat Structure ... 4
- The Zohar on Shabbat Meals and Songs ... 5
- Hafrashat Chalah (Separating the Dough) ... 7
- Candle Lighting for Shabbat and Holidays ... 13

Kabbalat Shabbat Connection ... 21
- Mizmor LeDavid (A Psalm of David) ... 23
- Ana Beko'ach ... 27
  - Angels of Friday Night ... 29
  - Tikkun HaNefesh ... 30
- Lecha Dodi (Go My beloved) ... 31
- Mizmor Shir leYom HaShabbat (A Psalm, a Song for the Day of Shabbat) 34
  - Bar Yochai ... 38
  - Kegavna (Just as They) ... 41

First Meal Connection-Chakal Tapuchin Kadishin (Friday Night) .. 43
- Shalom Alechem (Peace Be Upon You) ... 45
  - Ribon Kol HaOlamim (Master of the Worlds) ... 46
- Eshet Chayil (Woman of Valor) ... 48
  - Blessing Over the Myrtle Branches ... 51
- Kiddush (Blessing Over the Wine) for Friday Night ... 52
  - Blessing for Children ... 54
- Atkinu-Azamer (Prepare the Feast-I Will Sing) ... 56
- Kol Mekadesh (Whoever Sanctifies) ... 60

Second Meal Connection-Atika Kadisha (Saturday Morning) ... 63
- Kiddusha Rabba (Blessing Over the Wine) of Saturday Morning ... 65
- Atkinu-Asader (Prepare the Feast-I Will Prepare) ... 67
- Baruch Hashem (Blessed is the Lord)-Bom Bom ... 69

Third Meal Connection-Zeir Anpin (Saturday Afternoon) ... 73
- Atkinu-Benei Hechala (Prepare the Feast-Members of the Chambers) ... 75
- Mizmor LeDavid (A Psalm of David) ... 78
- Yetzaveh (May the Rock Command) ... 79
- El Mistater (God is Concealed) ... 81
- Ein Kelokenu (There is None Like our God) ... 84
- Atah Hu Elokenu (You are our God) ... 85
- Kiddush (Blessing Over the Wine) of the Third Meal ... 86
- Yedid Nefesh (Beloved of the Soul) ... 87

Table of Contents

Blessings 89
   Blessings Before Food 91
      Netilat Yadayim (Washing of the Hands) 93
      Hamotzi (Blessing Over Bread) 94
   Birkat Hamazon (Blessing After the Meal) 95
      Sheva Berachot (Seven Blessings) 114
      Bore Peri HaGefen (Blessing Over the Wine) 116
Me'en Shalosh (Resembling Three)-Last Blessing 117
Bore Nefashot (Who Has Created Living Beings)-Last Blessing 119

Havdalah and Fourth Meal Connection 121
   Havdalah of Saturday night 123
   Melaveh Malkah Connection 127
      Hamavdil (He Who Separates) 128
      Yehi Hachodesh Hazeh (May this Month Be) 130
      Amar Hashem LeYaakov (The Lord Told Jacob) ... 131
      Veyiten Lecha (And may God give you)-Verses for Success 134

Additional Songs (alphabetic order) 139
   Aderaba (On the Contrary) 176
   Adir hu (Mighty is He) 176
   Ahalela (I Shall Praise) 203
   Ahavat Olam (Everlasting Love) 176
   Al Tira (Do Not Be Afraid) 178
   Al Tira—Utzu Etza (Do Not Be Afraid—Devise a Plan) 178
   Amar Rabbi Akiva (Rav Akiva Says) 179
   Ana Hashem (Please Lord) 179
   Ane'im Zemirot (Song of Glory) 169
   Ani Ma'amin (I Believe) 180
   Asher Bara (Who Created Joy) 181
   Ashirah Lashem (I Shall Sing to the Lord) 180
   Atah Takum (You Shall Rise) 181
   Atiti Lechanenach (I Have Come to Plead Before You) 205
   Avinu Av Harachaman (Our Father, Merciful Father) 175
   Avinu Malkenu (Our Father, Our King) 175
   Baruch El Elyon (Blessed is the Supernal God) 148
   Becha Batchu (In You They Trust) 182
   Beshem Hashem (In the Name of the Lord) 182
   Biglal Avot (For the Sake of the Ancestors) 181
   Bilvavi (In My Heart) 181
   Chasdei Hashem (The Mercy of the Lord) 190
   Chemdat Yamim (Most Coveted of Days) 190

TABLE OF CONTENTS

David Melech Israel (David, King of Israel)	183
Deror Yikra (Call for Freedom)	152
El Na (Please God)	177
Elecha (To You)	178
En Aroch Lecha (There is No Comparison to You)	177
Gam Ki Elech (Though I walk)	183
Harachaman (The Compassionate One)	185
Hashem Lo Gava Libi (Lord, my Heart is Not Proud)	184
Hashem Melech (The Lord is King)	183
Hashem Oz Le'amo Yiten (The Lord Gives Might To His People)	184
Hashivenu (Bring Us Back to You)	186
Hashmi'ini Et Kolech (Let Me Hear Your Voice)	206
Hatov (The Good One)	184
Hazor'im Bedim'ah (Those Who Sow With Tears)	208
Hineh Ma Tov (Behold, How Good)	185
Hineh Yamim Ba'im (Behold, the Days Come)	185
Hineni Beyadecha (I Am in Your Hands)	203
Hoshi'a et Amecha (Redeem Your Nation)	184
Im Eshkachech (If I Forget You)	179
Ish Yehudi (A Man From the Tribe of Yehuda)	209
Kanfei Ru'ach (Wings of Spirit)	204
Ke'ayal Ta'arog (As the Hart is Longing)	193
Ki Besimcha Tetze'u (For You Shall Go Out with Joy)	194
Ki Eshmera Shabbat (When I Guard the Shabbat)	150
Ki Hirbeta (Since You Have Given Much)	194
Ki Lishu'atcha (Because it is For Your Salvation)	194
Kol Ha'olam Kulo (The Whole World)	195
Kol Zeman (As Long)	195
Lema'an Achay vere'ay (Because of My Brothers and Friends)	196
Lema'anche (For Your Sake)	204
Leshanah Haba'ah (Next Year)	196
Lo Yisa (Nation Shall not Lift Up)	195
Lulei Toratcha (Unless Your Torah)	195
Mah Yedidut (How Beloved is Your Tranquility)	143
Melech Rachman (Compassionate King)	197
Menucha Vesimcha (Contentment and Gladness)	141
Mi Ha'ish (Who is the Man)	194
Mi Shema'amin (He Who Believes)	197
Mikolot Mayim Rabim (Mightier Than the Noise of Many Waters)	206
Mimekomcha (From Your Place)	198
Min Hametzar (Out of My Distress)	198
Moshe Emet (Moses is True)	198
Na'ale (We Shall Go Up)	199
Ochila LaEl (I Shall Put My Hop in God)	205
Od Yishama (May There Ever be Heard)	199
Or Zaru'a Latzadik (Light is Sown for the Righteous)	177

TABLE OF CONTENTS

Orech Yamim (With Long Life)	180
Pitchu Li (Open to Me)	199
Shabechi Yerushalayim (Praise the Lord, Jerusalem)	200
Shifchi (Pour Out)	201
Shir Lama'alot (A Song of Ascents)	201
Shomer Israel (Guardian of Israel)	200
Shomrim (Watchmen)	200
Shoshanat Yaacov (Lily of Jacob)	208
Simcha Le'artzecha (Gladness to Your Land)	201
Tefilah Le'ani (A Prayer of the Poor)	202
Tehe Hasha'a Hazot (May This Time Be)	202
Tov Lehodot (It is Good to Say Thanks)	190
Tzam'ah Nafshi (My Soul Thirsts)	146
Tzur Meshelo Achalnu (The Rock, Whose Food We Have Eaten)	160
Ufduye (And the Redeemed)	189
Ufros (And Spread)	189
Umacha (And the Lord Will Wipe Away)	188
Uva'u Ha'ovdim (They Who Lose Shall Come Back)	186
Va'amartem Ko Lechai ("And You Should Say: Live Long")	162
Ve'afilu Behastara (Even in a Concealment)	207
Ve'ata Banim (And Now, Sons)	188
Veha'er Enenu (Enlighten Our Eyes)	186
Vehar'enu (And Show Us)	187
Vehi She'amda (It is This That Has Stood)	187
Vekarev Pezurenu (Draw Near Our Scattered)	189
Velirushalayim (And to Jerusalem)	187
Venisgav (And the Lord Will be Exalted)	188
Vesamachta Bechagecha (And You Shall Rejoice in your Feast)	189
Vetaher Libenu (And Purify Our Hearts)	187
Veten Banu (Give Us a Virtuous Desire)	190
Yachad (Together)	191
Yah Echsof (Yah, How I Yearn for the Bliss of Shabbat)	173
Yah Ribon Olam (Yah, Master of the World)	145
Yamim (Days)	191
Yasis (Your God Will Rejoice)	192
Yehi Shalom (May There be Peace)	191
Yerushalayim Oro Shel Olam (Jerusalem is the Light of the World)	192
Yibane Hamikdash (May the Temple be Rebuilt)	191
Yifrach Beyamav Tzadik (In His Days May the Righteous Flourish)	192
Yisrael Betach Bahashem (Israel, Trust in the Lord)	193
Yitbarech Shimcha (May Your Name be Blessed)	193
Yoducha Ra'ayonai (My Thoughts Thank You)	161
Yom Shabbaton (The Resting Day)	158
Yom Zeh LeYisrael (This Day is for Israel)	153
Yom Zeh Mechubad (This Day is Most Honored)	156

Introduction

RAV BERG ON THE NATURE OF SHABBAT
SHABBAT STRUCTURE
THE ZOHAR ON SHABBAT MEALS AND SONGS
HAFRASHAT CHALAH (SEPARATING THE DOUGH)
CANDLE LIGHTING FOR SHABBAT AND HOLIDAYS

INTRODUCTION: RAV BERG ON THE NATURE OF SHABBAT

RAV BERG ON THE NATURE OF SHABBAT

Why is the Seventh Day called *Shabbat*?

Some say it comes from the word *vayishbot* (Genesis 2:2), which is related to the word *shvita*, meaning "not to work." However, the *Zohar* (Vayakhel 180) explains that this meaning is superficial, that, in fact, the inner meaning of the word *Shabbat* goes far beyond the aspect of *shvita*, "not working."

There are the six days of the week and then there is the creation of the Seventh Day. On the Seventh Day, the Lord injected the aspect of automatic balance within the Universe.

The *Zohar* (Zohar Chadash, Yitro 89) brings to our attention that the third day is the *Sefira* of *Tiferet*, which is also a balancing energy-intelligence. In fact the third day is considered a *good day* because while in the case of almost all of the other days it says *Vayar Elokim ki tov* (and God saw that it was good), on the third day the Torah writes *ki tov*, twice (Genesis 1:9 and 1:12). It is from this that the idea has emerged that Tuesday (the third day) is a good day to begin a venture.

The *Zohar* (Ibid 82) says the third day is good because it is *Tiferet*, and *Tiferet* has the power to balance. Similarly, *Yesod* (the sixth day) also has the power to balance. If we consider the *Magen David* (Star of David), *Tiferet* is the balancing agent in the Upper Triad and *Yesod* is the balancing agent in the Lower Triad.

Why is it written (Genesis 2:3) that *Shabbat* is something special, *vayekadesh Oto*, made it holy? *Shabbat* (שבת) is *Shin*(ש)-*Bet*(ב)-*Tav*(ת), which is the *Sefira* of *Malchut*, the code name for the seventh day. *Malchut* is the manifestation of everything that preceded it. It all becomes manifested as one complete unit in *Malchut*. The *Zohar* says (Vayakhel 180), *hamita'achadim bevat yechida shehi haMalchut*, *Malchut* combines everything into one unified whole.

God made the Seventh Day holy because He injected and infused the cosmos with a built-in filament. The *Zohar* asks, "How is it different from Tuesday?" It also has an infusion of this neutralizing, harmonizing power, the filament. On Tuesday (third day, *Tiferet*) and Friday (sixth day, *Yesod*) God also injected into the universe a force of balance. The difference is that on the third day and the sixth day the harmonizing force by and within itself will not combine Right and Left. It is up to man. On Tuesday and Friday humanity has to work at bringing about the symmetry of that day, the thought energy-intelligence of restriction. It has been established and is available in a potential form, but we have to work for it.

The *Zohar* says, *Shabbat: Hi me'ateret et kulam*—She crowns all of the days of the week. This means that on *Shabbat* there is no effort required on our part to create the symmetry. It was created as an all-inclusive, all harmonized state without our intervention—this is what God created. And it is called *Shabbat* because *Shin*(ש) represents the Three Columns, all six days crowned into one unified whole. *Shabbat* is the unification of all three diversified forces.

Without the six components, *Shabbat* could not be revealed. Why do we have to go through these six stages? Because this is the way of Creation: To ultimately arrive at the fruit, which then again bears the seed in this physical world, we must go through a series of six energy-intelligences. *Shabbat* is the harmonization, the completion of all six, it is the fruit, which also bears the seed. It is the first aspect all over again.

INTRODUCTION: RAV BERG ON THE NATURE OF SHABBAT

The third day and the sixth day, which are *Tiferet* and *Yesod*, are not harmonizing energy-intelligences, by and within themselves. On Tuesday and Friday, *Tiferet* and *Yesod* are activated by our effort, we create the balance and harmony between Right and Left, between *erev* and *boker* (evening and morning). However, on the seventh day, the Bible does not say, *vayehi erev vayehi boker* (and there was evening and there was morning) as was done in the other six days, because *Shabbat* is not another Third-Column force that was created. No. She is the culmination of everything into one unified whole.

With this explanation from the *Zohar*, we can come to better understand the concept of work.

We now understand that on the seventh day, God did work, He brought together all of the *Sefirot* into a unified whole. So what does the Bible mean when it says (Exodus 20:10): *Ki sheshet yamim asa HaShem et hashamayim ve'et ha'aretz et hayam ve'et kol asher bam, vayanach bayom hashevi'i*. (And in six days the Lord made Heaven and Earth and the sea, and all that is within them, and rested on the seventh day)? If God created the Heaven and the Earth, the sea and all that is within them, is this not everything in the universe? The **Heavens** contain all the stars. The **Earth** contains all people and living creatures. And the **sea**, has life in concealment of water. These are the three aspects, each one, on an essential level, representing the elements of Right, Left, and Center. But the Bible says, **vayanach** *bayom hashevi'i* (And He **rested** on the seventh day). The Creator was very busy on the seventh day. There is no question that God was not resting. He was working, crowning all the differentiated, separate thought energy-intelligences, and bringing them into one unified whole. This is what God does, and this is what the ancient kabbalists would do on *Shabbat*. And therefore, on *Shabbat*, God was not resting.

What the *Zohar* is telling us is that by crowning all of the separate, individual, differentiated thought energy-intelligences—by bringing together the plus and minus, Left and Right—they do not remain in the constant battle, and thus God brought <u>them</u> to a rest!

He brought not only positive and negative to a rest, but even Central Column was brought to a rest. Because Central Column is a thought energy-intelligence that, like the filament, brings positive and negative together to produce a circuit of energy, the Central Column must work. If the filament does not work then plus and minus revert back to a short-circuit. The battle of Right and Left poles would continue. So, for the filament to do its job, it must be constantly working in its form of restriction.

On *Shabbat*, however, *vayanach*, everything rested, all three components, Right, Left and Central; both of the Upper Triad and the Lower Triad. All six were put to rest. No action. *Vayanach*, is not referring to God's activity, it is referring to the inactivity of the six. And why does the Bible not say *vayanchu*, (plural of *vayanach* in plural)? Because on *Shabbat* all six are one. *Vayanach* is singular, as they all rested as one. *Vayanach* indicates unity, whereas *vayanchu* is separation.

If we say that *Shabbat* is a day where everything is laid to rest, the Right is not winning, nor is the Left winning, and the Central is not bringing all these forces together. The battle that takes place in the physical dimension during the six days of the week, does not take place on *Shabbat*.

The Lord, in His infinite wisdom, created one day where there would be no effort on our part to put it together, where there is no engaging in the battling of Right and Left. *Shabbat* was created for this purpose—in potential—at the time of Creation (Genesis 2). And at the time of Revelation on Mount Sinai (Exodus 20), we received the instruction to: Observe the *Shabbat*. Does this mean we are being commanded not to work?

No. This Utterance is not a commandment but rather a guidance, informing us that on the seventh day we should refrain from initiating the battle between the forces that take place throughout the six days of the week. This is not referring to physical labor.

Therefore, we understand, when we strike a match, it is not that it requires a physical effort on our part (work). Rather by striking a match we are activating a Right (the match), we are activating a Left, (the carbon). Before we ignite the match, it is in the condition of rest. The Utterance of: Observe the *Shabbat*, is telling us to not upset rest. This is the requirement of *Shabbat*.

Revelation is telling us that if we participate in an action that takes something out of a state of rest, even one's animals, then we return to the world of separation, fragmentation. At the time of Creation, everything on the seventh day was put in a restful state. To connect to that state we too need to be at rest. *Shabbat* permits us to have this complete unified whole. When we strike a match and initiate activity, we set into motion dissension.

And why do we not want activity? Because where there is activity there is no peace of mind. People seek one aspect in life: Peace of mind. *Shabbat* connects us to the reality of quietness, of peace, to the ultimate oneness. The igniting of the match, the flipping of the switch, is creating movement in electrons, creating movement in atoms. When we initiate this activity, we have taken ourselves out of the state of peace of mind.

With the help of the *Zohar* we can now understand what constitutes work and what is not work. There are thirty-nine basic elements that the *Talmud* defines as activity. According to the *Torah*, peace of mind is the state where there is no activity.

When this power of *Shabbat* comes face-to-face with the energy-intelligence of the six other days, which are always in activity, they come to an abrupt halt. The arousal of a proton, of a neutron, or of an electron, by our initiation takes the world out of its cosmic tranquil state. Thereby, in essence, we have created fragmentation.

Observing *Shabbat* gives you the thought energy-intelligence that creates unity and peace of mind. This is why *Shabbat* is called a gift.

Shabbat means that everything has been laid to rest in the cosmos, nothing more. It is not a precept.

INTRODUCTION: Shabbat Structure

Shabbat Structure

We learn that the physical matter around us—including every human being—is merely an illusion. The reality is that we are all made up of one thing: Atoms. If someone created a pair of eyeglasses that could only see what lies beneath the illusion, imagine what we would see when you slipped them on. All the people, walls, furniture, buildings, trees, mountains, birds, dogs and cats, cars, and clouds would vanish. All we would perceive is a sea of atoms. Just as physics describes an atom as made up of three main particles, the electron, proton, and neutron, and that all three components are necessary to create circuitry in the physical reality, so too, the *Zohar* says there are three forces known as the Three-Column System that exist in the universe and that all three are necessary to create balance and reveal the Light of the Creator in this physical world:

1. A Vessel or negatively charged component (Left Column) – Desire to Receive;
2. The Light or positively charged component (Right Column) – Desire to Share;
3. Resistance or Balance (Central Column) – Desire to Receive for the Sake of Sharing (mediating between the positive and negative forces).

Shabbat is made up of this same Three-Column System—the basis of all reality—beginning every Friday evening, at sundown, and concluding on Saturday evening, at nightfall. On *Shabbat* it is our job, as human beings, to activate each of these components so that we can create circuitry and generate Light.

Friday Night: The function of Friday night is to create the Left Column energy, which the kabbalists call the Building of the Vessel. A vessel is a structure designed to receive energy. If we want a glass of water, first we need an empty glass; then we can pour water into it. Friday night is the building of the empty glass in preparation for the Divine Water (Light) that will be poured into it over *Shabbat*.

Saturday Morning: From Saturday morning to early Saturday afternoon our activities serve to assemble the Right Column energy. The Lightforce of the Creator or energy can only be released into our physical world by virtue of this positive component.

Saturday Afternoon: Saturday afternoon or the time of Third Meal is when we create the Central Column energy of balance or resistance. Only then can the full power and Light of *Shabbat* ignite in its entire splendor. For this reason, Saturday afternoon is considered to be the highest point of *Shabbat* because it is the moment when the Light becomes fully manifest.

INTRODUCTION: THE ZOHAR ON SHABBAT MEALS AND SONGS

THE ZOHAR ON SHABBAT MEALS AND SONGS

A powerful way of bringing the blessings and gifts of *Shabbat* to our life is through the three meals of *Shabbat*.

The *Talmud* says (Babylonian Talmud, Tractate Shabbat 30:2): "This teaches you that the Divine Presence rests upon man through a joy of precept ["precept" or *mitzvah* - מִצְוָה also means "to connect" or *tzavta* – צַוְתָּא], as it is said (Kings 2, 3:15): 'But now bring me a minstrel. And it came to pass, when the minstrel played, that the hand of the Lord came upon him.'"

The *Zohar* says (Ekev 31-32): "There are ten things one must do for the meal (of *Shabbat*): …(3) to eat of three meals and add from weekdays to holiness; On *Shabbat*, one should add from weekdays to holiness in everything he does, in his food and drink, his dress and his seating. He should prepare a comfortable reclining bed with many pillows and embroidered cushions from all that he has in his house, as when preparing the marriage canopy for the bride, because *Shabbat* is both a queen and a bride… There is a need to invoke, on that table, song and joy for her." And the *Zohar* continues (Ibid 48): "The third setting regarding the *Shabbat* table is to eat three meals on *Shabbat*… The secret of delight (Heb. oneg—עֹנֶג, Ayin—ע Nun—נ Gimel—ג) is the secret meaning of: "and a river went out of Eden to water that garden" (Genesis 2:10). For Eden means delight and the Garden is *Malchut*, the secret meaning of Shabbat. Also, Oneg—עֹנֶג is the initials of Eden—עֵדֶן, Nahar—נָהָר (Eng. 'river') and Gan—גַן (Eng. 'garden')… and it is written: 'then shall you delight yourself in the Lord (Isaiah 58:14)'"

The Zohar adds (Emor 117-118): "*Shabbat*, the feast of joy of the King with the Queen, who are *Zeir Anpin* and *Malchut*, and the joy of *Abba* and *Ima*. The higher and lower beings rejoice in it. Everyone has joy and have no pain in it. It is therefore written (Isaiah 58:13), 'and call the *Shabbat* a delight'. What is a delight? He answers, Delight only exists Above, where Supernal Holiness dwells, namely in Supernal *Abba* and *Ima*, as is written (Ibid. 14), "then shall you delight yourself in (lit. 'above') the Lord," namely, above *Zeir Anpin*. For that delight is above the Lord, namely in *Abba* and *Ima* that are above *Zeir Anpin*. That day, *Shabbat*, which is the feast of joy of the King, is adorned with that crown of delight from Supernal *Abba* and *Ima*. This is the meaning of, 'and call the *Shabbat* a delight,' which is not the case in other days. On that day, it behooves the King's children to prepare three meals and set the table in honor of the King, as we explained."

And continues (Zohar Beshalach 412-415): "Rav Yehuda said: Every single day, the world is blessed from that Supernal Day, for all the six days are blessed from the seventh day. And every day gives from that blessing that it receives on its own day… That night is the joy of the Queen with the King and their uniting, and all the six days are blessed, each one on its own. Therefore, a person must prepare his table on *Shabbat* night so that blessings from Above will dwell upon him, and a blessing is not present on an empty table."

In *Zohar Chadash* it says (Acharei Mot 93-95): "on this day of the *Shabbat*, a person needs to rejoice, day and night, and is required to prepare the table and cause joy to the higher and lower beings, meaning with a spiritual eating and physical eating. And when a person comes from the synagogue, holy angels accompany him from this side and angels from that side, and the *Shechinah* is over all of them, like a mother over her brood. And at that moment it is said regarding him (Psalms 91:7-10): 'A thousand shall fall at your side and ten thousand at your right side… Only with your eyes shall you behold… You, the Lord, are my refuge… No evil shall befall you…' All this is meant if a person proceeds into his home with gladness and receives guests with joy. And when the *Shechinah* arrives with the angels, and sees a candle lit and a table prepared, and the man and his wife are in happiness, at that moment the *Shechinah* says: 'This one belongs to me, Israel, in whom I will be glorified.' (Isaiah 49:3)"

INTRODUCTION: THE ZOHAR ON SHABBAT MEALS AND SONGS

Physicists and engineers figured out a way to make the invisible power of electricity a practical force, and without changing the electrical current itself, wires and cables acted as conduits, put to use to enrich our lives. The Light of the Creator—the God Current—works exactly the same way, and kabbalists use their own technology to create intermediary devices that allow us to use the God Current. This is the purpose of the food we eat and the songs we sing on *Shabbat*. The three meals, and food eaten at each meal, are wires, cables, tools, technology, devices to harness the God Current or Lightforce of the Creator so that we can be infused with Light to help us transform our lives in the ways that will bring us greater fulfillment. These tools (food, drink, and song) manifest spiritual energy in our physical world so we can use it practically.

The Hebrew word for meal is *se'uda*-סְעוּדָה, which connects to the Hebrew word *sa'ad*-סְעַד, meaning "to support." One of the purposes of *Shabbat* meals is for people to support one another as the intangible Light of the Creator becomes tangible and infused into us through the medium of the meal. Food becomes the conduit to transfer the energy of *Shabbat*. Connecting as a group with the consciousness to share, improves the effectiveness of the tools.

One of the foods we eat on Friday night (and also at other *Shabbat* meals) is fish. The kabbalists tell us that a spark of Light from the soul of a righteous person is within the fish we eat on *Shabbat*. This spark or atom in the fish is elevated by us when we eat the fish.

All food contains Divine sparks of Light, but if we are not consciously aware of the Light in the food we will only capture the physical benefit of the food. When we are conscious of the unique aspects of energy inside the food, we elevate not only the soul of the animal but all the sparks of Light in the food. By doing so, we elevate our own soul and inject more sparks of Light into our world. These elevated sparks help diminish the darkness that exists in the world.

When people are gathered at a table during *Shabbat* meals, another technology for igniting the Light is to share spiritual wisdom with one another. Injecting consciousness, thought, awareness and knowledge into the meal is so important. Kabbalists tell us, that without it, life drains out of the moment. On the other hand, in the presence of spiritual wisdom being shared between people, it is as if we were eating a meal in the Holy Temple of Jerusalem. The Holy Temple is not a symbol of religious significance; it is one of the greatest conduits ever built to draw down the Light of the Creator to this level of *Malchut*. When we say it is like being in the Holy Temple we are referring to the Temple as our tool for ultimate connection.

Rav Isaac Luria (the Ari) says that the songs of *Shabbat* have the power to cut off all the negative forces that prevent us from connecting to the Light. In the kabbalistic text (*Sefer Hechalot* or the Book of the Chambers, by Yishmael the High Priest – Israel, 1st century) it is written that the songs of *Shabbat* give life and power to all spiritual and physical entities and help us to elevate our soul into the Upper Worlds. Kabbalist Rav Pinchas of Koritz (Ukraine, 18th century) adds that the songs of *Shabbat* were written and composed with the inspiration of the songs of the Supernal Angels.

The singing and good cheer that takes place during *Shabbat* meals is an expression of our happiness, and happiness is one of the most effective tools to connect to the *Shechinah*, the female aspect of the Creator that is closest to us during the time of *Shabbat*. Our joy acts as a magnet to blessings and Light.

INTRODUCTION: Hafrashat Chalah (Separating the Dough)

Hafrashat Chalah (Separating the Dough)

It is stated in the Torah: "The first portion of your kneading, you shall offer up a cake (*chalah*)... of the first of your dough for a gift to the Lord." (Numbers 15:20-21)

The internal essence of bread is the force of receiving. It is Left Column and draws down energy. This means that it can attract negative as well as positive energies. Negative energies called *klipot* try to latch on to the bread and take the Light from it. From the moment we begin the process of making bread (preparing the dough), these *klipot* are waiting for the opportunity to take energy. At the time of the Temple in Jerusalem, the first piece of dough from the making of bread was given to the *Kohen* (or Priest) in order to protect it. Tithing (*ma'aser*) follows the same spiritual principle. One tenth of *se'ah* (the tenth Sefira – *Malchut*) was given to the Temple to protect negativity from attaching to its Light. Moreover, the first piece represents the seed that contains all the energy. By giving the first piece of the dough to the *Kohen*, who is the Right Column and the channel for the aspect of Mercy, we nullify the latching on of the *klipa*. In this way we can benefit from the Light the bread draws down without the attachment of the *klipot*. Today, we do not have the Temple's protection, so instead of giving it to the *Kohen*, we burn it.

The *Zohar* teaches that wheat embodies the same powerful desire that was found in the Tree of Knowledge Good and Evil (in the Garden of Eden). When Adam (who represents the Male aspect in the universe) and Eve (who represents the Female aspect) ate from it they fell from the spiritual dimension into the physical reality and brought about death and chaos. The *Midrash* (Midrash Tanchuma, Beresheet, 6:1) explains that one of the ways to correct the fall of Adam and Eve is for women (who represent Eve) to perform *Hafrashat Chalah* (Separating the Dough). Preparing a *chalah* or bread and performing *Hafrashat Chalah* any time is important but as the fall of Adam and Eve occurred on the eve of *Shabbat* it is more powerful to do so for *Shabbat*.

While separating the dough, a woman should meditate to draw livelihood and blessings back to all of existence—as the bread has within it the Four Foundations: Air (*Zeir Anpin* - as the dough rises), Earth (*Malchut* - where the wheat comes from), Water (*Ima* – which we add to the wheat) and Fire (*Abba* - where it is baked). She should also meditate to draw blessings and protection for her husband and family. Rav Shimon says that when a woman is separating the dough she brings protection and shields her house from any negativity (see Zohar Shelach Lecha 307).

How to perform *Hafrashat Chalah*?
The action of separating the dough is done only with dough that is made with flour produced from one (or a combination) of the five grains: wheat, barley, rye, oat and spelt.

The following are the quantities of flour (before adding anything to it) required for separating the dough:
When using at least 1,666.6 grams (3 lbs. & 10.8 oz.) of flour, it is recommended to separate the dough reciting the blessing below.
When using flour weighing between 1,230 and 1,666.6 grams, we separate the dough but no blessing is required.
When using less than 1,230 grams (2 lbs. & 11.4 oz.) of flour, separating of the dough is not required.

A woman should set aside a portion (28 grams, about an ounce) of the dough after it begins to rise (and before the baking process). However, if she forgets, she can perform *Hafrashat Chalah* even after baking, being mindful that the wheat represents the desire of the Tree of Knowledge. Then, the separated piece of dough should be burned, not simply discarded, as it contains a lot of energy that the *klipot* are seeking and burning eliminates the opportunity for them to attach themselves to this energy.

If the *chalah* or bread is being prepared for *Shabbat* we add the verse: *"lichvod Shabbat kodesh,"* (in honor of the holy *Shabbat*). In this way the energy of *Shabbat* is injected into the *chalah*.

INTRODUCTION: HAFRASHAT CHALAH (SEPARATING THE DOUGH)

HAFRASHAT CHALAH CONNECTION

> Before Separating the Dough (*Hafrashat Chalah*), meditate along with the actions as stated:
> Take one part of 48 parts, and meditate on the Name: יוד הא וו הה (=48) and the Name:
> יוד הי ואו (דס"ג) (=48). This is most important when making the twelve loaves for *Shabbat* meals.

Before Separating the Dough (*Hafrashat Chalah*)
scan or read the following sections of the *Zohar* (*Tikkunei Zohar—Tikkun Sixteen*):

(1) בְּרֵאשִׁית: דָּא וַחַלָּה. הֲדָא הוּא דִכְתִיב: רֵאשִׁית עֲרִיסֹתֵיכֶם חַלָּה תָּרִימוּ תְרוּמָה. וְהָא אוּקְמוּהוּ, דְּאָדָם וַחַלָּתוֹ שֶׁל עוֹלָם הֲוָה. וּמְנָא לָן דְּחַלָּה אִיהוּ רֵאשִׁית? דִּקְרָא אוּכַח, הֲדָא הוּא דִכְתִיב: רֵאשִׁית עֲרִיסֹתֵיכֶם חַלָּה תָּרִימוּ תְרוּמָה.

(2) מַאי וְחַלָּה? אֶלָּא שִׁבְעָה מִינִין אִינוּן: וְחִטָּה וּשְׂעוֹרָה וְגֶפֶן וּתְאֵנָה וְרִמּוֹן, אֶרֶץ זֵית שֶׁמֶן וּדְבָשׁ, דְּהוּא דְבַשׁ תְּמָרִים. וְחִטָּה, אִילָנָא אִיהוּ דְּאָכִיל מִנֵּיהּ אָדָם קַדְמָאָה, וְאִיהוּ לָא אַפִּיק מִתַּמָּן וְחַלָּה, וּבְגִין דָּא לָא וָזַל בֵּיהּ ה', וְשַׁרְיָא בֵּיהּ ו', ט', וְגָרִים לֵיהּ מוֹתָא. וְחַלָּה, אִיהִי שְׁכִינְתָּא, כְּלִילָא מִשִּׁבְעָה מִינִין אִלֵּין, וּבָהּ וָזָב אָדָם קַדְמָאָה.

HAFRASHAT CHALAH CONNECTION

1. Beresheet is Chalah. This is what is written, "You shall offer up a cake (chalah) of the first of your dough for a gift" (Numbers 15:20). HE ASKS, they have established that Adam, AFTER HE SINNED, was the sanctification of the world, AS IS WRITTEN, "BUT HE WHO EXACTS GIFTS OVERTHROWS IT" (Proverbs 29:4) WHICH REFERS TO ADAM WHO WAS THE FINAL SANCTIFICATION (CHALAH) OF THE WORLD. And how do we know that Chalah is first? The Torah proves it, as is written, "You shall offer up a cake of the first of your dough."

2. IF SO, what is chalah? AND HE ANSWERS, The seven kinds, THAT THE LAND OF ISRAEL IS PRAISED FOR, WHICH IS MALCHUT, and are, "Wheat, and barley, and vines, and fig trees, and pomegranate; a land of olive oil, and honey," (Deuteronomy 8:8) honey being date honey THAT COMES FROM THE TREE THAT GROWS FROM THE GROUND. Wheat is the tree that Primordial Adam ate of, FOR AN INFANT DOES NOT KNOW TO CALL "FATHER" OR "MOTHER" UNTIL HE TASTES GRAIN, AND THIS IS CALLED THE TREE OF KNOWLEDGE OF GOOD AND EVIL. But he did not separate chalah (the Priest's share of the dough) from it, therefore the Hei, WHICH IS MALCHUT, DID NOT REST ON HIM, AND THE LETTERS Chet and Tet settled on him, WHICH DENOTE THE GRASP OF THE EXTERNAL FORCES, and brought death on him. And chalah is the Shechinah composed of the seven kinds, and against her did Primordial Man sin.

INTRODUCTION: HAFRASHAT CHALAH (SEPARATING THE DOUGH)

(3) טִפָּה דָא י'. עִסָּה צָרִיךְ לְאַפָּקָא מִינָהּ וַלָּה. וּמִיָּד וָל עַל הַהִיא טִפָּה, וְיָהִיב לֵיהּ זֶרַע כְּלִיל מִתַּרְוַויְיהוּ, דְּאִיהוּ ו', וְרָזָא דְמִלָּה: הֵ"א לָכֶם זֶרַע.

(4) וּבְגִין דָּא וַלָּה וַדַּאי אִיהִי פְקוּדָא דְאִתְפַּקְּדַת אִתְּתָא, דִּבְגִינָהּ מֵת אָדָם, דְּאִיהוּ וַלָּתוֹ שֶׁל עוֹלָם, צְרִיכָה אִיהִי לְאַפְרָשָׁא וַלָּה, וּלְאַפָּקָא לָהּ מֵעִסָּתָהּ, דְּאִיהִי טִפָּה דִּילָהּ, לְהַחֲזִירָהּ עַל אָדָם.

(5) אִיהִי אַטְפַּת שְׁרָגָא דִּילֵיהּ, דְּאִתְּמַר בֵּיהּ, דְּאִתְּמַר בֵּיהּ: נֵר יְיָ' נִשְׁמַת אָדָם, צְרִיכָה לְאוֹקְדָא לֵיהּ בְּלֵיל שַׁבָּת, בְּאִתְעָרוּ דְשַׁלְהוֹבִין דְּאֶשָּׁא דִּרְחִימוּ לְגַבֵּי בַּעְלָהּ. וְרָזָא דְמִלָּה: מַיִם רַבִּים לֹא יוּכְלוּ לְכַבּוֹת אֶת הָאַהֲבָה. וְאִתְעָרוּ דְחֻמְּמוּתָא דְלֵיל שַׁבָּת מֵאִתְּתֵיהּ, צְרִיכָה בִּרְחִימוּ וּדְחִילוּ. וְדָא אִיהוּ: אִשָּׁה כִּי תַזְרִיעַ וְיָלְדָה זָכָר.

(6) עַל שְׁפִיכַת דָּמִים דְּאָדָם, אוֹדְרִיקַת דָּמָהּ. וְעַל דָּא, צְרִיכָה לְנַטְּרָא לֵיהּ מִדָּם נִדָּה. וּבְגִין דָּא, עַל תְּלַת מִלִּין אִלֵּין נָשִׁים זְהִירוֹת: בְּנִדָּה וּבְחַלָּה וּבְהַדְלָקַת הַנֵּר. עַד כַּאן רָזָא דְחִטָּה, דִּמְתַּמָּן וַלָּה. וְחִטָּ"ה, אִיהוּ רָזָא דְעֶשְׂרִין וּתְרֵין אַתְוָון דְּאוֹרַיְיתָא.

---

3. The drop of sperm is Yud, NAMELY CHOCHMAH. From the dough it is necessary to separate chalah, then immediately the Hei settles (Heb. chal), WHICH IS BINAH THAT SHINES WITH CHASADIM on this drop THAT IS CHOCHMAH, and he is given seed composed of both, CHOCHMAH AND CHASADIM, which is Vav (= 6). And the secret of it is, "lo here (Heb. he) is grain for you." (Genesis 47:23)

4. Therefore, certainly chalah is a Precept of which the woman is commanded, for since due to her Adam died, who was the sanctification (chalah) of the world, she needs to set aside a part of the dough (chalah.) And to remove it from her dough, which is her drop, and return it to Adam.

5. She extinguished his candle, of which is said, "The spirit of man is the candle of the Lord." (Proverbs 20:27) She needs to light it on Shabbat eve, by the arousal of the flames of fire of love for her husband. The secret of the matter is, "Many waters cannot quench love." (Song of Songs 8:7) And the arousal of the warmth from his wife on Shabbat eve must be with love and awe. This is, "If a woman have conceived, and born a man child." (Leviticus 12:2)

6. For this, FOR BRINGING bloodshed on Adam, SINCE HE WAS SENTENCED TO HAVING HIS LIMBS DROP OFF AND DEATH, her blood is thrown away MEANING THE FIVE IMPURE KINDS OF BLOODS, NIDAH (MENSTRUATING WOMAN). Therefore, she has to guard him from the menstruation blood. Therefore women are cautioned to observe three things, NAMELY, the laws of menstruation, setting aside a part of the dough and lighting the SHABBAT candles. Up to here the meaning of wheat (Heb. chitah=22) is related, and from which chalah IS SEPARATED. Wheat signifies the 22 letters of the Torah.

INTRODUCTION: HAFRASHAT CHALAH (SEPARATING THE DOUGH)

HAFRASHAT CHALAH - LESHEM YICHUD

לְשֵׁם leshem יִחוּד yichud קוּדְשָׁא kudsha בְּרִיךְ berich הוּא hu
וּשְׁכִינְתֵּיהּ ushchintei (יאהדונהי) בִּדְחִילוּ bid'chilu וּרְחִימוּ ur'chimu
(יאההויה), וּרְחִימוּ ur'chimu וּדְחִילוּ ud'chilu (איההיוהה),
לְיַחֲדָא leyachda שֵׁם shem יו״ד yud קֵי kei בְּוָא״ו bevav קֵי kei
בְּיִחוּדָא beyichuda שְׁלִים shelim (יהוה) בְּשֵׁם beshem כָּל kol יִלי
יִשְׂרָאֵל Yisrael, הֲרֵינִי hareni בָּאָה va'a לְקַיֵּם lekayem
מִצְוַת mitzvat עֲשֵׂה aseh שֶׁל shel הַצְּדָקָה hatzedakah ע״ה ריבוע אלהים
וַהֲרֵינִי vahareni נוֹתֶנֶת notenet שְׁתֵּי shetei פְּרוּטוֹת perutot
לִצְדָקָה litzdakah ע״ה ריבוע אלהים וְעוֹד ve'od הֲרֵינִי hareni נוֹתֶנֶת notenet
פְּרוּטָה peruta אַחַת achat לִצְדָקָה litzdakah ע״ה ריבוע אלהים לְתַקֵּן letaken
אֶת et שֹׁרֶשׁ shoresh מִצְוָה mitzva זוֹ zo וְכָל vechol יִלי תרי״ג taryag
מִצְוֹת mitzvot הַכְּלוּלוֹת hakelulot בָּהּ ba בִּמְקוֹם bemakom עֶלְיוֹן elyon.

Here a woman gives three coins for *tzedakah* (charity) before separating the dough and then continues:

וַהֲרֵינִי vahareni בָּאָה va'a לְקַיֵּם lekayem מִצְוַת mitzvat עֲשֵׂה aseh
דְרַבָּנָן derabanan שֶׁל shel הַפְרָשַׁת hafrashat חַלָּה chalah לחו מִן min
הָעִסָּה ha'isa לְתַקֵּן letaken שֹׁרֶשׁ shoresh מִצְוָה mitzva זוֹ zo
בִּמְקוֹם bemakom עֶלְיוֹן elyon. וִיהִי vihi נֹעַם no'am אֲדֹנָי Adonai ללה
אֱלֹהֵינוּ Elohenu ילה עָלֵינוּ alenu וּמַעֲשֵׂה uma'ase יָדֵינוּ yadenu
כּוֹנְנָה konena עָלֵינוּ alenu וּמַעֲשֵׂה uma'ase יָדֵינוּ yadenu כּוֹנְנֵהוּ konenehu:

HAFRASHAT CHALAH - LESHEM YICHUD

For the sake of unification between the Holy Blessed One and His Shechinah, with fear and love and with love and fear, in order to unify the Name Yud-Kei and Vav-Kei in perfect unity, and in the name of all Israel, I am hereby prepared to fulfill the obligatory precept of tzedakah, and hereby I am giving two coins for tzedakah and another one for tzedakah to correct the root of the precept of tzedakah with all the 613 other precepts that are included in it, in the Supernal Place, (here a woman gives three coins for tzedakah). And I hereby prepare to fulfill the obligatory precept from the sages of Separating the Dough to correct the root of the precept in the Supernal Place. "May the pleasantness of the Lord, our God, be upon us and may He establish the work of our hands for us and may the work of our hands establish Him." (Psalms 90:17)

INTRODUCTION: HAFRASHAT CHALAH (SEPARATING THE DOUGH)

Here the woman separates the dough, and recites the following blessing:

בָּרוּךְ baruch אַתָּה Ata יְהֹוָה‎אדניאהדונהי Adonai

אֱלֹהֵינוּ Elohenu ילה מֶלֶךְ melech הָעוֹלָם ha'olam אֲשֶׁר asher

קִדְּשָׁנוּ kideshanu בְּמִצְוֹתָיו bemitzvotav וְצִוָּנוּ vetzivanu

לְהַפְרִישׁ lehafrish חַלָּה chalah להו מִן min הָעִסָּה‎ ha'isa:

Holding the separated piece of dough, say:

הֲרֵי harei זוֹ zu וְחַלָּה chalah

Then burn the piece of the dough.

YEHI RATZON

Performing the action of *Hafrashat Chalah* (Separating the Dough) creates an opening in the Upper World (*Et Ratzon*—Time of Good Will) and therefore enables the woman who performs it to pray and ask for blessings and sustenance for the world, and especially for her husband and her children.

Hafrashat Chalah is considered to be a genuine act of sharing toward our family.

יְהִי yehi רָצוֹן ratzon מהש ע"ב, בריבוע קס"א, ע"ה, אל שדי ע"ה

מִלְּפָנֶיךָ milfanecha ס"ג מ"ה ב"ן יְהֹוָה‎אדניאהדונהי Adonai

אֱלֹהַי Elohai מילוי דע"ב, דמב ; ילה וֵאלֹהֵי velohei מילוי דע"ב, לכב ; ילה ; דמ"ב ; ילה

אֲבוֹתַי avotai שֶׁתָּווֹס shetachos וְתָרוּם utrachem ג"פ רי"ו ;

עָלַי alai, וְתַגְדִּיל vetagdil וְחַסְדְּךָ chasdecha עִמָּדִי imadi כָּלֵת latet

לִי li זֶרַע zera אֲנָשִׁים anashim עוֹשֵׂי osei רְצוֹנֶךָ retzonecha◆

וְעוֹסְקִים ve'oskim בְּתוֹרָתְךָ betoratcha לִשְׁמָהּ lishma◆

---

*Blessed are You, Lord, our God, King of the world,
Who has sanctified us with His commandments and obliged us to separate chalah from the dough.*
Holding the separated piece of dough, say: *This is a chalah.*

YEHI RATZON

May it be pleasing before You, Lord, my God, and God of my forefathers, that You will take pity and be merciful to me, and may You increase Your compassion to me by granting me, for offspring, ones who do Your bidding and who occupy themselves in Your Torah for Its own sake.

INTRODUCTION: HAFRASHAT CHALAH (SEPARATING THE DOUGH)

batorah בַּתּוֹרָה me'irim מְאִירִים (ייא״י מילוי דס״ג) אל veyih'yu וְיִהְיוּ

zo זוֹ, chalah וְחַלָּה hafrashat הַפְרָשַׁת bizchut בִּזְכוּת

utrachem וּתְרַחֵם tachos תָּחוֹס vegam וְגַם

ג״פ רי״י ; וז״פ אל, רי״י ל״ב נתיבות החכמה, רמ״ז (אברים), עסמ״ב ט״ז אותיות פשוטות

ba'ali בַּעֲלִי al עַל

(Here a woman should meditate and mention her husband's name and his father's name)

yamim יָמִים orech אֹרֶךְ lo לוֹ ב״פ כהת vetiten וְתִתֶּן נלך

chayim וְחַיִּים ushnot וּשְׁנוֹת אהיה אהיה יהוה, בינה ע״ה

ut'saye'ehu וְתַסִּיעֵהוּ, vehatzlacha וְהַצְלָחָה beracha בְּרָכָה im עִם

yehi יְהִי ken כֵּן bishlemut בִּשְׁלֵמוּת ♦ retzoncha רְצוֹנְךָ la'asot לַעֲשׂוֹת

amen אָמֵן מהע ע״ה, ע״ב בריבוע וקס״א ע״ה, אל שדי ע״ה ratzon רָצוֹן יאהדונהי ♦

(42 letters in this verse—מ״ב אותיות בפסוק)

leratzon לְרָצוֹן מהע ע״ה, ע״ב בריבוע וקס״א ע״ה (ייא״י מילוי דס״ג) אל yih'yu יִהְיוּ אל שדי ע״ה

libi לִבִּי vehegyon וְהֶגְיוֹן ר״ת אֶלֶף = אלף למד דלת שין יוד דלת ע״ה fi פִי imrei אִמְרֵי

vego'ali וְגֹאֲלִי ♦ tzuri צוּרִי Adonai יְהֹוָהאדנילהאדונהי ס״ג מ״ה ב״ן lefanecha לְפָנֶיךָ :

---

*May they be resplendent in the Torah by virtue of this separating dough.
May You also take pity and be merciful to my husband*
(Here a woman should meditate and mention her husband's name and his father's name)
and may You grant him lengthy days and years of life, filled with blessings and success, and may You help him in doing Your bidding perfectly. May it so be Your desire, Amen. "May the words of my mouth and the thoughts of my heart be pleasing before You, God, my Rock and my Redeemer." (Psalms 19:15)

Introduction: Shabbat and Holiday Candle Lighting

Meditation of the Preparation of Shabbat Candles

It is good to have two candles made of olive oil and not wax, because they are the secret of *Netzach* and *Hod* of *Abba* (that is called "oil") inside *Netzach* and *Hod* of *Ima* (that is called "olive") that receives them. In *Tikkunei HaZohar* there is another explanation: *Keli* (Vessel) is the Angel מטטרון (do not pronounce), the wick is *Nukva* of *Zeir Anpin* and the Light is the abundance of *Yesod*. Meditating on this candle (*ner*) 250, is equal to the 248 organs of *Malchut* with the two arms of the King and then it is called *ner Shabbat chova* (lit: lighting *Shabbat* candle is a must) and corresponds to *Binah* (the Holy Name: אהיה, which equals the numerical value of the word *chova* - 21). As the *Shabbat* candle's essence is *Ima* unified with *Abba* in three places, which creates three *Yichudim*:

In *Keter* - יאהדונהי (=47)

In *Chochmah, Binah, Da'at* - יאהלוההים (=112)

In *Zayin Tachtonot* (Seven Lower *Sefirot*) - יאהדונהי (=91)

The above three *Yichudim* (Unifications) add up to the numerical value of *ner*, candle. They also refer to the *Nukva* because when She ascends, She gets a new Name: אלף למד אדני (before, She had the Name: אל אדני) for the unification, which also adds up to 250. Therefore, light another candle for *Malchut*, which is the illumination of the Supernal *Ima* in *Nukva*. Also, the value of the spelling out of the Name שד"י (יו"ד דל"ת יו"ד) - the *Yesod* where all the above *Yichudim* occur) has the numerical value of 500, which is equal to two times candle (*ner*).

Meditation of the Lighting of Shabbat Candles

When lighting the candles, you should meditate that there are four flames corresponding to the four letters of the Name: יהוה. The two flames that are closer to the wick and can be seen by our sense of sight stand for the two letters *Vav* and *Hei* (ו"ה). However, the two above, are concealed from us and not seen, and they are hinted at by the letters *Mem* and *Tzadik* (מ"צ) of the word מצוה (*mitzvah* or "precept" but also "connection" and "unity," as the letters מ"צ in *AtBash* are replaced by the letters *Yud* and *Hei* - י"ה).

Then meditate to extinguish the two candles of the Other Side (*Abba* and *Ima*, *Zeir* and *Nukva* of the *klipa* which is called: שבתי – **Do not pronounce**) so they will not control the energy of *Shabbat*: *Ner* (candle) adds up to 250. When we remove the two *kolels* (2) for the *Nefesh* (נפש) and *Ruach* (רוח) [the acronym of the word *Ner* נ"ר], and also remove the three *Alefs* (3) of the Names: אהיה אלהים אדני [which are part of the three *Yichudim* above, and because they (the *Alefs*) are the root, the *klipot* have a grasp on them], from the *Nukva* aspect, we are left with 245. The two candles now add up to 490, which is equal to: ת"ץ (lit: shattered) from אבגית"ץ. And by this Name ת"ץ the *klipa* will be shattered. Also meditate that the above mentioned *klipa* will fade away like smoke [the secret of the verse "touch (*ga*) the mountains and they will be reduced to smoke" (Psalms 144:5)] by the Name יוד הי ואו הי with its ten letters (73), as it is the numerical value of the word "*ga*."

Karen's Meditation for Lighting Shabbat Candles

Breathe deeply and relax your body. Visualize the Holy Temple in Jerusalem, walk towards it and climb the stairs. See all your relatives and the people you love in your mind's eye. Invite them to join you and holding their hands continue climbing. When you come to the Holy Temple, connect to your *Tzadik* (righteous soul), the one you feel closest to and ask the *Tzadik* to bless you and to remain with you for the whole Shabbat. Feel the warmth and love coming from your *Tzadik*. Look into the eyes of your relatives and the people you love and tell them, in your heart, how much you love them. Make a circle in your mind's eye and bring them closer together, so that the *Tzadik* is above the whole circle. See a white light above the circle with the love that you are sharing with them. Speak to each soul in the circle, and with each candle you light meditate to bring them closer and tell them "*Shabbat Shalom*" and how much you love them and express your desire to be together with them on the *Shabbat*.

Shabbat Candle Lighting

We light the *Shabbat* candles to draw the spiritual Light into our personal lives. Every physical action in our world initiates a corresponding reaction in the Upper Worlds. The *Zohar* tells us that lighting the *Shabbat* candles is like turning on a switch that banishes all darkness from this world. By lighting the physical candles of *Shabbat* with the consciousness and intent to connect to the energy of *Shabbat* in the Upper Worlds, we arouse and draw spiritual Light into our physical world.

A secret of the candles can be found in their numerical value of 250. When we light two candles their numerical value is 250 x 2 = 500. A man has 248 bone segments and joints, whereas a woman has 252. Together, 248 + 252 = 500, the same value as two candles.

There are different customs regarding how many candles to light. Our teacher, Karen Berg, lights ten candles, which connect her and her loved ones to the Ten Dimensions (*Sefirot*) (see meditation above).

When a woman lights the *Shabbat* candles, she is also helping to correct the sin of Eve, which was a Desire to Receive for the Self Alone. The action of lighting the candles becomes an act of sharing. As a married woman's husband and children are closest to her, they receive the benefit of this action.

Although candle lighting is done by a woman, the preparation of the candles is done by a man. It is said about some great kabbalists like the Gaon of Vilna and the Chafetz Chaim that they would prepare the *Shabbat* candles and would not allow anyone else to do so. A woman lights the *Shabbat* candles before sundown Friday evening, just prior to the entry of the *Shabbat*.

It is recommended that a woman give three coins of charity before she lights. Charity—an act of sharing—causes the woman to become a pure Vessel. It is a perfect time to pray for children, for a soul mate, and for peace in the world.

Introduction: Shabbat and Holiday Candle Lighting

LeShem Yichud

hu הוּא berich בְּרִיךְ kudsha קוּדְשָׁא yichud יִחוּד leshem לְשֵׁם

ur'chimu וּרְחִימוּ bid'chilu בִּדְחִילוּ (יאהדונהי) ushchintei וּשְׁכִינְתֵּיהּ

(איההויהה), ud'chilu וּדְחִילוּ ur'chimu וּרְחִימוּ (יאההויהה),

kei קֵי bevav בְּוָא"ו kei קֵי yud יוּ"ד shem שֵׁם leyachda לְיַחֲדָא

ילי kol כָּל beshem בְּשֵׁם (יהוה) shelim שָׁלִים beyichuda בְּיִחוּדָא

Yisrael יִשְׂרָאֵל, hareni הֲרֵינִי va'a בָּאָה lekayem לְקַיֵּם

mitzvat מִצְוַת ase עֲשֵׂה shel שֶׁל hatzedakah הַצְּדָקָה ע"ה רִבּוּעַ אלהים

perutot פְּרוּטוֹת shetei שְׁתֵּי notenet נוֹתֶנֶת vahareni וַהֲרֵינִי

notenet נוֹתֶנֶת hareni הֲרֵינִי ve'od וְעוֹד ע"ה רִבּוּעַ אלהים litzdakah לִצְדָקָה

letaken לְתַקֵּן ע"ה רִבּוּעַ אלהים litzdakah לִצְדָקָה achat אַחַת peruta פְּרוּטָה

taryag תַּרְיָ"ג ילי vechol וְכָל zo זוֹ mitzva מִצְוָה shoresh שֹׁרֶשׁ et אֶת

♦elyon עֶלְיוֹן bemakom בִּמָּקוֹם ba בָּהּ hakelulot הַכְּלוּלוֹת mitzvot מִצְוֹת

Here a woman gives three coins for charity before lighting the candles and then continue,

ase עֲשֵׂה mitzvat מִצְוַת lekayem לְקַיֵּם va'a בָּאָה vahareni וַהֲרֵינִי

lichvod לִכְבוֹד nerot נֵרוֹת shenei שְׁנֵי lehadlik לְהַדְלִיק derabanan דְּרַבָּנָן

♦Shabbat שַׁבָּת echad אֶחָד keneged כְּנֶגֶד (מזבח, דאגה אהבה, זן, אל יהוה)

zachor זָכוֹר (ע"ב קס"א, יהי אור ע"ה סוד המשכת השפע מן ד' שמות ליסוד הנקרא זכור)

shamor שָׁמוֹר ve'echad וְאֶחָד keneged כְּנֶגֶד (מזבח, דאגה אהבה, זן, אל יהוה)

Shabbat Candle Lighting - LeShem Yichud

For the sake of unification between the Holy Blessed One and His Shechinah, with fear and love and with love and fear, in order to unify the Name Yud-Kei and Vav-Kei in perfect unity, and in the name of all Israel, I am hereby prepared to fulfill the obligatory precept of tzedakah, and hereby I'm giving two coins for tzedakah and another one for tzedakah to correct the root of the precept of tzedakah with all the 613 other precepts which are included in it, in the Supernal Place, (here a woman gives three coins for tzedakah). And I hereby prepare to fulfill the obligatory precept from the sages of lighting two candles for the honor of Shabbat — one corresponds to Zachor and one corresponds to Shamor

INTRODUCTION: SHABBAT AND HOLIDAY CANDLE LIGHTING

(candles ten lights she if: וְעוֹד ve'od הֲרֵינִי hareni מַדְלֶקֶת madleket
שְׁמוֹנָה shmona נֵרוֹת nerot. כְּדֵי kedei שֶׁיִּהְיֶה sheyihye ייי סַךְ sach
הַכֹּל hakol ילי עֲשָׂרָה asara שֶׁהֵם shehem מִנְיָן minyan עֶשֶׂר eser
הַסְּפִירוֹת hasefirot) לְתַקֵּן letaken שֹׁרֶשׁ shoresh מִצְוָה mitzva זוֹ zo
בִּמְקוֹם bemakom עֶלְיוֹן elyon. וִיהִי vihi נֹעַם no'am אֲדֹנָי Adonai כלה
אֱלֹהֵינוּ Elohenu ילה עָלֵינוּ alenu וּמַעֲשֵׂה uma'ase יָדֵינוּ yadenu
כּוֹנְנָה konena עָלֵינוּ alenu וּמַעֲשֵׂה uma'ase יָדֵינוּ yadenu כּוֹנְנֵהוּ konenehu:

Light the candles, cover your eyes after all the candles are lit and recite the following blessing:

בָּרוּךְ baruch אַתָּה Ata יְהֹוָה/אהדונהי Adonai
אֱלֹהֵינוּ Elohenu ילה מֶלֶךְ melech הָעוֹלָם ha'olam אֲשֶׁר asher
קִדְּשָׁנוּ kideshanu בְּמִצְוֹתָיו bemitzvotav וְצִוָּנוּ vetzivanu לְהַדְלִיק lehadlik
נֵר ner יהוה אהיה יהוה אלהים יהוה אדני שֶׁל shel שַׁבָּת Shabbat:

Then say "Yehi Ratzon" on pages 18-19.

(and more I hereby light eight candles — so it will add up to ten candles corresponding the number of the Ten Sefirot) to correct the root of the precept in the Supernal Place. "May the pleasantness of the Lord, our God, be upon us and may He establish the work of our hands for us and may the work of our hands establish Him." (Psalms 90:17)

Blessed are You, Lord, our God, King of the world,
Who has sanctified us with His commandments and obliged us with lighting the candles of Shabbat.

Introduction: Shabbat and Holiday Candle Lighting

Blessing for Holiday Candles

(Should be followed by the blessing of "Shehecheyanu" on page 18)

If a holiday falls on *Shabbat*, we should recite two blessings over the candles: one for *Shabbat* and one for the holiday. These special blessings are said only on holidays, and they connect us to the extra energy revealed on that holiday. We light the candles first, and then encircle the candles with our hands three times to draw the spiritual Light towards our face. We cover our eyes and recite the blessing.

בָּרוּךְ baruch אַתָּה Ata יְהוָֹה(אדנייאהדונהי) Adonai

אֱלֹהֵינוּ Elohenu ילה מֶלֶךְ melech הָעוֹלָם ha'olam

אֲשֶׁר asher קִדְּשָׁנוּ kideshanu בְּמִצְוֹתָיו bemitzvotav וְצִוָּנוּ vetzivanu

לְהַדְלִיק lehadlik נֵר ner יהוה אהיה יהוה אלהים יהוה אדני שֶׁל shel

(*if the holiday falls on Shabbat add* : שַׁבָּת Shabbat וְ ve) יוֹם yom טוֹב tov:

Blessing for Yom Kippur Candles

(Should be followed by the blessing of "Shehecheyanu" on page 18)

For *Yom Kippur*, there is a special blessing. We light the candles first, and then encircle the candles with our hands three times to draw the spiritual Light towards our face. We cover our eyes and recite the blessing.

בָּרוּךְ baruch אַתָּה Ata יְהוָֹה(אדנייאהדונהי) Adonai

אֱלֹהֵינוּ Elohenu ילה מֶלֶךְ melech הָעוֹלָם ha'olam

אֲשֶׁר asher קִדְּשָׁנוּ kideshanu בְּמִצְוֹתָיו bemitzvotav וְצִוָּנוּ vetzivanu

לְהַדְלִיק lehadlik נֵר ner יהוה אהיה יהוה אלהים יהוה אדני שֶׁל shel

(*if Yom Kippur falls on Shabbat add*: שַׁבָּת Shabbat וְ ve) יוֹם yom הַכִּפּוּרִים hakipurim:

Blessing for Holiday Candles
Blessed are You, Lord, our God, King of the world, Who has sanctified us with His commandments and obliged us with lighting the candles of (Shabbat and) the holiday.

Blessing for Yom Kippur Candles
Blessed are You, Lord, our God, King of the world, Who has sanctified us with His commandments and obliged us with lighting the candles of (Shabbat and) the Day of Atonement.

INTRODUCTION: SHABBAT AND HOLIDAY CANDLE LIGHTING

BLESSING OF SHEHECHEYANU

ילה Elohenu אֱלֹהֵינוּ Adonai יְהֹוָהאֲדֹנָיאהרונהי Ata אַתָּה baruch בָּרוּךְ

shehecheyanu שֶׁהֶחֱיָנוּ (*Right-Chesed*) ha'olam הָעוֹלָם melech מֶלֶךְ

vehigi'anu וְהִגִּיעָנוּ (*Central-Tiferet*) vekiyemanu וְקִיְּמָנוּ (*Left-Gevurah*)

hazeh הַזֶּה lazeman לַזְּמַן (*Malchut*):

YEHI RATZON

The power of righteous children and a righteous husband is given to us through this blessing. A woman's greatest opportunity for sharing is with her family, which is closest to her in her daily life. The definition of sharing with one's child or spouse takes on a whole new meaning when understood from a kabbalistic point of view. To help us understand what sharing genuinely means, we must first comprehend what is *not* sharing.

Our teacher, Rav Berg, explains that when parents raise their children, most acts of sharing are considered part of one's duty as a loving parent. In other words, there are no "merit points" in the Upper Worlds when we share with our loved ones. Real sharing occurs only when it is difficult for us to give; when we go outside of ourselves and leave our comfort zones. We ordinarily play with or give to our children when doing so pleases us. We derive as much pleasure as they do. If we can learn to share, and give our time and attention to them when it is difficult for us, we can reap far greater benefits. Lighting the *Shabbat* candles is considered to be a genuine act of sharing toward our family.

ע"ה עדי אל ע"ה, קס"א ע"ב בריבוע ע"ה, מהש ratzon רָצוֹן yehi יְהִי

Elohai אֱלֹהַי Adonai יְהֹוָהאֲדֹנָיאהרונהי ב"ן מ"ה ס"ג milfanecha מִלְּפָנֶיךָ

avotai אֲבוֹתַי ילה ; דמ"ב, דע"ב מילוי ; לכב velohei וֵאלֹהֵי דמב, דע"ב מילוי

רמ"ח (אברים), עסמ"ב וט"ז אותיות פשוטות ; אל רי"ו ; ג"פ יב"ק utrachem וּתְרַחֵם shetachus שֶׁתָּחוּס

chasdecha חַסְדְּךָ vetagdil וְתַגְדִּיל, alai עָלַי

osei עוֹשֵׂי anashim אֲנָשִׁים zera זֶרַע li לִי latet לָתֵת imadi עִמָּדִי

◆lishma לִשְׁמָהּ betoratcha בְּתוֹרָתְךָ ve'oskim וְעוֹסְקִים ◆retzonecha רְצוֹנֶךָ

BLESSING OF SHEHECHEYANU
Blessed are You, Lord, our God, King of the world,
who has kept us alive, sustained us, and brought us to this time.

YEHI RATZON
May it be pleasing before You, Lord, my God, and God of my forefathers,
that You will take pity and be merciful to me, and may You increase Your compassion to me by granting
me, for offspring, ones who do Your bidding and who occupy themselves in Your Torah for Its own sake.

Introduction: Shabbat and Holiday Candle Lighting

וְיִהְיוּ veyih'yu (יֵ"אי מילוי דס"ג) אל מְאִירִים me'irim בַּתּוֹרָה batorah

בִּזְכוּת bizchut נֵרוֹת nerot שַׁבָּת Shabbat (if a holiday falls on Shabbat add:

וְיוֹם veyom טוֹב tov) הַלָּלוּ halalu, כְּמוֹ kemo שֶׁנֶּאֱמַר shene'emar:

כִּי ki נֵר ner מִצְוָה mitzvah וְתוֹרָה vetorah אוֹר or רז, א"ס

וְגַם vegam תָּחוֹס tachos וּתְרַחֵם utrachem

ג"פ רי"ו ; וז"פ אל, רי"ו ל"ב נתיבות החוכמה, רמ"ח (אברים), עסמ"ב ט"ז אותיות פשוטות

עַל al בַּעֲלִי ba'ali

(Here a woman should meditate and mention her husband's name and his father's name)

וְתִתֵּן vetiten ב"פ כהת לוֹ lo אֹרֶךְ orech יָמִים yamim נלך

וּשְׁנוֹת ushnot חַיִּים chayim אהיה אהיה יהוה, בינה ע"ה

עִם im בְּרָכָה beracha וְהַצְלָחָה vehatzlacha, וְתַסִּיעֵהוּ ut'saye'ehu

לַעֲשׂוֹת la'asot רְצוֹנְךָ retzoncha בִּשְׁלֵמוּת bishlemut. כֵּן ken יְהִי yehi

רָצוֹן ratzon מהש ע"ה, ע"ב בריבוע וקס"א ע"ה, אל שדי ע"ה אָמֵן amen יאהדונהי.

(42 letters in this verse—מ"ב אותיות בפסוק)

יִהְיוּ yih'yu אל (יֵ"אי מילוי דס"ג) לְרָצוֹן leratzon מהש ע"ה, ע"ב בריבוע וקס"א ע"ה, אל שדי ע"ה

אִמְרֵי imrei פִּי fi ר"ת אֶלֶף = אלף למד דלת יוד ע"ה וְהֶגְיוֹן vehegyon לִבִּי libi

לְפָנֶיךָ lefanecha ס"ג ב"ן יְהֹוָהאדניאהדונהי Adonai צוּרִי tzuri וְגוֹאֲלִי vego'ali:

May they be resplendent in the Torah by virtue of these candles, as it is said:
"Because the precept is a candle and the Torah is Light." (Proverbs 6:23)
May You also take pity and be merciful to my husband
(Here a woman should meditate and mention her husband's name and his father's name)
and may You grant him lengthy days and years of life, filled with blessings and success, and may You help him in doing Your bidding perfectly. May it so be Your desire, Amen. "May the words of my mouth and the thoughts of my heart be pleasing before You, God, my Rock and my Redeemer." (Psalms 19:15)

Kabbalat Shabbat Connection

MIZMOR LEDAVID (A PSALM OF DAVID)
ANA BEKO'ACH
LECHA DODI (GO MY BELOVED)
MIZMOR SHIR LEYOM HASHABBAT (A PSALM, A SONG FOR THE
 DAY OF SHABBAT)
BAR YOCHAI
KEGAVNA (JUST AS THEY)

Kabbalat Shabbat

Kabbalat Shabbat

You should go out to the field (and if it is not possible, it is good to go outside to a courtyard, to a place that is empty and clear.) And you should stand in a high place and turn to the West. At the time of sunset, close your eyes and put your hands on your chest, right hand over the left and be with awe and fear as you stand in front of the King to receive the Holiness of *Shabbat*.

You should meditate that *Chakal* (וֹקֲל"ל field), which is the numerical value of 138 equals: הויה אהיה הויה אדני (יאהדונהי). Also it has the same numerical value of the *Milui* of the four Names (וד י י הי • וד י או י • וד י א או א • וד ה ו ה) with the ten letters. And also ס"ג (יוד הי ואו הי) with its ten letters and the Name אדני have the numerical value of 138.

Now in the field (*Sadeh* שדה) meditate that it is considered as the external part of the Four Worlds, and our goal, during *Kabbalat Shabbat* in the field, is to elevate the Inner aspect of the External part. You should visualize the Four Worlds in the following order:

Atzilut   יוד הי ויו הי
Beriah   יוד הי ואו הי
Yetzirah   יוד הא ואו הא
Asiyah   יוד הה וו הה

Say the following with all your might and with happiness:

לְשֵׁם leshem יִחוּד yichud קוּדְשָׁא kudsha בְּרִיךְ berich הוּא hu
וּשְׁכִינְתֵּיהּ ush'chintei (יאהדונהי) בִּדְחִילוּ bid'chilu וּרְחִימוּ ur'chimu
וּרְחִימוּ ur'chimu (יאההויהה), וּדְחִילוּ ud'chilu (איההויהה), לְיַחֲדָא leyachda
שֵׁם shem יוֹ"ד yud קֵי kei בְּוָא"ו bevav קֵי kei בְּיִחוּדָא beyichuda
שְׁלִים shelim (יהוה) בְּשֵׁם beshem כָּל kol יְלִי, יִשְׂרָאֵל Yisrael,
בּוֹאוּ bo'u וְנֵצֵא venetze לִקְרַאת likrat שַׁבָּת Shabbat מַלְכְּתָא malketa,
לַחֲקַל lachakal תַּפּוּחִין tapuchin קַדִּישִׁין kadishin.

Meditate to elevate the Inner aspect of the External part of the Worlds as *Chochmah, Binah, Da'at* of the Lower World are going up into *Netzach, Hod, Yesod* of the Upper World. And later on (while saying the word "havu," in Psalm 29, three times) meditate on the elevation of the Three Upper *Sefirot* of *Asiyah* (*Chochmah, Binah, Da'at*) into *Netzach, Hod, Yesod* of *Yetzirah*.

Kabbalat Shabbat
LeShem Yichud

For the sake of unification of the Holy Blessed One and His Shechinah with fear and love and with love and fear, in order to unify the Name Yud-Kei with Vav-Kei in perfect unity and in the name of all Israel, let us go out towards the Shabbat Queen, to the Field of the Holy Apples.

Kabbalat Shabbat

Mizmor LeDavid (A Psalm of David)

In this Psalm the word *Kol* קוֹל, which means "voice," is mentioned seven times. The voice is the Voice of the Creator—*Kol Adonai*. These seven voices represent seven dimensions of the Light. These seven dimensions (*Sefirot*) express themselves through the seven verses of the *Ana Beko'ach*, the 42-Letter Name of God. Whenever we make a connection to the 42-Letter Name of God, we are tapping the Primordial Force of Creation. This kind of energy brings new life, rejuvenation, and total positivity to our lives, and this helps awaken us to receive the Light of *Shabbat*.

In this Psalm we also find the Name: יהוה mentioned eighteen times. Eighteen is the same numerical value as the Aramaic word *Chai* חי meaning "life." Accordingly, we have 72 letters (4x18), which is equal to the numerical value of the Aramaic word *Chesed* חסד. *Chesed* represents the energy of Mercy. The construction of the prayer gives us the ability to surround ourselves with the energy of Mercy that flows into our world during *Shabbat*. It is said that, at this time of day (sunset), the universe is filled with the energy of Judgment. On *Shabbat*, however, we only connect to the Mercy, as *Shabbat* is a realm without Judgment. But there is a prerequisite: We have to be careful not to stand in judgment of others during the period just before *Shabbat*. During this time, the Satan always tries to incite hostilities and arguments between husbands and wives, families and friends. If the Satan succeeds and we are judgmental, we cannot connect to the Light of Mercy. We must put ourselves into a frame of total happiness.

In this Psalm there are 18 times יהוה that have 72 letters, which is the numerical value of *Chesed*, corresponding to the Mercy that descends from the Upper World. There are 11 verses, which is the same numerical value as ו"ה and 91 words, which is the numerical value for *Amen* אמן.

מִזְמוֹר mizmor לְדָוִד leDavid

הָבוּ havu אוֹר, אהבה, דאגה לַיהוָה(אדנייאהדונהי) ladonai (כ"ן - יוד הה וו הה)

Meditate to draw three times ב"ן from the Thirteen *Tikkunei Dikna* of *Arich Anpin* of *Asiyah* to *Da'at* of *Asiyah* in order to elevate it to *Yesod* of *Yetzirah* (*Keter* of *Asiyah* is elevated to *Hod* of *Yetzirah*).

בְּנֵי benei ר"ת הבל הבו יהוה בני אלים = יעקב אֵלִים elim

Meditate to unite your soul with the souls of Cain and Abel so it would be elevated with them.

הָבוּ havu אוֹר, אהבה, דאגה לַיהוָה(אדנייאהדונהי) la'donai (מ"ה - יוד הא ואו הא)

Meditate to draw three times מ"ה from the Thirteen *Tikkunei Dikna* of *Arich Anpin* of *Yetzirah* to *Binah* of *Asiyah* in order to elevate it to *Hod* of *Yetzirah* (*Keter* of *Asiyah* is elevated to *Netzach* of *Yetzirah*).

כָּבוֹד kavod ר"ת כלה (ב"ן) וג' ספירות (נה"י) וְעֹז va'oz

Mizmor LeDavid (A Psalm of David)

A Psalm of David:
Render to the Lord, you sons of the powerful ones, render to the Lord honor and might.

KABBALAT SHABBAT

הָבוּ havu אוֹר, אהבה, דאגה לַ**יהוה**אדניאהדונהי la'donai (ס״ג - יוד הי ואו הי)

Meditate to draw three times **ס״ג** from the Thirteen *Tikkunei Dikna* of *Arich Anpin* of *Beriah* to *Chochmah* of *Asiyah* in order to elevate it to *Netzach* of *Yetzirah* (*Keter* is elevated to *Tiferet*). Also, three times **הבו** is equal to **יוד הא ואו** (39), in which the last **הא** (*Nukva*) received from it.

כְּבוֹד kevod ר״ת כלה (ב״ן וג' ספירות נה״י) שְׁמוֹ shemo

ע״ב בריבוע וקס״א ע״ה, אל שדי ע״ה, מהש ע״ה ; הבו יהוה כבוד שמו = אדם דוד מעילוי

הִשְׁתַּחֲווּ hishtachavu לַ**יהוה**אדניאהדונהי la'donai (ע״ב - יוד הי ויו הי)

Meditate to draw three times **ע״ב** from the Thirteen *Tikkunei Dikna* of *Arich Anpin* of *Atzilut* to *Chochmah* of *Asiyah* (which is now in *Netzach* of *Yetzirah*) in order for **ס״ג** to go to *Binah* of *Asiyah* (which is now in *Hod* of *Yetzirah*) and **מ״ה** and **ב״ן** will go to *Da'at* of *Asiyah* (which is now in *Yesod* of *Yetzirah*), as this is Their place in the secret of *Chasadim* and *Gevurot* as it is known.

בְּהַדְרַת behadrat ר״ת הבל קֹדֶשׁ kodesh ר״ת קבלה (שביום שבת צריך ללמוד קבלה):

ז' קוֹלוֹת – Seven Voices

Seven Voices corresponding to the Seven Breaths of *Atzilut* and the 42-Letter Name of *Yetzirah*, to support the elevation of the Seven Lower *Sefirot* of *Asiyah* into *Yetzirah*.

קוֹל kol (*Chesed*) **יהוה**אדניאהדונהי Adonai (אבגיתץ) - (ו)

עַל- al הַמַּיִם hamayim ר״ת = אלף למד (וסד - ואל עני רמוז בגילה במועשר)

אֵל El יא״י (מילוי דס״ג) הַכָּבוֹד hakavod לאו הִרְעִים hir'im

ה״פ אדני (להמתיק עכ״ה דינים) **יהוה**אדניאהדונהי Adonai עַל- al מַיִם mayim

רַבִּים rabim ר״ת הרעים (עכ״ה דינים - וענין העכ״ה דינים נמתקים ע״י שמות א״ל הרמוזים לעיל):

קוֹל kol (*Gevurah*) **יהוה**אדניאהדונהי Adonai (קרעשטן) - (ד)

בַּכֹּחַ bako'ach ר״ת יב״ק, אלהים יהוה, אהיה אדני יהוה

קוֹל kol (*Tiferet*) **יהוה**אדניאהדונהי Adonai (נגדיכש) - (א)

בְּהָדָר behadar ר״ת יב״ק, אלהים יהוה, אהיה אדני יהוה:

Render to the Lord honor worthy of His Name, prostrate yourselves before the Lord in the glory of His Holiness. The voice of the Lord is upon the waters, The Lord of glory had thundered, the Lord is upon vast waters. The Voice of the Lord is powerful. The Voice of the Lord is majesty.

Kabbalat Shabbat

shover שֹׁבֵ֥ר (א - בְּטִרְצָתֵג) Adonai יְהוָ֑ה (Netzach) kol קֹ֣ול

arzei אַרְזֵ֣י et אֶת־ Adonai יְהוָ֑ה vayeshaber וַיְשַׁבֵּ֣ר arazim אֲרָזִ֑ים

egel עֵ֑גֶל kemo כְּמֹו־ vayarkidem וַיַּרְקִידֵ֥ם ר"ת האא: haLevanon הַלְּבָנֹ֗ון

re'emim רְאֵמִֽים: ven בֶן־ kemo כְּמֹ֥ו veSiryon וְ֝שִׂרְיֹ֗ן Levanon לְבָנֹ֥ון

(ו) - (וְיִקַבְטנע) Adonai יְהוָ֑ה (Hod) kol קֹול־

(Yesod) kol קֹ֥ול :esh אֵֽשׁ lahavot לַהֲבֹ֥ות chotzev חֹצֵ֗ב

יְהוָ֣ה אֲדֹנָי, לכלה ס"ת yachil יָחִ֣יל (א - יוּגוּלופוּוּוּקוּ) Adonai יְהוָ֑ה

Adonai יְהוָ֑ה yachil יָחִ֥יל קין = ר"ת midbar מִדְבָּ֑ר

קין: = ר"ת Kadesh קָדֵֽשׁ midbar מִדְבַּ֥ר

Meditate to elevate your soul with the sparks of the souls of Cain and Abel from the klipa to Yetzirah

Adonai יְהוָ֨ה (Malchut) kol קֹ֤ול

(עֲקוּצִית וִיכוּיָן לִכְלוֹל בּו כָּל עֲשִׂיָּה הָעוֹלָמוֹת הָאוֹחֲרִים - וְדָאוּא)

ye'arot יְעָרֹ֥ות vayechesof וַיֶּחֱשֹׂ֥ף ayalot אַיָּלֹ֗ות yecholel יְחֹולֵ֤ל

kavod כָּבֹֽוד: omer אֹמֵ֥ר kulo כֻּלֹּ֗ו uvchechalo וּ֝בְהֵיכָלֹ֗ו

הבל וס"ת ילי ר"ת yashav יָשָׁ֑ב lamabul לַמַּבּ֣וּל Adonai יְהוָ֭ה

Meditate on the Name ילי to draw a great Illumination to the inner part of the Worlds (their soul aspect) and to elevate the sparks of the souls of Cain and Abel and the rest of the souls that are stuck inside the klipa and cannot be elevated by themselves on Shabbat.

le'olam לְעֹולָֽם melech מֶ֣לֶךְ Adonai יְהוָ֥ה vayeshev וַיֵּ֥שֶׁב

yiten יִתֵּ֑ן le'amo לְעַמֹּ֣ו oz עֹ֭ז Adonai יְהוָ֗ה רביע ס"ג י אותיות דס"ג:

(למתק את ז' המלכים עמתו) עסמ"ב, הברכה yevarech יְבָרֵ֖ךְ Adonai יְהוָ֓ה ׀

יהו"ה: רביע ע"ב, ר"ת vashalom בַשָּׁלֹֽום amo עַמֹּ֣ו et אֶת־

The Voice of the Lord breaks cedars; the Lord breaks the cedars of Lebanon. He makes them dance around like a calf, Lebanon and Sirion like a wild young ox. The Voice of the Lord cleaves the flames of fire. The Voice of the Lord convulses the wilderness; the Lord convulses the wilderness of Kadesh. The Voice of the Lord frightens the hinds and strips the forests bare, and in His Temple all proclaim His glory. The Lord sat at the deluge, and the Lord sits as King forever. the Lord gives might to His people. The Lord will bless His people with peace. (Psalms 29)

Kabbalat Shabbat

Ana Beko'ach

The *Ana Beko'ach* is perhaps the most powerful prayer in the entire universe. Second-century Kabbalist Rav Nachunya ben HaKana was the first sage to reveal this combination of 42 letters, which encompass the power of Creation.

The *Ana Beko'ach* is a unique formula, built of 42 letters written in seven sentences, that gives us the ability to transcend this physical world with all its limitations. It is known as the 42-letter Name of God. The *Ana Beko'ach* can literally remove all friction, barriers, and obstacles associated with our physical existence. It injects order into chaos, removes Satan's influence from our nature, generates financial sustenance, arouses unity with, and love for, others, and provides healing energy to the body and soul. We can recite or scan the *Ana Beko'ach* every day, as many times as we want.

There are four elements that we connect to when using the *Ana Beko'ach*:

1) **Seven Sentences** - The seven sentences correspond to the seven *Sefirot*, from *Chesed* to *Malchut*. Although there are ten *Sefirot* in total, only the lower seven exert influence in our physical world. By connecting to these seven, we seize control over this physical world.

2) **Letters of the Month** - Abraham the Patriarch revealed the astrological secrets of the Aramaic letters and of the signs of the zodiac in his kabbalistic treatise, the *Book of Formation* (*Sefer Yetzirah*). Each month of the year is governed by a planet, and each planet has a corresponding verse in the *Ana Beko'ach*; therefore, we also meditate upon the planet and the Aramaic letter that created both the planet and the zodiac sign of each month. (See chart on pg. 29) In doing so, we connect to the positive energy of each planet and not to its negative influence. For example, the Aramaic letter *Ayin* created the sign of Capricorn, *Tevet*. Capricorn is governed by the planet Saturn. The Aramaic letter that gave birth to Saturn is *Bet*; therefore, each day during the month of *Tevet*, we meditate upon the the letters *Ayin* and *Bet* following the recital and meditation of the first verse of the *Ana Beko'ach*.

3) **Correction of the Soul** - *Tikkun HaNefesh* - Throughout history, kabbalists have used this healing meditation twice a day, seven days a week, to regenerate and revitalize all the organs of the body. When we reach the sentence in the *Ana Beko'ach* that governs the particular month we are in, we stop and meditate on the letters of that month, and then do the *Tikkun HaNefesh*. (See pg. 30) Using the chart as a guide, hold your right hand over the particular part of the body to which you are channeling energy. Look at the Aramaic letter combination for the specific area of the body that you are focusing on, and allow the Light to penetrate through your right hand, into that part of the body.

4) **Angels of the Day** - Angels are distinct packets of spiritual energy that act as a transportation system for our prayers. They carry our words and thoughts to the Upper Worlds. There is a line of *Ana Beko'ach* for each day of the week, and there are unique angels that govern each day. On *Shabbat*, as we ascend through our prayers to the Upper Worlds we can connect to the Angels of Friday night (See pg. 29).

Kabbalat Shabbat

Chesed, Sunday *(Alef Bet Gimel Yud Tav Tzadik)* אבג יתץ

ana אָנָּא	beko'ach בְּכֹחַ	gedulat גְּדוּלַת	yeminecha יְמִינְךָ
		tatir תַּתִּיר	tzerura צְרוּרָה

Gevurah, Monday *(Kuf Resh Ayin Sin Tet Nun)* קרע שטן

kabel קַבֵּל	rinat רִנַּת	amecha עַמְּךָ	sagevenu שַׂגְּבֵנוּ
	taharenu טַהֲרֵנוּ		nora נוֹרָא

Tiferet, Tuesday *(Nun Gimel Dalet Yud Kaf Shin)* נגד יכש

na נָא	gibor גִבּוֹר	dorshei דוֹרְשֵׁי	yichudecha יִחוּדְךָ
	kevavat כְּבָבַת		shomrem שָׁמְרֵם

Netzach, Wednesday *(Bet Tet Resh Tzadik Tav Gimel)* בטר צתג

barchem בָּרְכֵם	taharem טַהֲרֵם	rachamei רַחֲמֵי	tzidkatecha צִדְקָתֶךָ
	tamid תָּמִיד		gomlem גָּמְלֵם

Hod, Thursday *(Chet Kuf Bet Tet Nun Ayin)* חקב טנע

chasin וְחָסִין	kadosh קָדוֹשׁ	berov בְּרֹב	tuvcha טוּבְךָ
	nahel נַהֵל		adatecha עֲדָתֶךָ

Yesod, Friday *(Yud Gimel Lamed Pei Zayin Kuf)* יגל פזק

yachid יָחִיד	ge'eh גֵּאֶה	le'amecha לְעַמְּךָ	pene פְּנֵה
	zochrei זוֹכְרֵי		kedushatecha קְדֻשָּׁתֶךָ

Malchut, Saturday *(Shin Kuf Vav Tzadik Yud Tav)* שקו צית

shav'atenu שַׁוְעָתֵנוּ	kabel קַבֵּל	ushma וּשְׁמַע	tza'akatenu צַעֲקָתֵנוּ
	yode'a יוֹדֵעַ		ta'alumot תַּעֲלוּמוֹת

Baruch Shem Kevod

Whispering this final verse brings all the Light from the Upper Worlds into our physical existence.

(Whisper): יזו אותיות baruch בָּרוּךְ shem שֵׁם kevod כְּבוֹד malchuto מַלְכוּתוֹ
le'olam לְעוֹלָם ריבוע ס״ג ו״ו אותיות הס״ג va'ed וָעֶד׃

KABBALAT SHABBAT

The Month and the Letters		The Astrological Sign And the Letter		The Planet And the Letter		Ana Beko'ach meditation
Tevet	עב	Capricorn	ע	Saturn	ב	אבג יתץ
Shevat	צב	Aquarius	צ	Saturn	ב	אבג יתץ
Kislev	סג	Sagitarius	ס	Jupiter	ג	קרע שטן
Adar	קג	Pisces	ק	Jupiter	ג	קרע שטן
Nissan	דה	Aries	ה	Mars	ד	נגד יכש
Cheshvan	דנ	Scorpio	נ	Mars	ד	נגד יכש
Av	כט	Leo	ט	Sun	כ	בטר צתג
Iyar	פו	Taurus	ו	Venus	פ	וזקב טנע
Tishrei	פל	Libra	ל	Venus	פ	וזקב טנע
Sivan	רז	Gemini	ז	Mercury	ר	יגל פזק
Elul	רי	Virgo	י	Mercury	ר	יגל פזק
Tammuz	וזת	Cancer	וז	Moon	ת	שקו צית

Angels of Friday Night

יוֹד הֵי וָאו הֵי   שׁוֹעֲתֵנוּ קַבֵּל וּשְׁמַע צַעֲקָתֵנוּ יוֹדֵעַ תַּעֲלוּמוֹת
עַקְוצִית יְהוָה יְהוָה יְהוָה
שְׁמַעְיאֵל בֶּרְכִיאֵל אַהֲנִיאֵל ר"ת שׂוא
סַמְטוֹרְיָה גְּזוּרִיאֵל וְעַנָאֵל לְמוּאֵל ר"ת סגול   צוּרִיאֵל רְזִיאֵל יוֹפִיאֵל ר"ת צירי

ANA BEKO'ACH

Chesed, Sunday אבג יתץ
We beseech You, with the power of Your great right, undo this entanglement.

Gevurah, Monday קרע שטן
Accept the singing of Your Nation. Strengthen and purify us, Awesome One.

Tiferet, Tuesday נגד יכש
Please, Mighty One, those who seek Your unity, guard them like the pupil of the eye.

Netzach, Wednesday בטר צתג
Bless them. Purify them. Your compassionate righteousness always grant them.

Hod, Thursday וזקב טנע
Invincible and Mighty One, with the abundance of Your goodness, govern Your congregation.

Yesod, Friday יגל פזק
Sole and proud One, turn to Your people, those who remember Your sanctity.

Malchut, Saturday שקו צית
Accept our cry and hear our wail, You that knows all that is hidden.

BARUCH SHEM KEVOD
"Blessed is the Name of Glory. His Kingdom is forever and for eternity." (Pesachim 56a)

KABBALAT SHABBAT

	1 **Keter** Skull יְהֹוָה	
3 *Binah* Left Brain יֱהֹוִה		2 *Chochmah* Right Brain יְהוִה
5 Left Eye יהוה יהוה יהוה יהוה יהוה	9 8 Nose אֱלֹהִים	4 Right Eye יהוה יהוה יהוה יהוה יהוה
7 Left Ear יוד הי ואו הה		6 Right Ear יוד הי ואו הה

10
Mouth
יוד הי ואו הי (אהיה)
אוזה"ע גיכ"ק דטלנ"ת זסער"ץ בומ"ף

12 *Gevurah* Left Arm יֱהֹוִה	13 *Tiferet* Body יְהֹוָה	11 *Chesed* Right Arm יְהֹוָה
15 *Hod* Left Leg יְהֹוָה	16 *Yesod* Reproductive Organs לו הו וו הו	14 *Netzach* Right Leg יְהֹוָה

17
Malchut
עטרה
יהו(אדני)

Kabbalat Shabbat

Lecha Dodi (Go My beloved)

Lecha Dodi was written by Kabbalist Rav Shlomo Elkabetz, and contains ten verses that connect us to the Ten *Sefirot*—the transmitters by which the Light of God animates our universe, including our souls. During the week, we encounter many challenges and opportunities that may disrupt and misalign these ten energy forces on both a personal and universal level. The level of disruption is based on our individual and collective actions. On a personal level this can manifest in overreacting and anger to situations to which we would normally respond with restraint and patience. Each verse in *Lecha Dodi* adjusts a level of the Ten *Sefirot*, rearranging them into their correct positions in the universe. It also realigns each *Sefira* within our body, putting us into proper emotional, physical, and spiritual balance.

It is known (see Zohar Vayikra 81) that the elevation of *Malchut* is by *Tiferet*, which is the inner meaning of the verse "She is fallen, She shall no more rise" (Amos 5:2), meaning She shall no more rise by Herself but the Holy One Blessed Be He (*Tiferet*, which is called *dodi*-My beloved), shall raise Her.

Keter

לְכָה lecha דּוֹדִי dodi לִקְרַאת likrat כַּלָּה kalah.
פְּנֵי penei וחכמה בינה שַׁבָּת Shabbat נְקַבְּלָה nekabela:

Chochmah

שָׁמוֹר shamor וְזָכוֹר vezachor ע"ב קס"א יהי אור ע"ה
בְּדִבּוּר bedibur אֶחָד echad אהבה, דאגה. (סוד המשכת השפע מן ד' שמות ליסוד הנקרא זכור)
הִשְׁמִיעָנוּ hishmi'anu אֵל El יא"י (מילוי דס"ג) הַמְיוּחָד hameyuchad.
יְהוָֹה Adonai אֶחָד echad אהבה, דאגה ע"ב ברביעי קס"א ע"ה, וּשְׁמוֹ ushmo
וּלְתִפְאֶרֶת ultiferet וְלִתְהִלָּה velit'hila ע"ה אמת, אהיה פעמים אהיה, ז"פ ס"ג: Lecha
אֶחָד echad ע"ה מוהע"ה אל עדי ע"ה לְשֵׁם leshem אהבה, דאגה.

Binah

לִקְרַאת likrat שַׁבָּת Shabbat לְכוּ lechu וְנֵלְכָה venelcha.
כִּי ki הִיא hee מְקוֹר mekor הַבְּרָכָה haberacha.
מֵרֹאשׁ merosh ריבוע אלהים אלהים דיודין ע"ה מִקֶּדֶם mikedem נְסוּכָה nesucha.
סוֹף sof מַעֲשֶׂה ma'ase בְּמַחֲשָׁבָה bemachashava תְּחִלָּה techila: Lecha

---

Lecha Dodi (Go My beloved)

Keter — Go My beloved towards the bride, let us welcome the presence of the Shabbat!
Chochmah — "Safeguard" and "remember" as one utterance. The unique God made us hear. God is One and His Name is One, for renown, for splendor and for praise.
Binah — Come, let us go towards the Shabbat, for It is the source of blessing. From the beginning, from antiquity, It was honored. The end of deed was first in thought.

KABBALAT SHABBAT

Chesed

מִקְדַשׁ mikdash מֶלֶךְ melech עִיר ir סֶדֶלְפּוֹן, סֶזָוֶר, עָרֵי מְלוּכָה melucha◆

קוּמִי kumi צְאִי tze'i מִתּוֹךְ mitoch הַהֲפֵכָה hahafecha◆

רַב rav לָךְ lach שֶׁבֶת shevet בְּעֵמֶק be'emek הַבָּכָא habacha◆

וְהוּא vehu יַחֲמוֹל yachmol עָלַיִךְ alayich וְחֶמְלָה chemla: Lecha

Gevurah

הִתְנַעֲרִי hitna'ari מֵעָפָר me'afar קוּמִי kumi◆ לִבְשִׁי livshi בִּגְדֵי bigdei

תִפְאַרְתֵּךְ tifartech עַמִּי ami◆ עַל al יַד yad בֶּן ben יִשַׁי Yishai בֵּית bet

הַלַּחְמִי halachmi◆ קָרְבָה korva אֶל el נַפְשִׁי nafshi גְאָלָהּ ge'ala :Lecha

Tiferet

הִתְעוֹרְרִי hit'oreri הִתְעוֹרְרִי hit'oreri◆ כִּי ki בָא va אוֹרֵךְ orech קוּמִי kumi

אוֹרִי ori◆ עוּרִי uri עוּרִי uri שִׁיר shir דַּבֵּרִי daberi◆ כְּבוֹד kevod

יְהֹוָה Adonai עָלַיִךְ alayich נִגְלָה nigla: Lecha

Netzach

לֹא lo תֵבוֹשִׁי tevoshi וְלֹא velo תִכָּלְמִי tikalmi◆

מַה ma תִּשְׁתּוֹחֲחִי tishtochachi וּמַה uma תֶּהֱמִי tehemi◆

בָּךְ bach יֶחֱסוּ yechesu עֲנִיֵּי aniyei עַמִּי ami◆

וְנִבְנְתָה venivneta עִיר ir עַל al תִּלָּהּ tila: Lecha

Chesed   Sanctuary of the King. Royal city. Arise and depart from amidst the upheaval. For too long you have dwelt in the valley of weeping. He will bestow His compassion upon you.

Gevurah   Shake off the dust, arise. Don your clothes of splendor, my people. Through the son of Jesse, from Bethlehem, will the redemption draw close to my soul.

Tiferet   Wake up. Wake up. For your Light has come, rise and shine. Awaken, awaken, and utter a song. The glory of God is revealed upon you.

Netzach   Feel no shame, do not be humiliated. Why are you downcast? Why are you disconsolate? In you will My people's afflicted find shelter, as the city is built upon its hilltop.

Kabbalat Shabbat

Hod

וְהָיוּ vehayu לִמְשִׁסָּה limshisa שׁוֹסָיִךְ shosayich ♦ וְרָחֲקוּ verachaku כָּל kol יְלִי
מִבַּלְּעָיִךְ meval'ayich ♦ יָשִׂישׂ yasis עָלַיִךְ alayich אֱלֹהָיִךְ Elohayich ילה♦
כִּמְשׂוֹשׂ kimsos חָתָן chatan עַל al כַּלָּה kalah: Lecha

Yesod

יָמִין yamin וּשְׂמֹאל usmol תִּפְרוֹצִי tifrotzi ♦ וְאֵת ve'et
יְהוָֹה Adonai תַּעֲרִיצִי ta'aritzi ♦ עַל al יָד yad
אִישׁ ish בֵּן ben פַּרְצִי Partzi ♦ וְנִשְׂמְחָה venismecha וְנָגִילָה venagila: Lecha

Malchut

בּוֹאִי bo'i בְּשָׁלוֹם veshalom עֲטֶרֶת ateret בַּעְלָהּ ba'la ♦
גַּם gam בְּשִׂמְחָה besimcha בְּרִנָּה berina וּבְצָהֳלָה uv'tzahola ♦
תּוֹךְ toch אֱמוּנֵי emunei עַם am סְגֻלָּה segula:

Bo'i Kalah (Come bride)

When we utter the words *Bo'i Kalah*, which means "draw near bride," we receive an extra soul that comes to us every *Shabbat* to help us capture the extra energy that is being revealed. For example, an eight-ounce glass cannot contain ten ounces of water. The glass would need to be enlarged. When we receive the extra soul, this enlarges our soul, thereby, increasing its overall capacity to receive the additional Light of *Shabbat*. This is a golden opportunity to join our souls through the Light of *Shabbat*, with the Light of the Creator.

We learn from this verse that to maximize our connection, we are supposed to treat the energy of *Shabbat* like a bride. After a man has been married for twenty years, he usually does not have the same feeling, passion, longing, and anticipation that he first had when his wife was still a bride, just a few brief moments before their wedding ceremony.

Hod — *May your oppressors be downtrodden, and may those who devoured you be driven far away. Your God will rejoice over you as a groom rejoices over a bride.*

Yesod — *To the right and to the left you shall spread, and you shall extol God through a man, a descendant of Perez. Then we shall be joyful and mirthful.*

Malchut — *Come in peace, crown of her husband. Even in joy, in song, and in cheer. Among the faithful of the treasured nation.*

Kabbalat Shabbat

Meditate to elevate the Seven Lower *Sefirot* of the World of *Yetzirah* (which means: *Malchut* is elevated to *Netzach, Hod, Yesod*, then *Netzach, Hod, Yesod* are elevated to *Chesed, Gevurah, Tiferet*, then *Chesed, Gevurah, Tiferet* are elevated to *Chochmah, Binah, Da'at*) by the seven *Margela'in*, which are derived from the two Holy Names: יה"ו אהי"ה (=42), the secret of the 42-Letter Name of the World of *Beriah*:

א יהוה ה יֱהוִה ה יה אדני י מצפ"ץ ה אלהים ו אל

Then meditate to elevate the Three Upper *Sefirot* of the World of *Yetzirah* (which means: *Chochmah, Binah, Da'at* are elevated to *Malchut* of *Beriah*) by the three times word *Bo'i*, which equals 13, like the words for love, unity and care (אחד, אהבה, דאגה), and also equals יאאא (=13).

בּוֹאִי bo'i ג"פ באי = יוד הא ואו kalah כַּלָּה   **Bow to the Right**
בואי כלה = אכדטם (כי על ידי זה נמתקו הדינים)   *Chochmah - Speach*

בּוֹאִי bo'i ג"פ באי = יוד הא ואו kalah כַּלָּה   **Bow to the Left**
בואי כלה = אכדטם (כי על ידי זה נמתקו הדינים)   *Binah - Action*

תּוֹךְ toch אֱמוּנֵי emunei עָם am סְגֻלָּה segula:

Meditate that the three lower joints of the letter ל of *Tzelem* of *Abba* and *Ima* are entering *Zeir Anpin*.

Meditate to receive the extra soul called: *Nefesh*
from the aspect of the night of *Shabbat*

The third "*bo'i kalah*" should be said silently, as it corresponds to *Da'at*
(and *Da'at* is not part of the Ten *Sefirot*).

בּוֹאִי bo'i ג"פ באי = יוד הא ואו kalah כַּלָּה   **Bow to the Center**
ג"פ באי כלה = צדיק ; בואי כלה = אכדטם (כי על ידי זה נמתקו הדינים)   *Da'at - Thought*

שַׁבָּת Shabbat מַלְכְּתָא malketa:

לְכָה lecha דוֹדִי dodi לִקְרַאת likrat כַּלָּה kalah.

פְּנֵי penei וחכמה בינה שַׁבָּת Shabbat נְקַבְּלָה nekabela:

MIZMOR SHIR LEYOM HASHABBAT (A PSALM, A SONG FOR THE DAY OF SHABBAT)
The initials of each word of *Mizmor shir layom haShabbat*, when rearranged, are: *LeMoshe* (for Moses), which the sages say connects us to quantum consciousness. After we sing the *Lecha Dodi*, we say two paragraphs that were recited by Adam during the first *Shabbat* in the Garden of Eden, a realm of pure Light and immortality. Adam signifies all the souls of humanity. At the time of Creation, all these souls that were, and ever will be, were unified as one soul we call Adam. The Aramaic letters that comprise this paragraph represent specific energy forces that nourish and fulfill this unified soul called Adam. The letters are a formula that acts as an antenna to draw these forces into our lives, thereby giving us a taste of the Garden of Eden.

BO'I KALAH (COME BRIDE)
(We bow to the Left) *Come bride.*   (We bow to the Right) *Come, bride,*
(We bow to the Center) *Among the faithful of the treasured nation, Come bride! Queen Shabbat!*
Go my beloved towards the bride; let us welcome the presence of the Shabbat!

KABBALAT SHABBAT

מִזְמוֹר mizmor שִׁיר shir לְיוֹם leyom ע"ה נגד, מזבח, זן, אל יהוה הַשַּׁבָּת haShabbat

Initials of *LeMoshe* (למשה) —*Moshe* is a code name for the world of *Atzilut*, which is where we are now elevating *Beriah* that gets illuminated from *Netzach, Hod, Yesod* of *Atzilut*. Also it is called *Moshe*, because now *Moshe* receives 1,000 illuminations (those he had lost because of the golden calf) and then gives us back what we lost. Also, *Moshe*, with tens of thousands of righteous souls are descending in order to elevate all the Holy Sparks and the souls that are in the depths of the *klipa* and all the souls of the living and dead that cannot elevate on their own.

טוֹב tov יהו לְהֹדוֹת lehodot ר"ת ט"ל (ג"פ באי וג"פ הבו דלעיל)

(טֹל = יוד הא ואו, שדהם ג"ר (וֹזב"ד) דבריאה שיעלו כעת לאצילות)
Meditate to elevate the Three Upper *Sefirot* of *Beriah* to *Malchut* of *Atzilut*

לַיהוָה(אדנייאהדונהי) ladonai

Meditate on the Holy Name: יוד הי ויו הי, *Malchut* of *Atzilut*,
where the Three Upper *Sefirot* of *Beriah* are now elevated.
Also meditate on the 42-Letter Name of *Mem-Hei* of *Atzilut*:

יהוה, יוד הא ואו הא, יוד ואו דלת הא אלף ואו אלף ואו הא אלף

As by this Name, the Seven Lower *Sefirot* of *Beriah* are going to be elevated to *Atzilut*.
Also meditate on the Holy Name: יוד הי ואו הי which is the secret of the world of *Beriah*,
which is now elevated to *Atzilut* by the 42-Letter Name mentioned above.

וּלְזַמֵּר ulzamer לְשִׁמְךָ leshimcha עֶלְיוֹן elyon: לְהַגִּיד lehagid בַּבֹּקֶר baboker
וְחַסְדֶּךָ chasdecha וֶאֱמוּנָתְךָ ve'emunat'cha בַּלֵּילוֹת balelot: עֲלֵי- alei
עֲשׂוֹר asor וַעֲלֵי va'alei נָבֶל navel עֲלֵי alei הִגָּיוֹן higayon בְּכִנּוֹר bechinor:
כִּי ki שִׂמַּחְתַּנִי simachtani יְהוָה Adonai בְּפָעֳלֶךָ befa'olecha
בְּמַעֲשֵׂי bema'asei יָדֶיךָ yadecha אֲרַנֵּן aranen: מַה ma גָּדְלוּ gadlu
מַעֲשֶׂיךָ ma'asecha יְהוָה Adonai מְאֹד me'od עָמְקוּ amku
מַחְשְׁבֹתֶיךָ machshevotecha (**Superiour** *Keter*) יהו: אִישׁ ish בַּעַר ba'ar
לֹא lo יֵדָע yeda וּכְסִיל uchsil לֹא- lo יָבִין yavin אֶת- et זֹאת zot:
בִּפְרֹחַ bifro'ach רְשָׁעִים resha'im כְּמוֹ kemo עֵשֶׂב esev כוונות הקדושה (ע"ב שמות)
The souls of the wicked are judged now to see if they are worthy of being elevated from *Gehenom*.

MIZMOR SHIR LEYOM HASHABBAT (A PSALM, A SONG FOR THE DAY OF SHABBAT)
"A Psalm, a song for the day of Shabbat:
It is good to say thanks to You, the Lord, and to sing Your Name, Exalted One, And to relate Your kindness in the morning and Your faithfulness in the evenings, upon a ten-stringed instrument and lyre, with singing accompanied by a harp. Because You have made me happy, Lord, with Your deeds, for the work of Your hands, I shall sing joyously. How great are Your deeds, Lord, and how greatly profound are Your thoughts. A boor cannot know nor can a fool understand this. When the wicked bloom like grass

KABBALAT SHABBAT

lehishamdam **לְהִשָּׁמְדָם** aven **אָוֶן** po'alei ילי **פֹּעֲלֵי** kol **כָּל־** vayatzitzu **וַיָּצִיצוּ**
:(The *klipa* that wants to be elevated with the Holiness but it is not allowed) ad **עַד** adei **עֲדֵי־**
אותיות דס"ג ריבוע דס"ג י' le'olam **לְעֹלָם** marom **מָרוֹם** veAta **וְאַתָּה**
Adonai יְהֹוָ֯ה(אדניאהדונהי) oyvecha **אֹיְבֶיךָ** hineh **הִנֵּה** ki **כִּי** :Adonai יְהֹוָ֯ה(אדניאהדונהי)
yitpardu **יִתְפָּרְדוּ** yovedu **יֹאבֵדוּ** oyvecha **אֹיְבֶיךָ** hineh **הִנֵּה** ki **כִּי**
(the Holiness) vatarem **וַתָּרֶם** :(the *klipa*) aven **אָוֶן** po'alei ילי **פֹּעֲלֵי** kol **כָּל־**
:ra'anan **רַעֲנָן** beshemen **בְּשֶׁמֶן** baloti **בַּלֹּתִי** karni **קַרְנִי** kir'em **כִּרְאֵים**
bakamim **בַּקָּמִים** beshurai **בְּשׁוּרַי** רביע דמ"ה eni **עֵינִי** vatabet **וַתַּבֵּט**
:יוד הי ואו הה oznai **אָזְנָי** tishmana **תִּשְׁמַ֫עְנָה** mere'im **בַּמְּרֵעִים** alai **עָלַי**
ג"פ באי כלה דלעיל tzadik **צַדִּיק** The souls of the righteous that are elevated now
(meditate to elevate the soul of *Korach*) ס"ת קרח yifrach **יִפְרָח** katamar **כַּתָּמָר**
shetulim **שְׁתוּלִים** :yisge **יִשְׂגֶּה** baLevanon **בַּלְּבָנוֹן** ke'erez **כְּאֶרֶז**
bechatzrot **בְּחַצְרוֹת** Adonai יְהֹוָ֯ה(אדניאהדונהי) ב"פ ראה bevet **בְּבֵית**
beseva **בְּשֵׂיבָה** yenuvun **יְנוּבוּן** od **עוֹד** :yafrichu **יַפְרִיחוּ** ילה Elohenu **אֱלֹהֵינוּ**
דס"ג) אל (ויא"י מילוי yih'yu **יִהְיוּ** vera'ananim **וְרַעֲנַנִּים** deshenim **דְּשֵׁנִים**
Adonai יְהֹוָ֯ה(אדניאהדונהי) yashar **יָשָׁר** ki **כִּי** lehagid **לְהַגִּיד**
:bo **בּוֹ** (כתיב: עלתה) avlata **עַוְלָ֫תָה** velo **וְלֹא** tzuri **צוּרִי**

ADONAI MALACH (THE LORD HAS REIGNED)

In this Psalm we have 45 words corresponding to the Holy Name: (מ"ה (יוד הא ואו הא
ge'ut **גֵּאוּת** malach **מָלֵךְ** (*Zeir Anpin*) Adonai יְהֹוָ֯ה(אדניאהדונהי)
(410 cords of *Arich Anpin* - where *Zeir Anpin* is elevated on *Shabbat* and He is clothing them)
hit'azar **הִתְאַזָּר** oz **עֹז** Adonai יְהֹוָ֯ה(אדניאהדונהי) lavesh **לָבֵשׁ** lavesh **לָבֵשׁ**

---

and all doers of iniquity blossom in order to destroy them forever. And You are exalted forever, Lord. For behold, Your enemies, Lord. Your enemies shall perish and all the doers of iniquity shall be dispersed And You shall lift up my worth like an ox and I will be drenched with fresh oil. And my eyes will see my foes and my ears will hear those who rise up to harm me. A righteous man will flourish like a palm leaf, like a cedar in Lebanon he will grow tall. They are planted in the House of the Lord, they shall flourish in the courtyards of our God. They will still be fruitful in old age, vigorous and fresh they shall be to declare that the Lord is just, my Rock in whom there is no wrong." (Psalms 92)

ADONAI MALACH (THE LORD HAS REIGNED)
"The Lord has reigned. He clothed Himself with pride. The Lord clothed and girded Himself with might.

Kabbalat Shabbat

ר"י ב"פ tevel תֵּבֵל tikon תִּכּוֹן אדני, אהיה, אלהים = ר"ת af אַף־
ומב me'az מָאָז kis'acha כִּסְאֲךָ nachon נָכוֹן timot תִּמּוֹט׃ bal בַּל־
neharot נְהָרוֹת nas'u נָשְׂאוּ׃ אלהים אדני, קנ"א = ר"ת Ata אַתָּה me'olam מֵעוֹלָם
(410 cords of *Arich Anpin*
that draw Light from the sea of *Chochmah* -מוֹחָא סְתִימָא דא"א- on *Shabbat* to *Zeir Anpin*).

יְהֹוָה Adonai

נְקִי = ר"ת yis'u יִשְׂאוּ kolam קוֹלָם neharot נְהָרוֹת קין = ר"ת nas'u נָשְׂאוּ
(Rearranged initials of the name Cain, as when *Beriah* is elevated his sparks are being corrected)

ר"ת דני׃ dochyam דָּכְיָם neharot נְהָרוֹת
Meditate that we are now in the World of *Atzilut* — and with the 42-Letter Name
(the Seven Voices) that come from *Abba* and *Ima*, we are elevating the World of *Beriah*.

ערי, סנדלפון, מזלוך = ר"ת rabim רַבִּים mayim מַיִם (410 cords) mikolot מִקֹּלוֹת
ילי yam יָם mishberei מִשְׁבְּרֵי הרי adirim אַדִּירִים (*Ima* - לעשות בה מ"ן שהם ה"ג)

Arich Anpin [has 221 *Ribo* (tens of thousands) of Illuminations],
He is giving 150 *Ribo* (tens of thousands) of Illuminations to *Zeir Anpin*.
Initials of אמי (my mother) because *Zeir Anpin* first goes up and takes *Mochin* from *Ima* (mother).

Adonai יְהֹוָה bamarom בַּמָּרוֹם הרי adir אַדִּיר
Initials of אבי (my father) because *Zeir Anpin* later goes up and takes *Mochin* from *Abba* (father).

levetcha לְבֵיתְךָ קין = ר"ת me'od מְאֹד ne'emnu נֶאֶמְנוּ edotecha עֵדֹתֶיךָ
le'orech לְאֹרֶךְ Adonai יְהֹוָה kodesh קֹדֶשׁ na'ava נָאֲוָה ב"פ ראה
yamim יָמִים׃ נלך; ר"ת ילי; ס"ת אדני; ה' לאורך ימים = שע"נ נהורים עם האותיות׃

Meditate on the Name ילי to elevate the Name: אדני and the sparks of the souls of *Beriah* that are captured by the *klipa* and cannot elevate by the above mentioned 42-Letter Name. Then meditate on the Name: יוֹ"ד הֵ"י וָי"ו הֵ"י, which is the *Atzilut* (where everything is being elevated).

He also established the world firmly, so that it would not collapse. Your Throne has been established. Ever since then, You have been forever. The rivers have lifted, Lord, the rivers have raised their voices. The rivers shall raise their powerful waves. More than the roars of many waters, and the powerful waves of the sea, You are immense in the high places, The Lord. Your testimonies are extremely trustworthy. Your House is the Holy Sanctuary. The Lord shall be for the length of days." (Psalms 93)

Kabbalat Shabbat

Bar Yochai

Kabbalists throughout history agree that a human being cannot overcome the force of negativity alone, without the teachings and knowledge of the *Zohar* and the technology of *Kabbalah*. Why is it that when we know that something is bad for us, we still engage in it? Why is it that when we know something is good for us, we abstain or procrastinate? Why do we forego positive actions in favor of negative ones, nine times out of ten? The reason, according to Kabbalah, is that we constantly battle an opponent in the Game of Life. This opponent is called Satan. It ignites all of our reactive negative thoughts and actions. For 5000 years, it has been beating us at this game that hovers on the narrow edge of life and death, pain and suffering, good and evil. The kabbalistic insight as to why our opponent has been so successful is that Satan convinces humankind that Satan does not even exist. Through the Light of the *Zohar*, Satan is exposed and once we know who the opponent really is, we have a chance of beating it. The *Zohar* not only exposes and identifies the real enemy, it also gives us the power to overtake and defeat him.

It is incumbent upon us to connect to the seed and origin of the *Zohar* itself—its author, Rav Shimon bar Yochai. And so each *Shabbat* we sing the song of *Bar Yochai* to make this vital connection.

בַּר Bar יוֹחָאי Yochai נִמְשַׁחְתָּ nimshachta אַשְׁרֶיךָ ashrecha
שֶׁמֶן shemen שָׂשׂוֹן sason מֵחֲבֵרֶיךָ: mechaverecha

Malchut

בַּר Bar יוֹחָאי Yochai שֶׁמֶן shemen מִשְׁחַת mishchat קֹדֶשׁ kodesh,
נִמְשַׁחְתָּ nimshachta מִמִּדַּת mimidat הַקֹּדֶשׁ hakodesh
נָשֵׂאתָ nasata צִיץ tzitz נֵזֶר nezer הַקֹּדֶשׁ hakodesh,
חָבוּשׁ chavush עַל al רֹאשְׁךָ roshcha פְּאֵרֶךָ: pe'erecha Yochai Bar

Yesod

בַּר Bar יוֹחָאי Yochai מוֹשַׁב moshav טוֹב tov וִהִי יָשַׁבְתָּ yashavta,
יוֹם yom ע"ה נֶגֶד מוֹבוֹ, אָז, אֶל יהוה נָסַתָּ nasta
יוֹם yom ע"ה נֶגֶד מוֹבוֹ, אָז, אֶל יהוה אֲשֶׁר asher בָּרוֹחֲתָ barachta
בִּמְעָרַת bim'arat צוּרִים tzurim שֶׁעָמַדְתָּ she'amadeta שָׁם sham
קָנִיתָ kanita הוֹדְךָ hodcha וַהֲדָרֶךָ: vahadarecha Yochai Bar

---

Bar Yochai
Bar Yochai, you are anointed and praises, drawing the oil of happiness from your friends.

Malchut   Bar Yochai, holy oil anointed you from the holy tribute.
You carried the tiara of the holy crown, on you head for beauty.

Yesod   Bar Yochai, you sat in good place, the day you run and escaped.
In the cave of rock you stood, to obtain your majesty and glory.

Kabbalat Shabbat

Netzach Hod

בַּר Bar יוֹחַאי Yochai עֲצֵי atzei שִׁטִּים shitim עוֹמְדִים omdim,
לִמּוּדֵי limudei יְהֹוָה Adonai הֵם hem לוֹמְדִים lomdim. אוֹר or רז׳, א״ס,
מֻפְלָא mufla אוֹר or רז׳, א״ס הַיְקוֹד hayekod הֵם hem יוֹקְדִים yokdim,
הֲלֹא halo הֵמָּה hema יוֹרוּךְ yorucha מוֹרֶךָ morecha: Bar Yochai

Tiferet

בַּר Bar יוֹחַאי Yochai וְלִשְׂדֵה velisde תַּפּוּחִים tapuchim,
עָלִיתָ alita לִלְקוֹט lilkot בּוֹ vo מֶרְקָחִים merkachim.
סוֹד sod מיכ, י״פ הֵאא תּוֹרָה torah כְּצִיצִים ketzitzim וּפְרָחִים ufrachim,
נַעֲשֶׂה na'ase אָדָם adam נֶאֱמַר ne'emar בַּעֲבוּרֶךָ ba'avurecha: Bar Yochai

Gevurah

בַּר bar יוֹחַאי yochai נֶאֱזַרְתָּ ne'ezarta בִּגְבוּרָה bigvura רי״ו,
וּבְמִלְחֶמֶת uvmilchemet אֵשׁ esh דָּת dat הַשַּׁעְרָה hasha'ra.
וְזֶרֶב vecherev רי״ו הוֹצֵאתָ hotzeta מִתַּעְרָהּ mita'ra,
שָׁלַפְתָּ shalafta נֶגֶד neged מזבזו, זז, אל יהוה צוֹרְרֶיךָ tzorerecha: Bar Yochai

Chesed

בַּר bar יוֹחַאי yochai לִמְקוֹם limkom אַבְנֵי avnei שַׁיִשׁ shayish,
הִגַּעְתָּ higata לִפְנֵי lifnei וחכמה בינה אַרְיֵה arye לַיִשׁ layish.
גַּם gam גֻּלַּת gulat כּוֹתֶרֶת koteret עַל al עַיִשׁ ayish,
תְּשׁוּרִי tashuri וּמִי umi ילי יְשׁוּרֶךָ yeshurecha: Bar Yochai

---

Netzach Hod Bar Yochai, the acacia wood stands for you to study God's teachings. A wonderful, shining light is aglow, as your teachers taught you.

Tiferet Bar Yochai, you came to a field of apples to gather potions. The secret of Torah is like buds and blossoms; "Let us create man" was stated with you in mind.

Gevura Bar Yochai, you take courage with vigor, and fight with fire. You drew a sword out of its sheath against your opponent.

Chesed Bar Yochai, to the place of marble stones, you arrived with lion's face. We will see even the headstone of lions, but who will see you?

Kabbalat Shabbat

Binah

בַּר Bar יוֹחָאי Yochai בְּקֹדֶשׁ bekodesh הַקֳּדָשִׁים hakodashim,
קַו kav יָרוֹק yarok מְחַדֵּשׁ mechadesh י"ב הויות, קס"א קנ"א chodashim וְחֳדָשִׁים.
שֶׁבַע sheva שַׁבָּתוֹת shabatot סוֹד sod מ"כ, י"פ האא chamishim וַחֲמִשִּׁים,
קָשַׁרְתָּ kasharta קִשְׁרֵי kishrei שִׁי"ן shin קְשָׁרֶיךָ kesharecha: Bar Yochai

Chochmah

בַּר Bar יוֹחָאי Yochai יוּ"ד yod וְחָכְמָה chochmah בְּמִלּוּי = תרי"ג (מצוות)
קְדוּמָה keduma, הִשְׁקַפְתָּ hishkafta לִכְבוֹדוֹ lichvodo פְּנִימָה penima.
לֵב lev ל"ב netivot נְתִיבוֹת רֵאשִׁית reshit תְּרוּמָה teruma,
אֶת at כְּרוּב keruv מִמְשַׁח mimshach זִיו ziv אוֹרֶךָ orecha: Bar Yochai

Keter

בַּר bar יוֹחָאי yochai אוֹר or רז, א"ס מֻפְלָא mufla רוֹם rom מַעְלָה ma'la,
יָרֵאתָ yareta מִלְּהַבִּיט milhabit כִּי ki רַב rav לָהּ la,
תַּעֲלוּמָה ta'aluma וְאַיִן ve'ayin קוֹרֵא kore לָהּ la,
נָמְתָּ namta עַיִן ayin רבוע דמ"ה לֹא lo תְשׁוּרֶךָ teshurecha: Bar Yochai

בַּר Bar יוֹחָאי Yochai אַשְׁרֵי ashrei יוֹלַדְתֶּךָ yoladetecha,
אַשְׁרֵי ashrei הָעָם ha'am הֵם hem לוֹמְדֶךָ lomdecha.
וְאַשְׁרֵי ve'ashrei הָעוֹמְדִים ha'omdim עַל al סוֹדֶךָ sodecha מ"כ, י"פ האא
לְבוּשֵׁי levushei וְחֹשֶׁן choshen תֻּמֶּיךָ tumeicha וְאוּרֶךָ ve'urecha: Bar Yochai

בַּר bar יוֹחָאי yochai נִמְשַׁחְתָּ nimshachta אַשְׁרֶיךָ ashrecha,
שֶׁמֶן shemen שָׂשׂוֹן sason מֵחֲבֵרֶיךָ mechavereicha:

Binah — Bar Yochai, in the Holy of Holies, a green line renews the months. Seven Shabbats are the secret of fifty, the letter Shins for your own connections.

Chochmah — Bar Yochai, the ancient Yud of Chochmah, you observed its inner honor. 32 paths are the beginning of offering; you are the Cherub from which brilliant light anoints.

Keter — Bar Yochai, a wonderful light of highest greatness, you feared looking to her greatness. A mystery no one can read, you sleep, and no eye can see you. Bar Yochai, praised be those who gave birth to you, praised be the people who study your writings. And praised be the people who can understand your secret, dress with armor of your breastplate and of your Urim VeTumim. Bar Yochai, you are anointed and praised, drawing the oil of happiness from your friends.

KABBALAT SHABBAT

KEGAVNA (JUST AS THEY)

Kegavna, a passage from the *Zohar* (Teruma 163-166), is read or sung after the song of *Bar Yochai* because it reveals a secret of *Shabbat*. It helps remove us from this physical world, acting as a rocket booster to escape the "gravitational pull" of our planet.

כְּגַוְנָא kegavna דְּאִנּוּן de'inun מִתְיַחֲדִין mityachadin לְעֵילָא le'ela
בְּאֶחָד be'echad אוֹף of הָכִי hachi אִיהִי ihi אִתְיַחֲדַת ityachadat
לְתַתָּא letata בְּרָזָא beraza דְּאֶחָד de'echad לְמֶהֱוֵי lemehevei
עִמְּהוֹן imehon לְעֵילָא le'ela חַד chad לָקֳבֵל lakavel וְחַד chad,
קוּדְשָׁא kudsha בְּרִיךְ berich הוּא hu אֶחָד echad,
לְעֵילָא le'ela לָא la יָתִיב yativ עַל al כּוּרְסַיָּא kursaya דִּיקָרֵיהּ dikarei,
עַד ad דְּאִיהִי de'ihi אִתְעֲבִידַת it'avidat בְּרָזָא beraza
דְּאֶחָד de'echad כְּגַוְנָא kegavna דִּילֵיהּ dilei, לְמֶהֱוֵי lemehevei
אֶחָד echad בְּאֶחָד be'echad וְהָא veha אוּקִימְנָא ukimna
רָזָא raza דַּיהוה dadonai אֶחָד echad
וּשְׁמוֹ ushmo אֶחָד echad:
רָזָא raza דְּשַׁבָּת deShabbat, אִיהִי ihi שַׁבָּת Shabbat,
דְּאִתְאַחֲדַת de'itachada בְּרָזָא beraza דְּאֶחָד de'echad
לְמִשְׁרֵי lemishrei עֲלָהּ ala רָזָא raza דְּאֶחָד de'echad
צְלוֹתָא tzelota דְּמַעֲלֵי dema'alei שַׁבְּתָא shabeta, דְּהָא deha
אִתְאַחֲדַת itachadat כּוּרְסַיָּא kursaya יַקִּירָא yakira קַדִּישָׁא kadisha,
בְּרָזָא veraza דְּאֶחָד de'echad וְאִתְתַּקְּנַת ve'itetakanat
לְמִשְׁרֵי lemishrei עֲלָהּ ala מַלְכָּא malka קַדִּישָׁא kadisha עִלָּאָה ila'a.

KEGAVNA (JUST AS THEY)

163. Just as They [the Six Edges of Zeir Anpin] unite Above [from the Chest of Zeir Anpin and Above] into One (meaning that there is no partnership with the Other Side), She [Malchut] also unites Below [from the Chest of Zeir Anpin and Lower] in the secret of One, in order to be with Them Above, One in correspondence with One. For the Holy One, blessed Be He [Zeir Anpin], who is One above, does not sit on His Throne of Glory [Malchut], until She also becomes in the secret of One like Him in order so it would be One in One. We have already established the secret of 'The Lord [Zeir Anpin] is One and His Name [Malchut] is One". 164. And this is the secret of Shabbat. Malchut is called 'Shabbat' when She is united in the secret of One, so that Zeir Anpin (the secret of One) should dwell upon Her. And this is the secret of the prayer of Shabbat eve, because then the Holy Throne of Glory [Malchut] is united in the secret of One. This was established so that the Supernal Holy King [Zeir Anpin] shall dwell upon Her.

Kabbalat Shabbat

kad כַּד	ayil עָיִיל	shabeta שַׁבְּתָא,	ihi אִיהִי	ityachadat אִתְיַחֲדַת
ve'itparshat וְאִתְפָּרְשַׁת	misitra מִסִּטְרָא			achara אָחֳרָא,
vechol וְכָל	dinin דִּינִין יְלֵי	mit'aberin מִתְעַבְּרִין	mina מִנָּהּ,	
ve'ihi וְאִיהִי	ishte'arat אִשְׁתְּאָרַת	beyichuda בְּיִחוּדָא	dinhiru דִּנְהִירוּ	
kadisha קַדִּישָׁא,	ve'itatrat וְאִתְעַטְּרַת	bechama בְּכַמָּה	itrin עִטְרִין	
legabei לְגַבֵּי	malka מַלְכָּא	kadisha קַדִּישָׁא,	vechol וְכָל יְלֵי	shultanei שׁוּלְטָנֵי
rugzin רוּגְזִין	umarei וּמָארֵי	dedina דְּדִינָא	kulhu כֻּלְּהוּ	arkin עַרְקִין,
velet וְלֵית	shultana שׁוּלְטָנָא	achara אָחֳרָא	bechulhu בְּכֻלְּהוּ	almin עָלְמִין.
ve'anpaha וְאַנְפָּהָא	nehirin נְהִירִין	binhiru בִּנְהִירוּ	ila'a עִלָּאָה,	
veitatrat וְאִתְעַטְּרַת	letata לְתַתָּא	be'ama בְּעַמָּא	kadisha קַדִּישָׁא,	
vechulhu וְכֻלְּהוּ	mit'atrin מִתְעַטְּרִין	benishmatin בְּנִשְׁמָתִין	chadetin וַחֲדָתִין.	
keden כְּדֵין	sheruta שֵׁרוּתָא	ditzlota דִּצְלוֹתָא,	levarcha לְבָרְכָא	
la לָהּ	bechedva בְּחֶדְוָה,	binhiru בִּנְהִירוּ	de'anpin דְּאַנְפִּין.	

Shabbat Candles Connection

Look at the candles and meditate (see more on page 13):

Zeir and Nukva	Abba and Ima
For the second candle:	For the first candle:
The three *Yichudim* of *Zeir* and *Nukva* that add up to 250 which is the numerical value of *Ner* (candle).	The three *Yichudim* of *Abba* and *Ima* that add up to 250 which is the numerical value of *Ner* (candle).
יאהדונהי יאהלוההים יאהחויהה	יאהדונהי יאהלוההים יאהחויהה

---

165. When Shabbat enters, She secludes and separates from the Other Side. All the Judgments pass away from Her, and She remains in the oneness with the Holy Light and She becomes adorned with many Tiaras before the Holy King. All the wrathful dominions and the instigators of Judgment flee, and there is no other dominion in all the Worlds, except Her. 166. And Her face [Her Three Upper Sefirot] shines with the Supernal Light and becomes adorned with the holy Nation below, for they all become adorned from Her with new souls. Then the prayer begins of blessing Her with joy and with shining face.

First Meal Connection

CHAKAL TAPUCHIN KADISHIN (FIELD OF HOLY APPLES)

SHALOM ALECHEM (PEACE BE UPON YOU)
RIBON KOL HAOLAMIM (MASTER OF THE WORLDS)
ESHET CHAYIL (WOMAN OF VALOR)
BLESSING OVER THE MYRTLE BRANCHES
KIDDUSH (BLESSING OVER THE WINE) OF FRIDAY NIGHT
BLESSING FOR CHILDREN
ATKINU—AZAMER (PREPARE THE FEAST—I WILL SING)
KOL MEKADESH (WHOEVER SANCTIFIES)

First Meal Connection – Chakal Tapuchin Kadishin

Shalom Alechem (Peace Be Upon You)
Greeting the Shabbat Angels

We sing an ancient song known as *Shalom Alechem* (Peace Be Upon You) to greet the angels of *Shabbat*. Angels are intelligent-energy forces that exert influence on our reality. The *Midrash* teaches that two angels come with us to the *Kiddush* (Blessing Over the Wine) of Friday night, as well as accompany us to the meal. One angel is comprised of the positive energy we created during the week, the other angel, the negative energy we created during the week. If we have done our work spiritually, the negative angel will become transformed into a positive angel. However, the opposite also holds true. This song helps to keep us in a positive state of consciousness. Singing *Shalom Alechem* gives us power over the angels, enabling us to convert all negative forces into positive, even the most negative angel of all, Satan.

According to Kabbalah, all the positive actions we do during the week create millions of positive angels. But these angels are in potential, and can be activated and receive life from the Light of *Shabbat*. When we sing *Shalom Alechem*, we activate those angels so they can bless us then become "agents" or advocates on our behalf in the Upper World, as well as support and assist us in our spiritual work in the coming week.

We say each verse three times:

שָׁלוֹם shalom עֲלֵיכֶם alechem מַלְאֲכֵי mala'achei הַשָּׁרֵת hasharet
מַלְאֲכֵי mala'achei עֶלְיוֹן elyon מִמֶּלֶךְ mimelech מַלְכֵי malchei
הַמְּלָכִים hamelachim הַקָּדוֹשׁ haKadosh בָּרוּךְ Baruch הוּא Hu:

בּוֹאֲכֶם bo'achem לְשָׁלוֹם leshalom מַלְאֲכֵי mala'achei הַשָּׁלוֹם hashalom
מַלְאֲכֵי mala'achei עֶלְיוֹן elyon מִמֶּלֶךְ mimelech מַלְכֵי malchei
הַמְּלָכִים hamelachim הַקָּדוֹשׁ haKadosh בָּרוּךְ Baruch הוּא Hu:

בָּרְכוּנִי barchuni לְשָׁלוֹם leshalom מַלְאֲכֵי mala'achei הַשָּׁלוֹם hashalom
מַלְאֲכֵי mala'achei עֶלְיוֹן elyon מִמֶּלֶךְ mimelech מַלְכֵי malchei
הַמְּלָכִים hamelachim הַקָּדוֹשׁ haKadosh בָּרוּךְ Baruch הוּא Hu:

Shalom Alechem (Peace Be Upon You)

עֲלֵיכֶם שָׁלוֹם *Peace upon you, ministering angels [the angels who serve the Throne], angels of the Exalted One, from the King who reigns over kings, the Holy One, Blessed be He.*
בּוֹאֲכֶם לְשָׁלוֹם *Come in peace, angels of peace [the angels who support us], angels of the Exalted One, from the King who reigns over kings, the Holy One, Blessed be He.*
בָּרְכוּנִי לְשָׁלוֹם *Bless me with peace, angels of peace [the angels who support us], angels of the Exalted One, from the King who reigns over kings, the Holy One, Blessed be He.*

First Meal Connection – Chakal Tapuchin Kadishin

בְּצֵאתְכֶם betzetchem לְשָׁלוֹם leshalom מַלְאֲכֵי mala'achei הַשָּׁלוֹם hashalom
מַלְאֲכֵי mala'achei עֶלְיוֹן elyon מִמֶּלֶךְ mimelech מַלְכֵי malchei
הַמְּלָכִים hamelachim הַקָּדוֹשׁ haKadosh בָּרוּךְ Baruch הוּא Hu:
כִּי ki מַלְאָכָיו mala'achav יְצַוֶּה yetzave לָךְ lach ס"ת שֵׁם קָדוֹשׁ יוהך
לִשְׁמָרְךָ lishmorcha בְּכָל bechol דְּרָכֶיךָ derachech ס"ת שֵׁם קָדוֹשׁ כלך
יְהֹוָה Adonai יִשְׁמָר yishmor צֵאתְךָ tzetcha וּבוֹאֶךָ uvo'echa,
מֵעַתָּה me'ata וְעַד ve'ad עוֹלָם olam.

Ribon Kol HaOlamim (Master of the Worlds)

One Friday night, Kabbalist Rav Baruch of Mezhibuzh (the grandson of the Baal Shem Tov) was singing the *Shalom Alechem* and *Ribon Kol HaOlamim*. When he got to the words *"I gratefully thank You… for all the kindness You have done with me, and which You will do with me,"* he paused and asked himself, "Why should I give God thanks for future goodness? When that kindness will come, I will give thanks then." The answer he heard was: "Maybe by the time God will do you kindness you will no longer be on the level where you can appreciate it properly and therefore a person needs to give God thanks in the present for future kindness." Rav Baruch shared this revelation with his students and immediately began to cry bitterly. His students asked him why he was crying and he replied: "I cry at the thought that I might fall and then not be at the proper level of appreciation." Saying *Ribon Kol HaOlamim* helps us to connect and appreciate the kindness of the Creator always.

רִבּוֹן Ribon כָּל kol הָעוֹלָמִים ha'olamim
אֲדוֹן Adon כָּל kol הַנְּשָׁמוֹת haneshamot אֲדוֹן Adon הַשָּׁלוֹם hashalom.
מֶלֶךְ melech אַבִּיר Abir. מֶלֶךְ melech בָּרוּךְ Baruch. מֶלֶךְ melech גָּדוֹל gadol.
מֶלֶךְ melech דּוֹבֵר dover שָׁלוֹם shalom. מֶלֶךְ melech הָדוּר hadur. מֶלֶךְ melech
וָתִיק vatik. מֶלֶךְ melech זָךְ zach. מֶלֶךְ melech וְחַי chei הָעוֹלָמִים ha'olamim.
מֶלֶךְ melech טוֹב tov וּמֵטִיב umetiv. מֶלֶךְ melech יָחִיד yachid וּמְיֻחָד umeyuchad.
מֶלֶךְ melech כַּבִּיר kabir. מֶלֶךְ melech לוֹבֵשׁ lovesh רַחֲמִים rachamim.

בצאתכם לשלום *Go with peace, angels of peace [the angels who support us], angels of the Exalted One, from the King who reigns over kings, the Holy One, Blessed be He. "He will commend His angels to protect you in all your ways."* (Psalms 91:11) *"The Lord will guard you when you go and return, from this time and forever."* (Psalms 121:8)

Ribon Kol HaOlamim (Master of the Worlds)

Master of all Worlds, Lord of all souls, Lord of Peace. King Who is mighty, King Who is blessed, King Who is great, King Who bespeaks peace, King Who is glorious, King Who is faithful, King Who is pure, King Who gives life to the universe, King Who is good and beneficent, King Who is unique and Whose uniqueness is proclaimed, King Who is powerful, King Who dons mercy,

First Meal Connection – Chakal Tapuchin Kadishin

מֶלֶךְ melech בַּמְלָכִים malchei מֶלֶךְ melech הַמְּלָכִים hamelachim • נִשְׂגָּב nisgav •
מַעֲשֵׂה ma'ase מֶלֶךְ melech סוֹמֵךְ somech נוֹפְלִים noflim • מֶלֶךְ melech עוֹשֶׂה oseh
מֶלֶךְ melech בְּרֵאשִׁית vereshit • מֶלֶךְ melech פּוֹדֶה podeh וּמַצִּיל umatzil •
מֶלֶךְ melech צַח tzach וְאָדוֹם ve'adom • מֶלֶךְ melech קָדוֹשׁ kadosh •
מֶלֶךְ melech רָם ram וְנִשָּׂא venisa • מֶלֶךְ melech שׁוֹמֵעַ shome'a תְּפִלָּה tefila •
מֶלֶךְ melech תָּמִים tamim דַּרְכּוֹ darko:

מוֹדֶה modeh אֲנִי ani לְפָנֶיךָ lefanecha יְהֹוָה Adonai אֱלֹהַי Elohai
וֵאלֹהֵי velohei אֲבוֹתַי avotai • עַל al כָּל kol הַחֶסֶד hachesed אֲשֶׁר asher
עָשִׂיתָ asita עִמָּדִי imadi וַאֲשֶׁר va'asher אַתָּה Ata עָתִיד atid לַעֲשׂוֹת la'asot
עִמִּי imi וְעִם ve'im כָּל kol בְּנֵי benei בֵּיתִי beti וְעִם ve'im כָּל kol
בְּרִיּוֹתֶיךָ beriyotecha בְּנֵי benei בְּרִיתִי beriti • וּבְרוּכִים uvruchim הֵם hem
מַלְאָכֶיךָ mal'achecha הַקְּדוֹשִׁים hakedoshim וְהַטְּהוֹרִים vehatehorim
שֶׁעוֹשִׂים she'osim רְצוֹנְךָ retzoncha • אֲדוֹן Adon הַשָּׁלוֹם hashalom
מֶלֶךְ melech שֶׁהַשָּׁלוֹם shehashalom שֶׁלּוֹ shelo בָּרְכֵנִי barcheni
בְשָׁלוֹם vashalom • וְתִפְקֹד vetifkod אוֹתִי oti וְאֶת ve'et כָּל kol בְּנֵי benei
בֵיתִי beti וְכֹל vechol עַמְּךָ amecha בֵּית vet יִשְׂרָאֵל Yisrael
לְחַיִּים lechayim טוֹבִים tovim וּלְשָׁלוֹם ulshalom:
מַלְאֲכֵי mala'achei הַשָּׁלוֹם hashalom בּוֹאֲכֶם bo'achem לְשָׁלוֹם leshalom •
בָּרְכוּנִי barchuni לְשָׁלוֹם leshalom וְאִמְרוּ ve'imru בָּרוּךְ baruch
לְשֻׁלְחָנִי leshulchani הֶעָרוּךְ he'aruch • וְצֵאתְכֶם vetzetchem לְשָׁלוֹם leshalom
מֵעַתָּה me'ata וְעַד ve'ad עוֹלָם olam אָמֵן Amen סֶלָה Selah:

King Who reigns over kings, King Who is exalted, King Who supports the fallen, King Who maintains the works of Creation, King Who redeems and rescues, King Who is pure yet ruddy, King Who is Holy, King Who is exalted and upraised, King Who hears prayer, King Whose way is wholesome. I gratefully thank you, the Lord, my God and the God of my forefathers, for all the kindness You have done with me, and which You will do with me, with all my household, and with all Your creatures who are my fellows. Blessed are Your Holy and pure angels who do Your will. Lord of peace, King to Whom peace belongs, bless me with peace, and consider me and my entire household, and Your entire people, Israel, for a good life and for peace.

Angels of peace may your coming be for peace. Bless me for peace, and say: "Blessed is your prepared table." May your departure be in peace, from this time and forever. Amen Selah.

First Meal Connection – Chakal Tapuchin Kadishin

Eshet Chayil (Woman of Valor)

This song was written by King Solomon in order to help us to connect to the "Woman of Valor": the *Shechinah* or the female aspect of the Light of God. It is sung according to the twenty-two letters of the Hebrew Alphabet. These letters act as twenty-two channels that God uses to keep this world moving. Our connection to these letters gives us a connection to the Lightforce that moves this world and moves our lives forward.

In the section of *Eshet Chayil* there are 22 verses corresponding to the 22 conduits that are open during Friday night and influence blessings from the Upper Pool and from the Head of Crowns.

אֵשֶׁת eshet וְחַיִל chayil ומב

(ביטוש והארות ס"ג (יוד הי ואו הי) במ"ה (יוד הא ואו הא),
שישפיע לכנסת ישראל (אשת וחיל = יוד פ' יוד, הי פ' הא, ואו פ' ואו, הי פ' הא)

מִי mi ילי (Fiftieth Gate of *Binah*) יִמְצָא yimtza

"Who can find" means who will merit having the *Shechinah's* perfection and protection.

וְרָחֹק verachok מִפְּנִינִים mipeninim מִכְרָהּ michra:

בָּטַח batach בָּהּ ba לֵב lev בַּעְלָהּ ba'ala

Zeir Anpin trusts Her and put Her in charge over the world to be guided by Her.

וְשָׁלָל veshalal לֹא lo ב"פ עס"מ יֶחְסָר yechsar:

He puts his armory in Her hands to take the Holy Sparks from the *klipa*.

גְּמָלַתְהוּ gemalathu טוֹב tov והי וְלֹא velo רָע ra י"פ זר

כֹּל kol ילי יְמֵי yemei חַיֶּיהָ chayeha:

When the *Sefirot* (days of Her life) of *Zeir Anpin* (Tree of Life) shine upon Her (Tree of Knowledge) and send Her life (*Mochin* from *Binah*) then He unites with Her properly.

דָּרְשָׁה darsha צֶמֶר tzemer מצר (*Binah*) וּפִשְׁתִּים ufishtim (*Malchut*)

וַתַּעַשׂ vata'as בְּחֵפֶץ bechefetz כַּפֶּיהָ kapeha:

She protects the world from the Satan (שטן) that is drawn by the action of שעטנז *shatnez* (mixture of wool and linen, שטן ע = strong Satan), and She (willingly) sweetens the Judgment.

הָיְתָה hayta כָּאֳנִיּוֹת ka'oniyot סוֹחֵר socher

מִמֶּרְחָק mimerchak תָּבִיא tavi לַחְמָהּ lachma:

Like the merchant's ships, She brings Her bread (illumination from *Chochmah*) to the Worlds of *Beriah*, *Yetzirah* and *Asiyah* from afar (Supernal *Chochmah*) as protection from the *klipot*.

Eshet Chayil (Woman of Valor)

א "Who can find a woman of valor [the congregation of Israel]? Her value is far greater rubies.
ב The heart of Her husband [Zeir Anpin] safely trusts Her and He shall have no lacks of gain.
ג She will do Him good and not evil [Tree of Knowledge Good and Evil] all the days of Her life.
ד She seeks for wool [Binah] and flax [Malchut – Shatnez], and works willingly with Her hands.
ה She is like the merchant's ships, She brings Her bread [illumination from Chochmah] from afar.

First Meal Connection – Chakal Tapuchin Kadishin

וַתָּקָם vatakom (Light of *Chochmah*) בְּעוֹד be'od לַיְלָה layla מלה
וַתִּתֵּן vatiten לְבֵיתָהּ leveta ב"פ ראה טֶרֶף teref רפ"ח ע"ה ב"פ כהת vatiten וַתִּתֵּן
וְחֹק vechok לְנַעֲרֹתֶיהָ lena'aroteha:

She receives the Light of *Chochmah* from *Zeir Anpin* in the middle of the night and shares it with *Asiyah*, *Yetzirah* (Her household) and the Seven Chambers of *Beriah* (Her maidens). And this Light (the Light of *Chochmah*) is now ruled by the law (order) that It can be illuminating only from Below to Above for the *tzadikim* who elevate *Mayin Nukvin*.

זָמְמָה zamema שָׂדֶה sadeh (Judgment aspect of *Malchut*) וַתִּקָּחֵהוּ vatikachehu
מִפְּרִי miperi כַפֶּיהָ chapeha נָטְעָה nat'a כָּרֶם karem:
חָגְרָה chagra בְעוֹז ve'oz מָתְנֶיהָ motneha
וַתְּאַמֵּץ vate'ametz זְרוֹעֹתֶיהָ zero'oteha:
טָעֲמָה ta'ama כִּי ki טוֹב tov סַחְרָהּ sachra והו
לֹא lo יִכְבֶּה yichbe בַלַּיְלָה balayla מלה נֵרָהּ nera:

The complete revelation of the Light of the *Torah* and its precepts (good merchandise) keeps the soul (candle) illuminated during the time of exile (night) and by that She is corrected.

יָדֶיהָ yadeha שִׁלְּחָה shilecha בַכִּישׁוֹר vakishor
וְכַפֶּיהָ vechapeha תָּמְכוּ tamchu פָלֶךְ falech:
כַּפָּהּ kapa פָּרְשָׂה parsa לֶעָנִי le'ani
וְיָדֶיהָ veyadeha שִׁלְּחָה shilecha לָאֶבְיוֹן la'evyon:

The Ari explains that the action of *tzedakah* is a connection to the Holy Name יהוה (the letter *Yud*—י represents the money that is being given to *tzedakah*, the letter *Hei*—ה represents the palm of the giver, the letter *Vav*—ו represents the arm that passes the money to the receiver, and the last letter *Hei*—ה represents the palm of the receiver.) One should give *tzedakah* before being asked to give, as the Name of God will be in the right order. If a person waits to be asked to give, it changes the order of the Name of God, from יהוה to היהו.

ו She rises also while it is yet night, and gives food to Her household and orders for Her maidens.
† She deliberates on a field and buys it and She plants a vineyard from Her earnings.
ח She girds Her loins with fortitude, and flexes Her arms with strength.
ט She sees that Her merchandise is good [Torah]; Her candle [soul] does not go out at night [exile].
י She puts Her hands on the spindle, and Her palms hold tight to the distaff.
כ She stretches Her palm to the poor, and offers Her hand to the needy.

First Meal Connection – Chakal Tapuchin Kadishin

לֹא lo תִירָא tira לְבֵיתָהּ leveta מִשָּׁלֶג mishaleg (white-*Chasadim*)
כִּי ki כָל chol יְלֹ beta בֵּיתָהּ lavush לָבֻשׁ shanim שָׁנִים (red-*Chochmah*):

She (*Kneset Yisrael*) nourishes from both sides, sometimes from Mercy (snow) and sometimes from Judgment (scarlet). White dwells in red and red dwells in white.

מַרְבַדִּים marvadim עָשְׂתָה asta כָּהּ la
שֵׁשׁ shesh וְאַרְגָּמָן ve'argaman ר"ת אוּרִיאֵל רָפָאֵל גַּבְרִיאֵל מִיכָאֵל נוּרִיאֵל לְבוּשָׁהּ levusha:
נוֹדָע noda בַּשְּׁעָרִים bashe'arim בַּעְלָהּ ba'ala

To he, who merits those Supernal Grades, which are the opening of the soul (gates), the Holy One, blessed be He, is made known. So He is conceivable by those Supernal Grades.

בְּשִׁבְתּוֹ beshivto עִם im זִקְנֵי ziknei אָרֶץ aretz:
סָדִין sadin עָשְׂתָה asta וַתִּמְכֹּר vatimkor
וַחֲגוֹר vachagor נָתְנָה natna לַכְּנַעֲנִי lakena'ani:
עֹז oz וְהָדָר vehadar לְבוּשָׁהּ levusha
וַתִּשְׂחַק vatis'chak לְיוֹם leyom אַחֲרוֹן acharon:
פִּיהָ piha פָּתְחָה patcha בְחָכְמָה vechochma
וְתוֹרַת vetorat חֶסֶד chesed עַל al לְשׁוֹנָהּ leshona:

All the Unifications from *Abba* and *Ima* of *Atzilut* (*Chochmah*) and Above are from the aspect of the *Neshikin* (kisses)—the Supernal Unification—The tongue is the *Da'at* that unifies the palate (*Yesod*) with the throat (*Malchut*). And each Unification is roused by the aspect of Mercy.

צוֹפִיָּה tzofiya הֲלִיכוֹת halichot בֵּיתָהּ beta
וְלֶחֶם velechem עַצְלוּת atzlut לֹא lo תֹאכֵל tochel:

ל *She is not afraid of the snow for Her household; for all Her household are clothed with scarlet.*
מ *She makes Her own bedspreads; Her clothing is fine linen and purple [protecting angels].*
נ *Her husband is known at the Gates [the Supernal Grades], and He sits with the elders of the land.*
ס *She makes linen garments and sells them; She provides the merchants with girdles.*
ע *Strength and dignity are Her garments; She will rejoice in the last day.*
פ *She has opened Her mouth with wisdom, and the teaching of Mercy is on Her tongue.*
צ *She watches the performance of Her household, and does not eat the bread of idleness.*

First Meal Connection – Chakal Tapuchin Kadishin

קָמוּ kamu בָּנֶיהָ vaneha וַיְאַשְּׁרוּהָ vayashruha
בַּעְלָהּ ba'ala וַיְהַלְלָהּ vayehalela:

רַבּוֹת rabot בָּנוֹת banot עָשׂוּ asu וָזָיִל chayil
וְאַתְּ ve'at עָלִית alit עַל al כֻּלָּנָה kulana:

Many (in Hebrew also means "great") daughters are the Supernal twelve tribes who have made a throne for the *Nukva* so she is over them and the Upper and Lower will rejoice in them.

שֶׁקֶר sheker הַחֵן hachen וְהֶבֶל vehevel הַיֹּפִי hayofi
אִשָּׁה isha יִרְאַת yir'at (complete 613 precepts) יְהֹוָהִאהדונהי Adonai
הִיא hi תִתְהַלָּל tit'halal:

תְּנוּ tenu לָהּ la מִפְּרִי mipri יָדֶיהָ yadeha
וִיהַלְלוּהָ vihaleluha בַשְּׁעָרִים vashe'arim מַעֲשֶׂיהָ ma'aseha:

Blessing Over the Myrtle Branches

One should hold two bundles of myrtles; each containing three branches and recite the blessing over them. The two bundles represent *Zeir Anpin* and *Nukva* unified together. The myrtle represents the three Patriarchs (Abraham, Isaac and Jacob) and the three *Sefirot Chesed*, *Gevurah* and *Tiferet* of *Zeir Anpin* who draw Surrounding Light to the *Mochin* of *Malchut*. Smelling the myrtle elevates all that is left from the Holiness of *Asiyah* back to *Yetzirah*.

Also meditate on the four words of the following verse (without pronouncing its words.) Each word represents one of the four stages of the elevation of the fragrance:

רֵיחַ נִיחוֹחַ אִשֶּׁה לַיהֹוָהִאהדונהי

The fragrance, before we smell it, is considered to be Judgment. As it enters the nose (*Zeir Anpin*) the fragrance starts to become sweetened. Then the fragrance travels up inside the nose—Central Column, to the forehead, and finally, reaches the *Mochin* (Brains): ע"ב ס"ג מ"ה ב"ן.

בָּרוּךְ baruch אַתָּה Ata יְהֹוָהִאהדונהי Adonai אֱלֹהֵינוּ Elohenu ילה
מֶלֶךְ melech הָעוֹלָם ha'olam בּוֹרֵא bore עֲצֵי atzei בְּשָׂמִים vesamim:

ק Her children arise and bless Her; Her husband [*Zeir Anpin*] acclaims Her:
ר Many daughters [12 tribes] have done virtuously, but You [*Malchut of Atzilut*] excel [to *Abba*] them all.
ש Grace is deceptive and beauty fades; but a woman that is in the awe of the Lord will be praised.
ת Give Her of the fruit of Her hands, and let Her actions glorify Her at the Gates." *(Proverbs 31:10-23)*

Blessing Over the Myrtle Branches
Blessed are You, Lord, our God, the King of the world, Who creates the plants of fragrance.

First Meal Connection – Chakal Tapuchin Kadishin

Kiddush (Blessing Over the Wine) of Friday night

Until now our prayers have aroused spiritual energy in the Upper Worlds. Now we want to manifest and express this energy in our physical world so that we can utilize it in a practical manner. The *Kiddush* of Friday night contains 72 words that connect us to the power of the 72 Names of God (the totality of mind over matter). Drinking of the wine is one of the methods for expressing this energy.

The power of the Left Column is embodied in the Blessing over the Wine. This blessing gathers all the Divine energy that we have accumulated until now and manifests it in physical form. Wine also has the innate power to rise above the law of cause and effect. According to Kabbalah, the law of cause and effect governs the world, in a way that the cause is always higher than the effect by virtue of being first. Wine is the exception.

When we squeeze a grape, crush it, heat it, ferment it and put it in darkness, the result is great wine. We, too, also transform from a simple grape into the finest wine only after having gone through the hardships that life places on us. This is one of the few instances where the effect (the wine) is actually of a higher essence than the cause (a grape). This is the reason wine can draw down tremendous forces of Divine energy, and induces a high or intoxicated state. The power of rising above the natural laws of the universe is imbued in us through the wine, and helps us to rise above the negative actions (the cause) that we have done in the past that can result in chaos (the effect) in our life.

The essence of red wine, according to Kabbalah, is Left Column energy (Judgment), which is why wine has the ability to attract energy. To counterbalance this negative receiving power of red wine, the kabbalist adds a drop of water to the wine because the essence of water is Right Column energy (Mercy).

The secret of the *Kiddush* is to draw the Inner Light of the Three Upper *Sefirot* of *Zeir Anpin*, which are called *kodesh* (holiness) into *Nukva*. When receiving the *Kiddush* cup in your hand (as explained below) meditate that you are corresponding to *Zeir Anpin* and that the *Kiddush* cup corresponds to *Malchut*, which receives the Inner Light to Her *Mochin*.

While saying the *Kiddush* (and with speech comes breath—*hevel*, which represents the Surrounding Light,) meditate to draw the Surrounding Light to *Nukva* and therefore, hold the *Kiddush* cup in alignment with your chest as the Head of *Nukva* is against the Chest of *Zeir Anpin*.

One should receive the *Kiddush* cup with both hands (the ten fingers represent the *Ten Sefirot* of Returning Light) from someone else who is also holding the *Kiddush* cup in both of his hands (his ten fingers representing the *Ten Sefirot* of Direct Light), which together creates a complete Vessel. At this point (while holding the cup with your two hands aligned with your chest), meditate to send to *Nukva* the revealed aspect of the *Chasadim*, from the lower third part of *Tiferet*, from *Netzach* and from *Hod*.

Let go of the cup with your left hand and keep holding the cup in the palm of your right hand, with the tips of your five fingers around the base of the cup, creating a shape of a rose (Zohar, Prologue 1), and meditate to sweeten the Five Aspects of Judgment.

The *Kiddush* cup will stay by your right hand throughout the entire *Kiddush*.

During the *Kiddush* also meditate on the Name יוד הי ויו הי (ע"ב=72) three times:
1) 72 words in the *Kiddush*; 2) The word *veyechulu* has the numerical value of 72; 3) The initials of the words: *yom hashishi veyechulu hashamayim* is the Name יהוה (from the Name ע"ב);

First Meal Connection – Chakal Tapuchin Kadishin

The cup must be rinsed both inside and out prior to pouring the wine into it. The *Kiddush* cup must hold a *revi'it* (approximately 2.8 ounces) of wine. While standing, raise the cup (as previously explained), a *tefach* (four inches) or more from the table and recite the *Kiddush*.

Meditate that the three upper parts of the Surrounding *Mochin* of the letter *Lamed* (ל) of the *Tzelem* (צל״ם) of *Abba* are entering *Zeir Anpin* (as the head of *Zeir Anpin* is expanding).

(say silently: וַיְהִי *vayehi* עֶרֶב *erev* וַיְהִי *vayehi* בֹּקֶר *voker*)

יוֹם ע"ה נגד, מזבח, ז, אל יהוה הַשִּׁשִּׁי

On Friday night we recite the paragraph of *Vayechulu* three times. The first *Vayechulu* (during *Amidah* of *Arvit*) is to elevate the *Nukva* into *Netzach*, *Hod* and *Yesod* of *Zeir Anpin*. The second *Vayechulu* (after *Amidah* of *Arvit*) is to elevate the *Nukva* into *Chesed*, *Gevurah* and *Tiferet*. The third *Veyechulu* (during the *Kiddush*) is to elevate the *Nukva* to *Chochmah*, *Binah* and *Da'at*.

Also in the *Veyechulu* we have three times the word *shevi'i* (the seventh) as the *Mochin* for *Nukva* are made of seven *Sefirot* (the *Mochin* travel from *Keter* to *Netzach* through seven *Sefirot*, from *Chochmah* to *Hod* through seven *Sefirot* and from *Binah* to *Yesod* through seven *Sefirot*).

וַיְכֻלּוּ *vayechulu* (י יה יהו יהוה) ע"ב, ריבוע יהוה הַשָּׁמַיִם *hashamayim* י"פ טל, י"פ כוזו

וְהָאָרֶץ *veha'aretz* אלהים דההין ע"ה ; ר"ת ודו וְכָל *vechol* י-לי צְבָאָם *tzeva'am* ס"ת צלם:

וַיְכַל *vayechal* אלהים ע"ה אֱלֹהִים *Elohim* אהיה אדני ; י-לה בַּיּוֹם *bayom* ע"ה נגד, מזבח, ז, אל יהוה

הַשְּׁבִיעִי *hashevi'i* מְלַאכְתּוֹ *melachto* אֲשֶׁר *asher* עָשָׂה *asa*

וַיִּשְׁבֹּת *vayishbot* בַּיּוֹם *bayom* ע"ה נגד, מזבח, ז, אל יהוה הַשְּׁבִיעִי *hashevi'i*

מִכָּל *mikol* י-לי מְלַאכְתּוֹ *melachto* אֲשֶׁר *asher* עָשָׂה *asa*: וַיְבָרֶךְ *vayvarech*

אֱלֹהִים *Elohim* אהיה אדני ; י-לה אֵת *et* עצמ"ב, הברכה (למתק את ז' המלכים שמתו)

יוֹם *yom* ע"ה נגד, מזבח, ז, אל יהוה הַשְּׁבִיעִי *hashevi'i* וַיְקַדֵּשׁ *vaykadesh* אֹתוֹ *oto*

כִּי *ki* בוֹ *vo* שָׁבַת *shavat* מִכָּל *mikol* י-לי מְלַאכְתּוֹ *melachto* אֲשֶׁר *asher*

בָּרָא *bara* קנ"א ב"ן, יהוה אלהים יהוה אדני, מילוי קס"א וס"ג, מ"ה ברבוע וע"ב ע"ה

אֱלֹהִים *Elohim* אהיה אדני ; י-לה לַעֲשׂוֹת *la'asot*:

Kiddush of Friday Night (Blessing over the Wine)

"And there was evening, and there was morning—Day Six." (Genesis 1:31)

"And the Heavens and the Earth were completed and all their hosts. And God completed, on the seventh day, His work that He had done. And He abstained, on the seventh day, from all His work that He had done. And God blessed the seventh day and He sanctified it, for on it He had abstained from all His work that God had created to do." *(Genesis 2:1-3)*

First Meal Connection – Chakal Tapuchin Kadishin

סָבְרִי savri מָרָנָן maranan עִם (י"פ יהוה (ה' דחסדים וה' דגבורות))

לְחַיִּים lechayim אהיה אהיה יהוה, בינה ע"ה (: The others reply)

While saying the word *bore* (*peri hagefen*) look at the wine in the *Kiddush* cup and meditate to draw to the Head of *Nukva* the aspect of Her *Keter* (as *Chochmah*, *Binah* and *Da'at* are there already). Also, in the blessing of *Bore peri hegefen* there are nine words, which correspond to the nine times letter *Yud* (=90) in the Names of God (ע"ב ס"ג מ"ה ב"ן), so meditate to draw them into the nine letters in the Name: יוד הה וו הה (ב"ן), which is the *Nukva*, the vessel (the cup).

ילה	Elohenu אֱלֹהֵינוּ	Adonai יְהֹוָה	Ata אַתָּה	baruch בָּרוּךְ
חזק"ל	hagefen הַגָּפֶן	peri פְּרִי	bore בּוֹרֵא	ha'olam הָעוֹלָם	melech מֶלֶךְ

Elohenu אֱלֹהֵינוּ	Adonai יְהֹוָה	Ata אַתָּה	baruch בָּרוּךְ	
kideshanu קִדְּשָׁנוּ	asher אֲשֶׁר	ha'olam הָעוֹלָם	melech מֶלֶךְ	
veshabat וְשַׁבַּת	vanu בָּנוּ	veratza וְרָצָה	bemitzvotav בְּמִצְוֹתָיו	
hinchilanu הִנְחִילָנוּ	uvratzon וּבְרָצוֹן	be'ahava בְּאַהֲבָה	kodsho קָדְשׁוֹ	
techila תְּחִלָּה	vereshit בְּרֵאשִׁית	lema'ase לְמַעֲשֵׂה	zikaron זִכָּרוֹן	
litziat לִיצִיאַת	zecher זֵכֶר	kodesh קֹדֶשׁ	lemikraei לְמִקְרָאֵי	
be'ahava בְּאַהֲבָה	kodshecha קָדְשֶׁךָ	veshabat וְשַׁבַּת	mitzrayim מִצְרָיִם	
Ata אַתָּה	baruch בָּרוּךְ	hinchaltanu הִנְחַלְתָּנוּ	uvratzon וּבְרָצוֹן	
haShabbat הַשַּׁבָּת	mekadesh מְקַדֵּשׁ		Adonai יְהֹוָה	

Blessing for Children

After the *Kiddush*, as it is a time of favor, blessings are abundant, and parents have the ability to infuse their children with Divine Energy, strengthening the connection of the child's body, soul and consciousness to the 99 Percent Reality. The pathways of blessings are open on *Shabbat*, and parents are the channels through which children receive their Light. Therefore, it is important that parents bless their children so that the abundance of Light, which is available on *Shabbat*, flows through them to their children.

With your permission, my masters.
(The others reply) To life [Binah.]
Blessed are You, Lord, Our God, King of the universe, Who creates the fruit of the vine.
Blessed are You, Lord, King of the world, Who sanctified us with His commandments, and desired us, and gave us, with love and favor His Holy Shabbat, as a heritage, a remembrance of Creation; The prologue to the Holy Convocations, a memorial of the exodus from Egypt. And Your Holy Shabbat, You gave us as a heritage, with love and favor. Blessed are You, Lord, Who sanctifies the Shabbat.

First Meal Connection – Chakal Tapuchin Kadishin

For a son: yesimcha אֱלֹהִים Elohim אהיה אדני ; ילה יְשִׂימְךָ
keEfrayim כְּאֶפְרַיִם vechiMenasheh וְכִמְנַשֶּׁה• Continue "yevarechecha"

For a daughter: yesimech אֱלֹהִים Elohim אהיה אדני ; ילה יְשִׂימֵךְ
keSara כְּשָׂרָה Rivka רִבְקָה Rachel רָחֵל veLeah וְלֵאָה•

Right: yevarechecha יְבָרֶכְךָ Adonai יְהוָֹהאדנייאהדונהי veyishmerecha וְיִשְׁמְרֶךָ
ר"ת = יהוה ; וס"ת = מ"ה:

Left: ya'er יָאֵר כף ויו זין ויו יְהוָֹהאדנייאהדונהי Adonai | פָּנָיו panav אֵלֶיךָ elecha
vichuneka וִיחֻנֶּךָּ מנד ; יהה אותיות בפסוק:

Center: yisa יִשָּׂא יְהוָֹהאדנייאהדונהי Adonai | פָּנָיו panav אֵלֶיךָ elecha
veyasem וְיָשֵׂם lecha לְךָ shalom שָׁלוֹם האא תיבות בפסוק:
vesamu וְשָׂמוּ et אֶת shemi שְׁמִי al עַל benei בְּנֵי Yisrael יִשְׂרָאֵל
va'ani וַאֲנִי avarchem אֲבָרֲכֵם:

hamal'ach הַמַּלְאָךְ פוי, אל אדני hago'el הַגֹּאֵל oti אֹתִי mikol מִכָּל ra רָע ילי
yevarech יְבָרֵךְ עסמ"ב (למתק הברכה ד' המלכים שמותו) et אֶת
hane'arim הַנְּעָרִים מטטרון וסנדלפון עם ה' אותיות = ב"פ קס"א veyikare וְיִקָּרֵא vahem בָהֶם
shemi שְׁמִי veshem וְשֵׁם avotai אֲבֹתַי Avraham אַבְרָהָם וז"פ אל, רי"י ול"ב נתיבות
veYitzchak וְיִצְחָק דה"פ ב"ן הוחכמה, רמז"ל, עסמ"ב (אברים), וט"ו אותיות פשוטות
veyidgu וְיִדְגּוּ larov לָרֹב bekerev בְּקֶרֶב ha'aretz הָאָרֶץ אלהים דההין ע"ה:
ben בֵּן porat פֹּרָת Yosef יוֹסֵף ציון, ו' הויות, קנאה ben בֵּן porat פֹּרָת alei עֲלֵי
ayin עָיִן רביעו מ"ה banot בָּנוֹת tza'ada צָעֲדָה alei עֲלֵי shur שׁוּר ושר:

Blessing for Children

For a son: *"May God make you as Ephraim and as Menashe."* (Genesis 48:20)
For a daughter: *May God make you as Sarah, Rivka, Rachel and as Leah.*
(Right) *"May the Lord bless you and guard you.*
(Left) *May the Lord shine His Face upon you and be gracious unto you.*
(Center) *May the Lord lift His Face upon you and give you peace.*
And they placed My Name on the children of Israel and I shall bless them." (Numbers 6:24-27)
*"The angel who redeemed me from all evil
will bless the lads, and may my name and the name of my forefathers, Abraham and Isaac,
be called upon them. And let them grow in multitude amidst the Earth."* (Genesis 48:16) *"A fruitful bough
is Joseph. A fruitful bough by the well, and whose branches ran over the wall."* (Genesis 49:22)

First Meal Connection – Chakal Tapuchin Kadishin

The Meal of *Chakal Tapuchin Kadishin* (Field of the Holy Apples)

During *Kabbalat Shabbat*, the *Nukva* begins ascending and separating from the *klipot*, and She is called *Chakal* or "Field," meaning, a place where things can grow, in contrast to the desert, which is the place of the *klipot*, a place where nothing can grow. At this stage, *Nukva* receives from *Netzach*, *Hod* and *Yesod* of (*Netzach*, *Hod* and *Yesod* of) *Zeir Anpin*.

During *Arvit* (after the second *Veyechulu*,) the *Nukva* continues ascending and She is called: *Chakal Tapuchin* or "Field of Apples," meaning, as the apple has three colors (white, red and green) She receives from: *Chesed* (Right-white), *Gevurah* (Left-red) and *Tiferet* (Central-green) of (*Netzach*, *Hod* and *Yesod* of) *Zeir Anpin*.

During *Kiddush*, *Nukva* is called: *Chakal Tapuchin Kadishin* or "Field of the Holy Apples," meaning, She is receiving *Mochin* from *Chochmah*, *Binah* and *Da'at* of (*Netzach*, *Hod* and *Yesod* of) *Zeir Anpin*.

The kabbalists explain that the fall of Adam and Eve in the Garden of Eden was a result of their mistimed unification because their joining was intended for the eve of *Shabbat*, Friday night. Instead their unification took place six hours prior. What is difficult to understand is that their intention was good. However, as we all know, intentions are only valuable insofar as they influence our actions. It was not a case of right or wrong, but a case of resisting or not resisting. We, too, can react and seek immediate pleasure instead of resisting a selfish impulse. Through the power of the Friday night meal and its songs, we are making the connections that Adam and Eve did not; we are elevating sparks of Light that have been concealed since the time of Creation.

Atkinu—Azamer (Prepare the Feast—I Will Sing)

The great Kabbalist, Rav Isaac Luria (the Ari), wrote three songs, one for each of the three meals of *Shabbat*. These songs express the Light that is revealed in each of the meals, and their words assist us in connecting to this Light. *Azamer* is the song written for the first meal of *Shabbat*. It compares the *Shabbat* Queen to a bride, and we, the congregation, are the bridesmaids. Through our meditations and prayers the Light is revealed at the table. In connecting to *Shabbat*, we can elevate to a spiritual dimension where no negativity exists.

atkinu אַתְקִינוּ	se'udata סְעוּדָתָא	♦dimhemnuta דִּמְהֵימְנוּתָא
shelemata שְׁלֵמָתָא	chedveta וְחֶדְוְתָא	‡kadisha קַדִּישָׁא
atkinu אַתְקִינוּ	se'udata סְעוּדָתָא	♦demalka דְּמַלְכָּא
da דָּא	hi הִיא	se'udata סְעוּדָתָא	daChakal דַּחֲקַל	Tafuchin תַּפּוּחִין
Kadishin קַדִּישִׁין	uZeir וּזְעֵיר	Anpin אַנְפִּין	veAtika וְעַתִּיקָא
♦Kadisha קַדִּישָׁא	atyan אַתְיָן	lesa'ada לְסַעֲדָא	‡bahadeh בַּהֲדֵהּ

Atkinu—Azamer (Prepare the Feast—I Will Sing)

Prepare the feast of perfect faith; the joy of the Holy King. Prepare the feast of the King. This is the feast of the Field of Holy Apples [Chakal Tapuchin Kadishin]; and the Small Face [Zeir Anpin] and the Holy Ancient One [Atika Kadisha] come to partake in the feast with Her.

First Meal Connection – Chakal Tapuchin Kadishin

אֲמַר azmer בִּשְׁבָחִין bishvachin ◆ לְמֵיעַל leme'al גּוֹ go פְּתוּחִין pit'chin ◆
דְבַחֲקַל devaChakal תַּפּוּחִין Tapuchin ◆ דְאִנּוּן de'inun קַדִּישִׁין kadishin׃
נְזַמִּין nezamin לַהּ la הַשְׁתָּא hashta ◆ בִּפְתוֹרָא biftora וַחֲדַתָּא chadeta ◆

By the invitation (Hebrew: *zimun*) over the table (Aramaic: *petora*) we empower the *Nukva*, as *petora* פתורא has the same numerical value as the Names (Seven Gemstones-*Margalain*):
ע״ב (יוד הי ויו הי), ס״ג (יוד הי ואו הי), מ״ה (יוד הא ואו הא), ב״ן (יוד הה וו הה),
קס״א (אלף הי יוד הי), קנ״א (אלף הה יוד הה), וקמ״ג (אלף הא יוד הא).

וּבִמְנַרְתָּא uvimnarta ◆ טָבְתָא tavta ◆ דְנַהֲרָא denahara עַל al רֵישִׁין reshin׃

The secret of Fine Oil שמן הטוב ("like fine oil poured on the head, running down on the beard..." Psalms 133:2), which in *atbash* (שמן) creates the Holy Name (do not pronounce): בי"ט (=אהי"ה), the illumination from the Head of *Arich Anpin* through the *Dikna* to the *Nukva* and from Her to us.

יְמִינָא yemina ◆ וּשְׂמָאלָא usmala ◆ וּבֵינַיְהוּ uvenayhu ◆ כַלָּה chala ◆
בְּקִשּׁוּטִין bekishutin ◆ אָזְלָא azla ◆ וּמָאנִין umanin ◆ וּלְבוּשִׁין ulvushin׃
יְחַבֵּק yechabek לַהּ la ◆ בַּעְלָהּ ba'la ◆ וּבִיסוֹדָא uvisoda ◆ דִילָהּ dila ◆
דְעָבֵיד de'aved נַיְחָא naycha לַהּ la ◆ יְהֵא yehe כָתִישׁ katish כַּתִּישִׁין katishin׃

The Unification between *Zeir Anpin* (Her Husband) and *Nukva* results in three aspects: it will cause any force of darkness to be crushed, it will awaken tremendous joy and cause the Light to rest upon us.

צְוָוחִין tzevachin ◆ אַף af ◆ עָקְתִין aktin ◆ בְּטֵלִין betelin ◆ וּשְׁבִיתִין ushvitin ◆
בְּרַם beram ◆ אַנְפִּין anpin ◆ וַחֲדָתִין chadetin ◆ וְרוּחִין veruchin ◆ עִם im ◆ נַפְשִׁין nafshin׃
וַחֲדוּ chadu ◆ סַגֵּי sagei ◆ יֵיתֵי yetei ◆ וְעַל ve'al ◆ חֲדָא chada ◆ תַּרְתֵּי tartei ◆
נְהוֹרָא nehora ◆ לַהּ la ◆ יִמְטֵי yimtei ◆ וּבִרְכָאָן uvircha'an ◆ דִנְפִישִׁין dinfishin׃

א I will sing [in Hebrew also means - cut off (the negative forces) by the] praises, in order to ascend and enter through the openings of the Apple Orchard [*Chakal Tapuchin-Beriah*] for they are Holy [*Atzilut*].
ב Let us now (upon the arrival of Shabbat) invite [the secret of the *zimun* that removes the *klipot*] Her with a new table (to draw blessings for the entire week) and with a fine menorah that illuminates on the heads.
ג Right [*Yetzirah* with *Asiyah*] and left [*Beriah*], among them the Bride [*Shabbat*,] She elevates with (Twenty Four) adornments, vessels and robes [the Illumination from *Abba* and *Ima*].
ד Her Husband [*Zeir Anpin*] embraces Her in Her intimacy [Illumination of the sweetening of Mercy and Judgment in *Yesod*]; (this Illumination) grants Her serenity; and causes (the forces of Judgment to) crush.
צ (this Illumination causes) Screaming and anguish [negative forces] to be voided and suspended, but (for those who connect to the power of Shabbat) a new face, spirit and soul come [the additional soul of Shabbat].
ח Abundant joy (that is created by sweetening the Judgment) arrives, and the single [the Light during the weekdays] is doubled (on Shabbat); brilliance [from *Zeir Anpin*] will reach Her, and blessings of the soul.

First Meal Connection – Chakal Tapuchin Kadishin

קָרִיבוּ kerivu •שׁוֹשְׁבִינִין shoshvinin עֲבִידוּ avidu תִּקּוּנִין tikunin•

לְאַפְשָׁא le'apasha •זִינִין zinin וְנוּנִין venunin עִם im רַחֲשִׁין rachashin:

לְמֶעְבַּד lemevad •נִשְׁמָתִין nishmatin וְרוּחִין veruchin וַחֲדָתִין chadtin•

בְּתַרְתֵּין betarten •וְתִלָּתִין utlatin וּבִתְלָתָא uvitlata שִׁבְעִין shivshin:

וְעִטּוּרִין ve'iturin, שַׁבְעִין shavin כָּה la וּמַלְכָּא umalka דִּלְעֵלָּא dilela•

דְּיִתְעַטַּר deyit'ater •כֹּלָּא kola בְּקַדִּישׁ bekadish קַדִּישִׁין kadishin:

In general, She receives six crowns (each containing Five Mercies and Five Judgments): (1) from *Netzach* and *Hod* of *Atik*, (2) from *Chesed* and *Gevurah* of *Arich Anpin*, (3) from the Eighth *Tikkun* and the Thirteenth *Tikkun* of *Tikkunei Dikna* of *Arich Anpin*, (4) from *Chochmah* and *Binah* of *Abba* and *Ima*, (5) from *Netzach* and *Hod* of *Abba* and *Ima*, (6) and from *Chochmah* and *Binah* of *Zeir Anpin*. But on *Shabbat*, She receives an extra crown (besides the six crowns mentioned above), which is given to Her from *Zeir Anpin*.

רְשִׁימִין reshimin וּסְתִימִין ustimin• בְּגוֹ bego כָּל kol עָלְמִין almin•

בְּרַם beram עַתִּיק atik יוֹמִין yomin• הֲלָא halo בָּטִישׁ batish בְּטִישִׁין batishin:

יְהֵא yehe רַעֲוָא ra'ava קָמֵיהּ kameh •דְּיִתִשְׁרֵי detishrei עַל al עֲמֵיהּ ameh•

דְּיִתְעַנֵּג deyitanag לִשְׁמֵיהּ lishme •בִּמְתִיקִין bimtikin וְדוּבְשִׁין veduvshin:

אֲסַדֵּר asader לִדְרוֹמָא lidroma• מְנַרְתָּא menarta דִסְתִימָא distima•

וְשֻׁלְחָן veshulchan עִם im נַהֲמָא nahama• בִּצְפוֹנָא bitzfona אַרְשִׁין arshin:

The *Menorah* corresponds to the eyes of *Leah* (*Netzach* and *Hod* of *Ima*) that are hidden and the south (*Chesed*) sweetening them. The table is in the north and corresponds to *Rachel* and by adding bread (לחם=three times the Name: יהוה—*Netzach*, *Hod* and *Yesod* of *Zeir Anpin*) we are sweetening Her. Also, the Light of *Chochmah* comes through *Chesed* (south) to *Malchut* (*Menorah*) and brings wisdom, and the Light of *Binah* comes through *Gevurah* (north) to *Malchut* (table) and brings wealth.

ק *Entourage, come close (to the table,) and make corrections (for Shabbat the Bride) with multiple delicacies, big [Yesod of Adam Kadmon] and small [Yesod of Arich Anpin] fish and fowl.*

ב *Creating (righteous) souls and new spirits from the Thirty-Two (Paths of Chochmah that are spread to) the triple-branched [Netzach, Hod and Yesod of Ima for the Unification of Zeir Anpin and Nukva].*

ו *And seventy [Seven Corrections of Gulgalta] crowns are given to Her, (from) the Supernal King [Yesod of Adam Kadmon] so all (the Atzilut) is crowned by the Holy Sanctifications [the Tiara of Adam Kadmon].*

ר *Inscribed and engraved in Her [Malchut of Atzilut] all the Worlds [Beriah, Yetzirah and Asiyah], for He of Ancient Days [Atik Yomin] struck the compounds (in order to create additional Illuminations).*

י *May it be Your [Atik Yomin] will that She [the Shechinah] rest on Your people to take pleasure for His [the Endless Light] sake in delicacies and sweets [the Light of the Torah].*

א *I will arrange a Menorah of hidden to the south [wisdom] and a table with bread to the north [wealth].*

First Meal Connection – Chakal Tapuchin Kadishin

בְּחַמְרָא bechamra   גוֹ go   כַּסָא chasa   וּמְדָאנֵי umdanei   אַסָא asa•
לְאָרוּס le'arus   וַאֲרוּסָה va'arusa•   לְהִתְתַּקְפָא lehatkafa   וְחַלָשִׁין chalashin:

The wine (=70 and represents the Judgment of *Nukva*) in the cup (=86=אלהים). All equal to 156, which is the same value of יוסף Joseph—*Yesod* where the Judgment is sweetened) and the two bundles of myrtle (each with three myrtle branches, together six myrtles. Six times יהוה = 156. The two brunches correspond to the *Sefirot* of *Netzach* [ע"ב וקס"א = זכור—*Zachor*=233] and *Hod* [ע"ב ומילוי אלהים = אלהים דיודין, ריבוע אלהים ומילוי ע"ב—*Shamor*=546] of *Ima*) and are giving power to the weak (*Zeir Anpin* זכור and *Nukva* שמור in the stage before the Unification) and preparing Them for the Unification (They receive the Illumination of *Arich Anpin*).

נְעַטֵר ne'ater   לְהוֹן lehon   כִּתְרִין kitrin•   בְּמִלִין bemilin   יַקִירִין yakirin•
בְּשַׁבְעִין beshavin   עִטוּרִין iturin•   דְעַל de'al   גַבֵּי gabei   וְחַמְשִׁין chamshin:
שְׁכִינְתָא shechinta   תִתְעַטֵר tit'atar•   בְּשִׁית beshit   נַהֲמֵי nahamei   לִסְטָר listar•
בְּוָיו bevavin   תִתְקַטָר titkatar•   וְזִינִין vezinin   דִכְנִישִׁין dichnishin:

Bevavin titkatar means that the *Shechinah* will be connected to the letter *Vav* (=6) in a few ways: *Zeir Anpin* Itself (the letter *Vav* in the Name: יהוה), Her *Yesod* with His *Yesod* (the sixth *Sefirah*), and to the six *Sefirot*, which Her *Mochin* come from: *Netzach*, *Hod* and *Yesod* of *Ima* and *Netzach*, *Hod* and *Yesod* of *Zeir Anpin*. *Vezinin dichnishin* means that She will be also connected to all of the energy that is gathered inside Him (sweetened Judgment from Ima.) Also, *Malchut* is the last letter *Hei* ה of the Name יהוה and it can be drawn with three letters *Vav*.

שְׁבִיתִין shevitin   וּשְׁבִיקִין ushvikin•   מְסָאֲבִין mesa'avin   דִרְוִיזִיקִין dirchikin•
וְזַבִילִין chavilin   דִמְעִיקִין dimikin•   וְכָל vechol   זִינֵי zinei   וְחַבוּשִׁין chavushin:

Singing this song and creating the Unification between the Bride and the Groom pushes all the negative forces to a place that is called: *Nukva deTehoma Raba* or "the Hole of the Great Abyss."

ב With a wine-filled cup [sweetened Judgment] and two myrtle branches [Zachor and Shamor] for the Groom and the Bride [Zeir Anpin and Nukva before the Unification], to strengthen the weak.
נ We will fashion Them [Zeir Anpin and Nukva] with crowns of precious words (of this song), with the Seventy Tiaras [from the Seven Tikkuns of Gulgalta] that exceeding the Fifty [Gates of Binah].
ש May the Shchinah be crowned with six loaves at each side [corresponding to the twelve signs of the zodiac]; With the six [the letter Vav] She will be bound and all that is concealed in Him [sweeten Judgment].
ש Suspended and abandoned be the abominations who cause distance (between us and the Light and between Nukva and Zeir Anpin), the afflicting destroyers, and all forms of captives [impure forces].

First Meal Connection – Chakal Tapuchin Kadishin

Kol Mekadesh (Whoever Sanctifies)

The song, *Kol Mekadesh*, was written by one of the earliest kabbalists, Rav Moshe, the son of Kelonimus the Elder (Germany, 10th century). His family was entrusted with carrying the teaching of Kabbalah in Europe, in a hidden way for one thousand years. This song extols the greatness of the Light of *Shabbat* and the great rewards for those who connect to it. The verses of *Kol Mekadesh* are written according to the Hebrew alphabet, which when structured this way, helps us to remove chaos and connect to the energy of *Shabbat*. This very powerful song, whose melody was composed by Kabbalist Rav Ashlag, awakens within us greater understanding and appreciation for the gifts we receive on *Shabbat*.

כֹּל kol מְקַדֵּשׁ mekadesh שְׁבִיעִי shevi'i כָּרָאוּי kara'uy לוֹ lo♦

כֹּל kol שׁוֹמֵר shomer שַׁבָּת Shabbat כְּדָת kadat מֵחַלְּלוֹ mechalelo♦

שְׂכָרוֹ secharo הַרְבֵּה harbeh מְאֹד me'od עַל al פִּי pi פָּעֳלוֹ fa'olo♦

אִישׁ ish עַל al מַחֲנֵהוּ machanehu וְאִישׁ ve'ish עַל al דִּגְלוֹ diglo:

אוֹהֲבֵי ohavei יְהֹוָאדֹנָהי Adonai

הַמְחַכִּים hamechakim בְּבִנְיַן bevinyan אֲרִיאֵל Ari'el♦

בְּיוֹם beyom הַשַּׁבָּת haShabbat שִׂישׂוּ sisu וְשִׂמְחוּ vesimchu

כִּמְקַבְּלֵי kimekablei מַתַּן matan נַחֲלִיאֵל nachali'el♦

גַּם gam שְׂאוּ se'u יְדֵיכֶם yedechem קֹדֶשׁ kodesh

וְאִמְרוּ ve'imru לָאֵל laEl♦ בָּרוּךְ baruch יְהֹוָאדֹנָהי Adonai

אֲשֶׁר asher נָתַן natan מְנוּחָה menucha לְעַמּוֹ le'amo יִשְׂרָאֵל Yisrael:

דּוֹרְשֵׁי dorshei יְהֹוָאדֹנָהי Adonai

זֶרַע zera אַבְרָהָם Avraham אוֹהֲבוֹ ohavo♦

הַמְאַחֲרִים hame'acharim לָצֵאת latzet מִן min הַשַּׁבָּת haShabbat

וּמְמַהֲרִים umemaharim לָבֹא lavo♦

Kol Mekadesh (Whoever Sanctifies)

Whoever sanctifies the seventh (day) as suits it (is able and take actions to connect to Shabbat); whoever guards Shabbat properly from desecration (is unable to take action but does restriction to connect to Shabbat), his reward is very great corresponding to his effort (regardless of the end results); (as it says:) "Each man to his own camp, each man at his own banner ([everyone according to his deeds]." (Numbers 1:52)
א *Lovers of the Lord who homiletically long for the restoration of the Lion of God [the Temple];*
ב *On Shabbat day rejoice and be happy as if receiving the gift of God's inheritance [the Torah];*
ג *And raise your hands in holiness and say to God: "Blessed be the Lord Who has given serenity to His people—Israel." (1 Kings 8:56)* ד *Seekers of the Lord, seed of His beloved Abraham,*
ה *who delay in departing from Shabbat [as in the first Shabbat in Marah] and rush its coming,*

First Meal Connection – Chakal Tapuchin Kadishin

וּשְׂמֵחִים semechim לְשָׁמְרוֹ leshomro וּלְעָרֵב ul'arev עֵרוּבוֹ eruvo ♦

זֶה zeh הַיּוֹם hayom עָשָׂה asa יְהֹוָה Adonai

נָגִילָה nagila וְנִשְׂמְחָה venismecha בּוֹ vo:

זִכְרוּ zichru תּוֹרַת torat מֹשֶׁה Moshe

בְּמִצְוַת bemitzvat שַׁבָּת Shabbat גְּרוּסָה gerusa ♦

וְזָרוּתָהּ charuta לַיּוֹם layom הַשְּׁבִיעִי hashevi'i

כְּכַלָּה kechala בֵּין ben רְעוּתֶיהָ re'uteha מְשֻׁבָּצָה meshubatza ♦

טְהוֹרִים tehorim יִרָשׁוּהָ yirashuha וִיקַדְּשׁוּהָ vikadeshuha בְּמַאֲמַר bema'amar

כֹּל kol אֲשֶׁר asher עָשָׂה asa ♦ וַיְכַל vaychal אֱלֹהִים Elohim

בַּיּוֹם bayom הַשְּׁבִיעִי hashevi'i מְלַאכְתּוֹ melachto אֲשֶׁר asher עָשָׂה asa:

יוֹם yom קָדוֹשׁ kadosh הוּא hu

מִבּוֹאוֹ mibo'o וְעַד ve'ad צֵאתוֹ tzeto ♦

כֹּל kol זֶרַע zera יַעֲקֹב Ya'akov יְכַבְּדוּהוּ yechabeduhu

כִּדְבַר kidvar הַמֶּלֶךְ hamelech וְדָתוֹ vedato ♦

לָנוּחַ lanu'ach בּוֹ bo וְלִשְׂמוֹחַ velismo'ach בּוֹ bo בְּתַעֲנוּג beta'anug אָכוֹל achol

וְשָׁתוֹ veshato ♦ כֹּל kol עֲדַת adat יִשְׂרָאֵל Yisrael יַעֲשׂוּ ya'asu אוֹתוֹ oto:

א *And who are happy in guarding it and staying within its parameters [to be protected from the klipa], (stating:) "This is the day the Lord created for you within which to rejoice and be happy." (Psalms 118:24)*

ד *Remember the Torah of Moses, in its precept of Shabbat's expounding [mentioned 12 times in the Torah];*

ה *(The Torah) Engraved for the seventh day [as the Revelation on Mount Sinai was on Shabbat (Babylonian Talmud, Tractate Shabbat 86:2)], like a bride adorned among her companions [the secret of her seven maidens];*

ט *Pure ones take possession of it and sanctify it by saying (in the Kiddush) "All that He had made" (Genesis 1) (and also) "And God completed, on the seventh day, His work that He had done." (Genesis 2:2)*

י *It is a holy day from its beginning to its end [as even at afternoon time there is no Judgment],*

כ *all of Jacob's offspring [there are two levels; Jacob and Israel. Jacob represents the lower level and Israel represents the higher level. Here, the song indicates that regardless to our spiritual level – even if it's Jacob – when we connect to Shabbat, we will have joy] will honor it as "the king's order and his edict:" (Esther 2:8)*

ל *(and what is the King's order?) to rest in it and rejoice with the pleasure of food and drink; [But here, the song indicates that those who are in the level of Israel, the higher level, will be able to connect to its highest level, to its essence "IT"] "The entire congregation of Israel will do it." (Exodus 12:47)*

First Meal Connection – Chakal Tapuchin Kadishin

מְשׁוֹךְ meshoch וְחַסְדְּךָ chasdecha לְיוֹדְעֶיךָ leyod'echa
אֵל El קַנֹּא kano וְנוֹקֵם venokem.

נוֹטְרֵי notrei לַיּוֹם layom הַשְּׁבִיעִי hashevi'i
זָכוֹר zachor וְשָׁמוֹר veshamor לְהָקֵם lehakem.

שַׂמְּחֵם samchem בְּבִנְיַן bevinyan שָׁלֵם shalem בְּאוֹר be'or
פָּנֶיךָ panecha תַּבְהִיקֵם tavhikem יִרְוְיֻן yirveyun מִדֶּשֶׁן mideshen
בֵּיתֶךָ betecha וְנַחַל venachal עֲדָנֶיךָ adanecha תַּשְׁקֵם tashkem:

עֲזוֹר azor לַשּׁוֹבְתִים lashovtim בַּשְּׁבִיעִי bashevi'i
בֶּחָרִישׁ becharish וּבַקָּצִיר uvakatzir עוֹלָמִים olamim.

פּוֹסְעִים pos'im בּוֹ bo פְּסִיעָה pesia קְטַנָּה ketana
סוֹעֲדִים so'adim בּוֹ bo לְבָרֵךְ levarech שָׁלֹשׁ shalosh פְּעָמִים pe'amim.

צִדְקָתָם tzidkatam תַּצְהִיר tatz'hir כְּאוֹר ke'or שִׁבְעַת shiv'at
הַיָּמִים hayamim יְהֹוָהֵ‑אֱלֹהֵי‑נוּ Adonai אֱלֹהֵי Elohei יִשְׂרָאֵל Yisrael
אַהֲבַת ahavat תָּמִים tamim יְהֹוָהֵ‑אֱלֹהֵי‑נוּ Adonai
אֱלֹהֵי Elohei יִשְׂרָאֵל Yisrael תְּשׁוּעַת teshu'at עוֹלָמִים olamim:

> Rav Ashlag explains that in the beginning of the process we see Creation with blemishes—*mumim*, because we still connect to the Left Column (the Desire to Receive). When we elevate (as we do on Shabbat) we can connect to *Emunah lema'ala min haDa'at* (Certainty Beyond Logic) and then we can see the perfection and completion in Creation (*tamim*).

מ *Extend Your kindness to those who know [or "connect to" (see Zohar Beresheet B, 324-338)] You, "God [force of Mercy who is Master (see Zohar Tzav 91-96 and below)] of jealousy and vengeance" (Nahum 1:2)* ;
נ *And to those who anticipate the seventh day, support them so they can remember and guard the Shabbat,*
(ש)ס *Make them happy [or if it is spelled with the letter Samech-ס it means: "support them"] with rebuilt Shalem [Jerusalem]; in the light of Your Face make them radiant ["When Shabbat enters, She unites and separates from the Other Side. All the Judgments pass away from Her... All the dominions of anger and the instigators of Judgment flee, and there is no other dominion in all the worlds, except Her. And Her Face shines with the Supernal Light and becomes adorned with the holy nation below, for they all become adorned from Her with new souls. (Zohar Terumah 165-166)]. May they "be saturated from the fatness of Your house and You make them drink from the river of Your pleasure" (Psalms 36:9)*
ע *Help those who desist on the seventh (day) and ignore (the need to) plow [the preparations] and harvest [the final results];* פ *who take small strides on it, who feast on it in order to bless (You) three times;*
צ *May their righteousness blaze like the light of the Seven Days [Or Haganuz—the Hidden Light], Lord, God of Israel, (You are) simple love. Lord, God of Israel, (You are) eternal salvation.*

Second Meal Connection

ATIKA KADISHA
(HOLY ANCIENT ONE)

KIDDUSH (BLESSING OVER THE WINE) OF SATURDAY MORNING
 —KIDDUSHA RABBA
ATKINU—ASADER (PREPARE THE FEAST—I WILL PREPARE)
BARUCH HASHEM (BLESSED IS THE LORD)—BOM BOM

SECOND MEAL CONNECTION – ATIKA KADISHA

KIDDUSHA RABBA (BLESSING OVER THE WINE) OF SATURDAY MORNING

Until now, our prayers have aroused spiritual energy in the Upper Worlds. Here we want to manifest and express this energy in our physical world so we can utilize it in a practical manner. The power of the Left Column is embodied in the Blessing over the Wine. The *Kiddush* essentially gathers all the Divine Energy that we have accumulated until now and manifests it in physical form. The drinking of the wine is one of the ways of expressing this energy.

The *Kiddush* of *Shabbat* Morning, though fewer in words than the *Kiddush* of Friday night, is called *Kiddusha Rabba* or "Great Kiddush" (Babylonian Talmud, Tractate Pesachim 106:1) because at this point of *Shabbat*, the actual aspect of our inner essence (*Zeir Anpin*) is elevated to a higher place called *Atika Kadisha* and becomes united and aligned with the potential aspect of our inner essence (*Abba*). As *Zeir Anpin* is elevated, all the Lower Worlds (including us) ascend with It and receive these great illuminations.

At this point (after the morning connection), *Zeir Anpin* and *Nukva* stand in the place of *Abba* and *Ima* (Their *Keter* is equal to the *Keter* of *Abba* and *Ima*), which means that They are standing below the Mouth of *Atika* and eating from It. And this is why this meal is called the meal of *Atika Kadisha*.

This is the reason *Shabbat* morning *Kiddush* is called "*Kiddusha Rabba*" (Great *Kiddush*), is because on Friday night the *Mochin*, that are called *Kodesh* (Holiness), come from *Zeir Anpin* (the Small Face), and on *Shabbat* Morning the *Mochin* come from *Abba* Itself, which is called "the Supernal *Kodesh*." So meditate on the Supernal Names: יוד הה, יוד הה, יוד הה (=90,) which are *Chochmah*, *Binah* and *Da'at* of the Upper Ear of *Atika Kadisha* (to where *Atika Kadisha* of *Atzilut* is now elevated).

Also, meditate to draw the Surrounding Light of the Three Lower parts of *Abba* to *Zeir Anpin*.

haShabbat הַשַּׁבָּת	et אֶת	Yisrael יִשְׂרָאֵל	venei בְנֵי	veshamru וְשָׁמְרוּ		
berit בְּרִית	ledorotam לְדֹרֹתָם	haShabbat הַשַּׁבָּת	et אֶת	la'asot לַעֲשׂוֹת		
hi הוּא	ot אוֹת	Yisrael יִשְׂרָאֵל	benei בְּנֵי	uven וּבֵין	beni בֵּינִי	olam עוֹלָם•
asa עָשָׂה	yamim יָמִים	sheshet שֵׁשֶׁת	ki כִּי	le'olam: לְעֹלָם		
ha'aretz הָאָרֶץ	ve'et וְאֶת	hashamayim הַשָּׁמַיִם	et אֶת	Adonai יהוה		
vayinafash• וַיִּנָּפַשׁ	shavat שָׁבַת	hashevi'i הַשְּׁבִיעִי	uvayom וּבַיּוֹם			

KIDDUSHA RABBA (BLESSING OVER THE WINE) OF SATURDAY MORNING

"And the children of Israel shall keep the Shabbat, to make the Shabbat an eternal covenant for all their generations. Between Me and the children of Israel, it is an eternal sign that in six days did the Lord make the Heavens and the Earth and on the Seventh day, He was refreshed." (Exodus 31:16-17)

SECOND MEAL CONNECTION – ATIKA KADISHA

The secret of these verses is the seventh *Tikkun* "*ve'emet*" – the two Apples (sides) of the Face of *Atika*. As the *Zohar* explains (Zohar Naso, Idra Raba, 141-147): "from these Apples in *Arich Anpin*, Light is sent to the 370 directions from Them and They show happiness to *Zeir Anpin*".

♦lekadesho לְקַדְּשׁוֹ haShabbat הַשַּׁבָּת yom יוֹם et אֶת zachor זָכוֹר

ילי kol כָּל ve'asita וְעָשִׂיתָ ta'avod תַּעֲבֹד yamim יָמִים sheshet שֵׁשֶׁת

Shabbat שַׁבָּת hashevi'i הַשְּׁבִיעִי veyom וְיוֹם ♦melachtecha מְלַאכְתֶּךָ

ta'ase תַעֲשֶׂה lo לֹא Elohecha אֱלֹהֶיךָ ladonai לַיהוה

uvitecha וּבִתֶּךָ uvincha וּבִנְךָ ata אַתָּה melacha מְלָאכָה ילי chol כָל

vegercha וְגֵרְךָ uvhemtecha וּבְהֶמְתֶּךָ va'amatcha וַאֲמָתְךָ avdecha עַבְדְּךָ

yamim יָמִים sheshet שֵׁשֶׁת ki כִּי ♦bish'arecha בִּשְׁעָרֶיךָ asher אֲשֶׁר

ve'et וְאֶת hashamayim הַשָּׁמַיִם et אֶת Adonai יהוה asa עָשָׂה

ילי kol כָּל ve'et וְאֶת hayam הַיָּם et אֶת ha'aretz הָאָרֶץ

hashvi'i הַשְּׁבִיעִי bayom בַּיּוֹם vayanach וַיָּנַח bam בָּם asher אֲשֶׁר

(Zeir Anpin) Adonai יהוה berach בֵּרַךְ ken כֵּן al עַל

♦vaykadshehu וַיְקַדְּשֵׁהוּ (Malchut) haShabbat הַשַּׁבָּת yom יוֹם et אֶת

סַבְרִי savri י"פ יהוה (ה' דחסדים וה' דגבורות) מָרָנָן maranan שם

אהיה אהיה יהוה, בינה ע"ה lechayim לְחַיִּים (: The others reply)

In the blessing of *Bore peri hegefen* there are nine words, which correspond to the nine times letter *Yud* (=90) in the Names of God (ע"ב ס"ג מ"ה ב"ן) and also correspond to the nine letters in the Name: יוד הה וו הה (ב"ן), which is the vessel to receive these nine *Yuds* (=90, the same numerical value as the Supernal Names: יוד הה, יוד הה, יוד הה, as mentioned above).

ילה Elohenu אֱלֹהֵינוּ Adonai יהוה Ata אַתָּה baruch בָּרוּךְ

:hagefen הַגָּפֶן peri פְּרִי bore בּוֹרֵא ha'olam הָעוֹלָם melech מֶלֶךְ

"Remember the Shabbat day by keeping it Holy. Six days you shall labor and do all your work, but the seventh day is a Shabbat to the Lord, your God. On it you shall not do any work, neither you, nor your son or daughter, nor your male or female servant, nor your animals, nor any foreigner residing in your towns. For in six days the Lord made the Heavens and the Earth, the sea, and all that is in them, but He rested (His Holiness is rested upon the entire world) on the seventh day. So the Lord blessed the day of Shabbat and made it Holy." (Exodus 20:8-11)

With your permission, my masters.
(The others reply) *To life (Binah).*
Blessed are You, Lord, Our God, King of the universe, Who creates the fruit of the vine.

SECOND MEAL CONNECTION – ATIKA KADISHA

ATKINU—ASADER (PREPARE THE FEAST—I WILL PREPARE)

Asader was written by Rav Isaac Luria (the Ari) for the second meal of *Shabbat*, to be sung on *Shabbat* morning. This song elevates us to a higher level on *Shabbat*; a level where all the secrets are revealed, and finally there can be complete harmony and unity in the world. This meal prepares us and purifies us for the high point of *Shabbat*, the Third Meal. The first letter of each verse creates the words *Ani Yitzchak* or "I am Isaac."

אַתְקִינוּ atkinu סְעוּדָתָא se'udata דִמְהֵימְנוּתָא dimhemnuta ♦

שְׁלֵמָתָא shelemata וְחֶדְוָתָא chedveta דְמַלְכָּא demalka קַדִּישָׁא kadisha ׃

אַתְקִינוּ atkinu סְעוּדָתָא se'udata דְמַלְכָּא demalka ♦

דָא da הִיא hi סְעוּדָתָא se'udata דְעַתִּיקָא deAtika קַדִּישָׁא Kadisha ♦

וּזְעֵיר uZeir אַנְפִּין Anpin וַחֲקַל vaChakal תַּפּוּחִין Tafuchin

קַדִּישִׁין Kadishin אַתְיָן atyan לְסַעֲדָא lesa'ada בַּהֲדֵהּ bahadeh ׃

אֲסַדֵּר asader לִסְעוּדָתָא lisudata ♦ בְּצַפְרָא betzafra דְשַׁבַּתָּא deshabata ♦

וְאַזְמִין ve'azmin בַּהּ ba הַשְׁתָּא hashta עַתִּיקָא Atika קַדִּישָׁא Kadisha ׃

At this point, after the morning connection, *Zeir Anpin* and *Nukva* are equal to *Abba* and *Ima* (They are next to the Mouth of *Atika* of *Atzilut*), which means that They eat from the Mouth of *Atika* and therefore we have the second meal of *Shabbat*. This is why the Ari says *"asder lese'udata"* (I'll prepare for the meal of *Atika* and not "I'll prepare the meal for *Atika*") as it is preparation to draw the illumination (manifested as *Shabbat* second meal energy) of *Atika*. In order to reject the *klipot* that were created from our own negativity, we perform *hazmana* or "invitation," so the *klipot* cannot prevent us from connecting to the Light of *Atika* (unlike the *hazmana* on Friday night, whose purpose is to reject the *klipa* that controls the night).

נְהוֹרָא nehore יִשְׁרֵי yishrei בַּהּ va ♦ בְּקִידּוּשָׁא bekidusha רַבָּא raba ♦

וּבְחַמְרָא uvchamra טָבָא tava ♦ דְּבֵהּ deve תֶּחֱדֵי techedei נַפְשָׁא nafsha ׃

At this time of *Kiddusha Rabba*, the Light of *Chasadim*—Mercies (from *Yesod* of *Adam Kadmon*) will rest upon It (the *Nukva*) by the two Attributes: *Notzer* and *Venakeh*. Although, the wine (=70) represents the *Gevurot*—aspect of Judgments (of *Notzer* and *Venakeh*) now brings happiness (the seven letters *Yud* =70, in the Names: יוֹד הֵי וָיו הֵי יוֹד הֵי וָאו הֵי) for the additional soul.

ATKINU—ASADER (PREPARE THE FEAST—I WILL PREPARE)

Prepare the feast of perfect faith; the joy of the Holy King. Prepare the feast of the King. This is the feast of the Ancient Holy One [Atika Kadisha]. And the Small Face [Zeir Anpin] and the Field of Holy Apples [Chakal Tapuchin Kadishin] come to partake in the feast with Her.

א *I will prepare for the feast on Shabbat morning and I will invite to it the Ancient Holy One.*

נ *May His radiance rest upon it in the Great Kiddush and in the tasty wine in which the soul rejoices.*

Second Meal Connection – Atika Kadisha

לִישַׁדֵּר yeshader לָן lan שׁוּפְרֵיהּ shufre ♦ וְנֶחֱזֵי venechezei בִּיקָרֵיהּ vikare ♦
וִיחַזֵי veyachazei לָן lan סִתְרָה sitre ♦ דְּאִתְאֲמַר de'itamar בִּלְחִישָׁא bilchisha:

And He will send us (from *Ima*) the *Shofar* of Messiah (as in *Rosh Hashanah*, the *Shofar* represents the sweetening of the Judgment) so, we shall see His Honor (*Dikna* of *Yesod* of *Arich Anpin*). And then He will let us be part of the secret of the Unification of *Arich Anpin*.

יְגַלֶּה yegale לָן lan טַעֲמֵי ta'amei ♦ דִּבְתְרֵיסַר devitresar נַהֲמֵי nahamei ♦
דְּאִינוּן de'inun אַת at בִּשְׁמֵיהּ bishme ♦ כְּפִילָא kefila וּקְלִישָׁא uklisha:

The secret of the 12 loaves: The 12 letter Name (יהוה יהוה יהוה) in the Head of *Atika*. Three times 26 (=יהוה) comes to 78, which is the same numerical value for *lechem* or "bread." 12 times לחם (=78) equal 936, the same numerical value as the 13 Attributes times the 72 Names of God. At *bishme* speaks about the letter *Vav* (=6) in the Name יהוה that represents *Yesod* of *Adam Kadmon* and as the Endless Light goes through It the letter *Vav* split into two (=12, *Netzach* and *Hod*).

Kabbalist Rav Brandwein teaches that *yegale lan ta'amei* means "he will reveal to us the taste of" and here we ask not just to have the intellectual or spiritual reason for the 12 loaves but actually to have the real "taste" of the Light of *Shabbat* that is revealed through the 12 loaves.

צְרוֹרָא tzerora דִּלְעֵילָא dil'ela ♦ דְּבֵי devei וַזֵּי chayei כֹּלָּא chola ♦
וְיִתְרַבֵּי veyitrabei וַזֵּילָא chela ♦ וְתִיסַק vetisak עַד ad רֵישָׁא resha:

Tzerora dil'ela speaks about the bonding (*zivug*) of *Notzer* and *Venakeh* (the two Attributes that correspond to *Yesod* and *Da'at*), from where life for *Atzilut* and the rest of the Worlds originates. And as this bonding is happening, *Nukva* will be empowered (become a complete structure of Ten *Sefirot*) and She will rise all the way to the Head of *Zeir Anpin* (Her *Keter* equals to the *Keter* of *Zeir Anpin* and equals to the *Keter* of *Abba* and *Ima*) and She will be in Face-to-Face form with Him.

וַחֲדוּ chadu וְצִדֵּי chatzdei וַחֲקלָא chakla ♦ בְּדִבּוּר bedibur וּבְקָלָא uvkala ♦
וּמַלְּלוּ umalelu מִלָּה mila ♦ מְתִיקָא metika כְּדוּבְשָׁא keduvsha:

קֳדָם kodam רִבּוֹן ribon עָלְמִין almin ♦ בְּמִלִּין bemilin סְתִימִין setimin ♦
תְּגַלּוּן tegalun פִּתְגָּמִין pitgamin ♦ וְתֵימְרוּן vetemrun וְחִדּוּשָׁא chidusha:

˒ May He dispatch His beauty [*Atika*] and may we see His honor [*Yesod* of *Arich Anpin*], and may He show us His mysteries [the Unification of *Arich Anpin*] that are uttered in whispers.
˒ May He reveal to us the purpose (or taste) of the twelve loaves which represent the letter [*Vav*=6] in His Name that splits [by the Endless into two=12] and becomes thinner.
צ The Supernal bundle, which has in it life for all, may It increase Her strength and She will rise to His head.
ח Rejoice, tillers of the field [those who study Kabbalah], in the sound [*Zeir Anpin*] and voice [*Malchut*] and speak word as sweet as honey [the secrets of the Torah (Song of Songs 4:11)].
ק Before the Master of the Universe [*Atika*, as He now reveals the secrets reveal too], in concealed words [the wisdom of Kabbalah] you should reveal the secrets [as there is no fear from the klipot on Shabbat] and proclaim new thoughts [as we now have a new additional soul].

SECOND MEAL CONNECTION – ATIKA KADISHA

לְעַטֵּר le'ater פָּתוֹרָא petora• בְּרָזָא beraza יַקִּירָא yakira•
עֲמִיקָא amika וּטְמִירָא utmira• וְלָאו velav מִלְּתָא milta אוֹשָׁא avsha:
וְאִלֵּין ve'ilen מִלַּיָא milaya• יְהוֹן yehon לִרְקִיעַיָא lirki'aya• וְתַמָּן vetaman
מַאן man שַׁרְיָא sharya• הֲלָא halo הַהוּא hahu אהוה שִׁמְשָׁא shimsha:
רְבוּ revu יַתִּיר yatir יַסְגֵי yasgei• לְעֵילָא le'ela מִן min דַּרְגֵּהּ darge•
וַיֵּסַב veyisav בַּת bat זוּגֵהּ zuge• דַּהֲוָת dahavat פְּרִישָׁא perisha:

Here we ask that the expansion of *Zeir Anpin* (from Six Edges to a complete structure of Ten *Sefirot* that comes from *Abba* on *Shabbat*) will last forever, even during the weekdays, and not just during *Shabbat*, so that the Unification of *Zeir Anpin* and *Nukva—Rachel* will be in the Face-to-Face form eternally.

BARUCH HASHEM (BLESSED IS THE LORD)—BOM BOM
(Based on the words of Rav Shimon Bar Yochai in the Jerusalem Talmud, Tractate Ta'anit 1:1)

When we review history, beginning with the Egyptian exile and the children of Israel's redemption to the exile and redemption during the Babylonian, Persian, and Greek eras, it seems as if the Light of the Creator only appears at the times of redemption. Yet the *Zohar* states (Korach 58): "*The Shechinah protects all who guard the Shabbat, and therefore the Shechinah never moved away from Israel (even in times of exile)*".

In this song, Kabbalist Rav Shimon Hagadol (Simon the Great, student of Rav Yitzchak Alfasi "the Rif," who lived in Germany during the 10th century) details all of the travails, and how, at the end of each exile came a new elevation. This song emphasizes the importance of the Light of *Shabbat* as protector in times of darkness. The last section of this song (which we sing during the Third Meal of *Shabbat*) speaks of the current and final exile. It foretells the downfall of all evil and the Final Redemption soon in our days (Amen).

בָּרוּךְ baruch אֲדֹנָי Adonai יוֹם yom יוֹם yom• יַעֲמָס ya'amos לָנוּ lanu
יֶשַׁע yesha וּפִדְיוֹם ufidyom• וּבִשְׁמוֹ uvishmo נָגִיל nagil כֹּל kol
הַיּוֹם hayom• וּבִישׁוּעָתוֹ uvishu'ato נָרִים narim רֹאשׁ rosh עֶלְיוֹן elyon•
כִּי ki הוּא hu מָעוֹז ma'oz לַדָּל ladal וּמַחֲסֶה umachase לָאֶבְיוֹן la'evyon:

ל To adorn [from Atika] the table [Malchut] in precious secret, profound and hidden [Yesod of Abba and Ima], that it should not be made known [is kept in Atzilut and does not go down from Atzilut].
ו Then these words [of the wisdom of Kabbalah that we study during Shabbat] will create (new) firmaments [as it is stated in the introduction to the Zohar 61], and who is there (in the new firmaments) [to receive all the illuminations]? This is the sun [Yesod of Zeir Anpin that influences the moon—Nukva].
ר May it [the oil that descends from Abba] increase and be greater, beyond His [Zeir Anpin's] level [the Six Edges, so He will have a complete structure of Ten Sefirot]. Then may He [Zeir Anpin] encircle His mate [Nukva—Rachel], so She will never be separated from him anymore.

BARUCH HASHEM (BLESSED IS THE LORD)—BOM BOM
Blessed is the Lord [the Shechinah] every day, He will bear for us salvation and redemption. And in His Name [Shabbat is the Name of the Creator (Zohar Yitro 460)] we will rejoice all the day, and in His salvation we will raise the Supernal Head; For He is the stronghold for the poor and a refuge for the pauper.

betzaratam בְּצָרָתָם	edut עֵדוּת	leYisrael לְיִשְׂרָאֵל	Yah יָהּ	shivtei שִׁבְטֵי	
belivnat בְּלִבְנַת	uv'avdut וּבְעַבְדוּת	besivlot בְּסִבְלוֹת	tzar צָר	lo לוֹ	
venigla וְנִגְלָה	yedidut יְדִידוּת	oz עוֹז	her'am הֶרְאָם	hasapir הַסַּפִּיר	
im עִם	ki כִּי	vadut וָדוּת	bor בּוֹר	me'omek מֵעוֹמֶק	leha'alotam לְהַעֲלוֹתָם
fedut פְדוּת	imo עִמּוֹ	veharbe וְהַרְבֵּה	hachesed הַחֶסֶד	Adonai יְהֹוָה	
legonenemo לְגוֹנְנֵימוֹ	betzilo בְּצִלּוֹ	chasdo וְחַסְדּוֹ	yakar יָקָר	ma מַה	
lema'anemo לְמַעֲנֵימוֹ	shulach שֻׁלַּח	bavela בְּבָלָה	begalut בְּגָלוּת		
venemo בֵּינֵימוֹ	nimna נִמְנָה	barichim בְּרִיוַזִים	lehorid לְהוֹרִיד		
shovemo שׁוֹבֵימוֹ	lifnei לִפְנֵי	lerachamim לְרַחֲמִים	vayitnem וַיִּתְּנֵם		
et אֶת	Adonai יְהֹוָה	yitosh יִטּוֹשׁ	lo לֹא	ki כִּי	
shemo שְׁמוֹ	hagadol הַגָּדוֹל	ba'avur בַּעֲבוּר	amo עַמּוֹ		
yedidav יְדִידָיו	lehatzil לְהַצִּיל	kiso כִּסְאוֹ	shat שָׁת	elam עֵילָם	
mordav מוֹרְדָיו	moznei מֹאזְנֵי	misham מִשָּׁם	leha'avir לְהַעֲבִיר		
avadav עֲבָדָיו	et אֶת	pada פָּדָה	bashelach בַּשֶּׁלַח	me'avor מֵעֲבוֹר	
tehila תְּהִלָּה	yarim יָרִים	le'amo לְעַמּוֹ	keren קֶרֶן		
hoga הוֹגָה	im אִם	ki כִּי	chasidav וַחֲסִידָיו	lechol לְכָל	
chasadav וַחֲסָדָיו	uchrov וּכְרוֹב	kerachamav כְּרַחֲמָיו	vericham וְרִחַם		

The Egyptian Exile - The tribes of Yah [the incomplete Name of God in exile] (the letters, Yud and Hei, in this Name are) evidence to Israel; (that) by their troubles He is troubled, in suffering and in slavery; In the Sapphire Stone He showed [the appearance of the Light of the redemption during the slavery in Egypt] them the strength of His love, and was revealed [in the burning bush] to lift them from the depth of pit and dungeon. "For with the Lord is unfailing Mercy and with him is full redemption [to redeem us before its time]." *(Psalms 130:7).*

The Babylonian Exile - How precious is His Mercy (as people) find shelter in the shadow (of His wings.) In the Babylonian exile, He was sent for their sake; when the vessels [the Chariots and the Angel's Camps from the Upper World] went down He was with them *(Zohar Shemot 11).* And He showed them compassion before their captors *(Jeremiah 42:12)*; For He will not forsake His people for His great Name.

The Persian-Median Exile - In concealment [Esther in Hebrew] He placed His Throne to rescue His loved ones to dispel from there [by the Half Shekel] the scales [the ten thousand Shekels *(Esther 3:9)*] of His rebels [Queen Vashti, Haman and his ten sons *(Babylonian Talmud Megilah 10b)*], from passage under the scythe (the Angel of Death) He redeemed His servants, a beam of Light [Queen Esther] to His nation will raise praise for all of His devotees. "Although there is grief (as a result of the negative deeds), He is merciful, as to His compassion and His great kindness." *(Lamentation 3:32).*

SECOND MEAL CONNECTION – ATIKA KADISHA

וּצְפִיר utzfir	הָעִזִּים ha'izim	הִגְדִּיל higdil	עֲצוּמָיו atzumav •
וְגַם vegam	וְזֹאת chazut	אַרְבַּע arba	עָלוּ alu	לִמְרוֹמָיו limromav •
וּבְלִבָּם uvlibam	דִּמּוּ dimu	לְהַשְׁחִית lehashchit	אֶת et	רְחוּמָיו rechumav
עַל al	יְדֵי yedei	כֹּהֲנָיו chohanav	מִגֵּר miger	מִתְקוֹמְמָיו mitkomemav •
וְחַסְדֵי chasdei	יְהוָֹה Adonai	כִּי ki	לֹא lo
תַּמְנוּ tamnu	כִּי ki	לֹא lo	כָלוּ chalu	רַחֲמָיו rachamav :
נִסְגַּרְתִּי nisgarti	לֶאֱדוֹם le'edom	בְּיַד beyad	רֵעַי re'ai	מְדָנָי medanai •
שֶׁבְּכָל shebchol	יוֹם yom	מְמַלְּאִים memalim	כְּרֵסָם keresam
מֵעֲדָנָי me'adanai •	עֶזְרָתוֹ ezrato	עִמִּי imi	לִסְמוֹךְ lismoch	אֶת et
אֲדֹנָי adanai •	וְלֹא velo	נְטַשְׁתַּנִי netashtani	כָּל kol	יְמֵי yemei	עֲדֹנָי idanai •
כִּי ki	לֹא lo	יִזְנַח yiznach	לְעוֹלָם le'olam	אֲדֹנָי Adonai :

This part of the song literally speaks about the final days (based on Isaiah chapter 63) but it also has a hidden aspect, which is the power of giving *tzedakah* (charity) as the most influential tool to bring the Messiah. The word "blood" in Hebrew (*dam*—דם) is similar to the word money in Aramaic (*damim*—דמים). The *Zohar* (Pinchas 93-103) explains that when someone is ill and weak there must be a physical bloodletting (the frequent withdrawal of small quantities of blood from a patient to cure or prevent illness and disease) from his body to heal him, so too, on the spiritual level, giving *tzedakah* is an action that affects the removal any illness or disease.

"Who is this that comes from Edom… It is I, who speak in righteousness (in Heb: *tzedakah*), mighty to save." (Isaiah 63:1) The *Midrash* (the book "Parashat Derachim") says on this verse: In the time of the Final Redemption the Creator will look for a reason to redeem us but will not find any angels that will have anything good to say about us. Even the Angel Michael will be silent. Then the Creator Himself will say: "I will save you because of the power of the actions of *tzedakah*." It appears as if the verses are speaking about the blood (*dam*) that will be shed in the final days but this is not so. It is talking about the power of giving money (*damim*) for *tzedakah* that will ignite the energy of the Lightforce of the Creator to bring an end to all pain and suffering.

The Greek Exile - *And the young goat [the Greek king (Daniel 8:8)] overcame his mighty ones, and the four [his kingdom divided into four (Daniel 8:22)] gathered together and rose on high, and in their hearts they fancied destroying His mercies, but by virtue of His priests [Matityahu the High Priest and his five sons] he smote those who rebelled against Him. (Because of) "The Lord's mercies [as the Kohen represents Mercy] we have not finished, nor has His mercy been ended." (Lamentations 3:22)*

The Roman Exile - *I (Jerusalem) was given over to Edom [Rome] by the hand of my antagonistic comrades [hatred for no reason] while they filled their stomachs with my treasures daily. His help remained with me to support my pillars. But He will not forsake me all the days of my time [until the end of the exile (Daniel 7:25)], "for the Lord [the Shechinah] will never abandon anyone." (Lamentations 3:31)*

Second Meal Connection – Atika Kadisha

zevach זֶבַח	•begadim בְּגָדִים	chamutz וְחָמוּץ	me'edom מֵאֱדוֹם	bevo'o בְּבֹאוֹ
•bevogdim בְּבוֹגְדִים	lo לוֹ	vetevach וְטֶבַח	bevatzra בְּבָצְרָה	lo לוֹ
•leha'adim לְהַאֲדִים	malbushav מַלְבּוּשָׁיו	nitzcham נִצְחָם	veyez וְיֵז
•negidim נְגִידִים	ruach רוּחַ	yivtzor יִבְצֹר	hagadol הַגָּדוֹל	bechocho בְּכוֹחוֹ
:kadim קָדִים	beyom בְּיוֹם	hakasha הַקָּשָׁה	berucho בְּרוּחוֹ	haga הָגָה

Here, the song speaks about the three mistakes Satan (Angel of Death) will make at the End of Days, facilitating the Final Redemption (Babylonian Talmud, Makot 12:1):

1. Satan will think that the name of the city of refuge is *Batzra* (בצרה—the city of Edom) instead of *Betzer* (בצר);
2. Satan will think that the city also protects those who killed intentionally and not just those who killed accidently;
3. Satan will think that an angel (like himself) is also protected in the city of refuge just as humans are protected;

If this is so, why do we keep singing this song? Surely it can remind Satan not to make these three mistakes. We are told that the melody Rav Ashlag composed for this song is so powerful that it confuses Satan and removes his power completely as long as we are singing it.

•ha'otzer הָעוֹצֵר	Adomi אֲדוֹמִי	chen כֵּן	ki כִּי	re'oto רְאוֹתוֹ
•keVetzer כְּבֶצֶר	tiklot תִּקְלוֹט	beVatzra בְּבָצְרָה	lo לוֹ	yachashov יַחֲשׁוֹב
•yinatzer יִנָּצֵר	betocha בְּתוֹכָהּ	ke'adam כְּאָדָם	umal'ach וּמַלְאָךְ
•ye'atzer יֵעָצֵר	bemiklat בְּמִקְלָט	kashogeg כְּשׁוֹגֵג	umezid וּמֵזִיד
chasidav וַחֲסִידָיו	kol כָּל	Adonai יְהֹוָאדֹנָהִילֶהִי	et אֶת	ehevu אֶהֱבוּ
:notzer נֹצֵר	emunim אֱמוּנִים

When (in the final days) "He comes from Edom with His garments stained crimson [from the removal of the negative forces as their color is red]," (Isaiah 63:1) "there will be sacrifices in Batzrah" (Isaiah 34:6) and a slaughter [zevach is a code name for the weakening and breaking of the forces of Judgment (Zohar Vayikra 53)] of traitors [elevation of all the souls from the klipa (Or HaChaim on Leviticus 7)]. "The drippings of their defeat" (Isaiah 63:3) will redden His clothes; His great power will eliminate the nobles' spirit. "He declares on the day before (Creation) His harsh wind [the spirit of God (Genesis 1:2)—the spirit of Messiah, that is awakened by the study of Kabbalah (Zohar Veyachi 631 and Tikkunei Zohar, Tikkun 30 9-11)]," (Isaiah 27:8) When the oppressive one from Edom [the Angel of Death] sees how it is (that it is time for Redemption), he will think (and will be mistaken) that: 1) (the city of) Batzrah will provide him with refuge like (the city of refuge named) Betzer; 2) An angel, like a man, is protected in it; 3) And the willful murderer, just as the unintentional killer, is detained in the refuge. [And because of the melody of Rav Ashlag we are now protected from Satan, so] "Love the Lord, all his faithful people, He protects the believers." (Psalms 31:24)

Third Meal Connection

ZEIR ANPIN
(SMALL FACE)

ATKINU—BENEI HECHALA (PREPARE THE FEAST—MEMBERS OF
   THE CHAMBERS)
MIZMOR LEDAVID (PSALM OF DAVID)
YETZAVEH (MAY THE ROCK COMMAND)
EL MISTATER (GOD IS CONCEALED)
EIN KELOHENU (THERE IS NONE LIKE OUR GOD)
ATAH HU ELOHENU (YOU ARE OUR GOD)
KIDDUSH (BLESSING OVER THE WINE) OF THE THIRD MEAL
YEDID NEFESH (BELOVED OF THE SOUL)

Third Meal Connection – Zeir Anpin

Saturday Afternoon – The Central Column

The Third Meal is the highest point of *Shabbat*. It is the moment when we capture all of the Light we might have missed in our earlier *Shabbat* connections. When we reach the time of the Third Meal of *Shabbat* we are achieving perfect oneness, where our 1 Percent Reality is connected to the 99 Percent Reality. The ancient kabbalists tell us that those who participate regularly in the Third Meal, with complete consciousness and understanding as to its power, will be protected and blessed, even during times of great chaos.

The Third Meal of *Shabbat* offers us an opportunity to ignite the Desire of all Desires, where our Desire to Share is unlimited and truly genuine. Although this kind of true desire is difficult to achieve, the spiritual energy available at this time infuses us with the desire to reveal the Light not only for ourselves but also for the world. And if we do not have this desire then we can ask for that as well, as this is the time to ask for a personal spiritual wish, and attain a desire to have a pure desire.

The great kabbalists tell us that the Final Redemption of humankind is connected to the Third Meal of *Shabbat*. According to the *Zohar*, the Light we receive in the Third Meal helps us to overcome the war of *Gog Umagog*, the War of Thoughts. It is one of the most powerful tools to help us resist the voice of our opponent. The magnitude of the spiritual energy being awakened strengthens our spiritual immune system and that of the Earth. Our work at this time is to employ the energy of *Shabbat* and the Third Meal to remove chaos from this world and ensure that the Final Redemption takes place swiftly and smoothly.

Atkinu—Benei Hechala (Prepare the Feast—Members of the Chambers)

"Those who yearn to see the glow of the Light of the Creator, only they may be at the table for the third and final meal of *Shabbat*, at which the greatest Light of *Shabbat* is revealed." This is the message of Rav Isaac Luria (the Ari) throughout his third and final song of *Shabbat*. At this time, all of the Supernal Gates are open, and there is no Judgment. When we connect with desire and yearning at this time, we can merit the greatest Light possible from the Creator.

♦dimhemnuta דִּמְהֵימְנוּתָא		se'udata סְעוּדָתָא		atkinu אַתְקִינוּ	
‡kadisha קַדִּישָׁא	demalka דְמַלְכָּא	chedveta וְחֶדְוָתָא	shelemata שְׁלֵימָתָא		
hi הִיא	da דָא	♦demalka דְמַלְכָּא	se'udata סְעוּדָתָא	atkinu אַתְקִינוּ	
veAtika וְעַתִּיקָא	Anpin אַנְפִּין	diZeir דִּזְעֵיר	se'udata סְעוּדָתָא		
Kadishin קַדִּישִׁין	Tapuchin תַּפּוּחִין	vaChakal וַחֲקַל	♦Kadisha קַדִּישָׁא		
‡bahadeh בַּהֲדֵהּ	lesa'ada לְסַעֲדָא	atyan אַתְיָן			

Atkinu—Benei Hechala (Prepare the Feast—Members of the Chambers)

Prepare the feast of perfect faith, the joy of the Holy King. Prepare the feast of the King. This is the feast of the Small Face [Zeir Anpin.] And the Holy Ancient One [Atika Kadisha] and Field of Holy Apples [Chakal Tapuchin Kadishin] come to partake in the feast with Him.

THIRD MEAL CONNECTION – ZEIR ANPIN

בְּנֵי benei הֵיכָלָא hechala ♦ דִּכְסִיפִין dichsifin ♦
לְמֶחֱזֵי lemechezei זִיו ziv דִּזְעֵיר diZeir אַנְפִּין Anpin:

In the time of *Minchah* (afternoon) of *Shabbat*, *Zeir Anpin* ascends to the Eighth *Mazal* ("*venotzer*"), but *Nukva* and the rest of the Worlds (the Seven Chambers of the World of *Beriah*, the World of *Yetzirah*, and the World of *Asiyah*) stay Below and cannot be elevated with Him (*Zeir Anpin*) to delight in the brilliant Lights that He now receives.

יְהוֹן yehon הָכָא hacha ♦ בְּהַאי behay תַּכָּא taka ♦
דְּבֵהּ deve מַלְכָּא malka בְּגִלּוּפִין begilufin:

We ask that even though They cannot be elevated with Him, His brilliant Lights will shine upon *Nukva*, the Worlds and us, as we participate in His meal during the time of *Minchah* of *Shabbat*.

צְבוּ tzevu ♦ לַחֲדָא lachada ♦ בְּהַאי behay וַעֲדָא va'ada ♦
בְּגוֹ bego עִירִין irin וְכָל vechol גַּדְפִין gadfin:

וְחֲדוּ chadu הַשְׁתָּא hashta ♦ בְּהַאי behai שַׁעְתָּא sha'ata ♦
דְּבֵהּ deve רַעֲוָא ra'ava וְלֵית velet זַעֲפִין za'afin:

The *Zohar* (Yitro 463) says: On all six days of the week when the hour of *Minchah* arrives, Harsh Judgment rules and all the chastisements are aroused [the Name: אלהים is in control and all the forces of negativity and the *klipot* are awakened, which causes sorrow in all the Worlds], but on *Shabbat*, at the time of *Minchah* the Will of all Wills [*Yesod* of *Atika* through the Forehead of *Arich Anpin*] is present and *Atika Kadisha* shows goodwill and all the Judgments rest [as It sweetens all the Judgments, in the secret of the verse (Psalms 69:14): "God (אלהים, the force of Judgments becomes) with the abundance of Your kindness"], and gladness and joy are everywhere [as happiness is a result of the Unification in *Yesod* that sweetens the Judgments.] Rav Ashlag adds (*Zohar, Sulam* commentary, *Idra Zuta*, 43) that we should be happy now (*chadu hashta* וְחֲדוּ הַשְׁתָּא), in this time of *Minchah* of *Shabbat* (*behai sha'ata* בְּהַאי שַׁעְתָּא), when the Forehead is revealed and the power of *Chasadim* (Mercies) is exposed, as we can see that the ruling of the world by *Chasadim* is a choice, a passion and a desire of the Creator for us (*deve ra'ava* דְּבֵהּ רַעֲוָא) and not just because of the need of the Second *Tzimtzum* (the elevation of *Malchut* to *Binah*) (*velet za'afin* וְלֵית זַעֲפִין). We see that even though *Malchut* descends back from *Binah*, the Creator selects the *Chasadim* over *Chochmah* from choice and passion.

Members of the Chambers [the Seven Chambers in the World of *Beriah* that ascend to *Netzach*, *Hod* and *Yesod* of *Atzilut*; this also corresponds to those who study Kabbalah and connect to the three meals of *Shabbat* (*Zohar Yitro* 458)], who yearn [as they do not ascend with Him] to see the glow of *Zeir Anpin*.
י May they [the brilliant Lights of *Zeir Anpin*] be here at this ark (*Nukva*, as She is without *Zeir Anpin* She is not called table but an ark, as Noah's ark that had inside it all species and creatures – the Worlds of *Beriah*, *Yetzirah*, and *Asiyah*] in which the King [the brilliant Lights of *Zeir Anpin*] is engraved.
צ Have yearning to be part of this assembly [of *Zeir Anpin* that He invites *Atika Kadisha* and *Chakal Tapuchin Kadishin* to join Him, and] the angels [from *Beriah*] and all the wings [the angel **(do not pronounce)** *Matatron* with the ten groups of angels from *Yetzirah* and *Asiyah*].
ח Rejoice now [as *Yesod* of *Atika* is revealed through the Forehead of *Arich Anpin* and sweetens all the Judgments] at this very hour in which there is favor [sweetened Judgments] but no anger [Judgments].

THIRD MEAL CONNECTION – ZEIR ANPIN

קְרִיבוּ kerivu לִי li וְחָזוּ chazu וְחֵילִי cheli• דְּלֵית delet דִּינִין dinin דְּתַקִיפִין ditkifin:

The *Shechinah* asks of us: "As its time of favor, desire and will, come closer and see how 'I am lovesick' (Song of Songs 2:5) and beseech and ask for the Final Redemption. And do not be afraid from the accusing of the Judgment Attribute, because now all 24 houses of Judgments that are in the Forehead of *Zeir Anpin* (from the aspect of the Tiara of *Gevurah*) are sweetened." (*Zohar, Idra Zuta* 134).

לְבַר levar נָטְלִין natlin• וְלָא vela עָאלִין alin• הַנֵּי hanei כַּלְבִּין chalbin דַּחֲצִיפִין dachatzifin:

And the *Shechinah* continues: "And do not be afraid of the *klipot*, because of the half good part of the *klipa* of *Nogah*—brightness ascends and is included in the Holiness of *Shabbat* (as part of the secret of the additional soul of *Shabbat*), and the other three *klipot* (**do not pronounce:** *ru'ach se'ara*—wind of storm, *anan gadol*—big cloud and *esh mitlakachat*—inflammable fire) descend to *Nukva deTehoma Raba*—the Hole of the Greater Abyss (the 7th Chamber of *Beriah* of the External Forces)."

וְהָא veha אוּמִין azmin• עַתִּיק Atik יוֹמִין Yomin• לְמִנְוָא lemincha לְמִצְחָא lemitzcha עֲדֵי adei יְהוֹן yehon וְחַלְפִין chalfin:

The *Zohar* (*Idra Rabba* 199) says: "We have learned that when the Forehead of *Zeir Anpin* is revealed, all the plaintiffs are aroused and the world at large is given to trial, except for that particular period that It ascends before *Atik Yomin* (Ancient of Days) so He (*Atik Yomin*) reveals His Forehead (the Will of all Wills) and illuminates with the Forehead of *Zeir Anpin* and Judgment is soothed."

רְעוּ re'u דִּילֵהּ dile• דְּגַלֵּי degalei לֵהּ le• לְבַטָּלָא levatala בְּכֹל bechol קְלִיפִין kelifin:

Yesod of *Reisha Dela Ityada*—the Unknown Head ["extended one force that is sweetened and beautiful" (*Zohar, Idra Zuta*, 43)] is revealed through the Forehead of *Arich Anpin* (*Ratzon*—Desire).

יְשַׁוֵּי yeshavei לוֹן lon• בְּנוּקְבֵיהוֹן benokvehon• וְיִטַמְּרוּן veyitamrun בְּגוֹ bego כֵּפִין chefin:

אֲרֵי arei הַשְׁתָּא hashta• בְּמִנְחָתָא beminchata• בְּחֶדְוָתָא bechedvata דִּזְעֵיר diZeir אַנְפִּין Anpin קַדִישִׁין kadishin:

ק (Members of the Chambers) come close to me [Zeir Anpin] and see my strength [as Zeir Anpin now has the power of Arich Anpin], when there are no Harsh Judgments (so they cannot disturb you from coming closer).
ל Outside [of the Holiness of Shabbat] let them [the klipot] remain, never to arise [with Nukva and the rest of the Worlds into the World of Atzilut], those brazen dogs [the forces of negativity Zohar Vayikra 331].
ו But I [Zeir Anpin] invite [by the secret of the zimun to reject the klipot] the Ancient of Days [Atik Yomin] (so His) forehead (will shine) at Minchah, the time when they fade away (for eternity).
ר His favor [the Forehead of Atik Yomin], when It is revealed, will nullify all of the klipot.
י May He place them in their pits [Nukva deTehoma Rabba] and hide them under the dome.
א (I ask this) now, at the time of Minchah, during the rejoicing of the Holy Zeir Anpin.

THIRD MEAL CONNECTION – ZEIR ANPIN

Mizmor LeDavid (A Psalm of David)

Written by King David, Psalms 23 speaks of the trust we must have if we wish to connect to the Light of the Creator. Just as the sheep trust the shepherd for all of their needs, we, too, must trust in the Lord as our shepherd. Then and only then will we never lack.

In *Mizmor LeDavid* there are 57 words, which is also the numerical value of the word *Zan* זן (sustenance). Reciting it will prevent lacking in both spiritual and physical sustenance.

mizmor מִזְמוֹר leDavid לְדָוִד Adonai יְהֹוָהֱאֱלֹהִיםאֲדֹנָי ro'i רֹעִי lo לֹא

echsar אֶחְסָר: bine'ot בִּנְאוֹת deshe דֶּשֶׁא yarbitzeni יַרְבִּיצֵנִי al- עַל-

mei מֵי ילי menuchot מְנֻחוֹת ר"ת עמם yenahaleni יְנַהֲלֵנִי: nafshi נַפְשִׁי

yeshovev יְשׁוֹבֵב yancheni יַנְחֵנִי vema'gelei בְמַעְגְּלֵי- tzedek צֶדֶק

lema'an לְמַעַן shemo שְׁמוֹ מהש ע"ב ברבוע וקס"א ע"ה, אל שדי ע"ה:

gam גַּם ki כִּי elech אֵלֵךְ begei בְּגֵיא tzalmavet צַלְמָוֶת lo לֹא- ira אִירָא

ra רָע ki כִּי Ata אַתָּה imadi עִמָּדִי shivtecha שִׁבְטְךָ

umish'antecha וּמִשְׁעַנְתֶּךָ hema הֵמָּה yenachamuni יְנַחֲמֻנִי: ta'aroch תַּעֲרֹךְ

lefanai לְפָנַי shulchan שֻׁלְחָן neged נֶגֶד מזבוז, זן, אל יהוה tzorerai צֹרְרָי

dishanta דִּשַּׁנְתָּ vashemen בַּשֶּׁמֶן roshi רֹאשִׁי kosi כּוֹסִי revaya רְוָיָה:

ach אַךְ אהיה tov טוֹב יהו vachesed וָחֶסֶד ע"ב, ריבוע יהוה (י יה יהו יהוה) ; ס"ת = יהוה

yirdefuni יִרְדְּפוּנִי ר"ת = יהוה kol כֹּל ילי yemei יְמֵי chayai חַיָּי

veshavti וְשַׁבְתִּי bevet בְּבֵית ב"פ ראה Adonai יְהֹוָהֱאֱלֹהִיםאֲדֹנָי le'orech לְאֹרֶךְ

yamim יָמִים נלך ; ר"ת ילי ; ס"ת = אדני ; יהוה לאורך ימים = שע' נהורים עם י"ג אותיות:

Mizmor LeDavid (A Psalm of David)

"A Psalm of David: The Lord is my Shepherd, I shall not lack. In lush meadows He lays me down, beside tranquil waters He leads me. He restores my soul. He leads me on paths of justice for His Name's sake. Though I walk in the valley of the shadow of death, I will fear no evil for You are with me. Your rod and Your staff, they comfort me. You prepare a table before me in full view of my tormentors. You anointed my head with oil, my cup overflows. May only goodness and mercy pursue me all the days of my life, and may I dwell in the House of the Lord for long days." (Psalms 23)

Third Meal Connection – Zeir Anpin

Yetzaveh (May the Rock Command)

The words of this song are the completion of the song *"Baruch Hashem (Bom Bom)"* that is sung during the *Shabbat* Morning Meal (see page 69). This final section of the song speaks more specifically of the Final Redemption that will occur with the attribute of Mercy. The Creator will gather all the sparks of Light from the four corners of the world and bring them all to the land of Israel.

The *Zohar* says (Emor 37): "We have so learned, happy are Israel, for wherever they were exiled, the *Shechinah* went into exile with them. When Israel will come out of exile, whose salvation shall this be, that of Israel or of the Holy One, blessed be He (as the *Shechinah* will go out of exile as well)? The verse says (Psalms 3:9): 'Salvation to the Lord.' When will that be? When 'Your blessings be upon Your people.' When the Holy One, blessed be He, cares for Israel with blessings so as to take them out of exile and help them, then 'Salvation to the Lord,' because the *Shechinah* will go out of exile. We therefore learned that the Holy One, blessed be He, will return from exile with Israel. This is the meaning of the verse (Deuteronomy 30:3): "Then the Lord, your God, will turn your captivity.' 'Turn' can be construed to mean He will return with Israel from exile."

❖lekabetz	לְקַבֵּץ	kehilotav	קְהִלּוֹתָיו	chasdo	וְחַסְדּוֹ	tzur	צוּר	yetzaveh	יְצַוֶּה
❖lehikavetz	לְהִקָּבֵץ	adav	עֲדֵי	ruchot	רוּחוֹת	me'arba	מֵאַרְבַּע		
❖leharbetz	לְהַרְבֵּץ	otanu	אוֹתָנוּ	harim	הָרִים	merom	מְרוֹם	uvhar	וּבְהַר
yashiv	יָשִׁיב	❖kovetz	קוֹבֵץ	nidachim	נִדָּחִים	yashuv	יָשׁוּב	ve'itanu	וְאִתָּנוּ
⁂vekibetz	וְקִבֵּץ	veshav	וְשָׁב	im	אִם	ki	כִּי	ne'emar	נֶאֱמַר	lo	לֹא
tov	טוֹב	asher	אֲשֶׁר	Elohenu	אֱלֹהֵינוּ	hu	הוּא	baruch	בָּרוּךְ
chasadav	וְחַסָדָיו	uchrov	וּכְרוֹב	kerachamav	כְּרַחֲמָיו	❖gemalanu	גְּמָלָנוּ		
	ב"פ אלה = וסד	vecha'ele	וְכָאֵלֶּה	ele	אֵלֶּה	❖אלהים	lanu	לָנוּ	higdil	הִגְדִּיל

The Attribute of Judgment (the word לָנוּ—*lanu* equals to the word אלהים=86) is sweetened by the power of the Attribute of Mercy (=72; is equal to the value of twice the word אלה—*ele*) during this time of *Minchah* of *Shabbat* and also in the time of the Final Redemption.

hagadol	הַגָּדוֹל	shemo	שְׁמוֹ	lehagdil	לְהַגְדִּיל	❖imanu	עִמָּנוּ	yosef	יוֹסֵף
⁂alenu	עָלֵינוּ	shenikra	שֶׁנִּקְרָא	vehanora	וְהַנּוֹרָא	hagibor	הַגִּבּוֹר

Yetzaveh (May the Rock Command)

May the Rock command His Mercy to gather in His congregations [sparks of Light], from the four winds [the klipa] to be gathered up to Him, upon the loftiest mountain [the Temple Mount] to set us down. He shall return with us [Rav Shimon Bar Yochai says: "Wherever Israel are exiled, the Shechinah accompanies them" (Babylonian Talmud, Tractate Megilah 29:1)], the Gatherer of exiles – 'He shall bring back' is not said; but (it says) "He shall turn your captivity… and turn and gather (you from all the nations)." (Deuteronomy 30:3) Blessed is our God [the Attribute of Judgment] Who did us good. According to His mercy and His abundant kindness He did great things for us. Both these [the miracles of the redemption from Egypt] and those [the miracles from all other redemptions] may He increase for us – to magnify His great, mighty, and awesome Name [from יה (exile) to יהוה (redemption)] which was proclaimed upon us (based on Zohar Shemot 132-133).

Third Meal Connection – Zeir Anpin

baruch בָּרוּךְ hu הוּא Elohenu אֱלֹהֵינוּ shebera'anu שֶׁבְּרָאָנוּ
lichvodo לִכְבוֹדוֹ lehalelo לְהַלְלוֹ ulshabchv וּלְשַׁבְּחוֹ ulsaper וּלְסַפֵּר
hodo הוֹדוֹ mikol מִכָּל om אוֹם gavar גָּבַר alenu עָלֵינוּ chasdo וְחַסְדּוֹ
lachen לָכֵן bechol בְּכָל lev לֵב uvchol וּבְכָל nefesh נֶפֶשׁ
uvchol וּבְכָל me'odo מְאוֹדוֹ namlicho נַמְלִיכוֹ unyachado וְנְיַחֲדוֹ:

The next paragraph is based on the *Talmud* (Babylonian Talmud, Tractate Baba Metzi'a, 85:1) that says: "He who is himself spiritual, and his son is spiritual, and his son's son too, the Torah will nevermore cease from his seed, as it is written (Isaiah 59:21): 'As for me, this is my covenant with them, said the Lord; My spirit is upon you, and my words that I have put in your mouth, shall not depart out of the mouth, nor out of the mouth of your offspring, nor out of the mouth of your children's offspring, said the Lord, from hereafter and forever.' We ask here to have the merit to be able to physically see our next two generations follow in our spiritual footsteps. By guiding our children along the spiritual path of Torah we increase the strength of peace in the worlds, as it says: "Spiritual students increase the peace in the world." (Ibid., Tractate Berachot, 64:1); and also says: "The Holy One, Blessed Be He, found no vessel that could contain blessing for Israel save that of peace." (Mishna, Tractate Uktzin 3:12)

shehashalom שֶׁהַשָּׁלוֹם shelo שֶׁלּוֹ yasim יָשִׂים alenu עָלֵינוּ beracha בְּרָכָה
veshalom וְשָׁלוֹם mismol מִשְּׂמֹאל umiyamin וּמִיָּמִין al עַל Yisrael יִשְׂרָאֵל
shalom שָׁלוֹם harachaman הָרַחֲמָן hu הוּא yevarech יְבָרֵךְ
et אֶת amo עַמּוֹ bashalom בְּשָׁלוֹם veyizku וְיִזְכּוּ lir'ot לִרְאוֹת
banim בָּנִים uvnei וּבְנֵי vanim בָּנִים oskim עוֹסְקִים batora בַּתּוֹרָה
uvmitzvot וּבְמִצְוֹת al עַל Yisrael יִשְׂרָאֵל shalom שָׁלוֹם (פלא)
yo'etz יוֹעֵץ El אֵל gibor גִּבּוֹר avi אֲבִי ad עַד sar שַׂר shalom שָׁלוֹם:

Blessed is our God [the Attribute of Judgment] Who created us for His glory; to praise Him, laud Him and relate His majesty. More than any nation He strengthened His kindness [in His Attribute of Judgment] over us. Therefore [as we say in the prayer of "Shema Yisrael":] with a complete heart [emotional], with a complete soul [spiritual], and with complete resources [physical] (based on Deuteronomy 6:5), let us proclaim Him King [over the four levels of life—human, animal, plants and inanimate] and proclaim Him Unique [so all will be elevated in one Unification]. May He, to Whom peace belongs, [Binah or Zeir Anpin (Zohar, Terumah, 687-688)] set upon us blessing and peace [the blessing of the Kohanim starts with the words "May the Lord bless you" and end with the words "will give you peace" (Numbers 6:24-26)] — from left [the Judgment aspect] and from right [the Mercy aspect], peace upon Israel. May the Merciful One bless His people with peace; and may they merit seeing children and grandchildren engaging in Torah and precepts, bringing peace upon Israel. "(You are Wondrous [Supernal Chochmah]) Adviser [Binah], God [Abraham—Chesed] Mighty [Isaac—Gevurah], Father of Eternity [Tiferet], Prince of Peace [Yesod]." (Zohar, Tzav 96 based on Isaiah 9:5)

Third Meal Connection – Zeir Anpin

El Mistater (God is Concealed)

This song, written by Kabbalist Rav Avraham Meimin (student of Rav Moshe Kordovero – 16th century), explains how the Light of the Creator is revealed in this world through the Ten *Sefirot*. Throughout this song we climb up and down, using the ladder of the Ten *Sefirot*.

Keter אֵל El יי"א (מילוי דס"ג) מִסְתַּתֵּר mistater בְּשַׁפְרִיר beshafrir
וְחֶבְיוֹן chevyon, הַשֵּׂכֶל hashechel הַנֶּעְלָם hane'elam מִכָּל mikol יכלי
רַעְיוֹן ra'ayon, עִלַּת ilat הָעִלּוֹת ha'ilot מוּכְתָּר muchtar בְּכֶתֶר becheter ה' מלך
ה' מלך ה' ימלוך לעולם ועד ובאתב"ש גאל עֶלְיוֹן elyon, כֶּתֶר Keter ה' מלך
ה' מלך ה' ימלוך לעולם ועד ובאתב"ש גאל יִתְּנוּ yitnu לְךָ lecha יְהוָה Adonai◆

Chochmah בְּרֵאשִׁית bereshit תּוֹרָתְךָ toratcha הַקְּדוּמָה hakeduma,
רְשׁוּמָה reshuma וְחָכְמָתְךָ chochmatcha הַסְּתוּמָה hasetuma, מֵאַיִן me'ayin
תִּמָּצֵא timatze וְהִיא vehi נֶעְלָמָה ne'elama, רֵאשִׁית reshit
Chochmah חָכְמָה במילוי תרי"ג (מצוות) יִרְאַת yir'at יְהוָה Adonai◆

Binah רְחוֹבוֹת rechovot הַנָּהָר hanahar נַחֲלֵי nachalei אֱמוּנָה emuna,
מַיִם mayim עֲמוּקִים amukim יִדְלֵם yidlem אִישׁ ish תְּבוּנָה tevuna,
תּוֹצְאוֹתֶיהָ totzoteha וַחֲמִשִּׁים chamishim שַׁעֲרֵי sha'arei בִּינָה Binah
אֲמוּנִים emunim נֹצֵר notzer יְהוָה Adonai◆ ע"ה אהיה יהוה, ע"ה וזיי"ן ע"ה חיים

El Mistater (God is Concealed)

Keter – "God is concealed" (Isaiah 45:15) in a canopy (Jeremiah 43:10) of secrecy, the Hidden Brain [Yechidah] from all notion (Tikkunei Zohar, Patach Eliyahu); The Cause of Causes [the Endless Blessed Be He], crowned with the Supernal Crown [Keter] (Zohar Bo, 222); A crown [the angel Sandal-fon (**do not pronounce**) crowns the Creator with a crown from our prayers] will give to You, Lord.
Chochmah - In the beginning [before the creation of the Worlds] there was Your ancient Torah (Midrash Beresheet Rabba, 8:2), inscribed with Your hidden Wisdom; It originated from nothing [Ayin – Keter] but It still hidden. "The source of wisdom is awe of the Lord." (Psalms 111:10, Zohar, Prologue 120-124)
Binah - The breadth of the river [Binah (Etz Chaim A, pg. 114)], like a stream of faith [Amen is called the spring of the flowing river, which is Binah (Zohar, Veyelech, 39)]. "(Counsel in the heart [Binah (Tikkunei Zohar, Patach Eliyahu)] of man is like) deep waters [water—Mayim has the numerical value of 90, which is the same as the Hebrew letter Tzadik—צ, which also means righteous] (but) a man of understanding [Joseph the righteous—Yesod of Binah—Netzach, Hod, and Yesod of Tevunah (Zohar, Miketz, 183)] will draw it out." (Proverbs 20:5) Its results are the Fifty Gates of Binah [seven included in seven are drawn from Binah and the 50th is in Binah (Etz Chaim B, pg. 8)]; "the Lord preserves the faithful." ["He who sanctifies the Holy Name by meditating properly on Amen (=91=יאהדונהי)—Unifying Yesod (יהוה) and Malchut (אדני)." (Zohar, Vayelech, 46 based on Psalms 31:24)

THIRD MEAL CONNECTION – ZEIR ANPIN

Chesed הָאֵל haEl לאה, ייא"י (מילוי דס"ג) לההו, עם ד' אותיות מבה, יזל, אום hagadol הַגָּדוֹל
עֵינֵי enei ריבוע מ"ה כֹּל chol ילי נֶגְדֶּךָ negdecha זך, מזבוז, אל יהוה רַב rav
וְחֶסֶד Chesed ע"ב, ריבוע יהוה לההו, עם ד' אותיות מבה, יזל, אום גָּדוֹל gadol עַל al
הַשָּׁמַיִם hasamayim י"פ טל, ט"פ כוזו וְחַסְדְּךָ chasdecha, אֱלֹהֵי Elohei מילוי ע"ב, דמב ; ילה
אַבְרָהָם Avraham וז"פ אל, רי"ו ול"ב נתיבות החכמה, רמ"ח (אברים), עסמ"ב וט"ז אותיות פשוטות
זְכֹר zechor ע"ב קס"א, יהי אור ע"ה לְעַבְדֶּךָ le'avdecha פוי, אל אדני וְחַסְדֵי chasdei
◆Adonai יְהֹוָהֵאדֹנָיאהדונהי tehilot תְּהִלּוֹת azkir אַזְכִּיר Adonai אֲדֹנָיאהדונהי

Gevurah מָרוֹם marom נֶאְדָּר ne'edar בְּכֹחַ becho'ach וּגְבוּרָה uGvurah רי"ו
מוֹצִיא motzi אוֹרָה ora רז, א"ס מֵאַיִן me'en תְּמוּרָה temura, פּוֹזֵר pachad
יִצְחָק Yitzchak ד"פ ב"ן מִשְׁפָּטֵינוּ mishpatenu ע"ה ה"פ אלהים הָאִירָה ha'ira,
אַתָּה Ata גִּבּוֹר gibor לְעוֹלָם le'olam ריבוע ס"ג עם י' אותיות יְהֹוָהֵאדֹנָיאהדונהי Adonai◆

Initials of the Holy Name: אִגְלָא, which Yehuda, the head of the tribe, used to conquer (in Hebrew the word is "*lehitgaber*", which comes from the same root as the word *Gevurah*) the negative forces.

Tiferet בְּי mi ילי אֵל El (מילוי) ייא"י (מילוי דס"ג) כָּמוֹךָ kamocha
עֹשֶׂה oseh גְּדֹלוֹת gedolot לההו, עם ד' אותיות מבה, יזל, אום, אֲבִיר avir הרוז nora נוֹרָא
יַעֲקֹב Ya'akov ד"פ יהוה, יאהדונהי = אביר יעקב = רבי עקיבא nora
תְּהִלּוֹת tehilot, תְּפִלוֹת tefilot, שׁוֹמֵעַ shome'a יִשְׂרָאֵל Yisrael Tiferet תִּפְאֶרֶת
כִּי ki שׁוֹמֵעַ shome'a אֶל el אֶבְיוֹנִים evyonim יְהֹוָהֵאדֹנָיאהדונהי Adonai◆

Chesed - Great [*Chesed*] God, the eyes of all [*Yesod*] are upon You; Great and abounding with kindness [one of the Attributes of the Upper Beard of Arich Anpin, which is Chesed in the Lower Beard of Zeir Anpin (Zohar, Sifra Detzniuta, 37)], "on the Heavens [Zeir Anpin] is Your kindness [as Mercy—Chesed is the highest Sefira in Zeir Anpin];" (Psalms 108:5) God of Abraham, remember Your servant; "Lord's benevolence I will proclaim in praises of the Lord." (Isaiah 63:7)

Gevurah - The Supernal One [the source of Binah (Zohar, Pekudei 214)] is adorned in power and might [*Gevurah*]; draws light from that which is beyond compare [by the power of Sefirat Gevurah to divide and create a border over the Light]. The fear of Isaac [Gevurah, the most valuable Sefira (Zohar Vayechi 48)], illuminate our sentencing [as the prosecutors will be afraid of it], You are mighty forever, Lord.

Tiferet – "Who is a God like You [the Thirteen Attributes of Arich Anpin (Zohar, Idra Rabba, 89)]," (Micah 7:18) "He who performs greatness? [by the Name of Ayin Bet (Tikkunei Zohar Tikkun 22, 124)]" (Job 9:10) "The mighty One of Jacob [the letter Vav, which is Zeir Anpin-Tiferet (Zohar, Acharei Mot, 193)]" (Genesis 49:24) and "fearful in praises [Zeir Anpin-Tiferet connects Binah and Malchut (Zohar, Prologue, 29)]" (Exodus 15:11) The Splendor of Israel hears prayers [the blessing of "Shome'a Tefilah" in the Amidah connected to Tiferet], "for the Lord hears [the ears of Zeir Anpin-Tiferet (Zohar, Idra Rabba, 235-236)] the poor" (Psalms 69:34)

Third Meal Connection – Zeir Anpin

Netzach	Yah יָהּ	הה"ה	zechut זְכוּת	avot אָבוֹת	yagen יָגֵן	alenu, עָלֵינוּ
נִצּוֹ Netzach	Yisrael יִשְׂרָאֵל		mitzarotenu מִצָּרוֹתֵינוּ		ge'alenu, גְּאָלֵנוּ	
lenatze'ach לְנַצֵּחַ,	veha'alenu וְהַעֲלֵנוּ,	delenu דְּלֵנוּ	galut גָּלוּת	umibor וּמִבּוֹר		
al עַל	melechet מְלֶאכֶת	bet בֵּית	ב"פ ראה	Adonai יְהֹוָאדֹנָיאֱהֹדִילְהִיּ.		
Hod	miyamin מִיָּמִין	umismol וּמִשְּׂמֹאל	yenikat יְנִיקַת	hanevi'im הַנְּבִיאִים,		
נִצּוֹ Netzach	vaHod וְהוֹד	הה"ה	mehem מֵהֶם	nimtza'im נִמְצָאִים,		
יָכִין Yachin	uVo'az וּבוֹעַז	beshem בְּשֵׁם	nikra'im נִקְרָאִים,			
וְכֹל vechol	ילי	banayich בָּנַיִךְ	limudei לִמּוּדֵי	Adonai יְהֹוָאדֹנָיאֱהֹדִילְהִיּ.		
Yesod	Yesod יְסוֹד	הה"ע	tzadik צַדִּיק	beshiv'a בְּשִׁבְעָה	ne'elam נֶעְלָם,	
אוֹת ot	berit בְּרִית	hu הוּא	le'olam לְעוֹלָם	רביעי ס"ג עם י'	אותיות,	
הה"ע	Yesod יְסוֹד	tzadik צַדִּיק	haberacha הַבְּרָכָה	me'en מֵעֵין		
Adonai יְהֹוָוֹהִיאֱלֹהִים	Ata אַתָּה	tzadik צַדִּיק,	olam עוֹלָם			

Netzach - Yah, may the merit of the Patriarchs [Chesed, Gevurah and Tiferet] protects us, the Eternal One [as Netzach that was weakened by the Angel of Esau was corrected by the prophet Samuel (Zohar, Beresheet A, 145)] of Israel [Zeir Anpin in greatness] will redeem us from our troubles and from the pit of exile He will draw us and raise us up "to be victorious in the service of the House of the Lord." (Ezra 3:8)

Hod - From right and from left are the prophets nurtured [from Netzach and Hod of Atzilut (Zohar, Pekudei, 533)], Netzach and Hod are found with them [the Right Column—Mercy and the Left Column—Judgment]; they are called by the names Yachin and Boaz [the two pillars that King Solomon built in the Temple (1 Kings 7:21)]. "And all of your children will think of the Lord [the aspects of Netzach and Hod known as "thought of the Lord", as prophecy stems from there (Zohar, Trumah 805)]" (Isaiah 54:13)

Yesod - The foundation (of the world is Joseph) the righteous; as it [Yesod] is concealed in seven ["Furthermore, this pillar, namely Yesod of Zeir Anpin, takes more. This is a highly secret matter to expound on because He takes in the Seventh Chamber (Zohar, Beresheet B, 135 and see the Writings of the Ari, Etz Chaim, Gate 46, Chapter 4)], He is the sign of the covenant [of the rainbow (Malchut) and the sign of Shabbat and the sign of the festivals, and the sign of the Tefilin, and the sign of the circumcision (Zohar, Pinchas, 583)] for the world. A fountain of blessing ["Blessed is the source of blessings from the source of life and the place from which all watering goes forth to water everything, namely Yesod of Binah. It is the source that provides in the secret of the sign of the covenant, namely Yesod of Zeir Anpin, which we call 'the blessed' for it is the fountain of the well (Malchut)" (Zohar, Trumah, 169)] "the righteous man (as he) is the foundation of the world ["He is the pillar that upholds the world, which is Malchut. That is why He is called the foundation of the world. And what is this Yesod? It is the righteous" (Zohar, Noach, 8)]" (Proverbs 10:25) "You are the righteous, Lord." (Psalms 119:137)

THIRD MEAL CONNECTION – ZEIR ANPIN

Malchut נָא na הָקֵם hakem הקם מַלְכוּת malchut דָוִד David
וּשְׁלֹמֹה uShlomo, בַּעֲטָרָה ba'atara עֲטָרָה she'itra לוֹ lo אִמּוֹ imo,
כְּנֶסֶת keneset יִשְׂרָאֵל Yisrael כַּלָּה kala קְרוּאָה keru'a בִּנְעִימָה bane'ima,
עֲטֶרֶת ateret תִּפְאֶרֶת Tiferet בְּיַד beyad יְהוָֹה Adonai ♦

וְחֹזֶק chazak פהל meyached מְיֻוָּחָד ke'echad כְּאֶחָד אהבה דאגה eser עֶשֶׂר
סְפִירוֹת sefirot, וּמְאוֹחָד um'ached אַלּוּף aluf יִרְאֶה yir'eh רי"ו
מְאוֹרוֹת me'orot, סַפִּיר sapir גִּזְרָתָם gizratam יַחַד yachad מְאִירוֹת me'irot,
תִּקְרַב tikrav רִנָּתִי rinati לְפָנֶיךָ lefanecha ס"ג מ"ה ב"ן יְהוָֹה Adonai ♦

EIN KELOHENU (THERE IS NONE LIKE OUR GOD)

When we speak of the Creator's manifold providence in this world, we connect to His Light. This is the purpose of this second to last song of the Third Meal of *Shabbat*.

אֵין en	כֵּאלֹהֵינוּ ♦kelohenu	אֵין en	כַּאדוֹנֵינוּ ♦kadonenu
אֵין en	כְּמַלְכֵּנוּ ♦kemalkenu	אֵין en	כְּמוֹשִׁיעֵנוּ ♦kemoshi'enu
מִי mi	כֵּאלֹהֵינוּ ♦chelohenu	מִי mi	כַּאדוֹנֵינוּ ♦chadonenu
מִי mi	כְּמַלְכֵּנוּ ♦chemalkenu	מִי mi	כְּמוֹשִׁיעֵנוּ ♦chemoshi'enu
נוֹדֶה nodeh	לֵאלֹהֵינוּ lelohenu	נוֹדֶה nodeh ילה	לַאדוֹנֵינוּ ♦ladonenu
נוֹדֶה nodeh	לְמַלְכֵּנוּ ♦lemalkenu	נוֹדֶה nodeh	לְמוֹשִׁיעֵנוּ lemoshi'enu:
בָּרוּךְ baruch	אֱלֹהֵינוּ ♦Elohenu	בָּרוּךְ baruch	אֲדוֹנֵינוּ ♦adonenu
בָּרוּךְ baruch	מַלְכֵּנוּ ♦malkenu	בָּרוּךְ baruch	מוֹשִׁיעֵנוּ ♦moshi'enu

---

Malchut - Restore the kingdoms of David and Solomon *[by Tamar and Ruth (Zohar Vayeshev 194)]* with the Tiara *[Mochin of the Three Upper Sefirot (Sulam commentary on Zohar Beresheet A, 86)]* by which his mother crowned him *(See the Writings of the Ari, the Gate of Meditation B, 94-95).* The congregation of Yisrael *[Nukva of Zeir Anpin in Gadlut—greatness (Sulam commentary on Zohar, Prologue 1)]* is called a bride in her pleasantness; she is a crown of beauty in the Lord's hand. Strength unifies us as one – the Ten Luminous Emanations, and unites the chief who will see lights. The lights together were carved from sapphire, "draw my song near before You, Lord." *(Psalms 119:169)*

EIN KELOHENU (THERE IS NONE LIKE OUR GOD)
There is none like our God. There is none like our Master.
There is none like our King. There is none like our Redeemer. Who is like our God?
Who is like our Master? Who is like our King? Who is like our Redeemer? We shall give thanks to our God, we shall give thanks to our Master, we shall give thanks to our King, we shall give thanks to our Redeemer. Blessed is our God. Blessed is our Master. Blessed is our King. Blessed is our Redeemer.

Third Meal Connection – Zeir Anpin

Atah Hu Elohenu (You are our God)

We find the 22 letters of the Hebrew alphabet encoded into this song. The first letter in each of the first 22 phrases is in its correct alphabetical order. Because the Hebrew letters are the actual instruments of Creation, this song helps to inject order and the power of Creation into our lives. We are gaining control over our world by tapping the forces that created it.

אַתָּה Ata	הוּא hu	אֱלֹהֵינוּ Elohenu:	בַּשָּׁמַיִם bashamayim	וּבָאָרֶץ uva'aretz:	
גִּבּוֹר gibor		וְנֶעֱרָץ vena'aratz:		דָּגוּל dagul	מֵרְבָבָה mervava:
הוּא hu	שָׂח sach	וַיֶּהִי vayehi:	וְצִוָּה vetziva	וְנִבְרָאוּ venivra'u:	
זִכְרוֹ zichro		לָנֶצַח lanetzach:	חַי chai	עוֹלָמִים olamim:	
טָהוֹר tehor		עֵינַיִם enayim:	יוֹשֵׁב yoshev	סֵתֶר seter:	
כִּתְרוֹ kitro		יְשׁוּעָה yeshu'a:	לְבוּשׁוֹ levusho	צְדָקָה tzedaka:	
מַעֲטֵהוּ ma'atehu		קִנְאָה kin'a:	נֶאְפָּד ne'epad	נְקָמָה nekama:	
סִתְרוֹ sitro		יֹשֶׁר yosher:	עֲצָתוֹ atzato	אֱמוּנָה emuna:	
פְּעֻלָּתוֹ pe'ulato		אֱמֶת emet:	צַדִּיק tzadik	וְיָשָׁר veyashar:	
קָרוֹב karov	לְקוֹרְאָיו lekor'av:	בֶּאֱמֶת be'emet:	רָם ram	וּמִתְנַשֵּׂא umitnase:	
שׁוֹכֵן shochen	שְׁחָקִים shechakim:	תּוֹלֶה tole	אֶרֶץ eretz	עַל al	בְּלִימָה belima:
וָחַי chai	וְקַיָּם vekayam	נוֹרָא nora	וּמָרוֹם umarom	וְקָדוֹשׁ vekadosh:	

Atah Hu Elohenu (You are our God)

א *You are our God,* ב *in Heaven and on Earth,* ג *heroic and esteemed,* ד *outstanding over myriads,* ה *He utters and it is so.* ו *When He commanded, they were created,* ז *they will remember it forever,* ח *everlasting* ט *and pure eyed,* י *dwells in concealment,* כ *His crown is salvation,* ל *His garment is charity,* מ *His cloak is zeal.* נ *He is garbed in vengeance,* ס *His secret is justness,* ע *His counsel is faith,* פ *His act is truth,* צ *righteous and just,* ק *He is close to those who call Him in truth,* ר *lofty and high,* ש *He dwells in the Heavens,* ת *He hangs the Earth on nothing,*
Living and enduring One, awesome, exalted and Holy.

Third Meal Connection – Zeir Anpin

Kiddush (Blessing Over the Wine) of the Third Meal

The *Kiddush* of Third Meal connects us to the energy of Moses, David and Joseph, who left this world at this time of *Shabbat*, and in so doing we receive protection from the *klipa* called "*maday*" (מדי - initials of Moses—משה, David—דוד and Joseph—יוסף). We also have the opportunity to overcome the Armageddon war (in Hebrew: *Gog Umagog*—גוג ומגוג, meaning the War of the Thoughts—הגיגים), as well as strengthen our immune system.

וַיֹּאמֶר vayomer מֹשֶׁה Moshe מהש, אל שדי אִכְלֻהוּ ichluhu הַיּוֹם hayom נגד, זן, מזבח

כִּי ki שַׁבָּת Shabbat הַיּוֹם hayom נגד, זן, מזבח לַיהוָה ladonai

הַיּוֹם hayom נגד, זן, מזבח לֹא lo תִמְצָאֻהוּ timtza'uhu בַּשָּׂדֶה basadeh:

רְאוּ re'u כִּי ki יְהוָה Adonai נָתַן natan אבגיתץ, ושר, אהבת חנם

לָכֶם lachem הַשַּׁבָּת haShabbat עַל al כֵּן ken הוּא hu

נֹתֵן noten אבגיתץ, ושר, אהבת חנם לָכֶם lachem בַּיּוֹם bayom

הַשִּׁשִּׁי hashishi לֶחֶם lechem ג"פ יהוה יוֹמָיִם yomayim שְׁבוּ shevu |

אִישׁ ish ע"ה קנ"א קס"א תַּחְתָּיו tachtav ע"ה קנ"א קס"א אַל al יֵצֵא yetze אִישׁ ish ע"ה קנ"א קס"א

מִמְּקֹמוֹ mimekomo בַּיּוֹם bayom נגד, זן, מזבח הַשְּׁבִיעִי hasehvi'i:

וַיִּשְׁבְּתוּ vayishbetu הָעָם ha'am בַּיּוֹם bayom נגד, זן, מזבח הַשְּׁבִיעִי hasehvi'i:

עַל al כֵּן, ken בֵּרַךְ berach יְהוָה Adonai

אֶת et יוֹם yom הַשַּׁבָּת haShabbat וַיְקַדְּשֵׁהוּ vaykadshehu.

סַבְרִי savri י"פ יהוה (ה' דחסדים וה' דגבורות) מָרָנָן maranan עם

(The others reply :) לְחַיִּים lechayim אהיה אהיה יהוה, בינה ע"ה

בָּרוּךְ baruch אַתָּה Ata יְהוָה Adonai אֱלֹהֵינוּ Elohenu ילה

מֶלֶךְ melech הָעוֹלָם ha'olam בּוֹרֵא bore פְּרִי peri הַגָּפֶן hagefen:

Kiddush (Blessing Over the Wine) of the Third Meal

"And Moses said: Feast today because the Sabbath is the day of the Lord; today you will not be found in the field. See that because the Lord gave to you the Sabbath, therefore on the sixth day, He gives you two days worth of bread. Everyone is to stay where they are on the Seventh day; no one is to go out. The people rested on the seventh day." (Exodus 16:25, 29-30)

"So the Lord blessed the day of Shabbat and made it Holy." (Exodus 20:11)

With your permission, my masters.

(The others reply) *To life [Binah.]*

Blessed are You Lord, Our God, king of the world, Who created the fruit of the vine.

Third Meal Connection – Zeir Anpin

Yedid Nefesh (Beloved of the Soul)

Rav Eliezer Azikri, one of the greatest Kabbalists of the 16th century, wrote this heartfelt song, which speaks of our tremendous yearning for a connection with the Light of the Creator, and ends with a prayer to reveal to us this complete and everlasting love and Light.

Our Master and Teacher, Rav Yehuda HaLevi Ashlag, composed the melody to awaken our soul to yearn to connect to the Light of the Creator.

♦ harachaman הָרַחֲמָן	av אָב	nefesh נֶפֶשׁ	yedid יְדִיד
♦ retzonecha רְצוֹנֶךָ	el פוי, אל אדני אֵל	avdecha עַבְדְּךָ	meshoch מְשׁוֹךְ
♦ ayal אַיָּל	kemo פוי, אל אדני כְּמוֹ	avdecha עַבְדְּךָ	yarutz יָרוּץ
hadarecha ב"פ יבק, ס"ג קס"א הֲדָרֶךָ	mul מוּל	el אֶל	yishtachave יִשְׁתַּחֲוֶה
♦ ילי ר"ת	yedidutecha יְדִידוּתֶךָ	lo לוֹ	ye'erav יֶעֱרַב
: ta'am טַעַם	vechol וְכָל	tzuf צוּף	minofet מִנּוֹפֶת
♦ ha'olam הָעוֹלָם	ziv זִיו	na'e נָאֶה	hadur הָדוּר
♦ ahavatecha אַהֲבָתֶךָ	cholat חוֹלַת	nafshi נַפְשִׁי
na נָא (מילוי) דס"ג יא"י	El אֵל ב"ן	ana אָנָּא
♦ (11-Letter Name for healing)	lah לָהּ	na נָא	refa רְפָא
♦ zivecha זִיוֶךְ	no'am נֹעַם	lah לָהּ	behar'ot בְּהַרְאוֹת
♦ vetitrape וְתִתְרַפֵּא	titchazek תִּתְחַזֵּק	az אָז
: olam עוֹלָם	simchat שִׂמְחַת	lah לָהּ	vehayta וְהָיְתָה

Yedid Nefesh (Beloved of the Soul)

י Beloved of the soul, Compassionate Father, draw Your servant to Your desire. Your servant will run like a hart, he will bow before Your majesty. Your friendship will be sweeter than the dripping of the honeycomb and any taste. ה Majestic, Beautiful, Radiance of the world, my soul pines for Your love. Please, God, heal her, by showing her the pleasantness of Your radiance. Then she will be strengthened and healed, and she will have the gladness of the world.

THIRD MEAL CONNECTION – ZEIR ANPIN

◆rachamecha רַחֲמֶיךָ	na נָא	yehemu יֶהֱמוּ	vatik וָתִיק	
◆ahuvecha אֲהוּבֶךָ	ben בֶּן	al עַל	na נָא	vechusa וְחוּסָה
◆nichsafti נִכְסַפְתִּי	nichsof נִכְסוֹף	kamah כַּמָּה	zeh זֶה	ki כִּי
◆uzecha עֻזֶּךָ		betiferet בְּתִפְאֶרֶת		lir'ot לִרְאוֹת
◆libi לִבִּי		chamda חָמְדָה		eleh אֵלֶּה
:tit'alem תִּתְעַלֵּם		ve'al וְאַל	na נָא	vechusa וְחוּסָה
◆chavivi וְחָבִיבִי		ufros וּפְרוֹשׂ	na נָא	higale הִגָּלֵה
◆shelomecha שְׁלוֹמֶךָ		sukat סֻכַּת	et אֶת	alai עָלַי
◆לכב	ב"ן,	mikevodecha מִכְּבוֹדְךָ	eretz אֶרֶץ	ta'ir תָּאִיר
◆vach בָּךְ		venismecha וְנִשְׂמְחָה		nagila נָגִילָה
◆mo'ed מוֹעֵד	va בָא	ki כִּי	ehov אָהוּב	maher מַהֵר
:olam עוֹלָם		kimei כִּימֵי		vechonenu וְחָנֵּנוּ

א *All Worthy One, may Your mercy be aroused and please take pity on the sons of Your beloved, because it is so very long that I have yearned intensely, speedily to see the splendor of Your strength. Only these my heart desires, so please take pity and do not conceal Yourself.*
ה *Reveal and spread upon me, my Beloved, the shelter of Your peace. Illuminate the world with Your glory that we may rejoice and be glad with You. Hasten, show love, for time has come, and show us grace as in days of old.*

Blessings

BLESSINGS BEFORE FOOD
NETILAT YADAYIM (WASHING OF THE HANDS)
HAMOTZI (BLESSING OVER BREAD)
BIRKAT HAMAZON—BLESSING AFTER THE MEAL
SHEVA BERACHOT—SEVEN BLESSINGS
BORE PRI HAGEFEN—BLESSING OVER THE WINE
LAST BLESSING—ME'EN SHALOSH
LAST BLESSING—BORE NEFASHOT

BLESSINGS BEFORE FOOD

"Blessing" is a confusing word. Its connotations suggest that we are praising or thanking God for the food we eat. However, the truth is that God does not need or want our thanks, nor did we come into this world to sing God's praises; we came here to become the cause and creator of our own joy, happiness, and Light. To give us this opportunity, the Light was concealed, and it is our job to find it.

Consider food: If we simply eat food without reciting the blessing, the spark of Light inside the food remains dormant and inactive; all we receive from the food is nutrition, which only constitutes one percent of the food's energy. When we recite a blessing over the food, we ignite the Divine spark within it, enabling us to receive both the one percent of its energy that nourishes our bodies as well as the 99 percent of its essence that feeds our souls.

By reciting the blessing, we become the cause of the Light's revelation in the food. Now the food can not only provide nutrition but also healing, wellness, and spiritual contentment. According to sixteenth-century Kabbalist Rav Isaac Luria (the Ari), a body only filled with nutrients inevitably becomes dark and spiritually weighted down. Moreover, food that is eaten without its Light being released through blessing will feed the negative forces that dwell within the body as a result of selfish, reactive behavior. When we bless the food, we ignite the Light, and any negative forces within us are deprived of nourishment.

To activate the Light within the food, we hold the food in our right hand and recite the blessing appropriate to the food we are about to eat.

Blessings: Blessings before Food

Mezonot – Blessing over Grains other than Bread or Matzah
(Pastas, cake, cookies, cereals, crackers, pies, pastry, rice, etc.)

בָּרוּךְ baruch מֶלֶךְ melech הָעוֹלָם ha'olam בּוֹרֵא bore מִינֵי minei אֱלֹהֵינוּ Elohenu יְהֹוָה Adonai אַתָּה Ata יְלֹה מְזוֹנוֹת mezonot:

Hagefen - Blessing over Wine or Grape Juice

בָּרוּךְ baruch מֶלֶךְ melech הָעוֹלָם ha'olam בּוֹרֵא bore פְּרִי pri אֱלֹהֵינוּ Elohenu יְהֹוָה Adonai אַתָּה Ata יְלֹה הַגָּפֶן hagefen:

Ha'etz – Blessing over Fruits that Come from a Tree
(Apples, pears, oranges, etc.)
If you are unsure whether the fruit comes from a tree, recite the blessing of *Ha'adama* below)

בָּרוּךְ baruch מֶלֶךְ melech הָעוֹלָם ha'olam בּוֹרֵא bore פְּרִי pri אֱלֹהֵינוּ Elohenu יְהֹוָה Adonai אַתָּה Ata יְלֹה הָעֵץ ha'etz:

Ha'adama – Blessing over Fruits and Vegetables that Come from the Ground
(Strawberries, carrots, bananas, beans, etc.)

בָּרוּךְ baruch מֶלֶךְ melech הָעוֹלָם ha'olam בּוֹרֵא bore פְּרִי pri אֱלֹהֵינוּ Elohenu יְהֹוָה Adonai אַתָּה Ata יְלֹה הָאֲדָמָה ha'adamah:

Shehakol – Blessing Over Foods with No Particular or Distinguishable Origin
(Dairy products, eggs, candy, meat and poultry, fish, water, drinks other than wine, etc.)

בָּרוּךְ baruch מֶלֶךְ melech הָעוֹלָם ha'olam שֶׁהַכֹּל shehakol נִהְיָה nih'ya אֱלֹהֵינוּ Elohenu יְהֹוָה Adonai אַתָּה Ata יְלֹה בִּדְבָרוֹ bidvaro:

Mezonot
Blessed are You, Lord, our God, King of the universe, Who creates species of nourishment.
Hagefen
Blessed are You, Lord, our God, King of the universe, Creator of the fruit of the vine.
Ha'etz
Blessed are You, Lord, our God, King of the universe, Who creates the fruit of the tree.
Ha'adama
Blessed are You, Lord, our God, King of the universe, Who creates the fruit of the ground.
Shehakol
Blessed are You, Lord, our God, King of the universe, through Whose word everything came to be.

BLESSINGS: NETILAT YADAYIM AND HAMOTZI

NETILAT YADAYIM - WASHING OF THE HANDS

The reason for the washing of the hands is that external negative forces grab their energy from the hands of *Zeir Anpin* of *Asiyah* (from the nails on the edge of the fingers) and with the water—energy of Mercy—we want to reject and nullify the *klipot* so they cannot take from the energy of our food.

While washing the hands, meditate that the ten fingers are corresponding to the Ten *Ma'amrot* (Utterances) of Creation ("and God says…" is written ten times in the Creation story of Genesis), which are the foundation of the world, and to the ten letters of the *miluy* (spelled out aspect) of the Tetragrammaton. Also meditate that the twenty-eight bones of the fingers (in both hands) corresponding to the twenty eight letters of the *miluy* of *miluy* of the Tetragrammaton and to the twenty-eight letters in the first verse of the *Book of Genesis*, which is the seed of Creation. The washing of the hands draws the Illumination of these letters of Creation to the world.

To wash our hands we hold the washing vessel in our right hand and fill it with water, and then hand it over to our left hand. Then, pour the water with the left hand over the right hand twice (corresponding to the two letters *Yud* and *Hei*) and then pour water with the right hand onto the left hand twice (corresponding to the letters *Vav* and the last *Hei*). We rub our hands together and raise them to eye level and say the blessing below before drying the hands.

Here, our teacher, the Rav, said the following verse:

וָאֶשָּׂא va'esa כַּפַּי chapai אֶל el מִצְוֹתֶיךָ mitzvotecha אֲשֶׁר asher אָהָבְתִּי ahavti:

בָּרוּךְ baruch (אל) אַתָּה Ata (רחום) יְהֹוָה Adonai (וחנון)

אֱלֹהֵינוּ Elohenu (ילה ארך) מֶלֶךְ melech (אפים) הָעוֹלָם ha'olam (ורב וחסד)

אֲשֶׁר asher (ואמת) קִדְּשָׁנוּ kideshanu (נצר וחסד) בְּמִצְוֹתָיו bemitzvotav (לאלפים)

וְצִוָּנוּ vetzivanu (נשא עון) עַל al (ופשע) נְטִילַת netilat (וחטאה) יָדָיִם yadayim (ונקה):

The last three words of this blessing are *Al Netilat Yadayim*: The first letter from each of these three words spells *ani* עֲנִי (=130), Aramaic for "a poor person," and has the same numerical value of one of the abbreviations of the Holy Name *Mem-Hei* (יוד יוד הא יוד הא ואו יוד הא ואו הא). The last two letters of each of these three words, *Ayin Lamed* עַל (=100), *Lamed Tav* לַת (=430), and *Yud Mem* יִם (=50), have the same numerical value as the word *ashir* עָשִׁיר (=580), meaning "a rich person."

MIZMOR LEDAVID (SEE PAGE 78)

Here, our teacher, the Rav, said *Mizmor LeDavid*.

On Friday night, while reciting the verse *ach tov vachesed yirdefuni* meditate on the Name יהוה (=26) spelled with the letter *Yud* (יוד הי ויו הי), as the initials of this verse adds up to the value of 26.)
On Saturday morning, meditate on the Name יהוה (=26) spelled with the letter *Hei* (יוד הה וו הה), as the initials of this verse adds up to the value of 26.)

NETILAT YADAYIM - WASHING OF THE HANDS
"I will lift up my hands to Your precepts, which I have loved" (Psalms 119:48)
Blessed are You, Lord, our God, the King of the world,
Who has sanctified us with His commandments and obliges us with the washing of the hands.

BLESSINGS: NETILAT YADAYIM AND HAMOTZI

HAMOTZI – BLESSING OVER BREAD
(Made of wheat, barley, rye, oats, or spelt)

Meditate to draw sustenance from *Binah* (the first letter *Hei* of the Name יהוה and of the word *hamotzi*—הַמוֹצִיא) to *Chesed*, *Gevurah* and *Tiferet* (bread—*lechem*—לחם has the same numerical value as three times the Name יהוה = 78) to *Malchut* (the last letter *Hei* of the Name יהוה and of the word *ha'aretz*—הָאָרֶץ.)

On Shabbat, meditate that the *Hamotzi* connection is in the frame of *Atzilut*. **During the weekdays,** meditate that the *Hamotzi* connection is in the frame of *Yetzirah*.

Three times the Name יהוה (=bread=78) connects to the Eighth *Tikkun*—*Notzer Chesed*—*Mazala*. Three times the Name יהוה (=salt=78) connects to the Thirteenth *Tikkun*—*Venakeh* and from their Unification (the Eighth *Tikkun* and the Thirteenth *Tikkun*) food comes to the Worlds.

Dip the bread in salt

The first slice of the *chalah*-bread corresponds to *Yesod* of *Zeir Anpin* from which sustenance comes. Each subsequent slice is dipped three times in salt (bread—*lechem*—לחם and salt—*melach*—מלח has the same letters). The bread has the same numerical value of three times the Name יהוה (the three Mercies that are revealed in the lower part of *Tiferet*, *Netzach* and *Hod*) and we sweeten the bitterness (three times the Name of יהוה, which is the numerical value of salt.)

Also meditate that the letter *Mem* (ם) in the word *melach*—salt—מלח is open and the letter *Mem* (ם) in the word *lechem*—bread—לחם is closed like we close the mouth of the *klipa* so she cannot get any of the energy embedded in the bread (in general we keep salt on the table while eating as its power is to push away the *klipa*.)

בָּרוּךְ baruch אַתָּה Ata יְהֹוָה (אֲדֹנָי/אֱלֹהֵינוּ) Adonai
אֱלֹהֵינוּ Elohenu יה מֶלֶךְ melech הָעוֹלָם ha'olam
הַמּוֹצִיא hahamotzi לֶחֶם lechem מִן min הָאָרֶץ: haha'aretz

It says (Midrash Beresheet Rabbah 38:6, Midrash Devrim Rabbah 3:10 and Zohar, Prologue 177-179) that Satan wants a piece of energy from our meal; otherwise he will bring accusations against us. Based on the *Midrash* (Beresheet Rabbah 57:4) our teacher, the Rav, gave the first piece of the bread to Satan so that Satan would be busy with it and not with our meal. (We break off a small piece of bread after the blessing of *Hamotzi* and throw this piece in the garbage.)

HAMOTZI
Blessed are You, Lord, our God, King of the universe, Who brings forth bread from the earth.

BIRKAT HAMAZON—BLESSING AFTER THE MEAL

Birkat Hamazon is the blessing we recite after we have eaten a meal that consisted of bread, and is our tool to assist the digestion and processing of physical and spiritual energies contained within the food so that we can benefit from this energy. From the Zohar we know food contains sparks of souls, and with this blessing we can elevate those souls that are in the food we eat, and help them with their *tikkun*.

MAYIM ACHRONIM – LAST WATER

At the conclusion of a meal that consisted of bread and other foods, before we say *Birkat Hamazon*, we rinse our fingertips. The *Zohar* says (Zohar Terumah 523): "After the person has eaten… he must give the part of the remnants to that side, to the *klipot*. What is it? It is the 'last water,' that dirt of the hands that he must give to that side, for it is the portion that it needs. It is certainly an obligation, because it is obligatory and they dwell in a place of obligation, namely the *klipot*, for it is obligatory upon every person to give it this portion. Therefore, it is not necessary to make a blessing at all over the 'last water,' because there is no blessing on that side."

SHIR HAMA'ALOT

The *Zohar* says (Zohar Terumah 769): "One verse says, 'And you shall eat before the Lord your God' and another verse says, 'And rejoice before the Lord your God.' These verses were fulfilled when the children of Israel dwelt in the Holy Land and appeared before the Holy One, Blessed Be He, in the Temple. How are they fulfilled today? Who can eat before the Lord and who can rejoice before the Lord?" Based on this section from the *Zohar*, Kabbalist Rav Yishayahu Horovitz (Israel, 17th century) said to recite this Psalm before saying *Birkat Hamazon* as it helps us to connect to the joy of the Final Redemption.

שִׁיר shir הַמַּעֲלוֹת hama'alot בְּשׁוּב beshuv יְהֹוָה Adonai
אֶת et שִׁיבַת shivat צִיּוֹן Tziyon הָיִינוּ hayinu כְּחֹלְמִים kecholmim:
אָז az יִמָּלֵא yimaleh שְׂחוֹק sechok פִּינוּ pinu וּלְשׁוֹנֵנוּ ulshonenu
רִנָּה rina אָז az יֹאמְרוּ yomru בַגּוֹיִם vagoyim הִגְדִּיל higdil
יְהֹוָה Adonai לַעֲשׂוֹת la'asot עִם im אֵלֶּה ele:
הִגְדִּיל higdil יְהֹוָה Adonai לַעֲשׂוֹת la'ashot עִמָּנוּ imanu
הָיִינוּ hayinu שְׂמֵחִים semechim: שׁוּבָה shuva יְהֹוָה Adonai
אֶת et שְׁבִיתֵנוּ shevitenu כַּאֲפִיקִים ka'afikim בַּנֶּגֶב banegev:
הַזֹּרְעִים hazor'im בְּדִמְעָה bedim'ah בְּרִנָּה berina יִקְצֹרוּ yiktzoru:
הָלוֹךְ haloch יֵלֵךְ yelech וּבָכֹה uvacho נֹשֵׂא noseh מֶשֶׁךְ meshech הַזָּרַע hazara
בֹּא bo יָבֹא yavo בְרִנָּה berina נֹשֵׂא noseh אֲלֻמֹּתָיו alumotav:

BIRKAT HAMAZON - SHIR HAMA'ALOT

"A song of Ascents: When the Lord will return the captivity of Zion, we will be like dreamers. Then our mouths will be filled with laughter and our tongue with glad song. Then they will declare among the nations: 'The Lord has done greatly with these.' The Lord has done greatly with us; we were gladdened. Lord, return our captivity like springs in the desert. Those who tearfully sow will reap in glad song. He who bears the measure of seeds walks along weeping, but will return in exultation, a bearer of his sheaves." (Psalms 126)

BIRKAT HAMAZON—BLESSING AFTER THE MEAL

ZIMUN - GATHERING

The Hebrew word *Zimun* means "invitation" or "gathering." At this stage of the meal, we want to gather all the sparks that were in the food and elevate them through the *Birkat Hamazon*.

The *Zohar* says (Zohar Terumah 569): "It [the cup of Wine] is used only when there are three who ate together... for *Malchut*, which is the secret of the Cup of Blessing, is blessed from *Chesed*, *Gevurah*, and *Tiferet* of *Zeir Anpin* that are called 'Patriarchs.' One should give the Cup of Blessing with both the right and left hands, and receive it in both, because *Malchut* is given between the Right and Left of *Zeir Anpin*. Afterwards, one should leave it only in his right hand, because from there it is blessed, meaning from the Light of the *Chasadim* that are in the Right of *Zeir Anpin*."

The *zimun* is recited when three men or more were eating bread together in the same meal.
If there is no *minyan* (less than ten men), the bracketed words are omitted.
The *zimun* is recited by the leader with a cup of wine in his right hand.

The leader says:

הַב hav כָן lan וּנְבָרֵך unvarech:

Everyone answer:

יְהִי yehi שֵׁם shem יְהֹוָאדֹנָיאהדונהי Adonai
מְבֹרָך mevorach מֵעַתָּה me'ata וְעַד ve'ad עוֹלָם olam:

The leader continues:

יְהִי yehi שֵׁם shem יְהֹוָאדֹנָיאהדונהי Adonai
מְבֹרָך mevorach מֵעַתָּה me'ata וְעַד ve'ad עוֹלָם olam:

ADDITIONAL BLESSING FOR A WEDDING AND THE WEEK OF SEVEN BLESSINGS
Written by Kabbalist Dunash, son of Labrat (Spain, 10th century)
The leader says:

דְּוַי devai	הָסֵר haser	וְגַם vegam	וְחָרוֹן charon,
וְאָז ve'az	אִלֵּם ilem	בְּשִׁיר beshir	יָרוֹן yaron,
נְחֵנוּ nechenu	בְּמַעְגְּלֵי bema'aglei		צֶדֶק tzedek,
שְׁעֵה she'e	בִּרְכַּת birkat		בְּנֵי benei
יְשׁוּרוּן Yeshurun,	בְּנֵי benei		אַהֲרֹן Aharon:

ZIMUN - GATHERING
Leader: Gentlemen, let us bless.
Everyone: Blessed be the Name of the Lord from time and forever!
Leader: Blessed be the Name of the Lord from this time and forever!

ADDITIONAL BLESSING FOR A WEDDING AND THE WEEK OF SEVEN BLESSINGS
Remove agony and also wrath, and then the mute will rejoice in song.
Guide us in trails of righteousness. Hear the blessing of the children of Yeshurun (and) the children of Aaron.

BIRKAT HAMAZON—BLESSING AFTER THE MEAL

ADDITIONAL BLESSING FOR BRIT MILAH (CIRCUMCISION)

The leader says this verse and everyone repeats it:

נוֹדֶה nodeh לְשִׁמְךָ leshimcha בְּתוֹךְ betoch אֱמוּנַי emunai,
בְּרוּכִים beruchim אַתֶּם atem לַיהוָֹהֽ ladonai:

The leader says:

בִּרְשׁוּת birshut אֵל El אָיוֹם ayom וְנוֹרָא venora,
מִשְׂגָּב misgav לְעִתּוֹת le'itot בַּצָּרָה batzara, אֵל El נֵזֶר nezar
בִּגְבוּרָה bigvura, אַדִּיר adir בַּמָּרוֹם bamarom יְהוָֹהֽ Adonai:

Everyone: נוֹדֶה nodeh לְשִׁמְךָ leshimcha בְּתוֹךְ betoch אֱמוּנַי emunai,
בְּרוּכִים beruchim אַתֶּם atem לַיהוָֹהֽ ladonai:

The leader says:

בִּרְשׁוּת birshut הַתּוֹרָה hatora הַקְּדוֹשָׁה hakedosha,
טְהוֹרָה tehora הִיא hi וְגַם vegam פְּרוּשָׁה perusha צִוָּה tziva לָּנוּ lanu
מוֹרָשָׁה morasha, מֹשֶׁה Moshe עֶבֶד eved יְהוָֹהֽ Adonai:

Everyone: נוֹדֶה nodeh לְשִׁמְךָ leshimcha בְּתוֹךְ betoch אֱמוּנַי emunai,
בְּרוּכִים beruchim אַתֶּם atem לַיהוָֹהֽ ladonai:

The leader says:

בִּרְשׁוּת birshut הַכֹּהֲנִים hakohanim וְהַלְוִיִּם vehalviyim,
אֶקְרָא ekra לֵאלֹהֵי lelohei הָעִבְרִיִּים ha'ivriyim, אֲהוֹדֶנּוּ ahodenu
בְּכָל bechol אִיִּים iyim, אֲבָרְכָה avarcha אֶת et יְהוָֹהֽ Adonai:

Everyone: נוֹדֶה nodeh לְשִׁמְךָ leshimcha בְּתוֹךְ betoch אֱמוּנַי emunai,
בְּרוּכִים beruchim אַתֶּם atem לַיהוָֹהֽ ladonai:

The leader says:

בִּרְשׁוּת birshut מָרָנָן maranan וְרַבָּנָן verabanan וְרַבּוֹתַי verabotai,
אֶפְתְּחָה eftecha בְּשִׁיר beshir פִּי pi וּשְׂפָתַי usfatai, וְתֹאמַרְנָה vetomarna
עַצְמוֹתַי atzmotai, בָּרוּךְ baruch הַבָּא haba בְּשֵׁם beshem יְהוָֹהֽ Adonai:

Everyone: נוֹדֶה nodeh לְשִׁמְךָ leshimcha בְּתוֹךְ betoch אֱמוּנַי emunai,
בְּרוּכִים beruchim אַתֶּם atem לַיהוָֹהֽ ladonai:

ADDITIONAL BLESSING FOR BRIT MILAH (CIRCUMCISION)

Leader and everyone: *We give thanks to Your Name among my faithful blessed are you to the Lord.*
Leader: *With permission of the Almighty – fearful and awesome, the Refuge in times of trouble, the Almighty girded with strength, the Mighty on high – the Lord.* (**Everyone:** *We give thanks…*)
Leader: *With permission of the Holy Torah, it is pure and explicit, commanded to us as a heritage, by Moses, servant of the Lord.* (**Everyone:** *We give thanks…*)
Leader: *With permission of the Kohanim (from) the tribe of Levi, I call upon the God of the Hebrews, I will thank Him unto all islands, I will give blessing to the Lord.* (**Everyone:** *We give thanks…*)
Leader: *With permission of the distinguished people present, I open in song my mouth and lips, and my bones shall proclaim, "Blessed is he who comes in the Name of the Lord."* (**Everyone:** *We give thanks…*)

BIRKAT HAMAZON—BLESSING AFTER THE MEAL

Shabbat:		
•malketa מַלְכְּתָא	Shabbat שַׁבָּת	birshut בִּרְשׁוּת
Holidays:		
•kadisha קַדִּישָׁא oshpiza אוּשְׁפִּיזָא	tava טָבָא yoma יוֹמָא	uvirshut וּבִרְשׁוּת
Sukkot:		
•kadishin קַדִּישִׁין ila'in עִלָּאִין ushfizin אֻשְׁפִּיזִין	shiva שִׁבְעָה	uvirshut וּבִרְשׁוּת
Third Meal:		
•veyosef וְיוֹסֵף david דָּוִד moshe מֹשֶׁה	birshut בִּרְשׁוּת	

The leader continues:

harabanit הָרַבָּנִית, mori מוֹרִי rabi רַבִּי harav הָרַב uvirshut וּבִרְשׁוּת
nevarech נְבָרֵךְ verabotai וְרַבּוֹתַי maranan מָרָנָן •morati מוֹרָתִי
(Elohenu אֱלֹהֵינוּ: with *minyan*)
(ve וְ bime'ono בִּמְעוֹנוֹ shehasimcha שֶׁהַשִּׂמְחָה: *wedding week of seven blessings*)
:mishelo מִשֶּׁלוֹ she'achalnu שֶׁאָכַלְנוּ

Everyone:

(Elohenu אֱלֹהֵינוּ: with *minyan*) baruch בָּרוּךְ
(ve וְ bime'ono בִּמְעוֹנוֹ shehasimcha שֶׁהַשִּׂמְחָה: *wedding week of seven blessings*)
:chayinu וְחָיִינוּ uvtuvo וּבְטוּבוֹ mishelo מִשֶּׁלוֹ she'achalnu שֶׁאָכַלְנוּ

The leader continues:

(Elohenu אֱלֹהֵינוּ: with *minyan*) baruch בָּרוּךְ
(ve וְ bime'ono בִּמְעוֹנוֹ shehasimcha שֶׁהַשִּׂמְחָה: *wedding week of seven blessings*)
:chayinu וְחָיִינוּ uvtuvo וּבְטוּבוֹ mishelo מִשֶּׁלוֹ she'achalnu שֶׁאָכַלְנוּ

The *Zohar* says (Zohar Terumah 775): When one say the word *"uvtuvo"* (by Whose goodness) he should aim the desire and meditate to connect up to the Most Ancient of All—*Atika De'atikin*.

Shabbat: *With the permission of Shabbat the Queen.*
Holidays: *With the permission of this holiday, the Holy guest.*
Sukkot: *With the permission of the Seven holy and exalted guests.*
Third Meal: *With the permission of Moses, David and Joseph.*

With the permission of the Rav my teacher, and of the Rabanit my teacher, and of the distinguished people present, let us bless (**with minyan:** *our God*), (**wedding week:** *in Whose dwelling there is joy*) *He of whose we have eaten.*
Everyone: *Blessed is* (**with minyan:** *our God*), (**wedding week:** *in Whose dwelling there is joy*) *He of whose we have eaten and through whose goodness we live.*
Leader: *Blessed is* (**with minyan:** *our God*), (**wedding week:** *in Whose dwelling there is joy*) *He of whose we have eaten and by Whose goodness we live.*

BIRKAT HAMAZON—BLESSING AFTER THE MEAL

BIRKAT HAMAZON

THE FIRST BLESSING - THE WORLD OF ATZILUT/EMANATION

The *Zohar* says (Zohar Terumah 776-777): "Why is it called 'goodness—*tov*' and why 'Mercy—*Chesed*,' which are two names? 'Goodness' is when the *Sefira* contains everything within itself and the Light does not spread or descend downward. *Chesed* or Mercy is when the Light descends below and does good for all the creations, the righteous and the wicked, without hesitation because it does not contain Judgments. If both of them are on one level, why do we need both? But, as mentioned above, 'goodness' means that it retains everything within itself and does not spread down, and *Chesed* descends and spreads down and nourishes everything, the righteous and wicked alike. And because here (during the *zimun*) it says: 'And by whose goodness we live,' which is possible to explain that the flow does not descend to the righteous and the wicked. Therefore, it says again (in the first blessing,) 'Who sustains the entire world with His goodness, with grace, with kindness and with Mercy.' And later on: 'Who gives bread to all flesh, for His steadfast Mercy endures forever.' Therefore, it says (at the end of the blessing): 'He provides food for all,' namely for the righteous and the wicked, for everyone."

(On Shabbat meditate: יוד ויו דלת)

(when *zimun* is recited we add: בָּרוּךְ baruch הוּא hu וּבָרוּךְ uvaruch שְׁמוֹ shemo:)

בָּרוּךְ baruch אַתָּה Ata יְ‑הֹ‑וָ‑ה Adonai אֱלֹהֵינוּ Elohenu מֶלֶךְ melech הָעוֹלָם ha'olam, הַזָּן hazan אֶת et הָעוֹלָם ha'olam כֻּלּוֹ kulo בְּטוּבוֹ betuvo בְּחֵן bechen בְּחֶסֶד bechesed בְּרַחֲמִים uv'rachamim, הוּא hu נֹתֵן noten לֶחֶם lechem לְכָל lechol בָּשָׂר basar כִּי ki לְעוֹלָם le'olam חַסְדּוֹ chasdo: וּבְטוּבוֹ uv'tuvo הַגָּדוֹל hagadol, תָּמִיד tamid לֹא lo חָסַר chasar לָנוּ lanu וְאַל ve'al יֶחְסַר yechsar לָנוּ lanu, מָזוֹן mazon לְעוֹלָם leolam וָעֶד va'ed, בַּעֲבוּר ba'avur שְׁמוֹ shemo הַגָּדוֹל hagadol, כִּי ki הוּא hu אֵל El זָן zan וּמְפַרְנֵס um'farnes לַכֹּל lakol וּמֵטִיב umetiv לַכֹּל lakol, וּמֵכִין umechin מָזוֹן mazon לְכֹל lechol בְּרִיּוֹתָיו beriyotav אֲשֶׁר asher בָּרָא bara כָּאָמוּר ka'amur:

BIRKAT HAMAZON
THE FIRST BLESSING - THE WORLD OF ATZILUT/EMANATION

Blessed is He and blessed is His Name.

Blessed are You, Lord, our God, King of the Universe, Who sustains the entire world, with His goodness, with grace, with kindness and with Mercy. He gives bread to all flesh, for His steadfast Mercy endures forever. And through His great goodness, we have never lacked, and may we never lack, nourishment, for all eternity. For the sake of His Great Name because He is God who nourishes and sustains all, and benefits all, and He prepares food for all His creatures that He has created. As it is said:

BIRKAT HAMAZON—BLESSING AFTER THE MEAL

POTEACH ET YADECHA

We connect to the letters פ—*Pei*, א—*Alef*, and י—*Yud* by opening our hands and holding our palms skyward. Our consciousness is focused on receiving sustenance and financial prosperity from the Light through our actions of personal tithing and sharing, our Desire to Receive for the Sake of Sharing. In doing so, we also acknowledge that the sustenance we receive comes from a higher source and is not of our own doing.

According to Kabbalah, if we do not meditate on this idea at this juncture, we must repeat the prayer.

פתחו (ע"ע"וז נהורין למ"ה ולס"ה)

פותחו את ידך	יוד הי ויו הי יוד הי ויו הי
ר"ת פאי גימ' יאהדונהי (וז"ן)	(ח' חיוורתי)
	אלף למד אלף למד (ש"ע)
אהדונה י	יוד הא ואו הא (לז"א)
יסוד דנוק' ו"ק וזכמה דז"א	אדני (ולנוקבא)

פּוֹתֵחַ pote'ach אֶת et יָדֶךָ yadecha ר"ת פאי וס"ת וזתך עם ג' אותיות = דִיקַרנוֹסָא

ובאתב"ע הוא סאל, פאי, אמן, יאהדונהי ; ועוד יכוין שם וזתך בשילוב יהוה – יוֹהַתוּכָה

Drawing abundance and sustenance from Chochmah of Ze'ir Anpin

יוד הי ויו הי יוד הי ויו הי ד'לת הי ויו יוד הי ויו הי יוד

וזתך סאל יאהדונהי

וּמַשְׂבִּיעַ umasbi'a וזתך עם ג' אותיות = דִיקַרנוֹסָא

ובא"ת ב"ע הוא סאל, אמן, יאהדונהי ; ועוד יכוין שם וזתך בשילוב יהוה – יוֹהַתוּכָה

Drawing abundance and sustenance from Chochmah of Ze'ir Anpin

יוד הי ויו הי יוד הי ויו הי ד'לת הי ויו יוד הי ויו הי יוד

לְכָל lechol יה אדני (להמשיך מוווזן ד-יה אל הנוקבא שהיא אדני)

חַי chai כל וזי = אהיה אהיה יהוה, בינה ע"ה, וזיים

רָצוֹן ratzon מהטע ע"ה, ע"ב בריבוע וקס"א ע"ה, אל שדי ע"ה

ר"ת רוזל שהיא המלכות הצריכה לעשיע

יוד יוד הי ויו יוד הי ויו הי יוד הי יסוד דאבא אלף הי יוד הי יסוד דאימא

להמתיק רוזל וב' דמעין שך פר

בָּרוּךְ baruch אַתָּה atah יְהֹוָאֲדֹנָי Adonai הַזָּן hazan אֶת et הַכֹּל hakol:

POTEACH ET YADECHA

"You open Your hands, and satisfy the desire of every living thing." (Psalms 145;16)
Blessed are you, Lord who provides food for all.

BIRKAT HAMAZON—BLESSING AFTER THE MEAL

THE SECOND BLESSING - THE WORLD OF BERI'AH/CREATION

The *Zohar* continues (Ibid 778): "After he is reciting the Blessing after a Meal, we have to attach the Land of the Living, which is *Malchut*, to the Right, so it is nourished from there to sustain and give nourishment to all."

(On Shabbat meditate: הִי יוד)

נוֹדֶה nodeh לְךָ lecha יְהֹוָהאדנייאהדונהי Adonai אֱלֹהֵינוּ Elohenu עַל al
שֶׁהִנְחַלְתָּ shehin'chalta לַאֲבוֹתֵינוּ la'avotenu, אֶרֶץ eretz וְחֶמְדָּה chemdah
טוֹבָה tova וּרְחָבָה urchava, וְעַל veal שֶׁהוֹצֵאתָנוּ shehotzetanu
יְהֹוָהאדנייאהדונהי Adonai אֱלֹהֵינוּ Elohenu מֵאֶרֶץ me'eretz מִצְרַיִם Mitzrayim,
וּפְדִיתָנוּ uf'ditanu מִבֵּית mibet עֲבָדִים avadim, וְעַל ve'al
בְּרִיתְךָ beritcha שֶׁחָתַמְתָּ shechatamta בִּבְשָׂרֵנוּ bivsarenu, וְעַל ve'al
תּוֹרָתְךָ toratcha שֶׁלִּמַּדְתָּנוּ shelimadetanu, וְעַל ve'al חֻקֶּיךָ chukecha
שֶׁהוֹדַעְתָּנוּ shehoda'atanu, וְעַל ve'al חַיִּים chayim וָחֵן chen וָחֶסֶד vachesed
שֶׁחוֹנַנְתָּנוּ shechonantanu, וְעַל ve'al אֲכִילַת achilat מָזוֹן mazon
שָׁאַתָּה she'atah זָן zan וּמְפַרְנֵס umfarnes אוֹתָנוּ otanu תָּמִיד tamid,
בְּכָל bechol יוֹם yom וּבְכָל uvechol עֵת et וּבְכָל uvechol שָׁעָה sha'ah:

CHANUKAH AND PURIM

These cosmic events generate an added dimension of the energy of miracles. This blessing helps us harness that power so that we can draw miracles into our life whenever they are truly needed.

וְעַל ve'al הַנִּסִּים hanisim וְעַל ve'al הַפֻּרְקָן hapurkan♦
וְעַל ve'al הַגְּבוּרוֹת hagevurot♦ וְעַל ve'al הַתְּשׁוּעוֹת hateshu'ot
וְעַל ve'al הַנִּפְלָאוֹת hanifla'ot וְעַל ve'al הַנֶּחָמוֹת hanechamot
שֶׁעָשִׂיתָ she'asita לַאֲבוֹתֵינוּ la'avoteinu בַּיָּמִים bayamim הָהֵם hahem
בַּזְּמַן bazeman הַזֶּה hazeh וּהוּ:

THE SECOND BLESSING - THE WORLD OF BERI'AH/CREATION

We thank you, Lord, our God, because You have given to our forefathers as a heritage a desirable, good and spacious land; because You removed us, Lord, our God, from the land of Egypt and You redeemed us from the house of bondage; for Your covenant which You sealed in our flesh; for Your Torah which You taught us and for Your statutes which You made known to us; for life, grace and loving kindness which You granted us; and for the provision of food with which You nourish and sustain us constantly, in every day, in every season and in every hour.

CHANUKAH AND PURIM
And also for the miracles, deliverance, the mighty acts, the salvation, wonders, and comforting deeds that You have performed for our forefathers, in those days and at this time.

Chanukah

בִּימֵי bimei מַתִּתְיָה Matitya בֶּן ven יוֹחָנָן Yochanan כֹּהֵן kohen מלה
גָּדוֹל gadol להו ; עם ד' אותיות = מבה, יזל, אום וְחַשְׁמוֹנַאי Chashmonai וּבְנָיו uvanav
כְּשֶׁעָמְדָה keshe'amda מַלְכוּת malchut יָוָן Yavan הָרְשָׁעָה harsha'a עַל al
עַמְּךָ amcha יִשְׂרָאֵל Yisrael לְשַׁכְּחָם leshakcham תּוֹרָתֶךָ toratach
וּלְהַעֲבִירָם ulha'aviram מֵחֻקֵּי mechukei רְצוֹנֶךָ retzonach · וְאַתָּה ve'ata
בְּרַחֲמֶיךָ verachameicha הָרַבִּים harabim עָמַדְתָּ amadeta לָהֶם lahem
בְּעֵת be'et צָרָתָם tzaratam · רַבְתָּ ravta אֶת et רִיבָם rivam · דַּנְתָּ danta אֶת et
דִּינָם dinam · נָקַמְתָּ nakamta מנק אֶת et נִקְמָתָם nikmatam מנק.
מָסַרְתָּ masarta גִּבּוֹרִים giborim בְּיַד beyad וְחַלָּשִׁים chalashim·
וְרַבִּים verabim בְּיַד beyad מְעַטִּים me'atim · וּרְשָׁעִים urshaim בְּיַד beyad
צַדִּיקִים tzadikim · וּטְמֵאִים utmeim בְּיַד beyad טְהוֹרִים tehorim·
וְזֵדִים vezedim בְּיַד beyad עוֹסְקֵי oskei תוֹרָתֶךָ toratecha · לְךָ lecha
עָשִׂיתָ asita שֵׁם shem גָּדוֹל gadol להו ; עם ד' אותיות = מבה, יזל, אום
וְקָדוֹשׁ vekadosh בְּעוֹלָמֶךָ be'olamach · וּלְעַמְּךָ ulamcha יִשְׂרָאֵל Yisrael
עָשִׂיתָ asita תְּשׁוּעָה teshu'a גְּדוֹלָה gedola וּפֻרְקָן ufurkan
כְּהַיּוֹם kehayom ע"ה נגד, מזבוז, זן, אל יהוה הַזֶּה hazeh והו · וְאַחַר ve'achar כָּךְ kach
בָּאוּ bau בָנֶיךָ vanecha לִדְבִיר lidvir רי"ו בֵּיתֶךָ beitecha ב"פ ראה
וּפִנּוּ ufinu אֶת et הֵיכָלֶךָ heichalecha · וְטִהֲרוּ vetiharu אֶת et
מִקְדָּשֶׁךָ mikdashecha · וְהִדְלִיקוּ vehidliku נֵרוֹת nerot בְּחַצְרוֹת bechatzrot
קָדְשֶׁךָ kodshecha · וְקָבְעוּ vekavu שְׁמוֹנַת shemonat יְמֵי yemei חֲנֻכָּה chanuka
אֵלּוּ elu בְּהַלֵּל behalel אדני, ללה · וּבְהוֹדָאָה uvehoda'a · וְעָשִׂיתָ ve'asita
עִמָּהֶם imahem נִסִּים nisim וְנִפְלָאוֹת veniflaot וְנוֹדֶה venodeh לְשִׁמְךָ leshimcha
הַגָּדוֹל hagadol להו ; עם ד' אותיות = מבה, יזל, אום סֶלָה sela:

CHANUKAH

In the days of Matityahu, the son of Yochanan, the High Priest, the Chashmonai and his sons, when the evil Greek Empire rose up against Your nation, Israel, to force them to forget Your Torah and to force them away from the laws of Your desire, You, with Your compassion, stood up for them, in their time of trouble. You fought their battles, sought justice for them, avenged them, and delivered the strong into the hands of the weak, the many into the hands of the few, the wicked into the hands of the righteous, the defiled into the hands of the pure. And the tyrants into the hands of those who occupy themselves with Your Torah. For Yourself, You made a Holy Name in Your world, and for Your people, Israel, You carried out a great salvation and deliverance on this day. Then, Your children came into the Sanctuary of Your House, they cleansed Your Palace, they purified Your Temple, they lit candles in the courtyards of Your Holy Domain, and they instituted those eight days of Chanukah for praise and thanksgiving. And You performed for them miracles and wonders. For that, we are grateful to Your Great Name, Selah!

BIRKAT HAMAZON—BLESSING AFTER THE MEAL

PURIM:

בִּימֵי bimei מָרְדְּכַי Mardechai וְאֶסְתֵּר veEster עִם הָאוֹתִיּוֹת = מִילוּי אֲדֹנָי
בְּשׁוּשָׁן beShushan הַבִּירָה habira. כְּשֶׁעָמַד keshe'amad עֲלֵיהֶם alehem
הָמָן Haman הָרָשָׁע harasha. בִּקֵּשׁ bikesh לְהַשְׁמִיד lehashmid לַהֲרֹג laharog
וּלְאַבֵּד ul'abed אֶת et כָּל kol יְהוּדִים haYehudim מִנַּעַר mina'ar וְעַד ve'ad
זָקֵן zaken טַף taf וְנָשִׁים venashim בְּיוֹם beyom ע"ה נגד, מזבח, זן, אל יהוה
אֶחָד echad אהבה, דאגה בִּשְׁלֹשָׁה bishlsha עָשָׂר asar לְחֹדֶשׁ lechodesh
שְׁנֵים shenem י"ב הויות, קס"א קנ"א עָשָׂר asar הוּא hu חֹדֶשׁ chodesh י"ב הויות, קס"א קנ"א
אֲדָר Adar וּשְׁלָלָם ushlalam לָבוֹז lavoz. וְאַתָּה veAta בְּרַחֲמֶיךָ verachamecha
הָרַבִּים harabim הֵפַרְתָּ hefarta אֶת et עֲצָתוֹ atzato וְקִלְקַלְתָּ vekilkalta
אֶת et מַחֲשַׁבְתּוֹ machashavto. וַהֲשֵׁבוֹתָ vahashevota לוֹ lo גְּמוּלוֹ gemulo
בְּרֹאשׁוֹ berosho. וְתָלוּ vetalu אוֹתוֹ oto וְאֶת ve'et בָּנָיו banav עַל al הָעֵץ ha'etz.
וְעָשִׂיתָ ve'asita עִמָּהֶם imahem נִסִּים nisim וְנִפְלָאוֹת venifla'ot וְנוֹדֶה venode
לְשִׁמְךָ leshimcha הַגָּדוֹל hagadol לְהוּ ; עִם ד' אוֹתיוֹת = מבה, יוֹל, אוֹם סֶלָה selah:

וְעַל ve'al הַכֹּל hakol יְהוָה Adonai אֱלֹהֵינוּ Elohenu
אֲנַחְנוּ anachnu מוֹדִים modim לָךְ lach, וּמְבָרְכִים umevarchim אוֹתָךְ otach,
יִתְבָּרַךְ yitbarach שִׁמְךָ shimcha בְּפִי befi כָּל kol חַי chai
תָּמִיד tamid לְעוֹלָם le'olam וָעֶד va'ed. כַּכָּתוּב kakatuv:
וְאָכַלְתָּ vachalta וְשָׂבָעְתָּ vesavata וּבֵרַכְתָּ uverachta אֶת et
יְהוָה Adonai אֱלֹהֶיךָ Elohecha עַל al הָאָרֶץ ha'aretz הַטֹּבָה hatova
אֲשֶׁר asher נָתַן natan לָךְ lach: בָּרוּךְ baruch אַתָּה Atah
יְהוָה Adonai עַל al הָאָרֶץ ha'aretz וְעַל ve'al הַמָּזוֹן hamazon:

PURIM:
In the days of Mordechai and Esther, in Shushan, the capital, when the evil Haman rose up against them, he sought to destroy, slay, and annihilate all the people of Judea, young and old, children and women, in one day, on the thirteenth day of the twelfth month, which is the month of Adar, and to take their spoils. But You, in Your great compassion, ruined his plan, foiled his design, and turned his due upon his own head. They hanged him and his sons upon the gallows. And You performed for them [Israel] miracles and wonders. We give thanks to Your Great Name, Selah!

For all, Lord, our God, we thank You and bless You. May Your Name be blessed by the mouth of all the living, continuously for all eternity; As it is written: "And you shall eat and you shall be satisfied and you shall bless the Lord, your God for the good land that He gave you." (Deuteronomy 8:10) Blessed are you, Lord, for the land and the nourishment.

BIRKAT HAMAZON—BLESSING AFTER THE MEAL

THE THIRD BLESSING - THE WORLD OF YETZIRAH/FORMATION

The word *rachem* (mercy) has a numerical value of 248, the same numerical value as the name *Avraham*. Abraham was known for his constant mercy for all people. There are also 248 spiritual and physical body parts of an individual. This blessing is our drawbridge to the Upper Worlds, bringing the healing Light to each of our 248 body parts. When we behave with mercy toward others, as Abraham did, this healing energy flows. On the other hand, when we behave otherwise, we cut off this flow of energy, preventing it from reaching us.

The *Zohar* says (Ibid 784): "After the Land of the Living (*Malchut*) is blessed from the Right side and receives food, as mentioned above, we ask for Mercy for everyone, and say: 'Have Mercy, please Lord, our God, upon Israel Your people...' From that food and sustenance that is in the Land of the Living, which is *Malchut*, shall we ourselves receive from them and the Temple will be rebuilt below through His Mercy.'

(On Shabbat meditate: ויו יוד ויו)

רַחֵם rachem נָא na יְהוָֹהֵאדֹנָי Adonai אֱלֹהֵינוּ Elohenu, עַל al
יִשְׂרָאֵל Yisrael עַמֶּךָ amecha, וְעַל ve'al יְרוּשָׁלַיִם Yerushalayim
עִירֶךָ irecha, וְעַל ve'al צִיּוֹן Tzion מִשְׁכַּן mishkan כְּבוֹדֶךָ kevodecha,
וְעַל ve'al מַלְכוּת malchut בֵּית bet דָּוִד David מְשִׁיחֶךָ meshichecha,
וְעַל ve'al הַבַּיִת habayit הַגָּדוֹל hagadol וְהַקָּדוֹשׁ vehakadosh
שֶׁנִּקְרָא shenikra שִׁמְךָ shimcha עָלָיו alav. אֱלֹהֵינוּ Elohenu, אָבִינוּ avinu,
רְעֵנוּ re'enu, זוּנֵנוּ zunenu פַּרְנְסֵנוּ parnesenu וְכַלְכְּלֵנוּ vechalkelenu,
וְהַרְוִיחֵנוּ veharvichenu, וְהַרְוַח veharvach לָנוּ lanu יְהוָֹהֵאדֹנָי Adonai
אֱלֹהֵינוּ Elohenu מְהֵרָה meherah מִכָּל mikol צָרוֹתֵינוּ tzarotenu. וְנָא vena,
אַל al תַּצְרִיכֵנוּ tatzrichenu יְהוָֹהֵאדֹנָי Adonai אֱלֹהֵינוּ Elohenu,
לֹא lo לִידֵי lide מַתְּנַת matnat בָּשָׂר basar וָדָם vadam וְלֹא velo לִידֵי lide
הַלְוָאָתָם halva'atam. כִּי ki אִם im לְיָדְךָ leyadecha הַמְּלֵאָה hamele'a,
הַפְּתוּחָה hapetucha, הַקְּדוֹשָׁה hakedosha וְהָרְחָבָה veharechava, שֶׁלֹּא shelo
נֵבוֹשׁ nevosh וְלֹא velo נִכָּלֵם nikalem לְעוֹלָם le'olam וָעֶד va'ed:

THE THIRD BLESSING - THE WORLD OF YETZIRAH/FORMATION

Have mercy; please Lord, our God, upon Israel Your people; on Jerusalem, Your city, on Zion, the resting place of Your glory; on the monarchy of the House of David Your anointed; and on the Great and Holy House upon which Your Name is called. Our God, our Father, tend us, nourish us, sustain us support us, relieve us; Lord, our God, grant us speedy relief from all our troubles. Please, make us not needful, Lord our God, of the gifts of human hands nor of their loans, but only of Your hand that is full, open, Holy and generous, that we not feel inner shame nor be humiliated for ever and ever.

BIRKAT HAMAZON—BLESSING AFTER THE MEAL

SHABBAT:
We add the paragraph of *retze vehachalitzenu* in the third blessing of *Birkat HaMazon*, to make the connection to the energy of *Shabbat*. The third blessing correlates to the realm of *Zeir Anpin*, the dimension and source for all the spiritual Light that flows into our realm.

Also, the word *hachalitzenu* means "releases us." The third blessing correlates to the World of *Yetzirah* or "Formation," which, during the weekdays, is ruled by the Angel (**do not pronounce**) Matat–ron, and is from where we receive our fulfillment. On *Shabbat* we would like to be disconnected from the World of *Yetzirah* and elevate to the higher dimensions of the World of *Atzilut* or "Emanation," and receive our fulfillment directly from the Light (with no intermediation of the angels).

רְצֵה retze וְהַחֲלִיצֵנוּ vehachalitzenu יְהֹוָאדֹנָיאהדונהי Adonai אֱלֹהֵינוּ Elohenu
בְּמִצְוֹתֶיךָ bemitzvotecha וּבְמִצְוֹת uv'mitzvat יוֹם yom הַשְּׁבִיעִי hashevi'i,
הַשַּׁבָּת haShabbat הַגָּדוֹל hagadol וְהַקָּדוֹשׁ vehakadosh הַזֶּה hazeh.
כִּי ki יוֹם yom זֶה zeh גָּדוֹל gadol וְקָדוֹשׁ vekadosh הוּא hu לְפָנֶיךָ lefanecha,
לִשְׁבָּת lishbot בּוֹ bo וְלָנוּחַ velanu'ach בּוֹ bo בְּאַהֲבָה be'ahava
כְּמִצְוַת kemitzvat רְצוֹנֶךָ retzonecha. וּבִרְצוֹנְךָ uvirtzoncha הָנִיחַ hani'ach
לָנוּ lanu יְהֹוָאדֹנָיאהדונהי Adonai אֱלֹהֵינוּ Elohenu, שֶׁלֹּא shelo
תְהֵא tehe צָרָה tzara וְיָגוֹן veyagon וַאֲנָחָה va'anachah בְּיוֹם beyom
מְנוּחָתֵנוּ menuchatenu. וְהַרְאֵנוּ vehar'enu יְהֹוָאדֹנָיאהדונהי Adonai אֱלֹהֵינוּ Elohenu
בְּנֶחָמַת benechamat צִיּוֹן Tzion עִירֶךָ irecha, וּבְבִנְיַן uvevinyan
יְרוּשָׁלַיִם Yerushalayim עִיר ir קָדְשֶׁךָ kodshecha, כִּי ki אַתָּה Ata
הוּא hu בַּעַל ba'al הַיְשׁוּעוֹת hayeshu'ot וּבַעַל uva'al הַנֶּחָמוֹת hanechamot:

ROSH CHODESH (NEW MOON) AND COSMIC EVENTS (HOLIDAYS):
During these cosmic windows in time, we find an extra surge of spiritual energy in our midst. We have an additional blessing that is our antenna for drawing this extra power.

אֱלֹהֵינוּ Elohenu וֵאלֹהֵי velohe אֲבוֹתֵינוּ avotenu יַעֲלֶה ya'aleh וְיָבֹא veyavo
וְיַגִּיעַ veyagi'a וְיֵרָאֶה veyera'e וְיֵרָצֶה veyeratze וְיִשָּׁמַע veyishama וְיִפָּקֵד veyipaked
וְיִזָּכֵר veyizacher זִכְרוֹנֵנוּ zichronenu וְזִכְרוֹן vezichron אֲבוֹתֵינוּ avotenu.

SHABBAT:
Favor and strengthen us, Lord, our God, through Your commandments and through the commandment of the Seventh Day, this great and Holy Shabbat. For this day is great and Holy before You to refrain (from work) and to rest on it in love, as ordained by Your will. And with Your will, Lord, our God, there be no distress, grief or lament on this day of our contentment. And show us, Lord, our God, the consolation of Zion, Your city, and the rebuilding of Jerusalem, city of Your Holiness, for You are the Master of salvation and Master of consolations.

ROSH CHODESH (NEW MOON) AND COSMIC EVENTS (HOLIDAYS):
Our God and God of our forefathers, may it rise, come, arrive, appear,
find favor, be heard, be considered, and be remembered, our remembrance and the remembrance of our forefathers:

BIRKAT HAMAZON—BLESSING AFTER THE MEAL

vezichron וְזִכְרוֹן	irach עִירָךְ	Yerushalayim יְרוּשָׁלַיִם	zichron זִכְרוֹן		
kol כָּל vezichron וְזִכְרוֹן	avdach עַבְדָךְ	David דָּוִד	ben בֶּן	Mashi'ach מְשִׁיחַ	
lifleta לִפְלֵיטָה	lefanecha לְפָנֶיךָ	Yisrael יִשְׂרָאֵל	bet בֵּית	amcha עַמְּךָ	
ulerachamim וּלְרַחֲמִים	lechesed לְחֶסֶד	lechen לְחֵן	letova לְטוֹבָה		
beyom בְּיוֹם:	uleshalom וּלְשָׁלוֹם	tovim טוֹבִים	lechayim לְחַיִּים		
hazeh הַזֶּה	hachodesh הַחֹדֶשׁ	rosh רֹאשׁ	:Rosh Chodesh		
hazeh הַזֶּה	haMatzot הַמַּצּוֹת	chag חַג	:Pesach		
hazeh הַזֶּה kodesh קֹדֶשׁ mikra מִקְרָא (tov טוֹב :mid holiday skip) beyom בְּיוֹם					
hazeh הַזֶּה	haSukkot הַסֻּכּוֹת	chag חַג	:Sukkot		
hazeh הַזֶּה kodesh קֹדֶשׁ mikra מִקְרָא (tov טוֹב :mid holiday skip) beyom בְּיוֹם					
hazeh הַזֶּה haAtzeret הָעֲצֶרֶת chag חַג shemini שְׁמִינִי :Shemini Atzeret					
hazeh הַזֶּה kodesh קֹדֶשׁ mikra מִקְרָא tov טוֹב beyom בְּיוֹם					
hazeh הַזֶּה	haShavo'ut הַשָּׁבוּעוֹת	chag חַג	:Shavout		
hazeh הַזֶּה kodesh קֹדֶשׁ mikra מִקְרָא tov טוֹב beyom בְּיוֹם					
hazeh הַזֶּה	haZikaron הַזִּכָּרוֹן	:Rosh Hashanah			
hazeh הַזֶּה	haKippurim הַכִּפֻּרִים	:Children eating on Yom Kippur			
zochrenu זָכְרֵנוּ	ulehoshi'enu וּלְהוֹשִׁיעֵנוּ	alenu עָלֵינוּ	bo בּוֹ	lerachem לְרַחֵם	
(amen) (אָמֵן)	letovah לְטוֹבָה	bo בּוֹ	Elohenu אֱלֹהֵינוּ	Adonai יְהֹוָה	
(amen) (אָמֵן)	livrachah לִבְרָכָה	vo בּוֹ	ufokdenu וּפָקְדֵנוּ		
(amen) (אָמֵן)	tovim טוֹבִים	lechayim לְחַיִּים	vo בּוֹ	vehoshi'enu וְהוֹשִׁיעֵנוּ	
chus וְחוּס	verachamim וְרַחֲמִים	yeshu'a יְשׁוּעָה	bidvar בִּדְבַר		
alenu עָלֵינוּ	verachem וְרַחֵם	vachamol וַחֲמוֹל	vechonenu וְחָנֵּנוּ		
enenu עֵינֵינוּ	elecha אֵלֶיךָ	ki כִּי	vehoshi'enu וְהוֹשִׁיעֵנוּ		
Ata אַתָּה:	verachum וְרַחוּם	chanun חַנּוּן	melech מֶלֶךְ	El אֵל	ki כִּי

The remembrance of Jerusalem Your city; the remembrance of Messiah, son of David, Your servant; the remembrance of Your entire people the house of Israel, before You for deliverance, for goodness, for grace, for kindness and for compassion, for good life and for peace on this day of:
   Rosh Chodesh: *This Rosh Chodesh;*
   Pesach: *This festival of Matzot, on this day of Holy Convocation;*
   Sukkot: *This holiday of Sukkot, on this day of Holy Convocation;*
   Shemini Atzeret: *Shemini Atzeret this holiday, on this day of Holy Convocation;*
   Shavout: *This holiday of Shavout, on this day of Holy Convocation;*
   Rosh Hashanah: *This Day of Remembrance;*
   Children eating on Yom Kippur: *This Day of Atonement;*
To take pity on us and to save us. Remember us on it, Lord, our God, for goodness; consider us on it for blessing; and help us on it for good life. In the matter of salvation and compassion, pity, be gracious and compassionate with us, and help us, for our eyes are turned to You, because You are God, the gracious and compassionate King.

Birkat Hamazon—Blessing After the Meal

Uvneh Yerushalayim

The third blessing ends with the verse *Jerusalem will be built with mercy*. The reason the Temple of Jerusalem was destroyed some 2000 years ago was due to *Hatred for No Reason*. This kind of hatred epitomizes a complete lack of mercy and tolerance of one person to another.

The only way the Holy Temple will be rebuilt, physically, is through the power of *Love for No Reason*, meaning unconditional mercy and human dignity toward our friends and enemies. Kabbalah teaches us that the Temple already exists spiritually and that we can bring it into physical manifestation by virtue of our unconditional love for others. Each year, the Temple does not appear, is as though we have destroyed it all over again. It is this destruction that brings about all the chaos in our world.

וּבְנֵה uvene יְרוּשָׁלַיִם Yerushalayim עִיר ir הַקֹּדֶשׁ hakodesh בִּמְהֵרָה bimhera

בְּיָמֵינוּ veyamenu • בָּרוּךְ baruch אַתָּה Atah יְהוָֹה(אדני/אהיה) Adonai

בּוֹנֶה boneh בְּרַחֲמָיו verachamav יְרוּשָׁלַיִם Yerushalayim • אָמֵן amen:

The Fourth Blessing–The World of Asiyah/Action

The *Zohar* continues (Ibid 786): "Afterwards we say 'who is good and does good,' because everything comes from the Right side and nothing from the Left side." Whatever God gives us is what we need and not necessarily what we might want. If we are missing anything in life, it means we are not supposed to have it. We should always try to receive everything that life can offer us, but we should not allow ourselves to be controlled by the outcome of our efforts to receive. We must learn to fully appreciate, and be completely happy with all that we have and not focus our efforts on attaining the next level of success as a condition for our happiness.

(On Shabbat meditate: הֹי יוד)

בָּרוּךְ baruch אַתָּה Ata יְהוָֹה(אדני/אהיה) Adonai אֱלֹהֵינוּ Elohenu מֶלֶךְ melech
הָעוֹלָם ha'olam, הָאֵל haEl אָבִינוּ avinu, מַלְכֵּנוּ malkenu, אַדִּירֵנוּ adirenu,
בּוֹרְאֵנוּ bor'enu, גּוֹאֲלֵנוּ go'alenu, יוֹצְרֵנוּ yotzrenu, קְדוֹשֵׁנוּ kedoshenu
קְדוֹשׁ kedosh יַעֲקֹב Yaakov, רוֹעֵנוּ ro'enu רוֹעֵה ro'eh יִשְׂרָאֵל Yisrael•
הַמֶּלֶךְ hamelech הַטּוֹב hatov, וְהַמֵּטִיב vehametiv לַכֹּל lakol•

Uvneh Yerushalayim
May You rebuild Jerusalem, the Holy city, soon and in our days.
Blessed are you, Lord, Who in mercy rebuilds Jerusalem. Amen.

The Fourth Blessing–The World of Asiyah/Action
Blessed are you, Lord, our God, King of the Universe, the Almighty, our Father, our King. Our Sovereign, our Creator, our Redeemer, our Maker, our Holy One, Holy one of Jacob, our Shepherd, the Shepherd of Israel, the King who is good and who does good for all.

BIRKAT HAMAZON—BLESSING AFTER THE MEAL

שֶׁבְּכָל shebechol יוֹם yom וְיוֹם vayom הוּא hu הֵטִיב hetiv, הוּא hu
מֵטִיב metiv, הוּא hu יֵיטִיב yetiv לָנוּ lanu. הוּא hu גְּמָלָנוּ gemalanu,
הוּא hu גּוֹמְלֵנוּ gomelenu, הוּא hu יִגְמְלֵנוּ yigmelenu לָעַד la'ad
לְחֵן lechen וּלְחֶסֶד ulechesed וּלְרַחֲמִים ulerachamim וּלְרֶוַח ulerevach,
הַצָּלָה hatzala וְהַצְלָחָה vehatzlacha, בְּרָכָה beracha וִישׁוּעָה vishu'a,
נֶחָמָה nechama, פַּרְנָסָה parnasa וְכַלְכָּלָה vechalkala, וְרַחֲמִים verachamim,
וְחַיִּים vechayim וְשָׁלוֹם veshalom, וְכֹל vechol טוֹב tuv,
וּמִכָּל umikol טוּב tuv לְעוֹלָם le'olam אַל al יְחַסְּרֵנוּ yechasrenu.

The leader puts down the wine cup.

HARACHAMAN

In these next blessings, we will ask God for everything: health, happiness, sustenance, and the Final Redemption. The kabbalists ask what the point is in praying for anything, either God has it in the cards for us to receive, or He does not. The reason for asking has to do with ego, which is the only stumbling block to receiving any form of lasting fulfillment. If a person cannot admit to himself that he needs God, then he can never receive Light. No matter how many positive actions we do, no matter how smart we are, without admitting and recognizing the need for the Light of the Creator, we can never receive permanent fulfillment.

הָרַחֲמָן harachaman,
הוּא hu יִמְלֹךְ yimloch עָלֵינוּ alenu לְעוֹלָם leolam וָעֶד va'ed.
הָרַחֲמָן harachaman,
הוּא hu יִתְבָּרַךְ yitbarech בַּשָּׁמַיִם bashamayim וּבָאָרֶץ uva'aretz.
הָרַחֲמָן harachaman, הוּא hu יִשְׁתַּבַּח yishtabach לְדוֹר ledor דּוֹרִים dorim,
וְיִתְפָּאַר veyitpa'ar בָּנוּ banu לָעַד la'ad וּלְנֵצַח ulnetzach נְצָחִים netzachim,
וְיִתְהַדַּר veyit'hadar בָּנוּ banu לָעַד la'ad וּלְעוֹלְמֵי ule'olme עוֹלָמִים olamim,
הָרַחֲמָן harachaman, הוּא hu יְפַרְנְסֵנוּ yefarnsenu בְּכָבוֹד vechavod.

For every single day He did good, He does good and He will do good to us. He was bountiful with us, He is bountiful with us and He will forever be bountiful with us, with grace and with kindness and with mercy, with relief, salvation, success, blessing, help, consolation, sustenance, support, mercy, life, peace and all good; and of all good things may He never deprive us.

HARACHAMAN
The compassionate One, may He reign over us forever.
The compassionate One, may He be blessed in Heaven and on Earth. The compassionate One, may He be praised throughout all generations, may He be glorified through us forever to the ultimate ends, and be honored through us forever and for all eternity. The compassionate One, may He sustain us in honor.

BIRKAT HAMAZON—BLESSING AFTER THE MEAL

הָרַחֲמָן, harachaman,
הוּא hu יִשְׁבֹּר yishbor עֻלֵּנוּ ulenu מֵעַל me'al צַוָּארֵנוּ tzavarenu
וְהוּא vehu יוֹלִיכֵנוּ yolichenu קוֹמְמִיּוּת komemiyut לְאַרְצֵנוּ le'artzenu.

הָרַחֲמָן harachaman, הוּא hu
יִשְׁלַח yishlach לָנוּ lanu בְּרָכָה beracha מְרֻבָּה meruba בַּבַּיִת babait
הַזֶּה hazeh וְעַל ve'al שֻׁלְחָן shulchan זֶה ze שֶׁאָכַלְנוּ she'achalnu עָלָיו alav.
הָרַחֲמָן harachaman, הוּא hu יִשְׁלַח yishlach לָנוּ lanu אֶת et אֵלִיָּהוּ Eliyahu
הַנָּבִיא hanavi זָכוּר zachur לַטּוֹב latov (3x) וִיבַשֶּׂר vivaser לָנוּ lanu)
בְּשׂוֹרוֹת besorot טוֹבוֹת tovot יְשׁוּעוֹת yeshu'ot וְנֶחָמוֹת venechamot.

הָרַחֲמָן harachaman,
הוּא hu יְבָרֵךְ yevarech אֶת et הָרַב haRav רַבִּי rabi מוֹרִי mori בַּעַל ba'al
הַבַּיִת habayit הַזֶּה hazeh, וְאֶת ve'et הָרַבָּנִית haRabanit מוֹרָתִי morati
בַּעֲלַת ba'alat הַבַּיִת habayit הַזֶּה hazeh, וְאֶת ve'et אוֹתָם otam וְאֶת ve'et בֵּיתָם betam
וְאֶת ve'et זַרְעָם zar'am וְאֶת ve'et כָּל kol אֲשֶׁר asher לָהֶם lahem.

Here, one can add a personal blessing for their family:
הָרַחֲמָן harachaman, הוּא hu יְבָרֵךְ yevarech אוֹתִי oti (וְאָבִי ve'avi וְאִמִּי ve'imi)
וְאִשְׁתִּי ve'ishti וְזַרְעִי vezar'i וְאֶת ve'et כָּל kol אֲשֶׁר asher לִי li.

וְאֶת ve'et כָּל kol הַחֲבֵרִים hachaverim בְּכָל bechol מְקוֹמוֹתָם mekomotam
אוֹתָם otam וְאֶת ve'et בֵּיתָם betam וְאֶת ve'et זַרְעָם zar'am וְאֶת ve'et
כָּל kol אֲשֶׁר asher לָהֶם lahem אוֹתָנוּ otanu וְאֶת ve'et כָּל kol אֲשֶׁר asher
לָנוּ lanu, כְּמוֹ kemo שֶׁנִּתְבָּרְכוּ shenitbarchu אֲבוֹתֵינוּ avotenu:

The compassionate One, may He break the yoke of oppression from our necks and guide us erect to our land. The compassionate One, may He send us abundant blessing, to this house, and upon this table at which we have eaten. The compassionate One, may he send us Elijah the prophet – he is remembered for good – to proclaim to us good tidings, salvations and consolations. The compassionate One, may He bless the Rav, my rabbi, my teacher, the master of this house and the Rabanit, my teacher, the lady of this house; them, their house, their family and all that is theirs;

Here, one can add a personal blessing for their family:
The compassionate One, may He bless me (my father and my mother), my wife, my family and all that is mine.

All the friends, wherever they are, their houses, their families, and all that is theirs; Ours and all that is ours; just as our forefathers:

BIRKAT HAMAZON—BLESSING AFTER THE MEAL

אַבְרָהָם Avraham יִצְחָק Yitzchak וְיַעֲקֹב veYaakov: בַּכֹּל bakol,
מִכֹּל mikol, כֹּל kol. כֵּן ken יְבָרֵךְ yevarech אוֹתָנוּ otanu כֻּלָּנוּ kulanu
יַחַד yachad, בִּבְרָכָה bivracha שְׁלֵמָה shelema, וְנֹאמַר venomar אָמֵן amen:
בַּמָּרוֹם bamarom יְלַמְּדוּ yelamdu עֲלֵיהֶם alehem וְעָלֵינוּ ve'alenu
זְכוּת zechut, שֶׁתְּהֵא shetehe לְמִשְׁמֶרֶת lemishmeret שָׁלוֹם shalom,
וְנִשָּׂא venisa בְּרָכָה beracha מֵאֵת me'et יְהֹוָה Adonai
וּצְדָקָה utzedakah מֵאֱלֹהֵי meElohe יִשְׁעֵנוּ yish'enu, וְנִמְצָא venimtza חֵן chen
וְשֵׂכֶל vesechel טוֹב tov בְּעֵינֵי be'ene אֱלֹהִים Elohim וְאָדָם ve'adam.

After the meal following a circumcision, we recite the following:

Chesed   חסד

הָרַחֲמָן harachaman, הוּא hu יְבָרֵךְ yevarech אֶת et אֲבִי avi הַיֶּלֶד hayeled
וְאִמּוֹ ve'imo, וִיזַכּוּ veyizku לְגַדְּלוֹ legadlo וּלְחַנְּכוֹ ulechanecho וּלְחַכְּמוֹ ulechakemo,
מִיּוֹם miyom הַשְּׁמִינִי hashemini וָהָלְאָה vahal'a יֵרָצֶה yeratze דָּמוֹ damo,
וִיהִי vihi יְהֹוָה Adonai אֱלֹהָיו Elohav עִמּוֹ imo. (אָמֵן amen)

Gevurah   גבורה

הָרַחֲמָן harachaman, הוּא hu יְבָרֵךְ yevarech בַּעַל ba'al בְּרִית berit
הַמִּילָה hamila, אֲשֶׁר asher שָׂשׂ sas לַעֲשׂוֹת la'asot צֶדֶק tzedek בְּגִילָה begila,
וִישַׁלֵּם vishalem פָּעֳלוֹ pa'olo וּמַשְׂכֻּרְתּוֹ umaskurto כְּפוּלָה kefula,
וְיִתְּנֵהוּ veyitnehu לְמַעְלָה lemala לְמַעְלָה lemala. (אָמֵן amen)

Abraham, Isaac and Jacob were blessed in everything, from everything, with everything. So may He bless us all together with a perfect blessing. And let us say: Amen. May there be advocacy on high for their merit and for ours, for a safeguard of peace. May we receive a blessing from the Lord and just kindness from the God of our salvation and find favor and good understanding in the eyes of God and man.

After the meal following a circumcision, we recite the following:

Chesed - *The compassionate One, may He bless the father and mother of the child; may they merit raising him, to train him, and to educate him to be a scholar. From the eighth day onward his blood is accepted; may the Lord, his God, be with him.*

Gevurah - *The compassionate One, may He bless the godparent at the circumcision, who happily performed this good deed in joy. May He reward his deed and double his recompense and exalt him higher and higher.*

BIRKAT HAMAZON—BLESSING AFTER THE MEAL

Tiferet / תפארת

הָרַחֲמָן, harachaman, הוּא hu, יְבָרֵךְ yevarech, רַךְ rach, הַנִּימוֹל hanimol לִשְׁמוֹנָה lishmona, וְיִהְיוּ veyihyu, יָדָיו yadav, וְלִבּוֹ velibo, לָאֵל laEl אֱמוּנָה emunah, וְיִזְכֶּה veyizkeh, לִרְאוֹת lir'ot, פְּנֵי penei הַשְּׁכִינָה hashechinah, שָׁלֹשׁ shalosh פְּעָמִים pe'amim בַּשָּׁנָה bashana. (אָמֵן amen)

Netzach / נצח

הָרַחֲמָן, harachaman, הוּא hu, יְבָרֵךְ yevarech, הַמָּל hamal, בְּשַׂר besar הָעָרְלָה ha'orla, וּפָרַע ufara וּמָצַץ umatzatz דְּמֵי deme הַמִּילָה hamila, אִישׁ ish הַיָּרֵא hayare וְרַךְ verach הַלֵּבָב halevav עֲבוֹדָתוֹ avodato פְּסוּלָה pesula, שָׁלֹשׁ shelosh אֵלֶּה ele לֹא lo יַעֲשֶׂה ya'ase לָהּ la. (אָמֵן amen)

Hod / הוד

הָרַחֲמָן, harachaman, הוּא hu, יִשְׁלַח yishlach לָנוּ lanu מְשִׁיחוֹ meshicho הוֹלֵךְ holech תָּמִים tamim, בִּזְכוּת bizchut חֲתַן chatan לַמּוּלוֹת lamulot דָּמִים damim, לְבַשֵּׂר levaser בְּשׂוֹרוֹת besorot טוֹבוֹת tovot וְנִחוּמִים venichumim, לְעַם le'am אֶחָד echad מְפֻזָּר mefuzar וּמְפֹרָד umeforad בֵּין ben הָעַמִּים ha'amim. (אָמֵן amen)

Yesod / יסוד

הָרַחֲמָן, harachaman, הוּא hu, יִשְׁלַח yishlach לָנוּ lanu כֹּהֵן Kohen צֶדֶק tzedek אֲשֶׁר asher לֻקַּח lukach לְעֵילוֹם le'elom, עַד ad הוּכַן huchan כִּסְאוֹ kise'o כַּשֶּׁמֶשׁ kashemesh וְיַהֲלֹם veyahalom, וַיָּלֶט vayalet פָּנָיו panav בְּאַדַּרְתּוֹ be'adarto וַיִּגְלֹם vayiglom, בְּרִיתִי beriti הָיְתָה hayta אִתּוֹ ito הַחַיִּים hachayim וְהַשָּׁלוֹם vehashalom: (אָמֵן amen)

Tiferet - The compassionate One, may He bless the tender infant who has been circumcised on the eighth day; may his hands and heart be faithful to the Almighty, and may he merit to behold the Divine Presence three times a year.
Netzach - The compassionate One, may He bless the mohel who performed the circumcision, the periah and metzitzah. If a timid or faint-hearted man fails to perform these three parts of the mitzvah, his service is invalid.
Hod - The compassionate One, may He send us His Messiah who walks in perfection, in merit of the groom's bloodshed of circumcision, to bring good tidings and consolations to the one nation dispersed and scattered among the nations.
Yesod - The compassionate One, may He send us [Elijah] the righteous priest, who was taken into concealment, until his seat resplendent as the sun and precious stones is prepared for him; who covered his face with his mantle and enwrapped himself, with whom was made My covenant of life and peace.

BIRKAT HAMAZON—BLESSING AFTER THE MEAL

SHABBAT:

הָרַחֲמָן, harachaman, הוּא hu יַנְחִילֵנוּ yanchilenu יוֹם yom שֶׁכֻּלּוֹ shekulo
שַׁבָּת Shabbat וּמְנוּחָה umenuchah לְחַיֵּי lechaye הָעוֹלָמִים ha'olamim.

ROSH CHODESH:

הָרַחֲמָן, harachaman, הוּא hu יְחַדֵּשׁ yechadesh עָלֵינוּ alenu אֶת et
הַחֹדֶשׁ hachodesh הַזֶּה hazeh לְטוֹבָה letova וְלִבְרָכָה velivracha.

HOLIDAYS:

הָרַחֲמָן, harachaman,
הוּא hu יַנְחִילֵנוּ yanchilenu יוֹם yom שֶׁכֻּלּוֹ shekulo טוֹב tov.

ROSH HASHANAH:

הָרַחֲמָן, harachaman, הוּא hu יְחַדֵּשׁ yechadesh עָלֵינוּ alenu
אֶת et הַשָּׁנָה hashana הַזֹּאת hazot לְטוֹבָה letova וְלִבְרָכָה velivracha.

SUKKOT:

הָרַחֲמָן harachaman, הוּא hu
יָקִים yakim לָנוּ lanu אֶת et סֻכַּת sukkat דָּוִד David הַנּוֹפֶלֶת hanofelet.

הָרַחֲמָן, harachaman, הוּא hu יְזַכֵּנוּ yezakenu לִימוֹת limot
הַמָּשִׁיחַ hamashi'ach וּלְחַיֵּי ulchaye הָעוֹלָם ha'olam הַבָּא haba.
(Shabbat, Holidays and Rosh Chodesh: מִגְדּוֹל migdol) (otherwise: מַגְדִּיל magdil)
יְשׁוּעוֹת yeshu'ot מַלְכּוֹ malko וְעוֹשֶׂה ve'ose חֶסֶד chesed
לִמְשִׁיחוֹ limshicho לְדָוִד leDavid וּלְזַרְעוֹ ulezar'o עַד ad עוֹלָם olam.
עוֹשֶׂה ose שָׁלוֹם shalom בִּמְרוֹמָיו bimromav, הוּא hu יַעֲשֶׂה ya'ase
שָׁלוֹם shalom, עָלֵינוּ alenu וְעַל ve'al כָּל kol יִשְׂרָאֵל Yisrael,
וְאִמְרוּ ve'imru אָמֵן amen.

Shabbat: The compassionate One,
may He cause us to inherit the day, which will be completely a Shabbat and rest day for eternal life.
Rosh Chodesh: The compassionate One, may He renew for us this month for good and for blessing.
Holidays: The compassionate One, may He let us inherit that day which is all good.
Rosh Hashanah: The compassionate One, may He renew for us this year for good and for blessing.
Sukkot: The compassionate One, may He restore for us the fallen sukkah of David.

The compassionate one, may He make us worthy of the days of Messiah and the life of the World to Come. "He who is a tower of salvation of His king [David]; He shows unfailing kindness to His anointed, to David and to his descendants forever." (II Samuel 22:51, Psalms 18:51) "He who makes peace in His heights" (Job 25:2) may He make peace upon us and upon all Israel. And let us say: Amen.

BIRKAT HAMAZON—BLESSING AFTER THE MEAL

יְראוּ yir'u אֶת et יְהֹוָה Adonai קְדֹשָׁיו kedoshav,
כִּי ki אֵין en מַחְסוֹר machsor לִירֵאָיו lire'av:
כְּפִירִים kefirim רָשׁוּ rashu וְרָעֵבוּ vera'evu וְדֹרְשֵׁי vedorshe
יְהֹוָה Adonai לֹא lo יַחְסְרוּ yach'seru כָל kol טוֹב tov: הוֹדוּ hodu
לַיהֹוָה ladonai כִּי ki טוֹב tov, כִּי ki לְעוֹלָם le'olam וְחַסְדּוֹ chasdo:

POTEACH ET YADECHA
(See meditations on page 100)

פּוֹתֵחַ pote'ach אֶת et יָדֶךָ yadecha

פאי סאל וזתך דיקרנוסא
אמן יאהדונהי יוזהתוכה

וּמַשְׂבִּיעַ umasbi'a לְכָל lechol חַי chai רָצוֹן ratzon ר"ת רוזל:
בָּרוּךְ baruch הַגֶּבֶר hagever אֲשֶׁר asher יִבְטַח yivtach
בַּיהֹוָה badonai וְהָיָה vehaya יְהֹוָה Adonai
מִבְטַחוֹ mivtacho: נַעַר na'ar הָיִיתִי hayiti גַּם gam זָקַנְתִּי zakanti וְלֹא velo
רָאִיתִי ra'iti צַדִּיק tzadik נֶעֱזָב ne'ezav וְזַרְעוֹ vezar'o מְבַקֶּשׁ mevakesh
לָחֶם lachem: יְהֹוָה Adonai עֹז oz לְעַמּוֹ le'amo יִתֵּן yiten
יְהֹוָה Adonai יְבָרֵךְ yevarech אֶת et עַמּוֹ amo בַשָּׁלוֹם bashalom:

If there is a Seven Blessings connection, continue on page 114.
If there is *zimun* with a cup of wine, continue on page 116.

"Fear the Lord, you, His holy ones, for those who fear him lack nothing. Young lions go hungry and may starve, but those who seek the Lord will not lack any good" *(Psalms 34:10-11).* "Give thanks to the Lord for He is good. His kindness endures forever." *(Psalms 136:1)*

POTEACH ET YADECHA
"You open Your hand and satisfy the desire of every living thing." *(Psalms 145:16)*
"Blessed is the man who trusts in the Lord, then the Lord will be his security." *(Jeremiah 17:7)* "I have been young and now I am old, and I have not seen a righteous one forsaken neither his seed seeking bread." *(Psalms 37:25)* "The Lord will give might to His people; the Lord will bless His people with peace." *(Psalms 29:11)*

Sheva Berachot – Seven Blessings

During the first seven days after the wedding, the vessel of the newly married couple is being created. Each of these days connects the *chatan* (groom) and the *kalah* (bride) to one of the seven dimensions (*Sefirot*) from *Chesed* to *Malchut*, which directly imbue positivity into their physical realm, igniting the Light in their new relationship. Just as an apple seed contains within it the entire tree that will grow in the future, the Light received on their first *Shabbat* as a married couple, is the seed that contains all the Light necessary for building a transformative life together.

The *Zohar* (Terumah, 788-801) teaches us that the purpose of the Seven Blessings is to elevate the bride of Below and the bride of Above (the *Shechinah*) to receive all the blessings from *Zeir Anpin*.

Before *Birkat Hamazon*, two full cups of wine are prepared: One for the individual who leads the *Birkat Hamazon*, and the other cup for the Seven Blessings. The one who leads the *Birkat Hamazon* adds some words to the *zimun* (see page 96 and on). After *Birkat Hamazon* is completed, seven of the guests are invited to take the cup of wine of the Seven Blessings and recite one of the blessings below.

(The vowels of the Tetragrammaton is according to Kabbalist Rav Shabtai of Roshkov)

Chesed / חסד

baruch בָּרוּךְ Ata אַתָּה Adonai יְהוָוָהֹ(אדני/אהדונהי) Elohenu אֱלֹהֵינוּ
melech מֶלֶךְ ha'olam הָעוֹלָם shehakol שֶׁהַכֹּל bara בָּרָא lichvodo לִכְבוֹדוֹ:

Gevurah / גבורה

baruch בָּרוּךְ Ata אַתָּה Adonai יְהוָֹוָה(אדני/אהדונהי) Elohenu אֱלֹהֵינוּ
melech מֶלֶךְ ha'olam הָעוֹלָם yotzer יוֹצֵר ha'adam הָאָדָם:

Tiferet / תפארת

baruch בָּרוּךְ Ata אַתָּה Adonai יְהוָֹוָה(אדני/אהדונהי) Elohenu אֱלֹהֵינוּ melech מֶלֶךְ
ha'olam הָעוֹלָם asher אֲשֶׁר yatzar יָצַר et אֶת ha'adam הָאָדָם
betzalmo בְּצַלְמוֹ, betzelem בְּצֶלֶם demut דְּמוּת tavnito תַּבְנִיתוֹ,
vehitkin וְהִתְקִין lo לוֹ mimenu מִמֶּנּוּ binyan בִּנְיַן adei עֲדֵי ad עַד.
baruch בָּרוּךְ Ata אַתָּה Adonai יְהוָֹוָה(אדני/אהדונהי) yotzer יוֹצֵר ha'adam הָאָדָם:

Sheva Berachot – Seven Blessings

Chesed - *Blessed are You, Lord, our God, King of the Universe, who created everything for His Glory.*
Gevurah - *Blessed are You, Lord, our God, King of the Universe, who creates man.*
Tiferet - *Blessed are You, Lord, our God, King of the Universe, who creates man in His image, fashioning perpetuated life. Blessed are You, Lord, creator of man.*

SHEVA BERACHOT – SEVEN BLESSINGS

Netzach · נצח

akara עֲקָרָה vetagel וְתָגֵל tasis תָּשִׂישׂ sos שׂוֹשׂ
bimhera בִּמְהֵרָה letocha לְתוֹכָהּ baneha בָּנֶיהָ bekibutz בְּקִבּוּץ
Adonai יְהֹוָה Ata אַתָּה baruch בָּרוּךְ besimcha בְּשִׂמְחָה
bevaneha בְּבָנֶיהָ: tziyon צִיּוֹן mesame'ach מְשַׂמֵּחַ

Hod · הוד

ahuvim אֲהוּבִים, re'im רֵעִים tesamach תְּשַׂמַּח same'ach שַׂמֵּחַ
eden עֵדֶן began בְּגַן yetzircha יְצִירְךָ kesamechacha כְּשַׂמֵּחֲךָ
Adonai יְהֹוָה Ata אַתָּה baruch בָּרוּךְ mikedem מִקֶּדֶם
vechala וְכַלָּה: chatan וְחָתָן mesame'ach מְשַׂמֵּחַ

Yesod · יסוד

melech מֶלֶךְ Elohenu אֱלֹהֵינוּ Adonai יְהֹוָה Ata אַתָּה baruch בָּרוּךְ
ha'olam הָעוֹלָם, asher אֲשֶׁר bara בָּרָא sason שָׂשׂוֹן vesimcha וְשִׂמְחָה,
ditza דִּיצָה rina רִנָּה gila גִּילָה vechala וְכַלָּה chatan חָתָן
shalom שָׁלוֹם ve'achva וְאַחֲוָה ahava אַהֲבָה vechedva וְחֶדְוָה
Elohenu אֱלֹהֵינוּ Adonai יְהֹוָה mehera מְהֵרָה, vere'ut וְרֵעוּת,
uvchutzot וּבְחוּצוֹת Yehuda יְהוּדָה be'arei בְּעָרֵי yishama יִשָּׁמַע od עוֹד
simcha שִׂמְחָה vekol וְקוֹל sason שָׂשׂוֹן kol קוֹל Yerushalayim יְרוּשָׁלָיִם
mitz'halot מִצְהֲלוֹת kol קוֹל kala כַּלָּה vekol וְקוֹל chatan וְחָתָן kol קוֹל
mimishte מִמִּשְׁתֵּה un'arim וּנְעָרִים, mechupatam מֵחֻפָּתָם chatanim חֲתָנִים
Adonai יְהֹוָה Ata אַתָּה baruch בָּרוּךְ neginatam נְגִינָתָם
hakala הַכַּלָּה: im עִם hechatan הֶחָתָן mesame'ach מְשַׂמֵּחַ

Netzach – May the barren one exult and be glad as her children are joyfully gathered to her. Blessed are You, Lord, who gladden Zion with her children.

Hod – Grant perfect joy to these loving companions, as you did Your creations in the Garden of Eden. Blessed are You, Lord, who grants the joy of groom and bride.

Yesod – Blessed are You, Lord, our God, King of the Universe, who created joy and gladness, groom and bride, mirth, song, delight and rejoicing, love and harmony and peace and companionship. Soon, Lord our God, may there ever be heard in the cities of Judah and in the streets of Jerusalem voices of joy and gladness, voices of groom and bride, the jubilant voices of those joined in marriage under the bridal canopy, the voices of young people feasting and singing. Blessed are You, Lord, who causes the groom to rejoice with his bride.

BORE PERI HAGEFEN - BLESSING OVER WINE OR GRAPE JUICE

The *Zohar* says (Zohar Terumah 792): "Why are most blessings recited over wine? He answers: Wine is the aspect that causes everyone to rejoice, the wine that is always kept in its grapes... because wine produces fruits both Above in *Binah* and Below in *Malchut*. The vine, which is *Malchut*, receives everything and brings forth fruits to the world, for after receiving the aspect of wine, *Malchut* is named Lower *Chochmah*. And before She receives *Chochmah*, She is not able to give birth. The arousing of joy, meaning the beginning of the union of *Zeir Anpin* and *Malchut*, is the Left, as it is written: 'His left hand is under my head' and afterwards, 'And His right hand embraces me." That Tree of Life, which is *Zeir Anpin*, produces fruits and plants with this arousal of the Left because before it receives *Chochmah* from the Left of *Binah*, it cannot beget."

If there is a Seven Blessings Connection the seventh person holds the second cup of wine in his right hand, recites the blessing of *Hagefen* as the seventh blessing, and then drinks from it. Then the leader of *Birkat Hamazon* holds the first cup of wine, recites the blessing of *Hagefen*, and then drinks from it. Then wine from the two cups is mixed together, adding the blessing of *Birkat Hamazon* (the first cup) to the groom and the bride (the second cup) three times. Then the second cup is given to the groom and the bride to recite the blessing of *Hagefen* on it and drink from it. Then the leader of *Birkat Hamazon* will say the last blessing over the wine (see pages 117-119.)

In case of *zimun* (without the Seven Blessings connection), the leader of *Birkat Hamazon* holds the wine cup, recites the blessing of *Hagefen*, and then drinks from it. Then the leader of *Birkat Hamazon* will say the last blessing over the wine (see pages 117-119.)

עם maranan מָרָנָן (ה' דחסדים וה' דגבורות) י"פ יהוה savri סַבְרִי

אהיה יהוה, בינה ע"ה lechayim לְחַיִּים (: The others reply)

Malchut				מלכות
Elohenu אֱלֹהֵינוּ	Adonai יְהֹוָה(אדני/אהדונהי)	Ata אַתָּה	baruch בָּרוּךְ
hagefen הַגָּפֶן:	peri פְּרִי	bore בּוֹרֵא	ha'olam הָעוֹלָם	melech מֶלֶךְ

BORE PERI HAGEFEN - BLESSING OVER WINE OR GRAPE JUICE

With your permission, my masters.
(The others reply) *To life [Binah.]*
Malchut - Blessed are You, Lord, our God, King of the Universe, Who created the fruit of the vine.

LAST BLESSING

ME'EN SHALOSH (RESEMBLING THREE)—LAST BLESSING

Food contains different sparks of Light needed for our daily spiritual work. By reciting a blessing before and after we eat, we activate and elevate these sparks.

Just as we have specific blessings for the different foods before we eat, so too, there are different blessings that are recited after we have eaten. The following blessing is recited after eating food that was produced from the seven species of the land of Israel (food containing wheat, barley, rye, oats or spelt, grapes, wine or grape juice, figs, pomegranates, dates and olives). The *land of Israel* is a code name for the source and origin of the energy in our world. Reciting this blessing helps us to reconnect with the source.

בָּרוּךְ baruch אַתָּה Atah יְהֹוָאֲדֹנָי Adonai

אֱלֹהֵינוּ Elohenu מֶלֶךְ melech הָעוֹלָם ha'olam, עַל al

On food from the five grains:
(Wheat, barley, rye, oats & spelt)
הַמִּחְיָה hamichya וְעַל ve'al הַכַּלְכָּלָה hakalkala

On wine or grape juice:
הַגֶּפֶן hagefen וְעַל ve'al פְּרִי peri הַגֶּפֶן hagefen

On the five fruits of the tree:
(Grapes, figs, pomegranates, dates, olives)
הָעֵץ ha'etz וְעַל ve'al פְּרִי peri הָעֵץ ha'etz

On wine or grape juice and food from the five grains:
הַמִּחְיָה hamichya וְעַל ve'al הַכַּלְכָּלָה hakalkala
וְעַל ve'al הַגֶּפֶן hagefen וְעַל ve'al פְּרִי peri הַגֶּפֶן hagefen

וְעַל ve'al תְּנוּבַת tenuvat הַשָּׂדֶה hasade וְעַל ve'al אֶרֶץ eretz
חֶמְדָּה chemda טוֹבָה tova וּרְחָבָה ur'chava שֶׁרָצִיתָ sheratzita
וְהִנְחַלְתָּ vehinchalta לַאֲבוֹתֵינוּ la'avotenu לֶאֱכֹל le'echol מִפִּרְיָהּ mipirya
וְלִשְׂבּוֹעַ velisbo'a מִטּוּבָהּ mituva• רַחֵם rachem יְהֹוָאֲדֹנָי Adonai
אֱלֹהֵינוּ Elohenu עָלֵינוּ alenu וְעַל ve'al יִשְׂרָאֵל Yisrael עַמָּךְ amach וְעַל ve'al
יְרוּשָׁלַיִם Yerushalayim עִירָךְ irach וְעַל ve'al הַר har צִיּוֹן Tzion
מִשְׁכַּן mishkan כְּבוֹדָךְ kevodach• וְעַל ve'al מִזְבְּחָךְ mizbachach•

ME'EN SHALOSH (RESEMBLING THREE)—LAST BLESSING

Blessed are You, Lord our God, King of the universe;
On food from the five grains: *for the food and for the sustenance;*
On wine or grape juice: *for the vine and for the fruit of the grapevine;*
On the five fruits of the tree: *for the trees and for the fruit of the trees;*
On wine or grape juice and food from the five grains:
for the food and for the sustenance and for the vine and for the fruit of the grapevine;
And for the produce of the field and for the fine, fertile and great Land, that You have given our fathers as an inheritance to eat of its crop and to be satiated with its goodness. Be merciful the Lord, our God on Israel, Your people, and on Jerusalem Your city and on Mount Zion, the place of Your glory, and on Your Altar;

Last Blessing

ve'al וְעַל hechalach הֵיכָלֶךָ uvne וּבְנֵה Yerushalayim יְרוּשָׁלַיִם
ir עִיר hakodesh הַקֹּדֶשׁ bimhera בִּמְהֵרָה •veyamenu בְיָמֵינוּ
•veha'alenu וְהַעֲלֵנוּ letocha לְתוֹכָהּ vesamchenu וְשַׂמְּחֵנוּ •bevinyana בְּבִנְיָנָהּ
un'var'chach וּנְבָרֶכְךָ aleha עָלֶיהָ bikdusha בִּקְדֻשָּׁה •uv'tahara וּבְטָהֳרָה

Shabbat:
•urtze רְצֵה vehachalitzenu וְהַחֲלִיצֵנוּ beyom בְּיוֹם haShabbat הַשַּׁבָּת hazeh הַזֶּה•

Rosh Chodesh:
•vezochrenu וְזָכְרֵנוּ letova לְטוֹבָה beyom בְּיוֹם rosh רֹאשׁ hachodesh הַחֹדֶשׁ hazeh הַזֶּה.

Rosh Hashanah:
•vezochrenu וְזָכְרֵנוּ letova לְטוֹבָה beyom בְּיוֹם hazikaron הַזִּכָּרוֹן hazeh הַזֶּה•

Pesach:
•vesamchenu וְשַׂמְּחֵנוּ beyom בְּיוֹם chag וְחַג hamatzot הַמַּצּוֹת hazeh הַזֶּה•
•beyom בְּיוֹם (tov טוֹב: mid-holiday skip) mikra מִקְרָא kodesh קֹדֶשׁ hazeh הַזֶּה•

Shavuot:
•vesamchenu וְשַׂמְּחֵנוּ beyom בְּיוֹם chag וְחַג haShavout הַשָּׁבוּעוֹת hazeh הַזֶּה•
•beyom בְּיוֹם tov טוֹב mikra מִקְרָא kodesh קֹדֶשׁ hazeh הַזֶּה•

Sukkot:
•vesamchenu וְשַׂמְּחֵנוּ beyom בְּיוֹם chag וְחַג haSukkot הַסֻּכּוֹת hazeh הַזֶּה•
•beyom בְּיוֹם (tov טוֹב: mid-holiday skip) mikra מִקְרָא kodesh קֹדֶשׁ hazeh הַזֶּה•

Simchat Torah:
vesamchenu וְשַׂמְּחֵנוּ beyom בְּיוֹם Shemini שְׁמִינִי chag וְחַג Atzeret עֲצֶרֶת
•hazeh הַזֶּה• beyom בְּיוֹם tov טוֹב mikra מִקְרָא kodesh קֹדֶשׁ hazeh הַזֶּה•

---

ki כִּי Ata אַתָּה tov טוֹב umetiv וּמֵטִיב •lakol לַכֹּל

And on Your Temple. And reconstruct Jerusalem the Holy City speedily in our days and bring us there and gladden us with its rebuilding and we will bless You for it in holiness and purity.

> **Shabbat:** *and accept favourably and console us on this day of Shabbat;*
> **Rosh Chodesh:** *and remember us on this day of the New Moon;*
> **Rosh Hashanah:** *and remember us on this day of Remembrance;*
> **Pesach:** *and bring us joy on this Matzot festival, on this day of Holy Convocation.*
> **Shavuot:** *and bring us joy on this festival of Shavuot, on this day of Holy Convocation.*
> **Sukkot:** *and bring us joy on this festival of Sukkot, on this day of Holy Convocation.*
> **Simchat Torah:** *and bring us joy on this festival of Shemini Atzeret, on this day of Holy Convocation.*

For You are good and do good to all.

Last Blessing

Elohenu אֱלֹהֵינוּ   Adonai יְהֹוָה   lecha לְךָ   venode וְנוֹדֶה

ve'al וְעַל   ha'aretz הָאָרֶץ   al עַל

On food from the five grains: hakalkala הַכַּלְכָּלָה ve'al וְעַל hamichya הַמִּחְיָה

On wine or grape juice: hagefen הַגֶּפֶן peri פְּרִי

On the five fruits of the tree: ha'etz הָעֵץ peri פְּרִי

ve'al וְעַל ha'aretz הָאָרֶץ al עַל Adonai יְהֹוָה Ata אַתָּה baruch בָּרוּךְ

On food from the five grains: hakalkala הַכַּלְכָּלָה ve'al וְעַל hamichya הַמִּחְיָה

On food from the land of Israel, say this instead: kalkalata כַּלְכָּלָתָהּ ve'al וְעַל michyata מִחְיָתָהּ

On wine / grape juice: hagefen הַגֶּפֶן peri פְּרִי

On wine from the land of Israel, say this instead: gafna גַּפְנָהּ peri פְּרִי

On five fruits of the tree: haperot הַפֵּרוֹת

On fruit from the land of Israel, say this instead: peroteha פֵּרוֹתֶיהָ

Bore Nefashot (Who Has Created Living Beings)—Last Blessing
This blessing is recited after any other food.

melech מֶלֶךְ Elohenu אֱלֹהֵינוּ Adonai יְהֹוָה Ata אַתָּה baruch בָּרוּךְ

vechesronan וְחֶסְרוֹנָן, rabot רַבּוֹת nefashot נְפָשׁוֹת bore בּוֹרֵא ha'olam הָעוֹלָם

bahem בָּהֶם lehachayot לְהַחֲיוֹת shebarata שֶׁבָּרָאתָ ma מַה kol כָּל al עַל

ha'olamim הָעוֹלָמִים: chei חֵי baruch בָּרוּךְ, chai חַי kol כָּל nefesh נֶפֶשׁ

And we will give thanks to You, the Lord our God, for the land and for:
On food from the five grains: *for the food.*
On wine or grape juice: *for the fruit of grapevine.*
On the five fruits of the tree: *for the fruit of the trees.*
Blessed are You, Lord, for the land and
On food from the five grains: *for the (**from Israel**: its) food and for the (**from Israel**: its) sustenance.*
On wine or grape juice: *for the (**from Israel**: its) fruit of the grapevine.*
On the five fruits of the tree: *for the (**from Israel**: its) fruits of the tree.*

Bore Nefashot (Who Has Created Living Beings)—Last Blessing
Blessed are You,
Lord our God, King of the universe Who has created many living beings and everything to satisfy their needs; for all that You have created to maintain all life. Blessed is the One Who is the life giver of the worlds.

Havdalah and Fourth Meal (MELAVEH MALKAH) Connection

HAVDALAH OF SATURDAY NIGHT

MELAVEH MALKAH SONGS:
    HAMAVDIL (HE WHO SEPARATES)
    YEHI HACHODESH HAZEH (MAY THIS MONTH BE)
    AMAR HASHEM LEYAAKOV (THE LORD TOLD JACOB)

VEYITEN LECHA (AND MAY GOD GIVE YOU)—VERSES FOR SUCCESS

HAVDALAH OF SATURDAY NIGHT

HAVDALAH OF SATURDAY NIGHT

Throughout *Shabbat*, our soul elevates to the highest levels of the spiritual worlds. To avoid a sudden drop when we re-enter the days of the week, the kabbalists have instituted a technology known as *Havdalah* or "separation," that ensures a safe and soft landing. Meditating while we use the technology of Havdalah—the wine, myrtle branches, and a special candle—gives us the ability to differentiate between what is good and what is not, for us personally. This technology assists us to achieve a sense of peace and serenity in our lives. It is said that all those who smile and laugh during this connection arouse the forces of financial sustenance.

The *Talmud* says (Babylonian Talmud, Tractate Eruvin 65:1): "A person in whose house wine is not poured like water has not attained the state of blessedness," therefore, our teacher, the Rav, would pour the wine of the *Havdalah* into the cup until it overflows, so as to bring blessings for the coming week.

We do not add water to the *Havdalah* wine.

Some start here:

אָנָּא ana ב"ן יְהֹוָהאדנילאהדונהי Adonai הוֹשִׁיעָה hoshi'a יהוה וע"ע נהורין אָ na׃

אָנָּא ana ב"ן יְהֹוָהאדנילאהדונהי Adonai הוֹשִׁיעָה hoshi'a יהוה וע"ע נהורין אָ na׃

אָנָּא ana ב"ן יְהֹוָהאדנילאהדונהי Adonai הַצְלִיחָה hatzlicha אָ na׃

אָנָּא ana ב"ן יְהֹוָהאדנילאהדונהי Adonai הַצְלִיחָה hatzlicha אָ na׃

הַצְלִיחֵנוּ hatzlichenu. הַצְלִיחַ hatzli'ach דְּרָכֵינוּ deracheinu. הַצְלִיחַ hatzli'ach

לִמּוּדֵינוּ limudenu. וְשַׁלַּח ushlach בְּרָכָה beracha רְוָחָה revacha

וְהַצְלָחָה vehatzlacha בְּכָל bechol ב"ן, לכב מַעֲשֵׂה ma'ase יָדֵינוּ yadenu,

כַּדִכְתִיב kedichtiv׃ יִשָּׂא yisa בְרָכָה veracha מֵאֵת me'et ר"ת יבמ, ב"ן

יְהֹוָהאדנילאהדונהי Adonai וּצְדָקָה utzdaka ע"ה ריבוע אלהים; יהה מֵאֱלֹהֵי melohei

יִשְׁעוֹ yish'o ילה; דמב, ס"ת יהוה ע"ה עצכינה; ס"ת יהוה ע"ה מלה לַיְּהוּדִים layehudim׃

הָיְתָה hayta אוֹרָה ora וְשִׂמְחָה vesimcha וְשָׂשׂוֹן vesason וִיקָר vikar,

וּכְתִיב uchtiv׃ וַיְהִי vayhi דָוִד David לְכָל lechol יה אדני דְּרָכָיו derachav

מַשְׂכִּיל maskil וַיְהֹוָהאדנילאהדונהי vadonai עִמּוֹ imo׃ כֵּן ken יִהְיֶה yihye ""

עִמָּנוּ imanu ריבוע ס"ג, ע"ה קס"א ו"ד אותיות ע"ה קס"א קנ"א קמ"ג׃ תָּמִיד tamid ע"ה קס"א קנ"א קמ"ג׃

Continue "*kos yeshu'ot esa...*" on the bottom of the next page.

HAVDALAH OF SATURDAY NIGHT

"Please, Lord, save us. Please, Lord, save us. Please, Lord, give us success. Please, Lord, give us success." (Psalms 118:25) Give us success, make our ways successful, make our studies successful, and send blessing and tranquility to all the work of our hands, as it was written: 'He shall receive blessing from Lord and righteousness from the God of his salvation." (Psalms 24:5) "And to the Judeans it was Light and gladness and joy and honor." (Esther 8:16) And it was also written: "And David was successful in all his ways and the Lord is with him. May He be so with us always." (I Samuel 18:14)

Havdalah of Saturday Night

Meditation for spiritual memory (before saying *Havdalah*):

משבענא עליך פורה שר של שכוחה שתסיר לב טפש ממני
ותשליכהו על טורי רומיא ארמיא רמיא מיא ימ"ס מ"ס ס'.

וְנֹחַ veNo'ach מָצָא matza וְחֵן chen מילוי ריבוע מ"ה, מוזי
בְּעֵינֵי be'enei יְהֹוָאדֹנָהִאהְדֹונָהי Adonai ריבוע מ"ה:

הִנֵּה hineh אֵל el יא"י (מילוי דס"ג) יְשׁוּעָתִי yeshu'ati אֶבְטַח evtach
וְלֹא velo אֶפְחָד efchad כִּי ki עָזִּי ozi אלהים ע"ה, אהיה אדני ע"ה וְזִמְרָת vezimrat
יָהּ Yah הֲהַה יְהֹוָאדֹנָהִאהְדֹונָהי Adonai וַיְהִי vayehi לִי li לִישׁוּעָה lishu'a:
וּשְׁאַבְתֶּם ush'avtem מַיִם mayim בְּשָׂשׂוֹן besason מִמַּעַיְנֵי mima'aynei
הַיְשׁוּעָה hayeshu'a: לַיהֹוָאדֹנָהִאהְדֹונָהי ladonai הַיְשׁוּעָה hayeshu'a עַל al
עַמְּךָ amecha בִרְכָתֶךָ virchatecha סֶלָה sela: יְהֹוָאדֹנָהִאהְדֹונָהי Adonai
צְבָאוֹת Tzeva'ot עִמָּנוּ imanu ריבוע פני שכינה ס"ג, קס"א ע"ה ור אותיות
מִשְׂגָּב misgav מהש, ע"ב בריבוע קס"א, אל שדי, ד"פ אלהים ע"ה לָנוּ lanu אלהים, אהיה אדני
אֱלֹהֵי Elohei מילוי ע"ב, ; ילה, דמב יַעֲקֹב Yaakov י הויות, יאהדונהי אידהנויה סֶלָה sela:
יְהֹוָאדֹנָהִאהְדֹונָהי Adonai צְבָאוֹת Tzeva'ot פני שכינה אַשְׁרֵי ashrei אָדָם adam מ"ה;
בֹּטֵחַ bote'ach בָּךְ bach אדם בוטח בך = אמן (יאהדונהי) ע"ה; תפארת אשרי צבאות יהוה
יְהֹוָאדֹנָהִאהְדֹונָהי Adonai: הוֹשִׁיעָה hoshi'a ע"ב מילוי ע"ה: בוטח בך = יהוה ויש"ע נהורין
הַמֶּלֶךְ hamelech ר"ת יהה יַעֲנֵנוּ ya'anenu בְיוֹם veyom ע"ה נגד, מזבוז, זן, אל יהוה
קָרְאֵנוּ kor'enu ר"ת יב"ק, אלהים יהוה = אהיה אדני יהוה; ס"ת = ב"ן ועם כ' דהמלך = ע"ב:
לַיְּהוּדִים layehudim מלה הָיְתָה hay'ta אוֹרָה ora וְשִׂמְחָה vesimcha
וְשָׂשֹׂן vesason וִיקָר vikar כֵּן ken תִּהְיֶה tihye לָנוּ lanu אלהים, אהיה אדני:
כּוֹס kos אלהים, אהיה אדני; ובמילוי (כף וו סמך) = עסמ"ב, הברכה (למתק ח' המלכים שמתו)
יְשׁוּעוֹת yeshu'ot אֶשָּׂא esa וּבְשֵׁם uvshem יְהֹוָאדֹנָהִאהְדֹונָהי Adonai אֶקְרָא ekra:

"Behold God is my salvation, I will trust and not be afraid. Indeed, the Lord is my strength and my song and He has become my salvation. You shall draw water with joy from the wells of salvation." *(Isaiah 12:2-3)* "Salvation belongs to the Lord, may Your blessings be upon Your people, Selah." *(Psalms 3:9)* "The Lord of Hosts is with us, the God of Jacob is a refuge for us, Selah." *(Psalms 84:13)* "Lord of Hosts, happy is the man who trusts in You. Lord save us; may the King answer us on the day we call." *(Psalms 20:10)* "The Judeans had radiance and happiness, joy and honor." *(Esther 8:16)* "So may it be for us. I will raise the cup of salvations and invoke the Name of the Lord." *(Psalms 116:13)*

Havdalah of Saturday Night

סַבְרִי savri מָרָנָן (ה' דחסדים וה' דגבורות) maranan עם י"פ יהוה

(The others reply :) לְחַיִּים lechayim אהיה אהיה יהוה, בינה ע"ה

Bore Peri HaGefen

בָּרוּךְ baruch אַתָּה Ata יְהֹוָהאדניאהדונהי Adonai (יוד הי ויו הי) אֱלֹהֵינוּ Elohenu יל"ה מֶלֶךְ melech הָעוֹלָם ha'olam בּוֹרֵא bore פְּרִי peri הַגָּפֶן׃ hagefen

Bore Atzei Besamim

Havdalah includes smelling the fragrance of the myrtle branch to fill the void created by the departure of the extra soul that was present within us throughout the Shabbat. When we connect to the sweet aroma of the leaves of the myrtle branches, the additional soul leaves. The instant it does, Satan is back. For this reason, we often experience confusion and find it easy to lose our temper Saturday evening as the Satan works overtime to regain a foothold in our lives. As this time is the metaphysical seed for the coming week, it is especially important to maintain a positive consciousness and not react to chaos. (If you do not have a myrtle branch you can use another source of natural fragrance.)

You should take one bundle of the three myrtles (the one that you used on *Shabbat*) and meditate that they correspond to *Nefesh, Ruach* and *Neshamah* in order to save the energy of the additional soul (from all three aspects) of *Shabbat* and that is done right now by these three myrtles and the action of smelling them. Hold the myrtles in your right hand and when you smell them inhale their fragrance deeply into your nostrils three times (corresponding to *Nefesh, Ruach* and *Neshamah*). Also meditate on the four words as follows (without pronouncing them):

רֵיחַ נִיחוֹחַ אִשֶּׁה לַיְהֹוָהאדניאהדונהי׃

בָּרוּךְ baruch אַתָּה Ata יְהֹוָהאדניאהדונהי Adonai (יוד הי ואו הי) אֱלֹהֵינוּ Elohenu יל"ה מֶלֶךְ melech הָעוֹלָם ha'olam בּוֹרֵא bore עֲצֵי atzei (עִשְׂבֵי isbei) (מִינֵי minei) בְּשָׂמִים vesamim׃

Bore Me'orei HaEsh

We make our right hand into a fist, folding the thumb under the four fingers, and look at the reflection of the light from the *Havdalah* candle on the nails of our four fingers. The ancient kabbalists teach that the body of Adam was actually made of this enamel of the nails. As *Shabbat* concludes, negative forces and entities immediately swarm around us like hungry predators trying to rob us of our Light. The first place they strike are the fingers, specifically the fingernails. The candlelight reflected in our nails wipes all these negative forces and entities out.

With your permission, my masters. (The others reply) *To life [Binah.]*

Bore Peri HaGefen
Blessed are You, Lord, our God, the King of the world, Who creates the fruit of the vine.

Bore Atzei Besamim
Blessed are You, Lord, our God, the King of the world, Who creates the plants (spices) (varieties) of fragrance.

Havdalah of Saturday Night

We use a special candle made of wax that is lit like a torch for the connection with this blessing. You should fold the top of the right hand fingers into your right palm and cover the thumb underneath. The fingers should be folded tightly towards your face and towards the candle. You should hold the right hand and the fingers up by bending your elbow and facing your fingers towards your face and then you should fold the tops of the fingers into the palm and you should straighten the back of your fingers up against the candle. Indeed your fingers should be folded down on top of the thumb as it is mentioned and you should look only at the reflection of the Light that shines from your fingernails and not at the rest of your fingers. The reason for this is because within the four fingers there are 2500 outside forces that suck energy from the fingers, so we show them in front of the flame of the candle (which represents the *Shechinah*) to subdue them. We bless *bore me'orei ha'esh* because we want to connect to the Creator and not to them.

בָּרוּךְ baruch אַתָּה Ata יְהֹוָה֒אֲדֹנָי֒אֱלֹהִים Adonai (יוד הא ואו הא) אֱלֹהֵינוּ Elohenu ילה מֶלֶךְ melech הָעוֹלָם ha'olam בּוֹרֵא bore מְאוֹרֵי me'orei הָאֵשׁ ha'esh שאה:

Hamavdil

The final blessing separates the good from evil, giving us the ability to distinguish between these two forces in every area of our life.

בָּרוּךְ baruch אַתָּה Ata יְהֹוָה֒אֲדֹנָי֒אֱלֹהִים Adonai אֱלֹהֵינוּ Elohenu ילה מֶלֶךְ melech הָעוֹלָם ha'olam הַמַּבְדִּיל hamavdil בֵּין ben קֹדֶשׁ kodesh לְחוֹל lechol וּבֵין uven אוֹר or רו, א״ס לְחוֹשֶׁךְ lechoshech עוך נצוצות של ו׳ המלכים וּבֵין uven יִשְׂרָאֵל Yisrael לָעַמִּים la'amim וּבֵין uven יוֹם yom ע״ה נגד, מזלוח, זן, אל יהוה הַשְּׁבִיעִי hashevi'i לְשֵׁשֶׁת lesheshet יְמֵי yemei הַמַּעֲשֶׂה hama'ase ♦ בָּרוּךְ baruch אַתָּה Ata יְהֹוָה֒אֲדֹנָי֒אֱלֹהִים Adonai הַמַּבְדִּיל hamavdil בֵּין ben קֹדֶשׁ kodesh לְחוֹל lechol (יוד הה וו הה) (קליפת נגה):

The person performing the *Havdalah* should sit and drink a *revi'it* (approximately three ounces). Women can do Havdalah if there is no man present to do this for them. But it is recommended that they would do *Havdalah* on grape juice.

After drinking a *rev'it* of the wine, pour the remaining wine in the cup over the candle to extinguish it, meditating to extinguish the negative forces. Breathe in the smoke from the candle, meditating to connect to the smell of the Garden of Eden, and draw protection from evil spirits. Our teacher, the Rav, would dip his right index finger into the *Havdalah* wine left in the dish, touch both index fingers and then dab them next to each eye for greater spiritual and physical vision (see Babylonian Talmud, Tractate Berachot 43:2), and also in his pockets to draw sustenance.

Then say the last blessing (pages 117-119)

Bore Me'orei HaEsh
Blessed are You, Lord, our God, King of the world, Who creates the luminaries of fire.

Hamavdil
Blessed are You, Lord, our God, King of the world, Who separates between the Holy and the mundane and between Light and darkness, and between Israel and the other nations, and between the Seventh Day and the six days of action. Blessed are You, Lord, Who separates between the Holy and the mundane.

Fourth Meal – Melaveh Malkah (Escorting the Queen)

According to the *Zohar*, King David was destined to live for a short time on Earth and die on *Shabbat*. Adam foresaw this and gave King David seventy years from his own life so that David could accomplish all that he was meant to accomplish spiritually in this world. At the conclusion of every *Shabbat*, an unimaginably appreciative King David would sing praises and offer thanks to God and to Adam for giving him the gift of life. This gift of life is connected to the energy of immortality. Thus, every Saturday night, we re-enact King David's actions, employing the same technology he used. It is called the Fourth Meal or the Meal of King David, also known as Escorting the Queen. The Queen is the Light we experienced on *Shabbat* and now we are escorting Her out of our dimension as She returns to the 99 Percent Reality.

The Luz Bone

When Adam and Eve were first created, they were immortal. After eating from the Tree of Knowledge, their Desire to Receive created separation between them and the 99 Percent Reality. Death was born. Kabbalah tells us that there was one part of the body of Adam and Eve that was never nourished from the Tree of Knowledge, and therefore does not know death. It is called the Luz bone and it is found at the base of the skull. The Luz bone is immortal.

The secret of the Luz bone appears in other spiritual teachings as well. The prophet Muhammad said a special rain will come at the End of Days that will activate this bone and bring about resurrection. The *Zohar* says (See Sulam Commentary on Zohar Chayei Sarah 155) virtually the same thing, referring to the dew that will fall and ignite the resurrection through this unique bone. The kabbalists tell us the Luz bone is not nourished from any food during the week but only from the food we eat during the Fourth Meal; and only the Luz Bone is nourished at this time.

Consequently, the Light that is being released through the food of the Fourth Meal is obviously from the Tree of Life, the energy of immortality. Therefore, whoever participates in this meal connects to immortality and the power of the Resurrection of the Dead.

> The additional soul does not leave immediately. It only leaves after the Fourth Meal and this is why you should not eat or study spiritual matters until after the Fourth Meal.
>
> There are 31 kings in the *klipot* that Joshua conquered against 31 holy hours and this is the secret of *El* (31) *melech yoshev*. This means that from the midday of Friday until the night is six hours, *Shabbat* itself is 24 hours, and altogether this makes 30 hours. With the additional hour of the Fourth Meal, which is the meal of King David the Messiah, it adds up to 31. If a person does not do the meal of King David he leaves one *klipa* that is not surrendered. So after *Havdalah*, a person should perform the Fourth Meal on *mezonot* or bread and he should say:

דָא da הִיא hee סְעוּדָתָא se'udata

דְדָוִד deDavid מַלְכָּא malka מְשִׁיחָא meshicha

בִּזְכוּתוֹ bizchuto נִינָּצֵל ninatzel מֵחִיבּוּט michibut הַקֶבֶר hakever:

Blessings over the food can be found on pages 91-92.

Fourth Meal – Melaveh Malkah (Escorting the Queen)

This is the meal of David the anointed king.
With his merit we will be saved from the torture in the grave.

Fourth Meal – Melaveh Malkah (Escorting the Queen)

Hamavdil (He Who Separates)

Hamavdil was written by Rav Yitzchak Hakatan (the Small Isaac) Ibn Ghiyyat (Spain, 11th Century), as part of the prayer of *Neilah* that is recited at the end of *Yom Kippur* to awaken a desire for transformation and spiritual cleansing. The *Zohar* (see Zohar Chadash, Vayeshev 44) says that Saturday night is a time when the Light of the Messiah can appear. But, if we are not pure we cannot benefit from this Light. Therefore, the kabbalists added this song, which has the power of cleansing, to the *Melaveh Malkah* connection as it can help us prepare for the Light of Messiah.

הַמַּבְדִּיל hamavdil בֵּין ben קֹדֶשׁ kodesh לְחוֹל lechol ♦ וְחַטֹּאתֵינוּ chatotenu
הוּא hu יִמְחוֹל yimchol ♦ זַרְעֵנוּ zar'enu וְכַסְפֵּנוּ vechaspenu
יַרְבֶּה yarbe כַּחוֹל kachol ♦ וְכַכּוֹכָבִים vechakochavim בַּלַּיְלָה balayla ♦
יוֹם yom פָּנָה pana כְּצֵל ketzel תֹּמֶר tomer ♦ אֶקְרָא ekra לָאֵל laEl
עָלַי alai גּוֹמֵר gomer ♦ יוֹם yom אֲשֶׁר asher אָמַר amar שׁוֹמֵר shomer ♦
אָתָא ata בֹקֶר voker וְגַם vegam לַיְלָה layla ♦
צִדְקָתְךָ tzidkatcha כְּהַר kehar תָּבוֹר tavor ♦ עַל al חֲטָאַי chata'ai
עָבֹר avor תַּעֲבוֹר ta'avor ♦ כְּיוֹם keyom אֶתְמוֹל etmol כִּי ki יַעֲבוֹר ya'avor ♦
וְאַשְׁמוּרָה ve'ashmura בַּלַּיְלָה balayla ♦
וְחָלְפָה chalfa עוֹנַת onat מִנְחָתִי minchati ♦ מִי mi
יִתֵּן yiten מְנוּחָתִי menuchati ♦ יָגַעְתִּי yagati בְּאַנְחָתִי be'anchati ♦
אַשְׂחֶה asche בְּכָל bechol לַיְלָה layla ♦

Hamavdil (He Who Separates)

He Who separates between the Holy (Shabbat) and the secular (the rest of the week), may He forgive our sins; may He increase our offspring and wealth like the sand, like the stars at night [as it was promised to Abraham (Genesis 22:17)]. The day passed like a date-palm's shadow; I shall call out "to God, who vindicates me." (Psalms 57:3) The day about which the Guardian [the Holy One, Blessed Be He] said: "The morning comes [the redemption from Egypt], and also the night [the four exiles and the Final Redemption that follows them.] (Based on Isaiah 21:12; and see also Zohar Terumah 79) Your righteousness as Mount Tavor [the Attribute of Mercy is like a mountain and the Attribute of Judgment is like abyss (see Arvei Nachal on Beresheet)]; may You disregard my sins; like the yesterday that has passed, and a watch in the night (based on Psalms 90:4). The period of my gift [in Hebrew also midday, meaning time is lost] is over; who will grant me my rest? I am exhausted with my lament, I drench each night [as crying cleanses the blemishes of the in the internal organs and purifies them from the stains of the sins] (based on Psalms 6:7).

Fourth Meal – Melaveh Malkah (Escorting the Queen)

li לִי petach פְּתַח ♦yuntal יִנָּטֵל bal בַּל shima שִׁמְעָה koli קוֹלִי

♦tal טַל nimla נִמְלָא sheroshi שֶׁרֹאשִׁי ♦hamenutal הַמְּנוּטָל sha'ar שַׁעַר

♦layla לָיְלָה resisei רְסִיסֵי kevutzotai קְוֻצּוֹתַי

tena תְּנָה ashave'a אֲשַׁוֵּעַ ♦ve'ayom וְאָיוֹם nora נוֹרָא he'ater הֵעָתֵר

♦yom יוֹם be'erev בְּעֶרֶב beneshef בְּנֶשֶׁף ♦fidyom פִּדְיוֹם

♦layla לָיְלָה be'ishon בְּאִישׁוֹן

orach אֹרַח ♦hoshi'eni הוֹשִׁיעֵנִי Yah יָהּ keraticha קְרָאתִיךָ

♦tevatzeni תְּבַצְּעֵנִי midalut מִדַּלּוּת ♦todi'eni תּוֹדִיעֵנִי chayim חַיִּים

♦layla לָיְלָה ve'ad וְעַד miyom מִיּוֹם

yomru יֹאמְרוּ pen פֶּן ♦ma'asai מַעֲשַׂי tinuf טִנּוּף taher טַהֵר

♦osai עוֹשַׂי eloha אֱלוֹהַּ aye אַיֵּה ♦machisai מַכְעִיסַי

♦balayla בַּלַּיְלָה zemirot זְמִירוֹת noten נֹתֵן

al עַל na נָא selach סְלַח ♦kachomer כַּחוֹמֶר veyadcha בְּיָדְךָ nachnu אֲנַחְנוּ

♦omer אוֹמֵר yabia יַבִּיעַ leyom לְיוֹם yom יוֹם ♦vachomer וָחוֹמֶר kal קַל

♦lelayla לְלַיְלָה velayla וְלַיְלָה

chatotenu וְחַטֹּאתֵינוּ ♦lechol לְחוֹל kodesh קֹדֶשׁ ben בֵּין hamavdil הַמַּבְדִּיל

vechaspenu וְכַסְפֵּנוּ zar'enu זַרְעֵנוּ ♦yimchol יִמְחוֹל hu הוּא

♦balayla בַּלַּיְלָה vechakochavim וְכַכּוֹכָבִים ♦kachol כַּחוֹל yarbe יַרְבֶּה

Hear my voice; let it not be taken [by the angels]; open for me the Supernal Gate, "for my head is filled with dew, my locks with dewdrops at night." (Song of Songs 5:2) Please comply, Awesome and Frightful (see Zohar Terumah 11); I cry out, 'Bring the Redemption;' "at twilight, in the evening, in the blackness of night." (Proverbs 7:9) I called to You, Yah, save me; let me know the way of life (based on Psalms 16:11); spare me from poverty [or exile] (based on Isaiah 38:12) from day to night. Cleanse the filth of my deeds, lest my tormentors say: "Where is God [אֱלוֹהַּ: אל—Chesed, ו—Zeir Anpin and ה—Malchut], Who made me [as They make man and model him daily (Zohar Vayikra 395-400)], Who gives songs in the night [Malchut is constantly praising in order to receive the Supernal joyous Light of Zeir Anpin, because of this great joy that is aroused by reciting praises (Zohar Terumah 862)]?" (Job 35:10) We are in Your hands like clay ["What is this clay? It is the material of glass. Although it may break, it is mended and may be used again." (Zohar Vayishlach 253)]; please forgive for minor and serious; day to day utter words, as well as each night to night (based on Psalms 19:3). He Who separates between the Holy (Shabbat) and the secular (the rest of the week), may He forgive our sins; may He increase our offspring and wealth like the sand, like the stars at night.

Fourth Meal – Melaveh Malkah (Escorting the Queen)

Yehi Hachodesh Hazeh (May this Month Be)

Yehi Hachodesh Hazeh is an excerpt from a poem (*Bemotza'ei Yom Menuchah*) written by Rav Yaakov of Lunil (France, 12th Century). In it he expresses the difficulties and challenges we experience in our exile so as to awaken and increase our desire for the coming of the Final Redemption.

We sing only the last part of the song as it speaks about Saturday night as the time for the Final Redemption, the appearance of Elijah the prophet and the joy and the happiness that will surround us when Messiah will come.

kinevu'at כִּנְבוּאַת, hazeh הֲזֶה, hachodesh הַחֹדֶשׁ yehi יְהִי

,zeh זֶה bevayit בְּבַיִת veyishma וְיִשָּׁמַע ,choze חוֹזֶה avi אָבִי

⬥simcha שִׂמְחָה vekol וְקוֹל sason שָׂשׂוֹן kol קוֹל

amitz אַמִּיץ ,mish'alotenu מִשְׁאֲלוֹתֵינוּ yemaleh יְמַלֵּא chazak וְחָזָק

yishlach יִשְׁלַח vehu וְהוּא ,bakashatenu בַּקָּשָׁתֵנוּ ya'ase יַעֲשֶׂה

⬥vehatzlacha וְהַצְלָחָה beracha בְּרָכָה ,yadenu יָדֵינוּ bema'ase בְּמַעֲשֵׂה

shimcha שִׁמְךָ ,gila גִּלָה yom יוֹם bemotzaei בְּמוֹצָאֵי

tishbi תִּשְׁבִּי shelach שְׁלַח ,alila עֲלִילָה nora נוֹרָא

⬥vahanacha וְהֲנָחָה sason שָׂשׂוֹן revach רֶוַח ,segula סְגֻלָּה le'am לְעַם

az אָז sefatenu שְׂפָתֵינוּ ,verina וְרִנָּה tzahola צָהֳלָה kol קוֹל

,na נָא hoshia הוֹשִׁיעָה Adonai יְהוָה ana אָנָּא ,teranena תְּרַנֶּנָה

⬥na נָא hatzlicha הַצְלִיחָה Adonai יְהוָה ana אָנָּא

Yehi Hachodesh Hazeh (May this Month Be)

May this month (Exodus 12:1) be as prophesied by the father of the seers [Moses (see Midrash Vayikra Rabba 1)]; and may there be heard in this house [the Temple] "the sound of gladness, the sound of joy." (Jeremiah 33:11) The Mighty One [about these Name and appellatives of God see Zohar Pinchas 858-869] shall fulfill our requests, the Strong One shall implement our pleas; and He shall send into all our handiwork, blessing, prosperity and success. At the departure of the day of gladness, may You, Whose Name is Awesome in Deed, send the Tishbi to the chosen nation comfort, gladness and relief. The sound of jubilation and song shall our lips then sing out. We beseech You, Lord, save us now. We beseech You, Lord, give us success now.

FOURTH MEAL – MELAVEH MALKAH (ESCORTING THE QUEEN)

AMAR HASHEM LEYAAKOV (THE LORD TOLD JACOB)

The *Talmud* (Babylonian Talmud, Pesachim 88:1) says that the rebuilding of the Third Temple and the coming of the Final Redemption will be with the merit of Jacob the Patriarch. The *Zohar* (Hashmatot Zohar A, 254) asks about the verse (Micah 7:15) "As in the days when you came out of Egypt, I will show him marvelous," who is 'him'? And answers: "Jacob the Patriarch." Jacob the Patriarch guaranties the Final Redemption.

The song is written according to the Hebrew alphabet, and each of the sentences is from the Bible. In each sentence, God tells Jacob not to fear the power of the negative side and promises him that the Final Redemption will come. Kabbalist Rav Israel of Rujin (Ukraine, 19th century) says that in each line God gives Jacob a different reason for the Final Redemption to come, but Jacob is not convinced and still afraid that it will not come (Heaven forbid). Only in the last line, when God tells Jacob that the "truth" will guarantee the Final Redemption does Jacob then have certainty in the coming of the Final Redemption.

Kabbalist Rashi (Rav Shlomo son of Isaac, France, 11th century) says (Leviticus 26:42): "The name Jacob appears five times in the Bible with the letter *Vav* (יעקוב instead of יעקב) and the name Elijah appears five times in the Bible without the letter *Vav* (אליה instead of אליהו). The reason is that Jacob took the letter *Vav* as a guarantee that Elijah the Prophet will come and bring the Final Redemption." Kabbalist Maharal (Rav Shlomo Luria, Prague, 16th century) asks (Gur Aryeh on Ibid), "If a guarantee is taken from someone untrustworthy to assure his commitments, does Rashi consider Elijah unreliable?" And he answers, "Elijah was created for one purpose: to redeem us (the sons of Jacob). Elijah's essence is the Final Redemption. As long as Elijah's purpose is not actualized, his name cannot be completed, so Jacob is holding the *Vav* to complete Elijah's name thus completing his purpose." The Maharal continues and asks, "Why five times, is once not enough?" and he replies (based on the Tractate Ohalot that states: There are 30 pieces in the palm of the hand, and five times the letter *Vav* equals 30), "Five letter *Vavs* look like five fingers in the palm of a hand, which symbolizes a handshake guarantee between Jacob and Elijah."

אָמַר amar יְהֹוָה Adonai לְיַעֲקֹב leYa'akov◆

אַל al תִּירָא tira עַבְדִּי avdi יַעֲקֹב Ya'akov◆

בּוֹחֵר bachar יְהֹוָה Adonai בְּיַעֲקֹב beYa'akov◆

אַל al תִּירָא tira עַבְדִּי avdi יַעֲקֹב Ya'akov◆

גָּאַל ga'al יְהֹוָה Adonai אֶת et יַעֲקֹב Ya'akov◆

אַל al תִּירָא tira עַבְדִּי avdi יַעֲקֹב Ya'akov◆

דָּרַךְ darach כּוֹכָב kochav מִיַּעֲקֹב miYa'akov◆

אַל al תִּירָא tira עַבְדִּי avdi יַעֲקֹב Ya'akov◆

AMAR HASHEM LEYAAKOV – THE LORD TOLD JACOB

א *The Lord said to Jacob* (based on Isaiah 29:22): "Do not fear, My servant, Jacob." (Jeremiah 46:27)
ב *The Lord chose Jacob* (based on Psalms 135:4); "Do not fear, My servant, Jacob." (Jeremiah 46:27)
ג *The Lord redeemed Jacob* (based on Isaiah 44:23); "Do not fear, My servant, Jacob." (Jeremiah 46:27)
ד *"A star will shoot forth from Jacob"* (Numbers 24:17); "Do not fear, My servant, Jacob." (Jeremiah 46:27)

Fourth Meal – Melaveh Malkah (Escorting the Queen)

הַבָּאִים haba'im יַשְׁרֵשׁ yashresh יַעֲקֹב Ya'akov♦

♦Ya'akov יַעֲקֹב avdi עַבְדִּי tira תִּירָא al אַל

וַיֵּרְד veyerd מִיַּעֲקֹב miYa'akov♦

♦Ya'akov יַעֲקֹב avdi עַבְדִּי tira תִּירָא al אַל

זְכֹר zechor זֹאת zot לְיַעֲקֹב leYa'akov♦

♦Ya'akov יַעֲקֹב avdi עַבְדִּי tira תִּירָא al אַל

וְחֶדְוַת chedvat יְשׁוּעוֹת yeshu'ot יַעֲקֹב Ya'akov♦

♦Ya'akov יַעֲקֹב avdi עַבְדִּי tira תִּירָא al אַל

טוֹבוּ tovu אֹהָלֶיךָ ohalecha יַעֲקֹב Ya'akov♦

♦Ya'akov יַעֲקֹב avdi עַבְדִּי tira תִּירָא al אַל

יוֹרוּ yoru מִשְׁפָּטֶיךָ mishpatecha לְיַעֲקֹב leYa'akov♦

♦Ya'akov יַעֲקֹב avdi עַבְדִּי tira תִּירָא al אַל

כִּי ki לֹא lo נַחַשׁ nachash בְּיַעֲקֹב beYa'akov♦

♦Ya'akov יַעֲקֹב avdi עַבְדִּי tira תִּירָא al אַל

לֹא lo הִבִּיט hibit אָוֶן aven בְּיַעֲקֹב beYa'akov♦

♦Ya'akov יַעֲקֹב avdi עַבְדִּי tira תִּירָא al אַל

מִי mi מָנָה mana עֲפַר afar יַעֲקֹב Ya'akov♦

♦Ya'akov יַעֲקֹב avdi עַבְדִּי tira תִּירָא al אַל

ה "Those of Jacob who came, took root" (Isaiah 27:6); "Do not fear, My servant, Jacob." (Jeremiah 46:27)
ו "A ruler will emerge from Jacob" (Numbers 24:19); "Do not fear, My servant, Jacob." (Jeremiah 46:27)
ז Remember these things for Jacob (based on Isaiah 44:21); "Do not fear, My servant, Jacob." (Jeremiah 46:27)
ח The joy of salvation to Jacob (based on Isaiah 44:21); "Do not fear, My servant, Jacob." (Jeremiah 46:27)
ט "Your tents are good, Jacob" (Numbers 24:5); "Do not fear, My servant, Jacob." (Jeremiah 46:27)
י "They shall teach Your laws to Jacob" (Deuteronomy 33:10); "Do not fear, My servant, Jacob." (Jeremiah 46:27)
כ "For there is no sorcery among Jacob" (Numbers 23:23); "Do not fear, My servant, Jacob." (Jeremiah 46:27)
ל "He saw no iniquity in Jacob" (Ibid 21); "Do not fear, My servant, Jacob." (Jeremiah 46:27)
מ "Who can count the dust of Jacob" (Ibid 10); "Do not fear, My servant, Jacob." (Jeremiah 46:27)

Fourth Meal – Melaveh Malkah (Escorting the Queen)

נִשְׁבַּע nishba יְהֹוָה Adonai לְיַעֲקֹב leYa'akov ♦

♦ Ya'akov יַעֲקֹב avdi עַבְדִי tira תִּירָא al אַל

סְלַח selach נָא na לַעֲוֹן la'avon יַעֲקֹב Ya'akov ♦

♦ Ya'akov יַעֲקֹב avdi עַבְדִי tira תִּירָא al אַל

עַתָּה ata הָשֵׁב hashev שְׁבוּת shevut יַעֲקֹב Ya'akov ♦

♦ Ya'akov יַעֲקֹב avdi עַבְדִי tira תִּירָא al אַל

פָּדָה pada יְהֹוָה Adonai אֶת et יַעֲקֹב Ya'akov ♦

♦ Ya'akov יַעֲקֹב avdi עַבְדִי tira תִּירָא al אַל

צַוֵּה tzaveh יְשׁוּעוֹת yeshu'ot יַעֲקֹב Ya'akov ♦

♦ Ya'akov יַעֲקֹב avdi עַבְדִי tira תִּירָא al אַל

קוֹל kol קוֹל kol יַעֲקֹב Ya'akov ♦

♦ Ya'akov יַעֲקֹב avdi עַבְדִי tira תִּירָא al אַל

רָנִּי rani וְשִׂמְחִי vesimchi לְיַעֲקֹב leYa'akov ♦

♦ Ya'akov יַעֲקֹב avdi עַבְדִי tira תִּירָא al אַל

שָׁב shav יְהֹוָה Adonai אֶת et שְׁבוּת shevut יַעֲקֹב Ya'akov ♦

♦ Ya'akov יַעֲקֹב avdi עַבְדִי tira תִּירָא al אַל

תִּתֵּן titen אֱמֶת emet לְיַעֲקֹב leYa'akov ♦

♦ Ya'akov יַעֲקֹב avdi עַבְדִי tira תִּירָא al אַל

נ *The Lord swore to Jacob* (based on Exodus 32:13); *"Do not fear, My servant, Jacob."* (Jeremiah 46:27)

ס *Please forgive the sin of Jacob* (based on Amos 7:2); *"Do not fear, My servant, Jacob."* (Jeremiah 46:27)

ע *Return now the captivity of Jacob* (based on Ezekiel 39:25); *"Do not fear, My servant, Jacob."* (Jeremiah 46:27)

פ *"The Lord has delivered Jacob"* (Jeremiah 31:10); *"Do not fear, My servant, Jacob."* (Jeremiah 46:27)

צ *"Command salvations of Jacob"* (psalms 44:5); *"Do not fear, My servant, Jacob."* (Jeremiah 46:27)

ק *"The voice is the voice of Jacob"* (Genesis 27:22); *"Do not fear, My servant, Jacob."* (Jeremiah 46:27)

ר *Song and joy for Jacob* (based on Jeremiah 31:6); *"Do not fear, My servant, Jacob."* (Jeremiah 46:27)

ש *May the Lord return the captivity of Jacob* (based on Nahum 2:3); *"Do not fear, My servant, Jacob."* (Jeremiah 46:27)

ת *"You will give truth for Jacob"* (Micah 7:20); *"Do not fear, My servant, Jacob."* (Jeremiah 46:27)

Fourth Meal – Verses for Success

Veyiten Lecha (And may God Give you)

The Ari would recite these verses immediately after Shabbat to start the week off with an extra surge of positivity. These verses also help arouse greater financial sustenance and abundance.

וְיִתֶּן veyiten לְךָ lecha הָאֱלֹהִים haElohim אהיה אדני ; ילה מִטַּל mital יוד הא ואו, כוזו
הַשָּׁמַיִם hashamayim י"פ טל, י"פ כוזו וּמִשְׁמַנֵּי umishmanei הָאָרֶץ ha'aretz אלהים דההין ע"ה
וְרֹב verov דָּגָן dagan וְתִירֹשׁ vetirosh: יַעַבְדוּךָ ya'avducha עַמִּים amim
וְיִשְׁתַּחֲווּ veyishtachavu לְךָ lecha לְאֻמִּים le'umim הֱוֵה heve גְבִיר gevir
לְאַחֶיךָ le'achecha וְיִשְׁתַּחֲווּ veyishtachavu לְךָ lecha בְּנֵי benei אִמֶּךָ imecha
אֹרְרֶיךָ orarecha אָרוּר arur וּמְבָרֲכֶיךָ umvarachecha בָּרוּךְ baruch:
וְאֵל veEl (מילוי דס"ג) יא"י שַׁדַּי Shadai אל שדי = מהש, ע"ב בריבוע קס"א, ד"פ אלהים ע"ה
יְבָרֵךְ yevarech עסמ"ב, הברכה (למתק את ז' המלכים שמותו) אֹתְךָ otcha וְיַפְרְךָ veyafrecha
וְיַרְבֶּךָ veyarbecha וְהָיִיתָ vehayita לִקְהַל likhal עַמִּים amim: וְיִתֶּן veyiten
לְךָ lecha אֶת et בִּרְכַּת birkat אַבְרָהָם Avraham וז"פ אל, רי"ו ול"ב נתיבות החכמה,
לְךָ lecha וּלְזַרְעֲךָ ulzaracha אִתָּךְ itach רמ"ח (אברים), עסמ"ב וט"ו אותיות פשוטות
לְרִשְׁתְּךָ lerishtecha אֶת et אֶרֶץ eretz מְגֻרֶיךָ megurecha אֲשֶׁר asher נָתַן natan
אֱלֹהִים Elohim וז"פ אל, רי"ו ול"ב נתיבות החכמה, אהיה אדני ; ילה לְאַבְרָהָם leAvraham
מֵאֵל meEl יא"י (מילוי דס"ג), עסמ"ב וט"ו אותיות פשוטות, רמ"ח (אברים): אָבִיךָ avicha
וְיַעְזְרֶךָּ veyazereka וְאֵת ve'et שַׁדַּי Shadai וִיבָרֲכֶךָּ vivaracheka בִּרְכֹת birchot
שָׁמַיִם shamayim י"פ טל, י"פ כוזו מֵעָל me'al עֹלָם birchot בִּרְכֹת תְּהוֹם tehom
רֹבֶצֶת rovetzet תַּחַת tachat בִּרְכֹת birchot שָׁדַיִם shadayim וָרָחַם varacham
בִּרְכֹת birchot אברהם, וז"פ אל, רי"ו ול"ב נתיבות החכמה, רמ"ח (אברים), עסמ"ב וט"ו אותיות פשוטות:
אָבִיךָ avicha גָּבְרוּ gavru עַל al בִּרְכֹת birchot הוֹרַי horai עַד ad תַּאֲוַת ta'avat
גִּבְעֹת givot עוֹלָם olam תִּהְיֶיןָ tihyena לְרֹאשׁ lerosh ריבוע אלהים דיודין ע"ה
יוֹסֵף Yosef ציון, קנאה, ר הויות וּלְקָדְקֹד ulkodkod נְזִיר nezir אֶחָיו echav:

Veyiten Lecha (And may God Give you)

"And may God give you of the dew of the Heavens and of the fatness of the Earth, and abundant grain and wine. People will serve You and regimes will prostrate themselves to You. Be the lord of your brothers, and the offsprings of your mother will prostrate before you. They who curse you are cursed and they who bless you are blessed." (Genesis 27:28-29) "May El Shaddai bless you, make you fruitful and make you numerous, and may you be a congregation of people. May He grant you the blessing of Abraham, to you and to your offspring with you, so that you may possess the land of your sojourns that God gave to Abraham." (Genesis 28:3-4) "It is from the God of your father and He will help you and, with Shaddai, and He will bless you. Blessings of Heaven from Above, blessings of the deep crouching Below, blessings of breasts and womb. The blessings of your Father surpassed the blessings of my parents to the endless bounds of the world's hills. Let them be on Joseph's head and on the head of the one separated from his brothers." (Genesis 49:25-6)

Fourth Meal – Verses for Success

uverach וּבֵרַךְ	vehirbecha וְהִרְבֶּךָ	uverachecha וּבֵרַכְךָ	va'ahevcha וַאֲהֵבְךָ
degancha דְּגָנְךָ	admatecha אַדְמָתֶךָ	ufri וּפְרִי	vitnecha בִטְנְךָ	peri פְּרִי
alafecha אֲלָפֶיךָ	shegar שְׁגַר	veyitzharecha וְיִצְהָרֶךָ	vetiroshcha וְתִירשְׁךָ
asher אֲשֶׁר	ha'adama הָאֲדָמָה	al עַל	tzonecha צֹאנֶךָ	ve'ashterot וְעַשְׁתְּרֹת
tihye תִּהְיֶה	baruch בָּרוּךְ	lach לָךְ	latet לָתֶת	la'avotecha לַאֲבֹתֶיךָ	nishba נִשְׁבַּע
akar עָקָר	vecha בְךָ	yih'ye יִהְיֶה	lo לֹא	ha'amim הָעַמִּים	mikol מִכָּל
Adonai יְהֹוָה	vehesir וְהֵסִיר	uvivhemtecha וּבִבְהֶמְתֶּךָ	va'akara וַעֲקָרָה
madvei מַדְוֵי	vechol וְכָל	choli חֳלִי	kol כָּל	mimcha מִמְּךָ
lo לֹא	yadata יָדַעְתָּ	asher אֲשֶׁר	hara'im הָרָעִים	Mitzrayim מִצְרַיִם
son'echa שֹׂנְאֶיךָ	bechol בְּכָל	untanam וּנְתָנָם	bach בָּךְ	yesimam יְשִׂימֵם
Ata אַתָּה	uvaruch וּבָרוּךְ	ba'ir בָּעִיר	Ata אַתָּה	baruch בָּרוּךְ
ufri וּפְרִי	vitnecha בִטְנְךָ	peri פְּרִי	baruch בָּרוּךְ	basade בַּשָּׂדֶה
alafecha אֲלָפֶיךָ	shegar שְׁגַר	vehemtecha בְהֶמְתֶּךָ	ufri וּפְרִי	admat'cha אַדְמָתֶךָ
tanacha טַנְאֲךָ	baruch בָּרוּךְ	tzonecha צֹאנֶךָ	ve'ashterot וְעַשְׁתְּרוֹת
bevo'echa בְּבֹאֶךָ	Ata אַתָּה	baruch בָּרוּךְ	umishartecha וּמִשְׁאַרְתֶּךָ
Adonai יְהֹוָה	yetzav יְצַו	betzetecha בְּצֵאתֶךָ	Ata אַתָּה	uvaruch וּבָרוּךְ
uvchol וּבְכֹל	ba'asameicha בַּאֲסָמֶיךָ	haberacha הַבְּרָכָה	et אֶת	itcha אִתְּךָ
asher אֲשֶׁר	ba'aretz בָּאָרֶץ	uverachecha וּבֵרַכְךָ	yadecha יָדֶךָ	mishlach מִשְׁלַח
lach לָךְ	noten נֹתֵן	Elohecha אֱלֹהֶיךָ	Adonai יְהֹוָה
otzaro אוֹצָרוֹ	et אֶת	lecha לְךָ	Adonai יְהֹוָה	yiftach יִפְתַּח
hashamayim הַשָּׁמַיִם	et אֶת	hatov הַטּוֹב

"And He shall love you, and He shall bless you, and He shall make you numerous. He shall bless the fruit of your womb and the fruit of your land, your grain, your wine and your oil, the offspring of your cattle and the flocks of your sheep upon the land that He swore to your forefathers to give to you. Blessed shall you be above all peoples, there shall not be among you a barren man or woman, nor among your cattle. The Lord shall remove from you all illness, and all the evil sufferings of Egypt that you knew, He shall not place upon you, but He will set them upon your enemies." (Deuteronomy 7:13-15) "Blessed are you in the city, blessed are you in the field. Blessed is the fruit of your womb, the fruit of your land and the fruit of your animal, the offspring of your cattle and the flock of your sheep. Blessed is your fruit basket and your kneading trough. Blessed are you upon your arrival and blessed are you upon your departure." (Deuteronomy 28:3-6) "May the Lord command that blessing accompany you in your storehouse and wherever you set your hand. And may He bless you in the land that the Lord, your God, gives to you." (Deuteronomy 28:8) "May the Lord open for you His good treasury, the Heaven,

Fourth Meal – Verses for Success

latet **לָתֵת**	metar **מְטַר־**	artzecha **אַרְצְךָ**	be'ito **בְּעִתּוֹ**	ulvarech **וּלְבָרֵךְ**	et **אֵת**	
kol **כָּל־** יל'	ma'ase **מַעֲשֵׂה**	yadecha **יָדֶךָ**	vehilvita **וְהִלְוִיתָ**	goyim **גּוֹיִם**	rabim **רַבִּים**	
veAta **וְאַתָּה** יל'	lo **לֹא**	tilve **תִלְוֶה**:	ashrecha **אַשְׁרֶיךָ**	Yisrael **יִשְׂרָאֵל**	mi **מִי**	
chamocha **כָמוֹךָ**	am **עַם**	nosha **נוֹשַׁע**	badonai **בַּיהוה**	magen **מָגֵן**	גי"פ אל	
cherev **חֶרֶב**	va'asher **וַאֲשֶׁר־**	ezrecha **עֶזְרֶךָ** גבריאל מיכאל ר"ת; (וְיא"י מילוי דס"ג)				
ga'avatecha **גַּאֲוָתֶךָ**	veyikachashu **וְיִכָּחֲשׁוּ**	oyvecha **אֹיְבֶיךָ**	lach **לָךְ** ר"ת לאו			
veAta **וְאַתָּה**	al **עַל־**	bamotemo **בָּמוֹתֵימוֹ**	tidroch **תִדְרֹךְ**:	Yisrael **יִשְׂרָאֵל**		
nosha **נוֹשַׁע**	badonai **בַּיהוה**	teshu'at **תְּשׁוּעַת**	olamim **עוֹלָמִים**	lo **לֹא־**		
tevoshu **תֵבֹשׁוּ**	velo **וְלֹא־**	tikalmu **תִכָּלְמוּ**	ad **עַד־**	olmei **עוֹלְמֵי**	ad **עַד**:	
va'achaltem **וַאֲכַלְתֶּם**	achol **אָכוֹל**	vesavo'a **וְשָׂבוֹעַ**	vehilaltem **וְהִלַּלְתֶּם**	et **אֶת־**		
shem **שֵׁם**	Adonai **יהוה**	Elohechem **אֱלֹהֵיכֶם** ילה	asher **אֲשֶׁר־**	asa **עָשָׂה**		
imachem **עִמָּכֶם**	lehafli **לְהַפְלִיא**	velo **וְלֹא־**	yevoshu **יֵבֹשׁוּ**	ami **עַמִּי**		
le'olam **לְעוֹלָם** ריבוע ס"ג י' אותיות דס"ג	vida'atem **וִידַעְתֶּם**	ki **כִּי**	vekerev **בְקֶרֶב**			
Yisrael **יִשְׂרָאֵל**	ani **אָנִי** אני	va'ani **וַאֲנִי** אני	Adonai **יהוה**			
Elohechem **אֱלֹהֵיכֶם** ילה	ve'en **וְאֵין**	od **עוֹד**	velo **וְלֹא־**	yevoshu **יֵבֹשׁוּ**	ami **עַמִּי**	
le'olam **לְעוֹלָם** ריבוע ס"ג י' אותיות דס"ג	ufduyei **וּפְדוּיֵי**	Adonai **יהוה**				
yeshuvun **יְשֻׁבוּן**	uva'u **וּבָאוּ**	Tziyon **צִיּוֹן** יוסף, ו' הויות, קנאה	berina **בְּרִנָּה**			
vesimchat **וְשִׂמְחַת**	olam **עוֹלָם**	al **עַל־**	rosham **רֹאשָׁם**	sason **שָׂשׂוֹן**		
vesimcha **וְשִׂמְחָה**	yasigu **יַשִּׂיגוּ**	venasu **וְנָסוּ**	yagon **יָגוֹן**	va'anacha **וַאֲנָחָה**:		
ki **כִּי**	vesimcha **בְשִׂמְחָה**	tetze'u **תֵצֵאוּ**	uvshalom **וּבְשָׁלוֹם**	tuvalun **תּוּבָלוּן**		
heharim **הֶהָרִים**	vehageva'ot **וְהַגְּבָעוֹת**	yiftzechu **יִפְצְחוּ**	lifnechem **לִפְנֵיכֶם**			
rina **רִנָּה**	vechol **וְכָל־** ילי	atzei **עֲצֵי**	hasadeh **הַשָּׂדֶה**	yimcha'u **יִמְחֲאוּ**	chaf **כָף**:	

---

to give you rain to your land in its time and to bless your every handiwork. And may you lend many nations but you shall not borrow." (Deuteronomy 28:12) "Joyful are you, Israel, who is like you, a nation saved by God, Who is the shield of your help and Who is the sword of your majesty. Your enemies will be false with you, but you will tread upon their heights." (Deuteronomy 33:29) "Israel is saved by the Lord in an everlasting salvation. They shall not be shamed nor humiliated, forever and ever." (Isaiah 45:17) "You shall eat food and be satisfied and you shall praise the Name of the Lord, your God, Who has done wondrously with you. And My People shall not be shamed forever. And you shall know that I am in the midst of Israel, and I am the Lord, your God. There is none other, and My People shall not be shamed forever." (Joel 2:26-27) "And the redeemed of the Lord shall return, and they shall come to Zion with song and with everlasting happiness upon their heads. Gladness and joy shall they attain, and sorrow and sigh shall withdraw." (Isaiah 35:10) "For in gladness you shall go, and with peace you shall be led. The mountains and the hills will break out before you in glad song and the trees and the field will clap hands." (Isaiah 55:12)

Fourth Meal – Verses for Success

הִנֵּה hineh אֵל El יִשׁוּעָתִי yeshu'ati אֶבְטַח evtach וְלֹא velo
אֶפְחָד efchad כִּי ki עָזִּי ozi וְזִמְרָת vezimrat יָהּ Yah
יְהֹוָה Adonai וַיְהִי vayhi לִי li לִישׁוּעָה lishu'a: וּשְׁאַבְתֶּם ushavtem
מַיִם mayim בְּשָׂשׂוֹן besason מִמַּעַיְנֵי mima'aynei
הַיְשׁוּעָה hayeshu'a: וַאֲמַרְתֶּם va'amartem בַּיּוֹם bayom
הַהוּא hahu הוֹדוּ hodu לַיהֹוָה ladonai קִרְאוּ kir'u
בִשְׁמוֹ vishmo הוֹדִיעוּ hodi'u בָעַמִּים va'amim
עֲלִילוֹתָיו alilotav הַזְכִּירוּ hazkiru כִּי ki נִשְׂגָּב nisgav שְׁמוֹ shemo
זַמְּרוּ zameru יְהֹוָה Adonai כִּי ki גֵאוּת ge'ut
עָשָׂה asa מוּדַעַת muda'at זֹאת zot בְּכָל bechol
הָאָרֶץ ha'aretz צַהֲלִי tzahali וָרֹנִּי varoni יוֹשֶׁבֶת yoshevet
צִיּוֹן Tziyon כִּי ki גָדוֹל gadol
בְּקִרְבֵּךְ bekirbech קְדוֹשׁ kedosh יִשְׂרָאֵל: Yisrael וְאָמַר ve'amar בַּיּוֹם bayom
הַהוּא hahu הִנֵּה hineh אֱלֹהֵינוּ Elohenu זֶה ze קִוִּינוּ kivinu
לוֹ lo וְיוֹשִׁיעֵנוּ veyoshi'enu זֶה ze יְהֹוָה Adonai קִוִּינוּ kivinu לוֹ lo
נָגִילָה nagila וְנִשְׂמְחָה venismecha בִּישׁוּעָתוֹ: bishu'ato בּוֹרֵא bore נִיב niv
שְׂפָתָיִם sefatayim שָׁלוֹם shalom שָׁלוֹם shalom לָרָחוֹק larachok
וְלַקָּרוֹב velakarov אָמַר amar יְהֹוָה Adonai וּרְפָאתִיו: urfativ
וְרוּחַ veru'ach לָבְשָׁה lavsha אֶת et עֲמָשַׂי Amasai רֹאשׁ rosh
הַשָּׁלִישִׁים hashalishim לְךָ lecha דָוִיד David
וְעִמְּךָ ve'imcha בֶן ven יִשַׁי Yishai שָׁלוֹם shalom שָׁלוֹם shalom לְךָ lecha
וְשָׁלוֹם veshalom לְעֹזְרֶךָ le'ozrecha כִּי ki עֲזָרְךָ azarcha אֱלֹהֶיךָ Elhecha
וַיְקַבְּלֵם vaykablem דָּוִיד David וַיִּתְּנֵם vayitnem בְּרָאשֵׁי berashei הַגְּדוּד: hagedud

"Behold, God is my help, I shall trust and not fear, for God is my might and my praise, the Lord, and He was a salvation to me. And you shall draw water in joy from the springs of salvation. And you shall say on that day: Give thanks to the Lord, declare His Name, make His acts known among the nations. Remind one another for His Name is powerful. Play melodies to the Lord for He has established grandeur, this is known throughout the Earth. Exalt and sing for joy, inhabitants of Zion, for the Holy One of Israel has done greatly among you." (Isaiah 12:2-6) "And he shall say on that day: Behold this is our God, we had hoped for Him that He would save us. This is the Lord, we had hoped for Him. We shall be glad and rejoice at His salvation." (Isaiah 25:9) "I create fruit of the lips. Peace, peace for the far and the near, says the Lord, and I shall heal him." (Isaiah 57:19) "A spirit clothed Amasai, the head of the officers, for your sake, David, and to be with you, the son of Ishai. Peace, peace to you, and peace to the one who helps you, for your God had helped you. David accepted them and appointed them heads of the group." (I Chronicles 12:19)

Fourth Meal – Verses for Success

We recite the next verse seven times:

וַאֲמַרְתֶּם va'amartem כֹּה ko לֶחָי lechai
וְאַתָּה veAta שָׁלוֹם shalom
וּבֵיתְךָ uvetcha ב"פ ראה שָׁלוֹם shalom
וְכֹל vechol אֲשֶׁר asher לְךָ lecha שָׁלוֹם: shalom

בָּרוּךְ baruch הַגֶּבֶר hagever אֲשֶׁר asher יִבְטַח yivtach בַּיהוָֹה badonai
וְהָיָה vehaya יהוה ; יהה Adonai יְהוָֹה מִבְטַחוֹ: mivtacho
יְהוָֹה Adonai עֹז oz לְעַמּוֹ le'amo יִתֵּן yiten יְהוָֹה Adonai
יְבָרֵךְ yevarech עַמ"ב, (למתק הברכה ו' המלכים את עמיתו) אֶת et
עַמּוֹ amo בְּשָׁלוֹם vashalom ר"ת ע"ב, ריבוע יהוה:

We recite the following verse 130 times in order to correct the 130 years that Adam was without Eve. The *Zohar* (Acharei Mot 357-358) says: "We have learned that Adam lived apart from his wife for 130 years and did not beget children, since Adam did not want to copulate with his wife... from the time death was decreed for him and all mankind, he has said, why should I beget children that will be destroyed? He immediately separated from his wife. Two female spirits used to come and couple with him and they gave birth. They gave birth to demons called the plagues of mankind."

אֵלִיָּהוּ eliyahu לכב הַנָּבִיא hanavi
זָכוּר zachur ע"ב קס"א = יהי אור ע"ה (המושכת השופע מן ד' שמות ליסוד הנקרא זכור)
לְטוֹב letov יהו ; זכור לטוב = סֶזְוֹפָך, סנדלפון, ערי ; אליהו הנביא זכור לטוב = ת' כנגד ת' כוונות הס"א.

Then say *Petichat Eliyahu Hanavi*
(Found in the *Prayer of the Poor Kabbalistic Shabbat Prayer Book* page 186).

We recite the next verse seven times:
"And you shall say: So may it be as long as you live.
Peace for you, peace for your household and peace for all that is with you." (I Samuel 25:6)
"Blessed is the man who trusts in the Lord and the Lord becomes his sanctuary." (Jeremiah 17:7)
"The Lord endows His nation with strength, the Lord blesses His nation with peace." (Psalms 29:11)

Then recite the following verse 130 times:
Elijah the prophet is remembered for good.
Then say *Petichat Eliyahu Hanavi*.

Additional Songs

Songs

Menuchah Vesimchah (Contentment and Gladness)

Menuchah Vesimchah was written by one of the earliest kabbalists, Rav Moshe son of Kelonimus the Elder (Germany, 11th century). His family was entrusted with carrying the teaching of Kabbalah in secret for centuries in Europe.

During the *Shabbat* prayers we say that *Shabbat* is "The most coveted of days, You have called It". The *Talmud* says (Babylonian Talmud, Tractate Shabbat 10:2): "The Holy One, Blessed Be He, said to Moses, I have a precious gift in My treasure house, called the Sabbath, and I desire to give it to Israel; go and inform them."

This song extols the greatness of the Light of *Shabbat*, which brings with it contentment and happiness (the additional Soul) and prepares us for the Final Redemption. It also speaks about the elevation of the Worlds during the time of *Shabbat* and the Illumination all of Creation receives from *Shabbat*.

laYehudim לִיהוּדִים	or אוֹר	vesimcha וְשִׂמְחָה	menucha מְנוּחָה			
♦machamadim מַחֲמַדִּים	yom יוֹם	shabaton שַׁבָּתוֹן	yom יוֹם			
♦me'idim מְעִידִים	hema הֵמָּה	vezochrav וְזוֹכְרָיו	shomrav שׁוֹמְרָיו			
♦ve'omdim וְעוֹמְדִים	beru'im בְּרוּאִים	kol כָּל	leshisha לְשִׁשָּׁה	ki כִּי		
♦veyamim וְיַמִּים	eretz אֶרֶץ	shamayim שָׁמַיִם	shemei שְׁמֵי			
♦veramim וְרָמִים	gevohim גְּבוֹהִים	marom מָרוֹם	tzeva צְבָא	kol כָּל		
♦re'emim רְאֵמִים	vechayat וְחַיַּת	ve'adam וְאָדָם	tanin תַּנִּין			
♦olamim עוֹלָמִים	tzur צוּר	Hashem ה'	beYah בְּיָהּ	ki כִּי		

Menuchah Vesimchah (Contentment and gladness)

מ *Contentment and gladness is the light [as the Light of Shabbat that shines on our face is greater than the light of the rest of the week. (Midrash Beresheet Rabba 11)] for the Judeans [in Hebrew the people who give thanks (Chidushei Harim on Chanukah)], on this day of Shabbat, day (God) coveted; those who guard and those who remember it – they bear witness, that for six days all was created and still endures [and only the arrival of Shabbat gives meaning, life and existence to Creation, as the Zohar says: "When the Holy One, blessed be He, created the world, He endowed the earth with appropriate powers, so that everything was in the earth but it did not produce any fruit." (Zohar Vayera 1 and see also the Sulam commentary on Zohar, Prologue 4)]* ש *The Heaven of Heavens ["the Seven Chambers of Abba and Ima of Beriah {according to the Ari, during the six days of the week these Seven Chambers are from the aspect of Zeir Anpin of Beriah but on Shabbat the Seven Chambers are from the aspect of Abba and Ima of Beriah (the Writing of the Ari, gate of meditation B, pg. 90)}, which is Binah, is Heaven of Heavens and She influences Zeir Anpin which is Heaven (see the Sulam commentary on Zohar Beresheet B, 65; and on Zohar Pekudei 218-223)], Earth [Malchut of Zeir Anpin] and seas [Malchut of Atzilut and Worlds below Her,] all the Hosts of the Heavens [the Supernal Ministers who govern the people of the world (Zohar Noach 211)], high and exalted, crocodile [the Leviathan and his mate (Zohar Bo 39)], Adam [and Eve] and the mighty Oryx [the wild ox and his mate] – "for in Yah—* יה *["Rav Judah son of Rav Ila'I says: Yah refers to the two worlds which the Holy One, blessed be He, created, one with the letter Hei (* ה *Binah—Ima) and the other with the letter Yod (* י *Chochmah—Abba)" (Babylonian Talmud, Tractate Menachot 29:2)] the Lord, is the Rock of the Worlds" (Isaiah 26:4)*

Songs

הוּא hu	אֲשֶׁר asher	דִּבֶּר diber	לְעַם le'am	סְגֻלָּתוֹ segulato
שָׁמוֹר shamor	לְקַדְּשׁוֹ lekadsho	מִבֹּאוֹ mibo'o	וְעַד ve'ad	צֵאתוֹ tzeto
שַׁבָּת Shabbat	קֹדֶשׁ kodesh	יוֹם yom	וְחֶמְדָּתוֹ chemdato
כִּי ki	בוֹ vo	שָׁבַת shavat	אֵל El	מִכָּל mikol	מְלַאכְתּוֹ melachto
בְּמִצְוַת bemitzvat	שַׁבָּת Shabbat	אֵל El	יַחֲלִיצָךְ yachalitzach
קוּם kum	קְרָא kera	אֵלָיו elav	יְחִישׁ yachish	לְאַמְּצָךְ le'ametzach
נִשְׁמַת nishmat	כָּל kol	וְזִי chai	וְגַם vegam	נַעֲרִיצָךְ na'aritzach
אֱכוֹל echol	בְּשִׂמְחָה besimcha	כִּי ki	כְּבָר kevar	רָצָךְ ratzach
בְּמִשְׁנֶה bemishne	לֶחֶם lechem	וְקִדּוּשׁ vekidush	רַבָּה raba
בְּרוֹב berov	מַטְעַמִּים mat'amim	וְרוּחַ veru'ach	נְדִיבָה nediva
יִזְכּוּ yizku	לְרַב lerav	טוּב tuv	הַמִּתְעַנְּגִים hamit'anegim	בָּהּ ba
בְּבִיאַת bevi'at	גּוֹאֵל go'el	לְחַיֵּי lechayei	הָעוֹלָם ha'olam	הַבָּא haba

---

ה It is He Who spoke to His treasured nation (on Mount Sinai): 'Guard to hallow it from arrival to departure'; as the Holy Shabbat, day that He coveted, for on it God rested from all His work. Through the Shabbat precept God will strengthen you [in Hebrew can be translated as: God will release you. The Ari says that during the six days of the week the world is ruled by the angel Matat–ron **(do not pronounce)**, and is where we receive our fulfilment from. On Shabbat, we would like to disconnect from It and be elevated to higher dimensions, the World of Atzilut (Emanation) and receive our fulfilment directly from the Light, with no intermediation of the angels. (Writings of the Ari, Gate of Meditation B, pg. 87)]; arise, call Him, that He may rush to fortify you [as the power of guarding Shabbat can accelerate the coming of the Messiah (see Babylonian Talmud, Tractate Sanhedrin 98:1 on Isaiah 60:22 and also see Babylonian Talmud, Tractate Shabbat 118:1 on Isaiah 56:4)]; (So recite the prayer of) "The soul of every living being: Nishmat Kol Chai [Yesod of Zeir Anpin] and (also the prayer of) 'we revere You: Kedushat Keter'; "eat in gladness for He has already shown you favor." (Based on Ecclesiastes 9:7 and Babylonian Talmud, Tractate Pesachim 68:2) With the two loaves ["There are two kinds of breads, bread from Heaven, from Zeir Anpin, and bread from the earth, from the Nukva. This is millet bread, but the bread from the earth detached from the bread from heaven is the bread of poverty. On Shabbat, the lower bread of the Nukva is included within the Upper bread of Zeir Anpin, and the Lower is blessed by the Upper. This double bread of Shabbat, which is the bread of the Nukva, receives from the Supernal Shabbat, Binah, which flows and shines upon everything. The bread of the Nukva is united with the bread of Binah and becomes double." (Zohar Vayechi 754-755)] And the Great Kiddush [the revelation of Mochin from Abba], with abundant delicacies ["Therefore, he who has attained the grade of Faith must prepare a table and a meal on Shabbat eve so that his table may be blessed all through the other six days. For at that time, blessing is prevalent for all the six week days, for no blessing is found at an empty table… also during Shabbat day one should prepare the table with meals and draw blessing for the other six days… Therefore, it is necessary to prepare the table with three meals after the entrance of the Shabbat, and his table must not be empty. Thus, blessing will rest upon it during all the other week days, for therein depends the true Faith Above." (Zohar Yitro 446-450)] And a generous spirit [the extra soul]; those who take pleasure in Shabbat will merit much good (in this world), (they will merit) the coming of the redeemer and (they will merit) the life of the World to Come.

Songs

Mah Yedidut (How Beloved is Your Tranquility)

Mah Yedidut was composed by Kabbalist Rav Menachem son of Machir (student and friend of Rashi, Regensburg-Germany, 11th Century). He was known for his humbleness, and was one of the first to use the phrase "in my humble opinion" in his writings and teachings. This song speaks about the pleasure that our soul receives during *Shabbat*, and that even the physical pleasures, like eating, benefit our soul.

מַה ma יְדִידוּת yedidut מְנוּחָתֵךְ menuchatech, אַתְּ at שַׁבָּת Shabbat
הַמַּלְכָּה hamalka. בְּכֵן bechen נָרוּץ narutz לִקְרָאתֵךְ likratech,
בּוֹאִי bo'i כַלָּה chala נְסוּכָה nesucha. לְבוּשׁ levush בִּגְדֵי bigdei
חֲמוּדוֹת chamudot, לְהַדְלִיק lehadlik נֵר ner בִּבְרָכָה bivracha. וַתֵּכֶל vatechel
כָּל kol הָעֲבוֹדוֹת ha'avodot, לֹא lo תַעֲשׂוּ ta'ashu מְלָאכָה melacha.
לְהִתְעַנֵּג lehit'aneg בְּתַעֲנוּגִים beta'anugim.

בַּרְבּוּרִים barburim וּשְׂלָו uslav וְדָגִים vedagim.
מֵעֶרֶב me'erev מַזְמִינִים mazminim כָּל kol מִינֵי minei מַטְעַמִּים matamim,
מִבְּעוֹד mibod יוֹם yom מוּכָנִים muchanim תַּרְנְגוֹלִים tarnegolim
מְפֻטָּמִים mefutamim. וְלַעֲרוֹךְ vela'aroch כַּמָּה kama מִינִים minim,
שְׁתוֹת shetot יֵינוֹת yenot מְבֻשָּׂמִים mevushamim. וְתַפְנוּקֵי vetafnukei
מַעֲדַנִּים ma'adanim, בְּכָל bechol שָׁלוֹשׁ shalosh פְּעָמִים pe'amim.
(לְהִתְעַנֵּג lehitaneg בְּתַעֲנוּגִים beta'anugim...)

נַחֲלַת nachalat יַעֲקֹב Ya'akov יִירָשׁ yirash, בְּלִי beli מְצָרִים metzarim
נַחֲלָה nachala. וִיכַבְּדוּהוּ vichabduhu עָשִׁיר ashir וָרָשׁ varash,
וְתִזְכּוּ vetizku לִגְאֻלָּה ligula. יוֹם yom שַׁבָּת shabat
אִם im תִּשְׁמוֹרוּ tishmoru, וִהְיִיתֶם vihyitem לִי li סְגֻלָּה segula.

Mah Yedidut (How Beloved is Your Tranquility)

מ *How beloved is your tranquility, you are Shabbat, the Queen.* (Babylonian Talmud, Tractate Baba Kama 32:1) *So let us run to greet you (and say:) "Come, Princess Bride" (as we are) dressed in desirable clothes* (Ibid, Tractate Shabbat 113:1), *(and as we) light the (Shabbat's) candle with a blessing. "All the work was completed"* (Exodus 39:32); *(and as it is written:) "You shall do no work."* (Leviticus 23:3) *This is the time to enjoy pleasures: geese, quail and fish.*
In advance all is prepared, all sorts of tasty delicacies. While it is still daylight, the juicy, plump chickens are ready. We set a (table) with assorted foods, to drink fragrant wines, and (to taste) a connoisseur's special dainties, three times [the three Shabbat meals.] (This is the time to enjoy pleasures…)
נ *One (who connects to Shabbat) will inherit "Jacob's legacy,"* (Isaiah 58:14) *which is an inheritance without any boundaries* (Babylonian Talmud, Tractate Shabbat 118:1). *Both, rich and poor, should honor (Shabbat) and thereby all of you will merit redemption* (Midrash Kohelet Rabba 4:10). *So if you guard the day of Shabbat, "you will be a treasure [Chesed, Gevurah, and Tiferet* (Zohar Bamidbar 52)] *to Me."* (Exodus 19:5)

שֵׁשֶׁת sheshet יָמִים yamim תַּעֲבוֹדוּ ta'avodu, וּבַשְּׁבִיעִי uvashvi'i נָגִילָה nagila.
(לְהִתְעַנֵּג lehitaneg בְּתַעֲנוּגִים beta'anugim...)

וְחֶפְצֶיךָ chafatzecha אֲסוּרִים asurim, וְגַם vegam לַחֲשׁוֹב lachashov
וְעֶשְׂבּוֹנוֹת cheshbonot. הִרְהוּרִים hirhurim מֻתָּרִים mutarim, וּלְשַׁדֵּךְ ulshadech
הַבָּנוֹת habanvt. וְתִינוֹק vetinok לְלַמְּדוֹ lelamdo סֵפֶר sefer,
לַמְנַצֵּחַ lamnatze'ach בִּנְגִינוֹת binginot, וְלַהֲגוֹת velahagot בְּאִמְרֵי be'imrei
שֶׁפֶר shefer, בְּכֹל bechol פִּנּוֹת pinot וּמְחָנוֹת umachanot.
(לְהִתְעַנֵּג lehitaneg בְּתַעֲנוּגִים beta'anugim...)

הִלּוּכָךְ hiluchach תְּהֵא tehe בְנַחַת venachat, עֹנֶג oneg קְרָא kera
לַשַּׁבָּת laShabbat. וְהַשֵּׁנָה vehashena מְשֻׁבַּחַת meshubachat,
כְּדָת kedat נֶפֶשׁ nefesh מְשִׁיבַת meshivat, בְּכֵן bechen נַפְשִׁי nafshi
לְךָ lecha עָרְגָה arga, וְלָנוּחַ velanuach בְּחִבַּת bechibat.
כַּשּׁוֹשַׁנִּים kashoshanim סוּגָה suga, בּוֹ bv יָנוּחוּ yanuchu בֵּן ben וּבַת uvat.
(לְהִתְעַנֵּג lehitaneg בְּתַעֲנוּגִים beta'anugim...)

מֵעֵין me'en עוֹלָם olam הַבָּא haba, יוֹם yom שַׁבָּת shabat מְנוּחָה menucha,
כָּל kol הַמִּתְעַנְּגִים hamitangim בָּהּ ba, יִזְכּוּ yizku לְרוֹב lerov שִׂמְחָה shmecha,
מֵחֶבְלֵי mechevlei מָשִׁיחַ mashich, יֻצָּלוּ yutzalu לִרְוָחָה lirvacha.
פְּדוּתֵנוּ pedutenu תַצְמִיחַ tatzmiach, וְנָס venas יָגוֹן yagon וַאֲנָחָה va'anacha.
(לְהִתְעַנֵּג lehitaneg בְּתַעֲנוּגִים beta'anugim...)

"Six days [Chesed, Gevurah, Tiferet, Netzach, Hod, and Yesod (Zohar Vayikra 112)] you shall work," (Exodus 20:9) so on the seventh (day) let us be joyful (Ibid 115-117). (This is the time to enjoy pleasures...) א (Based on the Babylonian Talmud, Tractate Shabbat 150:1 and on Isaiah 58:13; pursuing) your business affairs are forbidden, as are computing your accounts. However purely mental calculations are permitted. So too are: matchmaking for your daughters (which often involves dowry calculations), teaching a child to study a book (or arranging to hire a teacher), singing melodies and contemplating, "beautiful words of wisdom" (Genesis 49: 21) wherever you are. (This is the time to enjoy pleasures...) ב Let your gait be relaxed, since "Shabbat is called a delight" (Isaiah 58:13). Sleep is highly recommended (see the Writings of the Ari, Gate of Meditation B, pg. 100), for it properly restores the soul. Hence my soul longs for you (Shabbat,) to rest with affection. (Shabbat is) "Encircled by lilies" (Song of Songs 7:3) (fenced in by protective prohibitions). Both son and daughter will rest (on Shabbat.) (This is the time to enjoy pleasures...) Shabbat, the day of rest, is a taste of the World to Come (Babylonian Talmud, Tractate Berachot 57:2) [but also can be translated that Shabbat is the spring and the source of the World to Come. All those who enjoy themselves on it will merit much happiness. They will be spared from the birth pangs of the Messiah (Ibid, Tractate Shabbat 118:1). (Because of the merit of Shabbat) Make our redemption flourish, so that sorrow and sighing will take flight. (This is the time to enjoy pleasures...)

Songs

YAH RIBON (YAH, MASTER OF THE WORLD)

Yah Ribon was written in Aramaic by Kabbalist Rav Yisrael son of Moshe Najara (student of the Ari, Gaza, 16th century). The Ari said about his songs that they are very precious in Heaven. This song does not speak directly about Shabbat but instead speaks about the creation of the World and the Final Redemption.

malka מַלְכָּא	hu הוּא	ant אַנְתְּ	ve'almaya וְעָלְמַיָּא	alam עָלַם	ribon רִבּוֹן	Yah יָהּ
gevurtech גְּבוּרְתֵּךְ		ovad עוֹבַד		malchaya מַלְכַיָּא		melech מֶלֶךְ
lehachavaya לְהַחֲוָיָא		kadamach קֳדָמָךְ		shefar שְׁפַר		vetimhaya וְתִמְהַיָּא
veramsha וְרַמְשָׁא		tzafra צַפְרָא		asader אֲסַדֵּר		shevachin שְׁבָחִין
nafsha נַפְשָׁא		chol כָּל		bera בְּרָא		kadisha קַדִּישָׁא	elaha אֱלָהָא	lach לָךְ
enasha אֱנָשָׁא			uvnei וּבְנֵי		kadishin קַדִּישִׁין		irin עִירִין
shemaya שְׁמַיָּא			ve'of וְעוֹף		bara בְּרָא		cheyvat וְחֵיוַת
vetakifin וְתַקִּיפִין			ovedech עוֹבְדָךְ				ravrevin רַבְרְבִין
kefifin כְּפִיפִין			vezakif וְזָקִיף		remaya רַמְיָא		machich מָכִיךְ
alfin אַלְפִין			shenin שְׁנִין		gevar גְּבַר		yichye יִחְיֶה	lu לוּ
bechushbenaya בְּחֻשְׁבְּנַיָּא			gevurtech גְּבוּרְתֵּךְ				ye'ol יֵעוֹל	la לָא
urvuta וּרְבוּתָא			yekar יְקָר		le לֵיהּ		di דִּי	Elaha אֱלָהָא
aryevata אַרְיְוָתָא			mipum מִפּוּם		anach עָנָךְ		yat יָת	perok פְּרוֹק
galuta גָּלוּתָא			migo מִגּוֹ		amech עַמָּךְ		yat יָת	ve'apek וְאַפֵּיק
umaya אֻמַּיָּא			mikol מִכָּל		vechart בְּחַרְתְּ		di דִּי	amech עַמָּךְ
kudshin קֻדְשִׁין			ulkodesh וּלְקֹדֶשׁ		tuv תּוּב			lemikdashech לְמִקְדָּשֵׁךְ
venafshin וְנַפְשִׁין			ruchin רוּחִין		yechedun יְחֶדוּן		ve בֵּיהּ	di דִּי	atar אֲתַר
verachashin וְרַחֲשִׁין			shirin שִׁירִין				lach לָךְ	vizamrun וִיזַמְּרוּן
deshufraya דְּשׁוּפְרַיָּא			karta קַרְתָּא					birushlem בִּירוּשְׁלֵם

YAH RIBON (YAH, MASTER OF THE WORLD)

י *Yah, Master of the World and the Universe, You are King over kings of kings; the deeds of Your might and wonders it is beautiful for me to relate. (Yah, Master of the World...)*

ש *Praises shall I arrange morning and evening to You, Holy God, Creator of all life; holy angels and mankind, beasts of the field and birds of the sky. (Yah, Master of the World...)*

ר *Great are Your deeds and mighty, You humble the haughty and straighten the bent; even were man to live a thousand years, he would be unable to make an accounting of Your might. (Yah, Master of the World...)*

א *God, to Whom belong glory and greatness, rescue Your sheep from the mouth of the lions, and bring out Your people from exile. Your people, when You chose from among the nations. (Yah, Master of the World...)*

ל *Return to Your Sanctuary and to the Holy of Holies, the place where spirits and souls will rejoice and will sing to You songs and praises, in Jerusalem, the city of beauty. (Yah, Master of the World...)*

Songs

TZAM'AH NAFSHI (MY SOUL THIRSTS)

Tzam'ah Nafshi was written by Kabbalist Rav Avraham Iben Ezra (Spain, 12th century) and speaks about the yearning and longing we have for the Light of the Creator. Kabbalist Chatam Sofer (Hungary, 18th century) said (Chut Hameshulash pg. 36:2) that the song is filled with very deep kabbalistic concepts and was written with Divine Inspiration.

צָמְאָה tzam'ah נַפְשִׁי nafshi לֵאלֹהִים lelokim לְאֵל leEl וָזִי chai.
לִבִּי libi וּבְשָׂרִי uvsari יְרַנְּנוּ yeranenu לְאֵל leEl וָזִי chai.
אֵל El אֶחָד echad בְּרָאַנִי bera'ani. וְאָמַר ve'amar וָזִי chai אָנִי ani.
כִּי ki לֹא lo יִרְאַנִי yirani. הָאָדָם ha'adam וָזִי vachai.
בָּרָא bara כֹּל kol בְּחָכְמָה bechochma. בְּעֵצָה be'etza וּבִמְזִמָּה uvimzima.
מְאֹד me'od נֶעְלָמָה ne'elama. מֵעֵינֵי me'enei כֹּל kol וָזִי chai.
(צָמְאָה tzam'ah נַפְשִׁי nafshi לֵאלֹהִים lelokim ...)

רָם ram עַל al כָּל kol כְּבוֹדוֹ kevodo. כָּל kol פֶּה pe יְחַוֶּה yechave הוֹדוֹ hodo.
בָּרוּךְ baruch אֲשֶׁר asher בְּיָדוֹ beyado. נֶפֶשׁ nefesh כָּל kol וָזִי chai.
הִבְדִּיל hivdil נִינֵי ninei תָם tam. וְחֻקִּים chukim לְהוֹרוֹתָם lehorotam.
אֲשֶׁר asher יַעֲשֶׂה ya'ash אוֹתָם otam. הָאָדָם ha'adam וָזִי vachai.
(צָמְאָה tzam'ah נַפְשִׁי nafshi לֵאלֹהִים lelokim ...)

מִי mi זֶה ze יִצְטַדָּק yitztadak. נִמְשַׁל nimshal לְאָבָק le'avak דַּק dak.
אֱמֶת emet כִּי ki לֹא lo יִצְדַּק yitzdak. לְפָנֶיךָ lefanecha כֹּל kol וָזִי chai.

TZAM'AH NAFSHI (MY SOUL THIRSTS)

"My soul thirsts for God, the living God," (Psalms 42:3)
"My heart and my flesh will sing to the living God." (Psalms 84:3)

א *The one God created me, and swore (to the prophets) "As sure as I'm alive"* (Numbers 14:21); *(and also said:) "No living man shall see My Face [Chochmah Ila'a] and live."* (Exodus 33:20)

ב *He [Binah-Ima] created all with Wisdom [Chochmah-Abba], purpose and secrecy. How it (Chochmah) "is hidden from the eyes of all the living."* (Job 28:20) *(My soul thirsts...)*

ר *Supreme above all His glory [Malchut] reigns; every mouth expresses His Majesty. Blessed "is He whose hand (maintains) the soul of all the living."* (Job 12:10)

ה *He dedicated the innocent's (Jacob) offspring, so statutes are going to be taught to them (also means "to give them light"), which indeed if any man follow them; His soul shall live. (My soul thirsts...)*

מ *Who is the one who justifies himself to thin dust [Adam; "the earth alone received the power of the three of them, so that all the four elements were in it, fire, air, water and dust; from the Heaven it received two, fire and air; from water one, water; and one was in it, dust. The earth brought forth the lifeless body mass of man"* (Zohar Chadash, Beresheet 677)] *In truth, "none living can justify before You."* (Psalms 143:2)

Songs

בְּלֵב belev יֵצֶר yetzer וְיָשׁוּב chashuv• כִּדְמוּת kidmut וְזָמַת chamat עַכְשׁוּב achshuv•
וְאֵיכָכָה ve'echacha יָשׁוּב yashuv• הַבָּשָׂר habasar הוֹי hechai•
(צָמְאָה tzam'ah נַפְשִׁי nafshi לֵאלֹקִים lelokim ...)

נְסוֹגִים nesogim אִם im אָבוּ avu• וּמִדַּרְכָּם umidarkam שָׁבוּ shavu•
טֶרֶם terem יִשְׁכְּבוּ yishkavu• בֵּית bet מוֹעֵד mo'ed לְכֹל lechol וְזִי vechai•
עַל al כֹּל kol אֲהוֹדֶךָ ahodecha• כָּל kol פֶּה pe תְּיַחֲדֶךָ teyachadecha•
פּוֹתֵחַ pote'ach אֶת et יָדֶךָ yadecha• וּמַשְׂבִּיעַ umasbi'a לְכֹל lechol וְזִי vechai•
(צָמְאָה tzam'ah נַפְשִׁי nafshi לֵאלֹקִים lelokim ...)

זְכֹר zechor אַהֲבַת ahavat קְדוּמִים kedumim• וְהַחֲיֵה vehachaye נִרְדָּמִים nirdamim•
וְקָרֵב vekarev הַיָּמִים hayamim• אֲשֶׁר asher בֶּן ben יִשַׁי yishai וְזִי vechai•
רְאֵה re'e לִגְבֶרֶת ligveret אֱמֶת emet• שִׁפְחָה shifcha נוֹאֶמֶת no'emet•
לֹא lo כִּי ki בְּנֵךְ venech הַמֵּת hamet• וּבְנִי uvni הוֹי hechai•
(צָמְאָה tzam'ah נַפְשִׁי nafshi לֵאלֹקִים lelokim ...)

אֶקֹּד ekod עַל al אַפִּי api• וְאֶפְרוֹשׂ ve'efros לְךָ lecha כַּפִּי kapi•
עֵת et אֶפְתַּח eftach פִּי pi• בְּנִשְׁמַת benishmat כֹּל kol וְזִי vechai•
(צָמְאָה tzam'ah נַפְשִׁי nafshi לֵאלֹקִים lelokim ...)

ב *Like serpent's poison venomous (based on Psalms 140:4), the (evil) inclination dwells in the heart. So how can any flesh (human being) return and be alive? [A phrase from Leviticus 13:16, which speaks about leprosy, and the Zohar explains (Zohar Tazria 135-136): "To You shall all flesh come." (Psalms 65:3) What is 'to You'? It refers to the Holy One, Blessed Be He... since all matters of purity and Holiness come from the Holy One, Blessed Be He" (My soul thirsts...)*

ג *If they have desire to withdraw (from their evil deeds), and return [teshuvah—repentance—*תשובה*] from their (negative) ways before they rest in the house (grave) that is appointed for all who live.*

ע *For everything I shall thank You (see Babylonian Talmud, Tractate Berachot 54:1) and every mouth shall acknowledge You for everything; As "You open Your hand to satisfy all living." (Psalms 145:16) (My soul thirsts...)*

ז *Remember the love of the ancients (the patriarchs), (and with their merit) bring to life the sleeping (dead). And bring closer "the days that the son of Jesse (Messiah) lives ["The illumination of Chochmah that is called life derives from the son of Jesse, namely Malchut—Kingdom of David, through which he ruled over all. And the Earth, which is Malchut, receives everything from Heaven." (Zohar Beresheet A, 304)]" (I Samuel 20:31)*

ר *Recognize the true Lady [the Shechinah], (and not) the handmaid [the klipa—Left of Left] who declares: "no, for your son is the dead [Chochmah-Wisdom without Chasadim-Mercy (see Sulam commentary on Zohar, Sifra detzniuta 54)] and my son is the live one" (I Kings 3:22) (My soul thirsts...)*

א *I shall bow down upon my face with my hands outspread as it time to open my mouth with (the praise of) 'the soul of every living being—Nishmat Kol Chai [Yesod of Zeir Anpin. "During Shabbat, Malchut receives blessings from the Upper souls of Atzilut." (Zohar Terumah 219)] (My soul thirsts...)*

BARUCH EL ELYON (BLESSED IS THE SUPERNAL GOD)

Baruch El Elyon was written by Kabbalist Rav Baruch Ben Shemuel (Germany, 12th century), one of the sages of the *Tosafot*.

The sages teach that *Shabbat* is *mekor haberachah* or "the source of all blessings." (Midrash Beresheet Rabba 11:1, Zohar Yitro 444-445, and the poem 'Lecha Dodi') Rav Ashlag (the Sulam commentary on Zohar Lech Lecha 237-243) explains that to draw *beracha* (blessing) we need first to elevate, from Below to Above, [*Zeir Anpin* (*ben*—the son) and *Nukva* (*bat*—the daughter) to *Binah* (*El Elyon*—the Supernal God)], and only then we can draw abundance from *Binah* (Above) to *Zeir Anpin*, to *Nukva* (Below) and the rest of the Lower Worlds. On *Shabbat* this happens on its own.

◆menucha מְנוּחָה	natan נָתַן	asher אֲשֶׁר	elyon עֶלְיוֹן	El אֵל	baruch בָּרוּךְ
◆va'anacha וַאֲנָחָה	mishet מִשֵּׂאת	fidyom פִּדְיוֹם	lenafshenu לְנַפְשֵׁנוּ
◆hanidacha הַנִּדָּחָה	ir עִיר	leTziyon לְצִיּוֹן	yidrosh יִדְרוֹשׁ	vehu וְהוּא
◆ne'enacha נֶאֱנָחָה	nefesh נֶפֶשׁ	tugyon תּוּגְיוֹן	ana אָנָה	ad עַד
◆habat הַבַּת	im עִם	haben הַבֵּן	Shabbat שַׁבָּת	hashomer הַשּׁוֹמֵר
◆machavat מַחֲבַת	al עַל	kemincha כְּמִנְחָה	yeratzu יֵרָצוּ	laEl לָאֵל
◆olamim עוֹלָמִים	melech מֶלֶךְ	ba'aravot בָּעֲרָבוֹת	rochev רוֹכֵב
◆bane'imim בַּנְּעִימִים	izen אֹזֶן	lishbot לִשְׁבֹּת	amo עַמּוֹ	et אֶת
◆mat'amim מַטְעַמִּים	beminei בְּמִינֵי	arevot עֲרֵבוֹת	bema'achalei בְּמַאֲכָלֵי
◆mishpacha מִשְׁפָּחָה	zevach זֶבַח	kavod כָּבוֹד	bemalbushei בְּמַלְבּוּשֵׁי

(hashomer הַשּׁוֹמֵר Shabbat שַׁבָּת...)

BARUCH EL ELYON (BLESSED IS THE SUPERNAL GOD)

ב *Blessed is the Supernal God [Right Column of Binah (Zohar Pekudei 801)] Who gave (us the Shabbat, which is) contentment; as for our souls it is a relief from ravage and groaning (based on Babylonian Talmud, Tractate Shabbat 118:1). May He seek out Zion ["from Zion, which is Yesod of Malchut, all blessings come out to all" (Zohar Shemini 11)] the outcast city, how long is the grieving for the groaning souls. He who guards the Shabbat [the righteous (Zohar Yitro 473)], the son [Zeir Anpin] and the daughter [Nukva] — may they find God's favor like a meal offering in a sacred pan [the poor offering, which upon it, it says: "The Holy One, Blessed Be He, said, 'Who is it that usually brings a meal-offering? It is the poor man. I account it as though he had offered his own soul to Me" (Babylonian Talmud, Tractate Menachot 104:2)]*

ר *He "Who rides upon the clouds ["Arich Anpin—the most ancient of all, the most concealed of all, which cannot be grasped, and will not be revealed. Upon what does He ride? The clouds, Yud-Hei, namely Abba and Ima," (Zohar Terumah 718-719)]" (Psalms 68:5) the King of the Universe, that His nation rest on the Shabbat He made it heard [also in Hebrew: balanced] with pleasantness, with tasty food and every manner of delicacy, with elegant garments and a family feast. (He who keeps the Shabbat...)*

Songs

וְאַשְׁרֵי ve'ashrei כָּל kol וְזוֹכֶה choche לְתַשְׁלוּמֵי letashlumei כֶּפֶל kefel

מֵאֵת me'et כָּל kol סוֹכֶה soche שׁוֹכֵן shochen בָּעֲרָפֶל ba'arafel

נַחֲלָה nachala לוֹ lo יִזְכֶּה yizke בָּהָר bahar וּבַשָּׁפֶל uvashafel

נַחֲלָה nachala וּמְנוּחָה umnucha כְּשֶׁמֶשׁ kashemesh לוֹ lo זָרְחָה zarcha

(הַשּׁוֹמֵר hashomer שַׁבָּת Shabbat...)

כָּל kol שׁוֹמֵר shomer שַׁבָּת Shabbat כַּדָּת kadat מֵחַלְּלוֹ mechalelo

הֵן hen הֶכְשֵׁר hechshar וְחִבַּת chibat קֹדֶשׁ kodesh גּוֹרָלוֹ goralo

וְאִם ve'im יָצָא yatza וְחוֹבַת chovat הַיּוֹם hayom אַשְׁרֵי ashrei לוֹ lo• אֵל el

אֵל el אָדוֹן adon מְחוֹלְלוֹ• mecholelo מִנְחָה mincha הִיא hi שְׁלוּחָה shelucha•

(הַשּׁוֹמֵר hashomer שַׁבָּת Shabbat...)

וְחֶמְדַּת chemdat הַיָּמִים hayamim• קְרָאוֹ kerao אֵלִי eli צוּר tzur•

וְאַשְׁרֵי ve'ashrei לִתְמִימִים litmimim• אִם im יִהְיֶה yihye נָצוּר natzur•

כֶּתֶר keter הִלּוּמִים hilumim• עַל al רֹאשָׁם rosham יָצוּר yatzur•

צוּר tzur הָעוֹלָמִים haolamim רוּחוֹ rucho בָּם bam נָחָה nacha•

(הַשּׁוֹמֵר hashomer שַׁבָּת Shabbat...)

זָכוֹר zachor אֵת et יוֹם yom הַשַּׁבָּת hashabbat לְקַדְּשׁוֹ lekadsho•

קַרְנוֹ karno כִּי ki גָבְהָה gavha נֵזֶר nezer עַל al רֹאשׁוֹ rosho•

א *"Praiseworthy are those who await"* (Isaiah 30:18) (as they will get) double reward (see Midrash Tehilim 92) from the One Who sees all but dwells in dense mist ["disagreement was aroused through the fierceness of the Left" (Zohar Beresheet A, 64)]. He will grant him an inheritance in mountain and valley, a heritage and a resting place like his upon whom the sun shone [Jacob (based on Genesis 32:32)]. (He who keeps the Shabbat...)

ב *Whomever properly "safeguards the Shabbat without desecrating it,"* (Isaiah 56:2) he is worthy and destined to receive the abundance of Holiness (that comes down for the rest of the week). And if he fulfills the day's obligation, praises are due him; to God, the Master Who formed him ["the Supernal Chesed, which is the light of Abba" (Zohar Beshalach 429)], it is sent as a meal-offering. (He who keeps the Shabbat...)

ו *The most coveted* (see Targum Jonathan on Genesis 2:2) *of days,' (Shabbat) is called by my God, my Rock. Praiseworthy are the undefiled who keep it guarded* [the secret of Shabbat — Malchut is called 'Shabbat' when She is united in the secret of one meaning that there is no partnership with the Other Side (Zohar Terumah 163-164)]. *A fitting crown is fashioned on their heads; the spirit of the Rock of the Universe will dwell upon them* ["An additional soul is bestowed upon man on Shabbat... the Holy Spirit, which dwells upon him and crowns man with the Holy Crown, the crowns of the angels. It is of the same spirit that will rest upon the righteous in the future to come. Man should therefore honor Shabbat, for the holy visitor that dwells with him." (Zohar Chadash Beresheet 708)] (He who keeps the Shabbat...)

ז *He who "remember(s) the Shabbat day to sanctify it,"* (Exodus 20:7) *his horn* [karan—shone is Malchut when She is clothing Binah Above and keren—horn is what kings are anointed with. So the tenth which is Malchut is crowned with Ima (Zohar, Sifra Detzniuta, 71-72)] *will rise like a coronet on his head.*

al עַל	ken כֵּן	yiten יִתֵּן	ha'adam הָאָדָם	lenafsho לְנַפְשׁוֹ
oneg עֹנֶג	vegam וְגַם	simcha שִׂמְחָה	bahem בָּהֶם	lemoshcha לְמָשְׁחָה

(הַשּׁוֹמֵר hashomer שַׁבָּת Shabbat...)

kodesh קוֹדֶשׁ	hi הִיא	lachem לָכֶם	shabat שַׁבָּת	hamalka הַמַּלְכָּה
el אֶל	toch תּוֹךְ	batechem בָּתֵּיכֶם	lehaniach לְהָנִיחַ	beracha בְּרָכָה	bechol בְּכָל
moshvotechem מוֹשְׁבוֹתֵיכֶם	lo לֹא	ta'asu תַּעֲשׂוּ	melacha מְלָאכָה
benechem בְּנֵיכֶם	uvnotechem וּבְנוֹתֵיכֶם	eved עֶבֶד	vegam וְגַם	shifcha שִׁפְחָה

(הַשּׁוֹמֵר hashomer שַׁבָּת Shabbat...)

KI ESHMERA SHABBAT (WHEN I GUARD THE SHABBAT)

Ki Eshmera Shabbat was written by Kabbalist Rav Avraham Iben Ezra (Spain, 12th century) and speaks about the protection the Light of *Shabbat* creates. Kabbalist Rav Yechezkel of Sieniawa (Poland, 19th century) says in the name of Kabbalist Rav Tzvi Hirsh of Rymanow (Poland, 19th century) that singing this song on *Shabbat* opens the channels of sustenance in the world.

ki כִּי	eshmera אֶשְׁמְרָה	Shabbat שַׁבָּת	El אֵל	yishmereni יִשְׁמְרֵנִי
ot אוֹת	hi הִיא	le'olmei לְעוֹלְמֵי	ad עַד	beno בֵּינוֹ	uveni וּבֵינִי
asur אָסוּר	metzo מְצֹא	chefetz וְחֵפֶץ	asot עֲשׂוֹת	derachim דְּרָכִים
gam גַּם	mildaber מִלְּדַבֵּר	bo בּוֹ	divrei דִּבְרֵי	tzerachim צְרָכִים
divrei דִּבְרֵי	sechora סְחוֹרָה	af אַף	divrei דִּבְרֵי	melachim מְלָכִים
ehge אֶהְגֶּה	betorat בְּתוֹרַת	El אֵל	utchakmeni וּתְחַכְּמֵנִי

(כִּי ki אֶשְׁמְרָה eshmera שַׁבָּת Shabbat...)

Therefore, let each man give to his soul, delight and also gladness with which to be anointed ["The Holy One, Blessed Be He, satiates him with all these delights of the Supernal Holy anointing oil that flows (from Abba) and is drawn constantly to that Supernal glory, as it is written: 'And satisfy the afflicted soul... Then shall you delight yourself in the Lord.' (Zohar Terumah 534-535)] (He who keeps the Shabbat...)

ק She is holy to you, the Shabbat Queen, to deposit within your homes blessing ["We have learned that all blessing from Above and from Below depends upon the Seventh Day" (Zohar Yitro 445)]. In all your lodgings do no work – your sons and daughters, slave and even maidservant. (He who keeps the Shabbat...)

KI ESHMERA SHABBAT (WHEN I GUARD THE SHABBAT)

When I guard the Shabbat then God will guard me ["The Holy One, Blessed Be He, said to them: 'If you keep this Supernal Seventh One, the attribute of Judgment will not be able to bring accusations against you.'" (Zohar Chadash, Vayeshev 32)]; it is a sign (see Zohar Pinchas 583) forevermore between Him and me.

א It is forbidden to pursue business or to engage with it, even to speak on it necessary matters; if it matters of commerce or matters of kings. I shall delve into the Torah of God, and it shall impact wisdom upon me ["your speech of Shabbat should not be like your speech of the weekday. Because that talk, secular speech that is spoken on Shabbat, rises and stimulates secular things Above. And the Shabbat becomes blemished. One who invites a guest should strive to please him, and not someone else... on Shabbat, it is necessary to awaken only in the words of the Name and the Holiness of the day" (Zohar Beshalach 72-74)] (When I guard the Shabbat...)

Songs

•lenafshi לְנַפְשִׁי	nofesh נוֹפֶשׁ	tamid תָּמִיד	emtza אֶמְצָא	bo בּוֹ
•kedoshi קְדוֹשִׁי	natan נָתַן	rishon רִאשׁוֹן	ledor לְדוֹר	hineh הִנֵּה
•bashishi בַּשִּׁשִּׁי	mishne מִשְׁנֶה	lechem לֶחֶם	betet בְּתֵת	mofet מוֹפֵת
•mezoni מְזוֹנִי	yachpil יַכְפִּיל	shishi שִׁשִּׁי	bechol בְּכָל	kacha כָּכָה
		(כִּי ki אֶשְׁמְרָה eshmera שַׁבָּת Shabbat...)		
•seganav סְגָנָיו	el אֶל	chok וְחֹק	haEl הָאֵל	bedat בְּדָת	rasham רָשַׁם
•befanav בְּפָנָיו	panim פָּנִים	lechem לֶחֶם	la'aroch לַעֲרוֹךְ	bo בּוֹ
•nevonav נְבוֹנָיו	pi פִּי	al עַל	bo בּוֹ	lehit'anot לְהִתְעַנּוֹת	ken כֵּן	al עַל
•avoni עֲוֹנִי	Kippur כִּפּוּר	miYom מִיּוֹם	levad לְבַד	asur, אָסוּר
		(כִּי ki אֶשְׁמְרָה eshmera שַׁבָּת Shabbat...)		
•ta'anugim תַּעֲנוּגִים	yom יוֹם	hu הוּא	mechubad מְכֻבָּד	yom יוֹם	hu הוּא
•vedagim וְדָגִים	basar בָּשָׂר	tov טוֹב	veyayin וְיַיִן	lechem לֶחֶם
•nesogim נְסוֹגִים	achor אָחוֹר	bo בּוֹ	hamit'abelim הַמִּתְאַבְּלִים
•utsamcheni וּתְשַׂמְּחֵנִי	hu הוּא	semachot שְׂמָחוֹת	yom יוֹם	ki כִּי
		(כִּי ki אֶשְׁמְרָה eshmera שַׁבָּת Shabbat...)		
•lehachrit לְהַכְרִית	sofo סוֹפוֹ	vo בוֹ	melacha מְלָאכָה	mechel מֵחֵל
•kevorit כְּבוֹרִית	libi לִבִּי	bo בּוֹ	achabes אֲכַבֵּס	ken כֵּן	al עַל
•veshacharit וְשַׁחֲרִית	arvit עַרְבִית	El אֵל	el אֶל	ve'etpalela וְאֶתְפַּלְלָה
•ya'aneni יַעֲנֵנִי	hu הוּא	mincha מִנְחָה	vegam וְגַם	musaf מוּסָף
		(כִּי ki אֶשְׁמְרָה eshmera שַׁבָּת Shabbat...)		

ב On it I shall always find rest for my soul *(Zohar Pinchas 568); behold, to the first generation (in the desert) did my Holy One give a wonder, by giving double-bread (the manna) on the sixth day. So, on every Friday, may He double my food (see Babylonian Talmud, Tractate Betza 16:1) (When I guard the Shabbat...)*

ר He inscribed in the Godly Ruling *(Leviticus 24:8)* a law for His assistants (priests), that on it (Shabbat) to set up (the twelve loaves of) the Showbread before Him; therefore, to fast on it, according to His wise sages, is prohibited *(Zohar Vayakhel 245-250),* except on the Day of Atonement of my sin. *(When I guard the Shabbat...)*

ה It is an honored day, it is a day of pleasures, bread and good wine, meat and fish; those who mourn on it (Shabbat) they must withdraw, for it is a day of joys, and may cause me to rejoice. *(When I guard the Shabbat...)*

מ The outcome of desecrating it (Shabbat) by performing labor *[extracting Mochin—brains (Zohar Mishpatim 3)]* is (spiritual) excision; I shall therefore cleanse my heart on it (the cleansing Light of Shabbat) as if it is soap *[so during the rest of the week I will be able the help others to cleanse (Kabbalist Rav Tzvi Hirsh of Rymanow)].* I shall pray to God evening (Arvit connection) and morning (Shacharit connection), Musaf (additional connection) as well as Michah (afternoon connection), and He will answer Me. *(When I guard the Shabbat...)*

Songs

Deror Yikra (Call for Freedom)

Deror Yikra was written by Kabbalist Dunash son of Labrat the Levite (Spain, 10th century) and speaks about the freedom that the Light of *Shabbat* can give us. Kabbalist Rav Baruch of Medzhybizh (Ukraine, 18th century) says in the name of his grandfather, the Baal Shem Tov, that singing *Deror Yikra* on *Shabbat* (and specifically at the Third Meal) gives life and vitality for the week to come.

deror דְּרוֹר	yikra יִקְרָא	leven לְבֵן	im עִם	bat בַּת.	veyintzarchem וְיִנְצָרְכֶם
kemo כְּמוֹ	vavat בָּבַת.	ne'im נָעִים	shimchem שִׁמְכֶם	velo וְלֹא
yushbat יוּשְׁבַּת.	shevu שְׁבוּ	venuchu וְנוּחוּ	beyom בְּיוֹם	Shabbat שַׁבָּת.
derosh דְּרוֹשׁ	navi נָוִי	ve'ulami וְאוּלָמִי.	ve'ot וְאוֹת	yesha יֶשַׁע
aseh עֲשֵׂה	imi עִמִּי.	neta נְטַע	sorek שׂוֹרֵק	betoch בְּתוֹךְ
karmi כַּרְמִי.	she'e שְׁעֵה	shav'at שַׁוְעַת	benei בְּנֵי	ami עַמִּי.
deroch דְּרוֹךְ	pura פּוּרָה	betoch בְּתוֹךְ	Batzra בְּצְרָה.	vegam וְגַם
Bavel בָּבֶל	asher אֲשֶׁר	gavra גָּבְרָה.	netotz נְתוֹץ	tzarai צָרָי
be'af בְּאַף	ve'evra וְעֶבְרָה.	shema שְׁמַע	koli קוֹלִי	beyom בְּיוֹם	ekra אֶקְרָא.

Deror Yikra (Call for Freedom)

He shall proclaim freedom for son and daughter ["All should rest from their work on Shabbat and holidays, each according to its own aspect... At the coming of Shabbat or a holiday, Binah descends, which is Yud-Hei-Vav – Chochmah, Binah, and Da'at of Binah – upon Hei, which is the Kingdom of Heaven, which is then an additional Neshamah. And She, Binah, is 'engraved (Heb. charut) upon the tablets' (Shemot 32:16). The tablets are Malchut, and the inspiration of Binah upon Her gives Her freedom (Heb. cherut) from all the Klipot." (Zohar Tzav 56-57)], *and watch over you like* [He—Arich Anpin watches] *the pupil* [Malchut, when She is in the first stage of Her emanation, which is in the secret of one small dot (Writings of the Ari, Gate of Meditations, pg. 358-359)]; *your pleasant name* ["refers to Malchut, called pleasant when the pleasantness Above rests upon her, which is of the World to Come, the secret of Binah." (Zohar Chadash Terumah 21) "When the World to Come is roused to bestow, all goodness, all joy, all the lights and all the freedom of the world are awakened. Therefore the World to Come, which is Binah, is called pleasantness" (Zohar Va'era 187)] *shall not cease* [if] *you cease work and rest on the day of Shabbat* ["all have joy and rest on Shabbat, once Shabbat enters." (Zohar Va'era 188)] *Seek my Dwelling Place and my Hall* (of the Holy Temple), *and grant me a sign* [in Hebrew also letter] *of salvation* ["the name Isaiah, which is composed of the letters Yesha (Eng. 'salvation') Yud, Hei, Vav, brings redemption and the return of the Supernal Light to its place, to Malchut, the rebuilding of the Temple, and ensures that every goodness and every Light will return as before... The Name causes, and the combination of the letters with each other brings about action... for the letters themselves cause Holy, Supernal secrets to appear in them." (Zohar Tetzaveh 7)] *Plant a choice vine in my vineyard* ["the children of Israel, who are called 'the choice vine.'" (Zohar Vayechi 588)]; *turn to the outcry of my people. Tread upon the winepress* [the negative forces] *in Batzrah* [the city of the Angel of Death], *as well as upon Babylon, which overpowered; smash my oppressors in wrath and anger, hear my voice on the day I call.*

Songs

hadas הֲדַס	•har הַר	bamidbar בַּמִדְבָּר	ten תֵּן	Elohim אֱלֹהִים
velamazhir וְלַמַזְהִיר	•tidhar תִּדְהָר	berosh בְּרוֹשׁ	shita שִׁטָּה
•nahar נָהָר	kemei כְּמֵי	ten תֵּן	shelomim שְׁלוֹמִים	•velanizhar וְלַנִּזְהָר
bemog בְּמוֹג	•kana קָנָא	El אֵל	kamai קָמַי	hadoch הֲדוֹךְ
pe פֶּה	venarchiv וְנַרְחִיב	•uvamgina וּבַמְּגִנָּה	levav לֵבָב
•rina רִנָּה	lecha לָךְ	leshonenu לְשׁוֹנֵנוּ	•unmal'ena וּנְמַלְּאֶנָה
vehi וְהִיא	•lenafshecha לְנַפְשֶׁךָ	chochma וְחָכְמָה	de'e דֵּעָה
mitzvat מִצְוַת	netzor נְצוֹר	•leroshecha לְרֹאשֶׁךָ	cheter כֶּתֶר
•kodshecha קָדְשֶׁךָ	Shabbat שַׁבָּת	shemor שְׁמוֹר	•kedoshecha קְדוֹשֶׁךָ

YOM ZEH LEYISRAEL (THIS DAY IS FOR ISRAEL)

Yom Zeh LeYisrael was written by Rav Isaac Luria (the Ari). The title of this song is based on the saying of the *Talmud* (Babylonian Talmud, Tractate Shabbat 86:2) that the Torah was given on *Shabbat*. Kabbalist Rashi says: "this day (of the giving of the Torah) is worthy for Israel." This song speaks about how the Light of *Shabbat* fulfills any deficiency in Creation.

vesimcha וְשִׂמְחָה	ora אוֹרָה	leYisrael לְיִשְׂרָאֵל	ze זֶה	yom יוֹם
		•menucha מְנוּחָה	Shabbat שַׁבָּת	

God, make the wilderness [place of klipot] (bloom) like mountains; (with) myrtles, acacia, cypress and maples (based on Isaiah 41:19 and see Midrash Bamidbar Rabba 21:22). To him who exhorts and is himself heedful [in Hebrew "shining," meaning the Illumination of Chochmah that shines to the Lower Worlds (Zohar Beresheet B, 115)], give peace (flowing) like the waters of a river [Yesod of Zeir Anpin] (based on Isaiah 48:18). Trample my enemies [the klipa], jealous God ["For I the Lord your God, am a jealous God' so that your heart should be directed upwards, and it should not descend below and approach the portal of the Other Side, for in that place lies jealousy" (Zohar Yitro 517)]. (Even) through melted heart [two hearts. "Meaning, with the Good Inclination and Evil Inclination that dwell in him; We must thank the Holy One, Blessed Be He, for everything, both with the Good Inclination and the Evil Inclination… and it behooves one to thank the Holy One, Blessed Be He, for everything that may come unto a person from either side" (Zohar Terumah 883)] and grief, we shall enlarge our mouths and fill it (based on Psalms 81:11), and our tongues sing Your joyful song. Acquire wisdom [Chochmah] for your soul, as it will be a crown [Keter] upon your head ["No man can reach the highest level of Keter except on Shabbat when all is elevated, so if one acquires the level of Chochmah it becomes for him as if he acquires the level of Keter (Arvei Nachal, Vayakhel 39:1)] (and how can you reach this high level? By) guarding the commandment of your Holy One and observe the Shabbat of your Holy One.

YOM ZEH LEYISRAEL (THIS DAY IS FOR ISRAEL)

י *This day is for Israel light and joy – Shabbat is tranquility.*

Songs

צִוִּיתָ tzivita ♦ פִּקּוּדִים pikudim ♦ בְּמַעֲמַד bema'amad סִינַי Sinai ♦
שַׁבָּת Shabbat וּמוֹעֲדִים umo'adim ♦ לִשְׁמוֹר lishmor בְּכָל bechol שָׁנַי shanai ♦
לַעֲרֹךְ la'aroch לְפָנַי lefanai ♦ מַשְׂאֵת mas'et וַאֲרוּחָה va'arucha ♦
שַׁבָּת Shabbat מְנוּחָה menucha ♦

וְזִמְרַת chemdat הַלְּבָבוֹת halevavot ♦ לְאֻמָּה le'uma שְׁבוּרָה shevura ♦
לִנְפָשׁוֹת linfashot נִכְאָבוֹת nich'avot ♦ נְשָׁמָה neshama יְתֵרָה yetera ♦
לְנֶפֶשׁ lenefesh מְצֵרָה metzera ♦ תָּסִיר tasir אֲנָחָה anacha ♦
שַׁבָּת Shabbat מְנוּחָה menucha ♦

קִדַּשְׁתָּ kidashta בֵּרַכְתָּ berachta ♦ אוֹתוֹ oto מִכָּל mikol יָמִים yamim ♦
בְּשֵׁשֶׁת besheshet כִּלִּיתָ kilita מְלֶאכֶת melechet עוֹלָמִים olamim ♦
בּוֹ bo מָצְאוּ matz'u עֲגוּמִים agumim הַשְׁקֵט hashket וּבִטְחָה uvitcha ♦
שַׁבָּת Shabbat מְנוּחָה menucha ♦

לֶאֱסוּר le'isur מְלָאכָה melacha ♦ צִוִּיתָנוּ tzivitanu נוֹרָא nora ♦
אֶזְכֶּה ezke הוֹד hod מְלוּכָה melucha ♦ אִם im שַׁבָּת Shabbat אֶשְׁמֹרָה eshmora ♦
אַקְרִיב akriv שַׁי shai לַמּוֹרָא lamora ♦ מִנְחָה mincha מֶרְקָחָה merkacha ♦
שַׁבָּת Shabbat מְנוּחָה menucha ♦

צ *You commanded precepts at the convocation at Mount Sinai; Shabbats and Holidays to keep through all My years, (and during these days) to prepare before Me dishes and meals; Shabbat is tranquility.*

ח *(Shabbat is) heart's desire of a broken people (from the length of the exile); for pained souls an additional soul (is given on Shabbat); for an anguished soul (Shabbat) takes away misery ["At the coming of Shabbat or a Holiday, Binah descends, which is Yud-Hei-Vav – Chochmah, Binah, and Da'at of Binah – upon Hei, which is the Kingdom of Heaven, which is then an additional Neshamah. And She, Binah, is "engraved (Heb. charut) upon the tablets" (Shemot 32:16). The tablets are Malchut, and the inspiration of Binah upon Her gives Her freedom (Heb. cherut) from all the klipot." (Zohar Tzav 57) (Also see Rashi on Babylonian Talmud, Tractate Betzah 16:1)] – Shabbat is tranquility.*

ק *You have sanctified [Central Column] and blessed [Right Column] it over all other days. In six (days) You completed the work of the Universe (see Sulam commentary on Zohar Beresheet B, 180-181). On Shabbat, the melancholies find quietness and trust – Shabbat is tranquility.*

ל *The prohibition of labor did the Awesome One command us. I shall merit the splendor of royalty [the coming of the Messiah (Midrash Yalkut Shimoni, portion Beshalach 16)] if I shall keep the Shabbat. I shall offer tribute to the Awesome One, a savory meal-offering – Shabbat is tranquility.*

Songs

וְשִׁיר veshir אֶעֱרֹךְ e'eroch לָךְ lecha ♦ בְּנִגּוּן benigun וּנְעִימָה un'ima♦
מוּל mul תִּפְאֶרֶת tiferet גָּדְלְךָ godlecha ♦ נַפְשִׁי nafshi לָךְ lecha כָּמְהָה chamha♦
לִסְגֻלָּה lisgula תְּמִימָה temima ♦ קַיֵּם kayem הַבְטָחָה havtacha♦
שַׁבָּת Shabbat מְנוּחָה menucha♦

רְצֵה retze תְּפִלָּתִי tefilati ♦ כְּמוֹ kemo קָרְבַּן korban נַחְשׁוֹן Nachshon♦
וְיוֹם veyom מְנוּחָתִי menuchati בְּרִנָּה berina וּבְשָׂשׂוֹן uvsason♦
חָבִיב chaviv כְּבַת kevat אִישׁוֹן ishon ♦ בְּרֹב berov הַצְלָחָה hatzlacha♦
שַׁבָּת Shabbat מְנוּחָה menucha♦

יֶשְׁעֲךָ yeshacha קִוִּינוּ kivinu ♦ יָהּ Yah אַדִּיר adir אַדִּירִים adirim♦
בֶּן ben דָּוִד David מַלְכֵּנוּ malkenu ♦ שְׁלַח shelach נָא na לָעִבְרִים laIvrim♦
וְיִקְרָא veyikra לִדְרוֹרִים lidrorim ♦ רֶוַח revach וַהֲנָחָה vahanacha♦
שַׁבָּת Shabbat מְנוּחָה menucha♦

אָנָּא ana עֶלְיוֹן elyon נוֹרָא nora ♦ הַבִּיטָה habita עֲנֵנוּ anenu♦
פְּדֵנוּ fedenu בִּמְהֵרָה vimhera ♦ וְחָנֵּנוּ chonenu וְחָנֵּנוּ chonenu♦
שַׂמַּח samach נַפְשֵׁנוּ nafshenu בְּאוֹר be'or ♦ וְשִׂמְחָה vesimcha♦
שַׁבָּת Shabbat מְנוּחָה menucha♦

וְחַדֵּשׁ chadesh מִקְדָּשֵׁנוּ mikdashenu זָכְרָה zochra נֶחֱרֶבֶת necherevet♦
טוּבְךָ tuvcha מוֹשִׁיעֵנוּ moshi'enu ♦ תְּנָה tena לַנֶּעֱצֶבֶת lane'etzevet♦
בְּשַׁבָּת beShabbat יוֹשֶׁבֶת yoshevet ♦ בְּזֶמֶר bezemer וְשִׁבְחָה ushvacha♦
שַׁבָּת Shabbat מְנוּחָה menucha♦

ו And I shall arrange a song for You, melodious and sweet, towards Your splendorous greatness my soul longs so for You. For Your perfect treasure fulfill the pledge – Shabbat is tranquility.

ר Accept favorably my prayer like the offering of Nachshon [son of Amminadab, the head of the tribe of Judah, who sacrificed himself and initiated by walking in head deep until the Red Sea split and with that merited the kinghood (Midrash Mechilta, Beshalach 5)], and the day of my tranquility with songs of praise and joy. As beloved as the apple of the eye [Bat Ayin – Malchut that receives from the Supernal Chochmah on Shabbat (Sulam commentary on Zohar Vayakhel 182)] with abundant success – Shabbat is tranquility.

י For Your redemption have we hoped, Yah, mightiest of the mighty. (The Messiah) Son of David, our king, please send to the Hebrews; and let he proclaim for freedom, comfort, and relief – Shabbat is tranquility.

א Please, Supreme One, Awesome One, see and answer us. Redeem us speedily. Favor us favor us. Bring happiness to our souls with Light and gladness – Shabbat is tranquility.

ח Renew our Sanctuary (the Holy Temple); remember the ruined. Your goodness, our Savior, grant to the saddened ones, who sit on the Shabbat in song and praise – Shabbat is tranquility.

zechor זְכוֹר	kadosh קָדוֹשׁ	lanu לָנוּ׃	bizchut בִּזְכוּת	yikrat יְקָרַת	hayom הַיּוֹם׃		
shemor שָׁמוֹר	na נָא	otanu אוֹתָנוּ׃	beyom בְּיוֹם	ze זֶה	uvchol וּבְכָל	yom יוֹם׃	
dodi דּוֹדִי	tzach צַח	ve'ayom וְאָיוֹם׃	tavi תָּבִיא	revacha רְוָחָה׃			
	Shabbat שַׁבָּת	menucha מְנוּחָה׃					
kol קוֹל	rina רִנָּה	vishu'a וִישׁוּעָה׃	leYisrael לְיִשְׂרָאֵל	hashmi'a הַשְׁמִיעָה׃			
bevo בְּבֹא	chezyon חֶזְיוֹן	teshu'a תְּשׁוּעָה׃	tzur צוּר	matzmi'ach מַצְמִיחַ׃			
yeshu'a יְשׁוּעָה׃	or אוֹר	shimshi שִׁמְשִׁי	hofi'a הוֹפִיעָה׃				
tamid תָּמִיד	hazricha הַזְרִיחָה׃	Shabbat שַׁבָּת	menucha מְנוּחָה׃				

YOM ZEH MECHUBAD (THIS DAY IS MOST HONORED)

Written by Yisrael Hager (11th century) and based on the early teaching of Kabbalah, *Yom Zeh Mechubad* speaks about the joy and contentment of *Shabbat*, and recommends honoring the *Shabbat* as it brings blessings, sustenance and illuminations from Above, as the *Zohar* states (Zohar Yitro 445): "We have learned that all blessing from Above and from Below depends upon the Seventh Day."

yom יוֹם	zeh זֶה	mechubad מְכֻבָּד	mikol מִכָּל	yamim יָמִים׃	
ki כִּי	vo בּוֹ	shavat שָׁבַת	tzur צוּר	olamim עוֹלָמִים׃	
sheshet שֵׁשֶׁת	yamim יָמִים	ta'ase תַּעֲשֶׂה	melachtecha מְלַאכְתֶּךָ׃	veyom וְיוֹם	
hashvi'i הַשְּׁבִיעִי	lelohecha לֵאלֹהֶיךָ׃	Shabbat שַׁבָּת	lo לֹא	ta'ase תַּעֲשֶׂה	vo בּוֹ
melacha מְלָאכָה׃	ki כִּי	chol כָל	asa עָשָׂה	sheshet שֵׁשֶׁת	yamim יָמִים׃
(yom יוֹם	zeh זֶה	mechubad מְכֻבָּד...)			

---

† Remember for us, Holy One, with the merit of the honor of the day (of Shabbat); please guard us, on this day ["Shabbat day is joy for all, and everything is protected Above and Below" (Zohar Vayakhel 204)] and every day. My beloved, pure [Chesed] and awesome [Gevurah], bring relief – Shabbat is tranquility.
ק The sound of song and salvation make heard to Israel with the coming of the prophecy of salvation. Rock, Who causes salvation to sprout, let the light of the sun appear, may it always shine [based on the verse "But to you who fear My Name the sun of righteousness shall arise with healing in its wings" (Malachi 3:20) the Zohar says: "For we have learned that the Holy One, blessed be He, made a lofty Light when He created the world, and treasured it for the righteous for the future to come… When the Holy One, blessed be He, saw the wicked that will live in the world, He concealed that Light… The Holy One, blessed be He, will shine it upon the righteous in the World to Come," (Zohar Emor 3-4)] – Shabbat is tranquility.

YOM ZEH MECHUBAD (THIS DAY IS MOST HONORED)
י This day is most honored of all days, for on it rested the Rock of the Universe.
ש Six days shall you do your work ["It is written, 'for six days the Lord made Heaven and Earth' and not 'in six days'. We have explained that each day did its work… They are the six Supernal Days, from which all the works of Creation were performed" (Zohar Emor 112)]; But the Seventh Day is for your God. Shabbat you shall perform no labor, for He completed everything in six days. (This day is most honored…)

•kodesh קֹדֶשׁ	lemikraei לְמִקְרָאֵי	hu הוּא	rishon רִאשׁוֹן	
•kodesh קֹדֶשׁ	Shabbat שַׁבַּת	yom יוֹם	shabaton שַׁבָּתוֹן	yom יוֹם
•yekadesh יְקַדֵּשׁ	beyeno בֵּינוֹ	ish אִישׁ	kol כָּל	ken כֵּן al עַל
•temimim תְּמִימִים	yivtze'u יִבְצְעוּ	lechem לֶחֶם	shetei שְׁתֵּי	al עַל

(yom יוֹם zeh זֶה mechubad מְכֻבָּד...)

•mamtakim מַמְתַקִּים	shete שְׁתֵה	mashmanim מַשְׁמַנִּים	echol אֱכוֹל	
•devekim דְּבֵקִים	bo בּוֹ	lechol לְכָל	yiten יִתֵּן	El אֵל ki כִּי
•chukim וְחֻקִּים	lechem לֶחֶם	lilbosh לִלְבּוֹשׁ	beged בֶּגֶד	
•matamim מַטְעַמִּים	vechol וְכָל	vedagim וְדָגִים	basar בָּשָׂר	

(yom יוֹם zeh זֶה mechubad מְכֻבָּד...)

•vesavata וְשָׂבָעְתָּ	ve'achalta וְאָכַלְתָּ	bo בּוֹ	kol כָּל	techsar תֶחְסַר lo לֹא
asher אֲשֶׁר •Elohecha אֱלֹהֶיךָ		Hashem ה'	et אֶת	uverachta וּבֵרַכְתָּ
•ha'amim הָעַמִּים	mikol מִכָּל	verachecha בֵּרַכְךָ	ki כִּי	•ahavta אֲהַבְתָ

(yom יוֹם zeh זֶה mechubad מְכֻבָּד...)

ha'aretz הָאָרֶץ	gam גַּם	•kevodo כְּבוֹדוֹ	mesaprim מְסַפְּרִים	hashamayim הַשָּׁמַיִם
asta עָשְׂתָה	ele אֵלֶּה	chol כָּל	ki כִּי	re'u רְאוּ •chasdo וְחַסְדּוֹ mal'a מָלְאָה
•tamim תָּמִים	pa'olo פָּעֳלוֹ	hatzur הַצּוּר	hu הוּא	ki כִּי •yado יָדוֹ

(yom יוֹם zeh זֶה mechubad מְכֻבָּד...)

ר It is the first to the Holy Convocations ["Shabbat is not called from Holiness (Kodesh—Supernal Abba and Ima), because Shabbat receives the inheritance of Holiness and is not called (from there). Hence all (the other Holidays) are called from Holiness, are attached to Shabbat and adorn themselves with it" (Zohar Emor 110)]; the day of rest, the holy Shabbat day. Therefore, let every person recite the Kiddush over his wine [also can be translated as: Every person sanctifies himself by the Kiddush wine (Chochmah) (Botzina Denehora, Rav Baruch of Medzhybizh)]; over two complete loaves shall ones break bread [also can be translated as: Even after the two loaves are broken they are still complete, meaning we also should be complete and whole. (Be'erot Hamayim, Rav Tzvi Hirsh of Rymanow, Beresheet)]. (This day is most honored...)

א Eat rich foods, drink sweet beverages, for God will give to all who cling to Him [also can be translated as: On Shabbat, God will give to all the gift of cleaving to the Creator (Shem MiShemuel, Emor, 1914)] clothes to wear, a daily portion of bread, meat, fish and all delicacies. (This day is most honored...)

ל You shall lack nothing on it, you will eat and you will be satiated. And you shall bless the Lord, your God, Whom you love, for He has blessed you over all peoples. (This day is most honored...)

ה The Heavens declare His glory ["When the day of Shabbat dawns, the joy ascends in all the worlds with satisfaction and gladness. Then 'The heavens declare the glory of God'... He questions: What is the meaning of 'declare'?... they illuminate and sparkle in the glitter of the Supernal Light" (Zohar Terumah 184-185)], ג the Earth too is filled with His kindness. ר See that all this His hand had made, for He is the Rock; His work is perfect. (This day is most honored...)

SONGS

YOM SHABBATON (THE RESTING DAY)

Yom Shabbaton was written by Kabbalist Rav Yehuda Halevi (Spain, 11th century) and portrays the connection between *Shabbat* and the dove from the biblical story of Noah. It emphasizes the protection we can receive on *Shabbat* from any disaster.

The *Zohar* says (Tikkunei Zohar, 6th Tikkun, 43): "As when the *Shechinah* is in exile, in *Beriah*, *Yetzirah*, and *Asiyah*, it is said concerning Her (Genesis 8:9): 'And the dove did not find a resting place…' except on *Shabbat* and the Holidays, when She rises to *Atzilut*." The *Zohar* also says (Tikkunei Zohar, 21st Tikkun, 74): "On week days, food is brought to Her through a messenger… But on *Shabbat* and the Holidays, food is brought to Her by the Holy One, blessed be He. Woe to the woman who is sustained through a messenger and not by her husband, himself. And it has been explained in relation to the dove, as is said (Genesis 8:11): 'in its beak was a freshly plucked olive leaf' Why an olive leaf? The dove said, 'Master of the Universe, may my food be as bitter as an olive but given over by Your hands (like on *Shabbat*), rather than sweet given over by the hands of an agent.'"

♦lishkoa'ch לִשְׁכּוֹחַ   en אֵין   shabaton שַׁבָּתוֹן   yom יוֹם
♦hanicho'ach הַנִּיחוֹחַ   kere'ach כְּרֵיחַ   zichro זִכְרוֹ
mano'ach מָנוֹחַ vo בּוֹ matz'a מָצְאָה yona יוֹנָה
ko'ach כֹּחַ yegi'ei יְגִיעֵי yanuchu יָנוּחוּ vesham וְשָׁם
(…mano'ach מָנוֹחַ vo בּוֹ matz'a מָצְאָה yona יוֹנָה)

♦emunim אֱמוּנִים   livnei לִבְנֵי   nichbad נִכְבָּד   hayom הַיּוֹם
♦uvanim וּבָנִים   avot אָבוֹת   leshomro לְשָׁמְרוֹ   zehirim וְזְהִירִים
♦avanim אֲבָנִים   luchot לוּחוֹת   bishnei בִּשְׁנֵי   chakuk וְחָקוּק
♦ko'ach כֹּחַ   ve'amitz וְאַמִּיץ   onim אוֹנִים   merov מֵרוֹב
(…mano'ach מָנוֹחַ vo בּוֹ matz'a מָצְאָה yona יוֹנָה)

YOM SHABBATON (THE RESTING DAY)

' *The Shabbat day shall not be forgotten, for its memory is like a pleasing fragrance [of Noah's sacrifices* "All the sweetening of the Judgments depend on the nose, and therefore it is written: 'And the Lord smelled the sweet savor.' (Beresheet 8:21) (This verse) does not speak of the smell of the sacrifice, but of the savory smell, because all Judgments that are connected to the nose are mitigated… the sweet savor (Heb. nicho'ach) indicates double satisfaction (Heb. nachat) on both sides, Right and Left. The one on the Right is satisfaction revealed from the most concealed Atika Kadisha, who brings pleasure and sweetening for everything, both to Chochmah and Chasadim. The one on the Left is sweetening coming from Below with the smoke and fire on the altar. Since it is sweetened on both sides from Atika and from Below, therefore it is written, 'nicho'ach,' which indicates double satisfaction. All this applies to Zeir Anpin." (Zohar Ha'azinu, Idra Zuta, 148-151 and Zohar Naso, Idra Rabba, 135/1 and see also the Writings of the Ari, Gates of Meditation B, 77)] *The dove finds rest on it,* "and there [in the Garden of Eden (see Midrash Beresheet Rabba 33:6)] the weary are at rest." [the righteous (Midrash Beresheet Rabba 9:6)]" (Job 3:17)
ה *This day is glorious for the children of the faithful one, those who diligently observe it — fathers and sons; engraved on two stone tablets,* "because of the greatness of His might [the Supernal Keter] and because He is strong in power [Chochmah (see Tikkunei Zohar, 49th Tikkun, 4)]" (Isaiah 40:26) (The dove finds rest …)

Songs

uva'u וּבָאוּ	chulam כֻּלָּם	bivrit בִּבְרִית	yachad יַחַד
na'ase נַעֲשֶׂה	venishma וְנִשְׁמָע	amru אָמְרוּ	ke'echad כְּאֶחָד
ufatchu וּפָתְחוּ	ve'anu וְעָנוּ	Hashem ה'	echad אֶחָד
baruch בָּרוּךְ	hanoten הַנּוֹתֵן	layaef לַיָּעֵף	ko'ach כֹּחַ
(yona יוֹנָה matz'a מָצְאָה vo בוֹ mano'ach מָנוֹחַ...)

diber דִּבֶּר	bekodsho בְּקָדְשׁוֹ	behar בְּהַר	haMor הַמּוֹר
yom יוֹם	hashevi'i הַשְּׁבִיעִי	zachor זָכוֹר	veshamor וְשָׁמוֹר
vechol וְכָל	pikudav פִּקּוּדָיו	yachad יַחַד	ligmor לִגְמוֹר
chazek חַזֵּק	motnayim מָתְנַיִם	ve'ametz וְאַמֵּץ	ko'ach כֹּחַ
(yona יוֹנָה matz'a מָצְאָה vo בוֹ mano'ach מָנוֹחַ...)

ha'am הָעָם	asher אֲשֶׁר	na נָע	katzon כַּצֹּאן	ta'a טָעָה
yizkor יִזְכּוֹר	lefokdo לִפְקְדוֹ	bivrit בִּבְרִית	ushvu'a וּשְׁבוּעָה
leval לְבַל	ya'avor יַעֲבוֹר	bam בָּם	mikrei מִקְרֵי	ra'a רָעָה
ka'asher כַּאֲשֶׁר	nishbata נִשְׁבַּעְתָּ	al עַל	mei מֵי	No'ach נֹחַ
(yona יוֹנָה matz'a מָצְאָה vo בוֹ mano'ach מָנוֹחַ...)

ו Then they all joined together in a covenant "We will do and obey [*"Before Israel arrived on the scene, the lofty angels in Heaven used to prepare and complete this work. As soon as Israel arrived and stood at Mount Sinai and said, 'Will we do and obey (lit. 'listen'),' they took over this task from the ministering angels and became part of His World... Therefore, at first, prior to the arrival of Israel, were 'mighty ones who perform His bidding' (Psalms 103:20), and after that... those 'mighty ones who perform His bidding' were Israel." (Zohar Balak 105)]"* (Exodus 24:7) they said as one. Then they opened (their mouth) and called: "The Lord is One"; Blessed is "He Who gives strength to the weary." (Isaiah 40:29) *(The dove finds rest...)*

ה He spoke through His holy one on the Mount of Myrrh: 'Remember the Seventh Day, (Exodus 20:8) and guard it (Deuteronomy 5:12) and all His statutes to be studied as well'; "Strengthen the loins *["(It says (Ezekiel 1:27)): 'From what appeared to be his loins upward, and from what appeared to be his loins downward'... they are in the Sefirot of Netzach and Hod. For Netzach and Hod are called 'loins'... The Holy One, blessed be He said to the ministering angels: 'Those who run... to hear the lesson on the Shabbat... they are to be received in the Temple of this appearance,' namely in the Temple of Netzach and Hod." (Zohar Pinchas 316-321)]* and fortify the power" (Nahum 2:2) *(The dove finds rest...)*

ה The people who have wondered like lost sheep (in the exile), may He remember for them the covenant and the oath that no evil happenings shall befall them, as You swore at the waters of Noah *["My father (Rav Shimon) said that the reason the redemption of Israel and the remembrance of Malchut are mentioned in the Torah is that "remember the everlasting covenant" refers to the redemption of Israel and the completion of Malchut. That is why, in reference to the time of redemption, it is written: 'For as I have sworn that the waters of Noah should no more go over the earth, so have I sworn that I would not be angry with you, nor rebuke you.' (Isaiah 54:9)" (Zohar Noah 292)]* *(The dove finds rest...)*

Tzur Meshelo Achalnu (The Rock, Whose Food We Have Eaten)

Tzur Mishelo is one of the ancient songs of *Shabbat* (about 1800 years) and its structure follows the order of *Birkat Hamazon*.

The *Talmud* (Babylonian Talmud, Tractate Sotah, 10:2) says about Abraham: "'And he called there on the Name of the Lord, the Everlasting God.' Resh Lakish said: Read not 'and he called' but 'and he made to call,' thereby teaching that our father Abraham caused the Name of the Holy One, blessed be He, to be uttered by the mouth of every passer-by. How was this? After travelers (who were hosted in the tent of Abraham and Sarah) had eaten and drunk, they stood up to bless Abraham; but, he said to them, 'Did you eat of mine? You ate of that which belongs to the God of the Universe. Thank, praise and bless Him who spoke and the world came into being.'"

The first verse says: "We are satiated and have left over, according to the word of the Lord." The question is where in the Torah does the Lord say anything about leaving food over? Regarding the verse, "and call the *Shabbat* a delight" the *Zohar* says that one should eat and drink on *Shabbat* meals until he is full. Kabbalist Rav Pinchas of Koritz asks: "How do you know if one is satiated, and with that he fulfills the obligation?" And he answers: "Only when he leaves some food over."

צוּר tzur מִשֶּׁלּוֹ mishelo אָכַלְנוּ achalnu. בָּרְכוּ barchu אֱמוּנַי emunai.

שָׂבַעְנוּ savanu וְהוֹתַרְנוּ vehotarnu כִּדְבַר kidvar ה' Hashem.

הַזָּן hazan אֶת et עוֹלָמוֹ olamo. רוֹעֵנוּ ro'enu אָבִינוּ avinu.

אָכַלְנוּ achalnu אֶת et לַחְמוֹ lachmo. וְיֵינוֹ veyeno שָׁתִינוּ shatinu.

עַל al כֵּן ken נוֹדֶה node לִשְׁמוֹ lishmo. וּנְהַלְלוֹ unhalelo בְּפִינוּ befinu.

אָמַרְנוּ amarnu וְעָנִינוּ ve'aninu. אֵין en קָדוֹשׁ kadosh כַּה' kaHashem.

בְּשִׁיר beshir וְקוֹל vekol תּוֹדָה toda נְבָרֵךְ nevarech לֵאלֹהֵינוּ lelokenu. עַל al

אֶרֶץ eretz חֶמְדָּה chemda טוֹבָה tova. שֶׁהִנְחִיל shehinchil לַאֲבוֹתֵינוּ la'avotenu.

מָזוֹן mazon וְצֵדָה vetzeda הִשְׂבִּיעַ hisbi'a לְנַפְשֵׁנוּ lenafshenu.

וְחַסְדּוֹ chasdo גָּבַר gavar עָלֵינוּ alenu. וֶאֱמֶת ve'emet ה' Hashem.

Tzur Meshelo Achalnu (The Rock, Whose Food We Have Eaten)

The Rock, Whose food we have eaten — bless, my faithful friends,
we are satiated and have left over, according to the word of the Lord.

He Who feeds His world, our Shepherd, our Father, we have eaten of His bread and have drunk of His wine. Therefore, we will give thanks to His Name, and praise Him with our mouths; we shall say and proclaim aloud: "There is none Holy as the Lord." (I Samuel, 2:2) With song and sound of thanksgiving shall we offer blessing to our God, for the good and the delightful land ["which is the secret of the lower world, Malchut" (Zohar Chadash, Ruth 589)] that He bequeathed to our forefathers, and food and sustenance He did adequately provide for our souls. "His kindness has overwhelmed us; and faithful is the Lord." (Psalms 117:2)

Songs

רַחֵם rachem • בַּחֲסָדֶךָ bechasdecha • עַל al עַמְּךָ amecha צוּרֵנוּ tzurenu•
עַל al צִיּוֹן Tziyon מִשְׁכַּן mishkan כְּבוֹדֶךָ kevodecha • זְבוּל zevul בֵּית bet
תִּפְאַרְתֵּנוּ tif'artenu • בֶּן ben דָּוִד David עַבְדְּךָ avdecha יָבֹא yavo
וְיִגְאָלֵנוּ veyig'alenu • רוּחַ ru'ach אַפֵּינוּ apenu • מְשִׁיחוֹ mesh'iach ה׳ Hashem•
יִבָּנֶה yibane הַמִּקְדָּשׁ hamikdash • עִיר ir צִיּוֹן Tziyon תִּמָּלֵא tima'le•
וְשָׁם vesham נָשִׁיר nashir שִׁיר shir חָדָשׁ chadash • וּבִרְנָנָה uvirnana נַעֲלֶה na'ale•
הָרַחֲמָן harachaman • הַמְקֻדָּשׁ hanikdash • יִתְבָּרַךְ yitbarach וְיִתְעַלֶּה veyit'ale•
עַל al כּוֹס kos יַיִן yayin מָלֵא maleh• כְּבִרְכַּת kevirkat ה׳ Hashem•

Yoducha Ra'ayonai (My Thoughts Thank You)

Yoducha Ra'ayonai was written by Kabbalist Rav Yisrael son of Moshe Najara (student of the Ari, Gaza, 16th century) and expresses the Holiness of Shabbat.

יוֹדוּךָ yoducha רַעְיוֹנַי ra'ayonai יְהֹוָה(אלהינוה) Adonai רוֹעִי ro'i•
בְּיוֹם beyom שַׁבַּת shabat קֹדֶשׁ kodesh יוֹם yom הַשְּׁבִיעִי hashvi'i•
יוֹם yom אֲשֶׁר asher כִּלִּיתָ kilita בּוֹ vo כָּל kol מְלַאכְתֶּךָ melachtecha•
אוֹמַר omar כִּי ki שָׂרִיתָ sarita עַל al כָּל kol זוּלָתֶךָ zulatecha•

Be merciful, in Your kindness, upon Your people, our Rock, upon Zion, the residence place of Your glory, the dwelling house of our splendor ["(King Solomon said:) 'I have surely built You a house to dwell in (Heb. zvul)' (1 Kings 8:13). 'A house to dwell in' most definitely. When all the stored treasures of the King, that is Zeir Anpin, were assigned in the hands of Malchut, and she has authority over them, she is called 'a house to dwell in.' There is one firmament that is called 'zvul,' since its function is to receive blessings and put everything in order. That one – Malchut, when she rules over everything – is also called 'a house to dwell in'". (Zohar Beha'alotcha 25)]. And let the son of David, Your servant, come and redeem us – "The breath of our nostrils, the anointed one of the Lord." (Ecclesiastes 4:20) May the Temple be rebuilt. May the city of Zion be filled, and there we shall sing a new song ["It is written: 'A psalm'... This is because the Holy Spirit is destined to sing it, when the Holy One, blessed be He, raises Israel from the dust. Therefore, David is not mentioned here. Then 'Sing to the Lord a new song,' for this is a new song that has not been sung since the world was created." (Zohar Chayei Sarah 29) "For it (this song) is called 'new' only with the renewal of the moon, which is Malchut, when it illuminates from the sun, which is Zeir Anpin. Then it is new, and this is 'a new song,' for each time Malchut ascends to pair with Zeir Anpin, She is transformed to become new... and it all amounts to the same, for the elevation of the Throne, which is Malchut, to ascend Above occurs on Shabbat. Therefore, the order of this praise is on the Shabbat." (Zohar Terumah 211-213)]; and there go up with joyous song. The Holy, Merciful One – may He be blessed and exalted over a filled cup [cup—kos—כוס spelled out: kaf—כף vav—וו samech—סמך=232] of wine, worthy the blessing [beracha—הברכה=232] of the Lord.

Yoducha Ra'ayonai (My Thoughts Thank You)

My thoughts thank You, Lord, my shepherd, on the day of the Holy Sabbath, the Seventh Day. On the day upon which You completed all Your works, I declare that You ruled over everything else,

levalotecha לְבַלּוֹתֶךָ	en אֵין	asita עָשִׂיתָ	uma'asim וּמַעֲשִׂים
lehargi'i לְהַרְגִּיעִי	chish וְחִישׁ	amatecha אֲמָתֶךָ	ven בֶּן	li לִי
haminyanim הַמִּנְיָנִים	mikol מִכֹּל	vacharta בָּחַרְתָּ	shevi'i שְׁבִיעִי
veshanim וְשָׁנִים	beshavuot בְּשָׁבוּעוֹת	kidashta קִדַּשְׁתָּ	ve'oto וְאוֹתוֹ
emunim אֱמוּנִים	legeza לְגֶזַע	nasata נָשָׂאתָ	asher אֲשֶׁר	chish וְחִישׁ
verivi וְרִבְעִי	archi אָרְחִי	me'asonim מֵאֲסוֹנִים	ufdem וּפְדֵם
menucha מְנוּחָה	yom יוֹם	ze זֶה	yom יוֹם	vimnuchati בִּמְנוּחָתִי	retze רְצֵה
harvacha הָרְוָחָה	li לִי	hamtzi הַמְצִיא	avodati עֲבוֹדָתִי	uvyom וּבְיוֹם
va'arucha וַאֲרוּחָה	maset מַשְׂאֵת	lishvitati לְשָׁבְתָּתִי	vehachen וְהָכֵן
sha'ashui שַׁעֲשׁוּעַי	yihye יִהְיֶה	vesimcha וְשִׂמְחָה	vesason וְשָׂשׂוֹן
tezakeni תְּזַכֵּנִי	Shabbat שַׁבָּת	shekulo שֶׁכֻּלוֹ	olam עוֹלָם	el אֵל
ba'adeni בַּעֲדֵנִי	or אוֹר	sim שִׂים	behilo בְּהִלּוֹ	venercha וְנֵרְךָ
ta'aleni תַּעֲלֵנִי	tashuv תָּשׁוּב	Shilo שִׁילֹה	mishkan מִשְׁכַּן	ve'el וְאֶל
veyish'i וְיִשְׁעִי	ori אוֹרִי	aneni עֲנֵנִי	mehera מְהֵרָה

VA'AMARTEM KO LECHAI ("AND YOU SHOULD SAY: LIVE LONG")

This song was written by Kabbalist Rav Yosef Chaim (the Ben Ish Chai – Iraq, 19th century) while he was visiting Meron, Israel, during the *Hilula* of Rav Shimon Bar Yochai on Lag Ba'Omer in 1869. It is written according to the Hebrew alphabet and lauds Kabbalist Rav Shimon Bar Yochai, the author of the *Zohar*.

The *Zohar* says (Zohar Bo 126): "Rav Chiya and Rav Yosi came and prostrated before Rav Shimon, and kissed his hands. They wept and said: Upper and lower images raise their heads through your merit. The Holy One, blessed be He, made terrestrial Jerusalem, which is *Malchut*, in the likeness of celestial Jerusalem, which is *Binah*. And He made the outer walls of the Holy City and its gates. One cannot enter until the gates are opened for him. One cannot ascend until the steps to the outer walls are prepared. Who can open the gates of the Holy City? And who can repair the steps to the outer walls? This is Rav Shimon bar Yochai, who opens the gates of the secrets of Wisdom and repairs the Upper Levels. And it is written: 'Every one of your males shall appear before the Master, the Lord (can be translated: 'shall be seen by the Face of the Master, the Lord)' (Exodus 34:23). Who is the Face of the Master the Lord? This is Rav Shimon bar Yochai."

---

and You have made deed that in no way diminished You. As for me, the son of Your maidservant (based on the words of king David in Psalms 116:16), hurry to bring me serenity.
ש *You selected the seventh, the start of all the numbers, and You sanctified it among weeks and years; hurry that which You swore to the offspring of the faithful. Rescue from disasters my going and my lying down.*
ר *Accept favorably my tranquility this day, the day of rest, and on the day that I work provide me with prosperity, and prepare for my rest a gift of food; and may joy and happiness be my delight.*
אל *A world that is all Shabbat allow me to merit. And Your lamp in its illumination grant as a light for me; and to the Tabernacle of Shiloh bring me up once more; speedily answer me, my Light and my Salvation.*

Songs

וַאֲמַרְתֶּם va'amartem כֹּה ko לֶחָי lechai
רַבִּי rabi שִׁמְעוֹן Shimon בַּר bar יוֹחַאי Yochai.
וַאֲמַרְתֶּם va'amartem כֹּה ko לֶחָי lechai
רַבִּי rabi שִׁמְעוֹן Shimon צַדִּיקַאי tzadikay.

אִישׁ ish אֱלֹהִים Elohim קָדוֹשׁ kadosh הוּא hu. אַשְׁרֵי ashrei עַיִן ayin
רָאַתְהוּ ra'at'hu. לֵב lev וְחָכָם chacham יַשְׂכִּיל yaskil פִּיהוּ pihu.
אֲדוֹנֵנוּ adonenu בַּר Bar יוֹחַאי Yochai. (וַאֲמַרְתֶּם va'amartem...)

בָּרוּךְ baruch הוּא hu מִפִּי mipi עֶלְיוֹן elyon. קָדוֹשׁ kadosh הוּא hu
מְהֵרָיוֹן meherayon. מְאוֹר me'or גָּלִיל Galil הָעֶלְיוֹן haelyon.
אֲדוֹנֵנוּ adonenu בַּר Bar יוֹחַאי Yochai. (וַאֲמַרְתֶּם va'amartem...)

גִּבּוֹר gibor וְאִישׁ ve'ish מִלְחָמָה milchama. בְּדַת bedat תּוֹרָה tora
תְּמִימָה temima. מָלֵא maleh מַדָּע mada וְחָכְמָה vechochma.
אֲדוֹנֵנוּ adonenu בַּר Bar יוֹחַאי Yochai. (וַאֲמַרְתֶּם va'amartem...)

VA'AMARTEM KO LECHAI ("AND YOU SHOULD SAY: LIVE LONG")

"And you should say: Live long" (I Samuel 25:6 and see Zohar Vayera 31) *(to) Rav Shimon son of Yochai.*
"And you should say: Live long" (I Samuel 25:6 and see Zohar Vayera 31) *(to) Rav Shimon the righteous.*

א *"He is a man of God"* [as it is written about Moses (Deuteronomy 33:1), which implies about the soul connection between Moses and Rav Shimon. (Likutei Hashas - The Ari on the Babylonian Talmud - on Tractate Shabbat 33:1) See also: "They heard a Divine voice that was saying: Get out of here, for Rav Shimon ben Yochai is here. Since the Holy One blessed be He, decrees, yet he cancels it. Rav Chanina was there. He came over and told Rav Meir. Rav Meir said to him: Who can bear Rav Shimon's greatness? Is he not as great as Moses?" (Zohar Chadash, Ruth 496) Also it speaks about the righteous aspect that Rav Shimon was, which is Yesod of Zeir Anpin, who causes Unification between Nukva and Zeir Anpin (see Zohar Terumah 89, 124 and Zohar Chadash, Ki Tisa 90)]; *"He is holy"* (as it is written about Elisha the prophet (II Kings 4:9) and the Zohar says: "Who is the holy one of the Lord? That is Rav Shimon bar Yochai, who is called honorable in this world and the World to Come (Zohar Naso, Idra Rabba 364)]. Fortunate is the eye that saw him [as it is says about the Messiah. (Midrash Pesikta of Rav Kahana) And also "Rav Shimon replied: How happy is my lot, that you have seen me so. Because if you had not seen me so, I would not have been so." (Zohar, Prologue 189)] *"His wise heart makes his mouth prudent."* (Proverbs 16:23) *Our master, the son of Yochai.* (And you should say...)

ב He is blessed by the mouth of the Most High ["This is Rav Shimon bar Yochai, with whom his Master glorifies Himself daily. Blessed is his portion Above and Below" (Zohar, Ha'azinu, Idra Zuta 201)]. He was dedicated (to holiness) from conception [see discussion in the Talmud (Babylonian Talmud Tractate Makot 17:2)]. His Light illuminated the Upper Galilee; *Our master, the son of Yochai.* (And you should say...)

ג *"He is a warrior and a man of war"* [(Isaiah 3:2) the spiritual war - "Rav Shimon says: Gather, friends, to the chamber, dressed in shields with swords and lances in your hands, which is the secret of the unifications to destroy the klipot" (Zohar Naso, Idra Rabba 2)] in [defending] the complete Torah (Psalms 19:8). He was filled with deep knowledge and wisdom; *Our master, the son of Yochai.* (And you should say...)

be'oz בְּעֹז		ta'alumot תַּעֲלוּמוֹת		kol כָּל		darash דָּרַשׁ
ramot רָמוֹת		ma'alot מַעֲלוֹת		ala עָלָה		veta'atzumot וְתַעֲצוּמוֹת

אֲדוֹנֵנוּ adonenu בַּר Bar יוֹחָאי Yochay • (וַאֲמַרְתֶּם...)va'amartem

hagzera הַגְּזֵרָה		mipnei מִפְּנֵי		me'ara מְעָרָה		betoch בְּתוֹךְ	huchba הֻחְבָּא
tora תּוֹרָה		sitrei סִתְרֵי		lamad לָמַד		sham שָׁם

אֲדוֹנֵנוּ adonenu בַּר Bar יוֹחָאי Yochay • (וַאֲמַרְתֶּם...)va'amartem

vecharuv וְחָרוּב		lo לוֹ		mayan מַעְיָן		nivra נִבְרָא	vesham וְשָׁם
vechevlo וְחֶבְלוֹ		chelko חֶלְקוֹ		tov טוֹב		ma מַה	lema'achalo לְמַאֲכָלוֹ

אֲדוֹנֵנוּ adonenu בַּר Bar יוֹחָאי Yochay • (וַאֲמַרְתֶּם...)va'amartem

recha רֵיקָא		din דִּין		livracha לִבְרָכָה		tzadik צַדִּיק	zecher זֵכֶר
zika זִכָּה		verabim וְרַבִּים		zacha זָכָה		recha רֵיקָא	uvar וּבַר

אֲדוֹנֵנוּ adonenu בַּר Bar יוֹחָאי Yochay • (וַאֲמַרְתֶּם...)va'amartem

bemishna בְּמִשְׁנָה		hen הֵן		halachot הֲלָכוֹת		kama כַּמָּה	chidesh וְחִדֵּשׁ
mamlachot מַמְלָכוֹת		hamargiz הַמַּרְגִּיז		ze זֶה		aruchot עֲרוּכוֹת

אֲדוֹנֵנוּ adonenu בַּר Bar יוֹחָאי Yochay • (וַאֲמַרְתֶּם...)va'amartem

---

ה He revealed all that was concealed ["Rav Shimon said: 'Now is the time of goodwill, and I want to come without shame into the World to Come. Here are holy matters that I have not revealed until now. I wish to reveal them before the Shechinah so it shall not be said that I have gone from this world in want.'" (Zohar Ha'azinu, Idra Zuta 26)] With invincible strength and courage. He ascended the highest rungs ["At the same time, all the friends and Rav Shimon, as well, stood up. Rav Shimon's Light reached up to the empyrean." (Zohar, Prologue 58)] Our master, the son of Yochai. (And you should say...)

ה He was hidden in a (rocky) cave [the same cave as Moses and Elijah (Livnat Hasapir on Beresheet 3:1)] to escape the death decree. There he learned the secrets of the Torah (see Babylonian Talmud, tractate Shabbat 33, Zohar Chadash, Ki Tavo 1 and Tikkunei Zohar, Prologue 1); Our master, the son of Yochai. (And you should say...)

ו A wellspring [Chesed] was created for him there, with a carob [=216=Gevurah—Judgment] tree for his food (Zohar Chadash, Ki Tavo 1). How good is his portion and his lot of faith (Ibid 9, Zohar, Prologue 188 and more); Our master, the son of Yochai. (And you should say...)

ז "The memory of the righteous is a blessing" (Proverbs 10:7), this king the son of a king ["Happy is the generation that Rav Shimon dwells therein... it is written (Ecclesiastes 10:17): 'Happy are you, land, when your king is free' Who is 'your king'? This refers to Rav Shimon bar Yochai, master of Torah, master of wisdom." (Zohar Acharei Mot 407)] He was worthy and brought many to merit ["Blessed is the generation in which Rav Shimon Bar Yochai lives, for even among the mountains there is wisdom." (Zohar Terumah 544)]; Our master, the son of Yochai. (And you should say...)

ח He innovated a number of practical laws, as arranged in the Mishnah [Rav Shimon Bar Yochai is mentioned in the Mishnah more than 300 times], this [tzadik] dared to challenge mighty empires (Zohar Ha'azinu, Idra Zuta 201); Our master, the son of Yochai. (And you should say...)

Songs

טָהֵר tiher אֶת et הָעִיר ha'ir טְבֶרְיָה Teverya. עָשָׂה asa אוֹתָה ota
נְקִיָּה nekiya. הוֹדוּ hodu לוֹ lo מִן min שְׁמַיָּא shemaya.
אֲדוֹנֵנוּ adonenu בַּר bar יוֹחַאי yochai. (וַאֲמַרְתֶּם va'amartem...)

יָדַע yada כָּל kol הַנִּסְתָּרוֹת hanistarot. דְּבָרָיו devarav
עוֹשִׂים osim פֵּרוֹת perot. בִּטֵּל bitel כַּמָּה kama גְּזֵרוֹת gezerot.
אֲדוֹנֵנוּ adonenu בַּר Bar יוֹחַאי Yochai. (וַאֲמַרְתֶּם va'amartem...)

כָּל kol יָמָיו yamav אֲשֶׁר asher וְזֶה chaya. אוֹת ot הַקֶּשֶׁת hakeshet
לֹא lo נִהְיָה nihya. כִּי ki הוּא hu אוֹת ot עוֹלָם olam. הָיָה haya.
אֲדוֹנֵנוּ adonenu בַּר Bar יוֹחַאי Yochai. (וַאֲמַרְתֶּם va'amartem...)

לְכָל lechol יִשְׂרָאֵל yisrael הֵאִיר he'ir. בְּסוֹד besod תּוֹרָה tora
הַבָּהִיר habahir. כְּאוֹר ke'or הַחַמָּה hachama מַזְהִיר mazhir.
אֲדוֹנֵנוּ adonenu בַּר Bar יוֹחַאי Yochai. (וַאֲמַרְתֶּם va'amartem...)

ט He purified and made clean the city of Tiberias (Zohar Bo 102, Midrash Kohelet Rabba 10:11 and Babylonian Talmud, Tractate Shabbat 33:2). Heaven concurred with him; Our master, the son of Yochai. (And you should say…)

י He knew all that is not disclosed ["Elijah said to him: Rav Shimon, happy is your portion, that the secrets of your Master shine before you like the rays of the sun." (Zohar Chadash, Song of Songs 496)] His words are still bearing fruit ["The Torah scholars, who are 'like the best wine'; just as the best wine is here yet its odor drifts afar, so do the Torah scholars stay in one place and their Torah (studies) drifts afar, to every place. And even when they are in the grave, their lips whisper their Torah. Even more so, in the place where the pillars of the world (like Rav Shimon) stand – many times more so. Because even the ministering angels are powerless before them." (Zohar Chadash, Ruth 493-494)] He nullified a number of [harsh] decrees ["A voice resounded from Heaven at that moment, saying, Happy is your portion, Rav Shimon, for the Holy One, blessed be He decrees, and yet you annul it down Below." (Zohar Chadash, Vayera 4) And also: "One time there was a plague in Lod. Rav Shimon bar Yochai came to the city. They said to him: What shall we do? Rav Shimon bar Yochai got up and went through the city, and he saw people dying. He said: All this happens in the city, while I am here? I demand that it, the plague, stop. They heard a Divine voice, saying: Get out of here, for Rav Shimon ben Yochai is here. Since the Holy One blessed be He, decrees, yet he cancels it." (Zohar Chadash, Ruth 495-496)]; Our master, the son of Yochai. (And you should say…)

כ Throughout the days of his life, the sign of the rainbow was not seen ["They said about Rav Shimon that the rainbow never appeared in his days, because he was a sign in this world, because his merits protected the world, hence they did not need a rainbow. (Zohar Chadash, Beresheet, 421 and see also Zohar Shemini 12)], for he himself was a sign to the world. Our master, the son of Yochai. (And you should say…)

ל He illuminated all of Israel with the secret radiance of the Torah ["How many lights shine because of Rav Shimon, who illuminates the world much more with the Torah, being the pillar of all pillars." (Zohar Vayetze 175) He continues to shine like the sun ["Rav Rechumai said to Rav Pinchas: I have heard that our friend Yochai has a jewel, a precious stone, namely a son. And I have observed the Light that shines from that jewel; and it shines like the radiance of the sun as it emerges out from its sheath and illuminates the whole world." (Zohar, Prologue 185)] Our master, the son of Yochai. (And you should say…)

Songs

im עִם	bishmaya בִּשְׁמַיָּא •	bachar בָּחַר	makom מָקוֹם
aliya עֲלָיָה •	mibnei מִבְּנֵי	ze זֶה	hanavi הַנָּבִיא • Achiya אֲחִיָּה •
(...va'amartem וַאֲמַרְתֶּם) •	Yochay יוֹחַאי •	Bar בַּר	adonenu אֲדוֹנֵנוּ
likar לִיקָר	zacha זָכָה	lemala לְמַעְלָה •	me'od מְאֹד nechmad נֶחְמַד
nigla נִגְלָה •	lo לוֹ	elyon עֶלְיוֹן	keter כֶּתֶר • ugdula וּגְדֻלָּה
(...va'amartem וַאֲמַרְתֶּם) •	Yochay יוֹחַאי •	Bar בַּר	adonenu אֲדוֹנֵנוּ
ari אֲרִי	nikra נִקְרָא •	lo לוֹ	sinai סִינַי sinai סִינַי
tora תּוֹרָה •	tetze תֵּצֵא	mimenu מִמֶּנּוּ	shebachavura שֶׁבַּחֲבוּרָה •
(...va'amartem וַאֲמַרְתֶּם) •	Yochay יוֹחַאי •	Bar בַּר	adonenu אֲדוֹנֵנוּ
yekarim יְקָרִים	tikunim תִּקּוּנִים •	shivim שִׁבְעִים	asa עָשָׂה
haelyonim הָעֶלְיוֹנִים •	tiken תִּקֵּן	bam בָּם	mipninim מִפְּנִינִים •

בּ He chose a place in Heaven with the prophet Achiyah [HaShiloni *(Zohar Chadash, Beresheet 803)*]. He was one of few who ascended so high [the Three Upper Sefirot of the Garden of Eden *(Sulam commentary on Zohar, Prologue 108 and see Babylonian Talmud, Tractate Sukah 45:2)*]; Our master, the son of Yochai. (And you should say...)

ג He is greatly beloved Above ["Elijah said to him: Master, upon your life! ... Happy are you in this world, that your Master on high is praised through you." *(Zohar Pinchas 558)*], he merited rare honor and greatness. The Supernal Crown was revealed to him ["This Atika, which is Arich Anpin, the oldest among the old, from which derive Supernal Abba and Ima that are considered old, is the Supernal Keter Above, namely Keter of Arich Anpin." *(Zohar ha'azinu, Idra Zuta 41)* "In the meantime, the most ancient among the old came down. Chochmah and Binah are called 'ancient' and Keter, which is above Chochmah and Binah, is called 'most ancient among the ancient'. And this is the secret of the soul of Yechidah that shall be revealed in the world at the End of Correction." *(Zohar Beresheet A, 262)*] Our master, the son of Yochai. (And you should say...)

ס He was described as Sinai, Sinai *(see Tikkunei Zohar, 22nd Tikkun 10 and 20)* (and he was also described as) a lion among his companions *(See Zohar Shemot 252, Zohar Acharei Mot 407 and Zohar Chadash, Ruth 491)*. From him the Torah went forth [Based on the verse *(Isaiah 2:3)*: 'For out of Zion (Yesod) shall go forth Torah'. Rav Aba says: "I wish to follow you and learn from the good things that you taste daily from the holy chamber of Rav Shimon bar Yochai." *(Zohar Naso 189)*]; Our master, the son of Yochai. (And you should say...)

ע He made seventy rectifications ["Rav Shimon opened and said, 'In the beginning God created' *(Genesis 1:1)*; 'The secret of the Lord is with them that awes him; and He will reveal to them His covenant' *(Psalms 25:14)*. 'Secret, numerically seventy, these are the seventy manners, by which the word 'Beresheet' in this passage is defined" *(Tikkunei Zohar, Prologue, Elijah opens 22)*], more precious than rubies ["which are the mysteries and inner meaning of the Torah" *(Zohar Tazria 6)*]. With them, he repaired the Upper Worlds [Kabbalist Rav Shalom Buzaglo *(introduction to his book Kiseh Melech)* asks, what so special in the Tikkunei Zohar, more than other part of Torah, to be able to correct the Worlds? And he answers quoting the Ari: "what is the reason that Rav Shimon, in the Tikkunei Zohar, explains all the verses, the words and the teachings, using 'small numbers' (all the 22 letters will have numerical value from 1 to 10. For an example, the letter Kaf, which has numerical value of 20 will have, in 'small number,' numerical value of 2), as small number represents energy of katnut—smallness? Could Rav Shimon not make 'the teaching based on 'big calculation' (as it represents gadlut (greatness), meaning more revelation of Light)? And the Ari answers: Rav Shimon intention in the Tikkunei Zohar is to correct the World of Asiyah, the dwelling place of the klipa, where the klipa is very sturdy and we need a great force to correct and elevate Her (and small numbers represent the World of Asiyah)". And he concludes that even though, any Torah study makes a correction in the Worlds, the Tikkunei Zohar makes the most valuable and important correction that all others are dependent on it.]

SONGS

אֲדוֹנֵנוּ adonenu בַּר Bar יוֹחָאי Yochay ♦ (וַאֲמַרְתֶּם va'amartem...)

פָּתַח patach פִּיהוּ pihu בְּחָכְמָה vechochma ♦ הוֹצִיא hotzi אוֹר or
תַּעֲלוּמָה ta'aluma ♦ תִּקֵּן tiken זָהֳרֵי zahorei וַחֲמָּה chama ♦

אֲדוֹנֵנוּ adonenu בַּר Bar יוֹחָאי Yochay ♦ (וַאֲמַרְתֶּם va'amartem...)

צַדִּיק tzadik יְסוֹד yesod עוֹלָם olam ♦ גִּלָּה gila מִדְרָשׁ midrash
הַנֶּעְלָם hane'elam ♦ יָכוֹל yachol לִפְטוֹר liftor הָעוֹלָם ha'olam ♦

אֲדוֹנֵנוּ adonenu בַּר Bar יוֹחָאי Yochay ♦ (וַאֲמַרְתֶּם va'amartem...)

קוֹלוֹ kolo זִמֵּר zimer עָרִיצִים aritzim ♦ וְהִכְרִית vehichrit
אֶת et הַקּוֹצִים hakotzim ♦ וְהִצִּיל vehitzil הַלְחוּצִים halechutzim ♦

אֲדוֹנֵנוּ adonenu בַּר Bar יוֹחָאי Yochay ♦ (וַאֲמַרְתֶּם va'amartem...)

Our master, the son of Yochai. (And you should say...)

פ He opened his mouth with Wisdom ["the secret of Malchut showering the Lower Worlds with Wisdom" (Sulam commentary on Zohar Toldot 184)], and brought forth the light of the mystery ["The two forming, one of the Upper beings and the other of the Lower beings, are symbolized by the two Yud's that appear at the beginning and end of the Name: Yud, Alef, Hei, Dalet, Vav, Nun, Hei, Yud, and represent Chochmah at the beginning (Binah) and Chochmah at the end (Malchut) of the Name. They are called the mysteries of wisdom, because they are concealed from the Supernal Chochmah, which is below the Supernal Keter." (Zohar Beresheet A, 253) "And when Zeir Anpin (the sun) receives from Binah (the Upper Chochmah) and showers it to Nukva (Malchut), then She (Nukva) is called the Lower Wisdom, and both (Binah and Malchut) are called the mysteries of Wisdom" (Sulam Commentary on Ibid)] and with that he perfected the rays of the sun [Zeir Anpin]; Our master, the son of Yochai. (And you should say...)

צ "Righteous is the foundation of the world" (Proverbs 10:25 and see Zohar Chadash, Vayera 4), he revealed the hidden teachings [Kabbalist Rav Shalom Buzaglo (Mikdash Melech on Zohar Vayera) quotes Kabbalist Rav Moshe Zachuta saying: "Most of the teachings of Midrash Hane'elam speak about the soul—Neshamah, whose source is from the World of Beriah, and as there are four levels in the revealed Torah, the third one, the Midrash, corresponds to Beri'ah but from the external aspect, so Midrash Hane'elam—the hidden teachings, is the third level of the Hidden Torah—the Zohar and corresponds to the World of Beriah from the internal aspect."] He could absolve the entire world [from Judgment (see Babylonian Talmud, tractate Sukah 45:2 and Midrash Beresheet Rabba, 35:2)]; Our master, the son of Yochai. (And you should say...)

ק His voice cut away the powers of tyranny ["'The time of the singing bird (also: pruning) is come' alludes to the fourth day, when the 'pruning of the tyrants' took place." (Zohar, Prologue 4) "] and cut down the thorns ["Before Adam was created, the klipa was able to suck energy from the holiness, in the secret of the verse (Genesis 2:5): "and there was no Adam to cultivate the ground" and one of the actions of cultivating the ground is cutting the thorns." (Writings of the Ari, Etz Chaim, The Nekudim Chamber, Gate Eight, chapter 6)]. He liberated the oppressed ["Worthy is Rav Shimon to be relied on him in time of stress." (Babylonian Talmud, Tractate Berachot 9:1) "For the sounds of the Teru'ah teach about duress after duress with no respite between them. And clearly, since the other nations make Israel's exile more difficult, it is the duress that they suffer that brings the redemption closer." (Zohar Pinchas 106) "With your composition, of Rav Shimon bar Yochai, which is the book of the Zohar, from the Light of the Supernal Ima called repentance. They do not require a test and, because Israel in the future will taste from the Tree of Life, which is this book of the Zohar, they will leave the exile with mercy." (Zohar Naso 90)] Our master, the son of Yochai. (And you should say...)

SONGS

רָאָה ra'a פָּנָיו fanav מְאִירִים me'irim• בְּשִׁבְתּוֹ beshivto עִם im
וַחֲבֵרִים chaverim• עֵת et גִּלָּה gila סוֹד sod נִסְתָּרִים nistarim•
אֲדוֹנֵנוּ adonenu בַּר Bar יוֹחַאי Yochay• (וַאֲמַרְתֶּם va'amartem...)

שָׁלוֹם shalom רַב rav עַל al מִשְׁכָּבוֹ mishkavo• מַה ma טוֹב tov
וְחֶלְקוֹ chelko וְטוּבוֹ vetuvo• דּוֹבֵר dover אֱמֶת emet בִּלְבָבוֹ bilvavo•
אֲדוֹנֵנוּ adonenu בַּר Bar יוֹחַאי Yochay• (וַאֲמַרְתֶּם va'amartem...)

תּוֹרָתוֹ torato מָגֵן magen לָנוּ lanu• הִיא hi מְאִירַת me'irat
עֵינֵינוּ enenu• הוּא hu יַמְלִיץ yamlitz טוֹב tov עָלֵינוּ alenu•
אֲדוֹנֵנוּ adonenu בַּר Bar יוֹחַאי Yochay• (וַאֲמַרְתֶּם va'amartem...)

ר He could see His Face illuminated, when he sat with the friends and revealed the secret of mysteries ["Rav Shimon said to the friends: I take upon myself as evidence the uppermost Heavens and the uppermost holy Earth that I now see what no human has seen since the day that Moses ascended Mount Sinai for the second time, since I perceive my face to be shining like the powerful sun that will heal the world in the future" (Zohar Naso, Idra Rabba 120)] Our master, the son of Yochai. (And you should say…) ש He attained great peace when he lay down ["After the bed left the house, it rose in the air and fire burned before it. They heard a voice: 'Come and gather to the feast of Rav Shimon, (Isaiah 57:2) He shall enter in peace to them that rest in their graves.'" (Zohar Ha'azinu 200)] How awesome is his portion and his goodness ["Messiah said, how happy are the righteous with their portion in the World to Come, and how happy is the portion of the son of Yochai, who has this distinction. He is described by the verse (Proverbs 8:21): 'I may cause those who love me to inherit substance; and I will fill their treasures'" (Zohar, prologue 60 and see Zohar Ha'azinu 201)] He speaks truth in his heart ["Rav Johanan said in the name of Rav Shimon bar Yochai: Verbal wrong is more heinous than monetary wrong." (Babylonian Talmud, Tractate Baba Metziah 58:2) Our master, the son of Yochai. (And you should say…) ת May his Torah learning protect us ["Elijah said: With your composition, of Rav Shimon bar Yochai, which is the book of the Zohar, from the Light of the Supernal Ima called repentance. They do not require a test and, because Israel in the future will taste from the Tree of Life, which is this book of the Zohar, they will leave the exile with mercy," (Zohar Naso 90)] it illuminates our eyes ["Rav Elazar and Rav Abba approached and kissed the hands of Rav Shimon. Rav Abba wept and said, Woe, when you are gone from the world because the world will remain orphaned from you. Who will then be able to illuminate the words of Torah?" (Zohar Va'era 29)]. May he promote good for us (see Babylonian Talmud, Tractate Shabbat 111:1, Ibid 138:2, Ibid, Tractate Megilah 29:1); Our master, the son of Yochai. (And you should say…)

SONGS

ANE'IM ZEMIROT (SONG OF GLORY)

This poem was written by Kabbalist Rav Yehuda Hachasid (the pious) son of Samuel (He, his father and his grandfather, Kelonimus the Elder, were the leading kabbalists in Germany during the 11-12th century. Rav Yehuda Hachasid established the concept that one should study Torah only for the purpose of spiritual transformation and not for intellectual stimulation). Composed according to the Hebrew alphabet, this song is based on the teachings of Kabbalists Rav Saadia Ga'on (Iraq, 9th century) and Kabbalist Rav Bachye Iben Paquda (Spain, 11th century) and in it Rav Yehuda describes his yearning for the Creator through the kabbalistic description of the Creator's actions and power.

אַנְעִים ane'im זְמִירוֹת zemirot וְשִׁירִים veshirim אֶאֱרוֹג e'erog.

כִּי ki אֵלֶיךָ elecha נַפְשִׁי nafshi תַעֲרוֹג ta'arog.

נַפְשִׁי nafshi וְזִמְדָה chamda בְּצֵל betzel יָדְךָ yadecha.

לָדַעַת lada'at כָּל kol רָז raz סוֹדֶךָ sodecha.

מִדֵּי midei דַבְּרִי daberi בִּכְבוֹדֶךָ bichvodecha.

הוֹמֶה homeh לִבִּי libi אֶל el דּוֹדֶיךָ dodecha.

עַל al כֵּן ken אֲדַבֵּר adaber בְּךָ becha נִכְבָּדוֹת nichbadot.

וְשִׁמְךָ veshimcha אֲכַבֵּד achabed בְּשִׁירֵי beshirei יְדִידוֹת yedidot.

אֲסַפְּרָה asapera כְּבוֹדְךָ chevodcha וְלֹא velo רְאִיתִיךָ re'iticha.

אֲדַמְּךָ adamecha אֲכַנְּךָ achanecha וְלֹא velo יְדַעְתִּיךָ yeda'aticha.

בְּיַד beyad נְבִיאֶיךָ nevi'echa בְּסוֹד besod עֲבָדֶיךָ avadecha.

דִּמִּיתָ dimita הֲדַר hadar כְּבוֹד kevod הוֹדֶךָ hodecha.

גְּדֻלָּתְךָ gedulatcha וּגְבוּרָתֶךָ ugvuratecha.

כִּנּוּ kinu לְתוֹקֶף letokef פְּעֻלָּתֶךָ pe'ulatecha.

ANE'IM ZEMIROT (SONG OF GLORY)

I shall compose pleasant psalms [in Hebrew also means cut off (the negative forces)] and weave songs [according to the Zohar (Shemot 324), song or shir is the secret of the illumination of Chochmah that is drawn through the Nukva] as by (singing) for You shall my soul yearn. My soul desired the shelter of Your hand [as protection from the flames of the angels (Zohar, prologue 66)], (so I could) know every mystery of Your secret. The more I speak of Your glory [illuminations from Dikna], my heart longs for Your love. Therefore, I shall speak of Your glories and Your Name I shall honor with Songs of Love [between Zeir Anpin and Malchut (Zohar Chadash, Chukat 63)].

א *(How can) I relate Your majesty, nonetheless I see You not [as the Light of Chayah does not exist (Zohar, Vayechi 4)]? (How can) I allegorize You, (or how can) I describe You, and yet I know You not?*
ב *through Your prophets, and through the Divine Inspiration of Your servants; You are imagined with the splendorous glory of Your power [Zeir Anpin receives the Light of Chochmah (Zohar Chadash, Chukat 88)].*
ג *(and when they used words like) Your greatness [the Mercy attribute] and Your strength [the Judgment attribute], they (actually) described the might of Your works (and not You or Your essence).*

Songs

דִּמּוּ otcha וְלֹא velo כְּפִי kefi יֶשְׁךָ yeshcha.
וַיְשַׁוּוּךָ vayashvucha לְפִי lefi מַעֲשֶׂיךָ ma'asecha.
הִמְשִׁילוּךָ himshilucha בְּרוֹב berov וְחֶזְיוֹנוֹת chezyonot.
הִנְּךָ hinecha אֶחָד echad בְּכָל bechol דִּמְיוֹנוֹת dimyonot.
וַיֶּחֱזוּ vayechezu בְךָ vecha זִקְנָה zikna וּבַחֲרוּת uvacharut.
וּשְׂעַר usar רֹאשְׁךָ roshcha בְּשֵׂיבָה beseva וְשַׁחֲרוּת veshacharut.
זִקְנָה zikna בְּיוֹם beyom דִּין din וּבַחֲרוּת uvacharut בְּיוֹם beyom קְרָב kerav.
כְּאִישׁ ke'ish מִלְחָמוֹת milchamot יָדָיו yadav לוֹ lo רָב rav.
חָבַשׁ chavash כּוֹבַע kova יְשׁוּעָה yeshua בְּרֹאשׁוֹ berosho.
הוֹשִׁיעָה hoshia לּוֹ lo יְמִינוֹ yemino וּזְרוֹעַ uzroa קָדְשׁוֹ kadsho.
טַלְלֵי talelei אוֹרוֹת orot רֹאשׁוֹ rosho נִמְלָא nimla.
קְוֻצּוֹתָיו kevutzotav רְסִיסֵי resisei לַיְלָה layla.
יִתְפָּאֵר yitpaer בִּי bi כִּי ki וָחֵפֶץ chafetz בִּי bi.
וְהוּא vehu יִהְיֶה yihye לִי li לַעֲטֶרֶת la'ateret צְבִי tzevi.
כֶּתֶם ketem טָהוֹר tahor פָּז paz דְּמוּת demut רֹאשׁוֹ rosho.
וְחַק vechak עַל al מִצְחוֹ metzach כְּבוֹד kevod שֵׁם shem קָדְשׁוֹ kadsho.

ד They allegorized You, but not according to Your reality, and they portrayed You according to Your deeds.
ה They embodied You in many visions; yet You are One containing all the metaphors.
ו They envisioned in You agedness [Arich Anpin—on Mount Sinai] and virility [Zeir Anpin—in the Red sea], and the hair [the root of the Judgment aspect] of Your head a hoary [white as pure wool—Amra Naki, still in the stage of Mercy (Zohar, Naso, Idra Rabba 24)] and yet black (ibid. 196).
ז Elderly (Ancient of Days—Atik Yomin) on Judgment Day (see Daniel 7) and virile on the day of battle, like a man of war (Zohar Beshalach 256-258) Whose hands shall contend for Him.
ח He put on His head [Arich Anpin] the helmet [Keter of Keter] of salvations [Shin-Ayin Nehorin (370 illuminations)]; "His Right Hand [Chesed] and His Holy Arm [Left—Gevurah] have gained Him the victory [when the Nukva's Light will be as the light of the sun (Zohar, Chayei Sarah 30)]" (Psalms 98:1)
ט With illuminating dew drops [from Gulgalta of Arich Anpin (Zohar Vayechi 465)] His [Zeir Anpin] head is filled [and becomes the Light of Chesed and Gevurah (Zohar Sifra Detzniuta 26)], (but) His locks [that cover the ears and obstruct the hearing of prayers (Zohar, Ha'azinu, Idra Zuta 126)] are the rains of the night [meaning, Judgment; so one should concentrate on mitigating this Judgment (Ibid.)].
י He shall be glorified in me [the secret of the servant (Left Column—Malchut) and the son (Right Column—Zeir Anin) when They are united as one (Zohar Behar 85)] for He desires me [simple desire with no conditions], so He shall be for me a crown of splendor [at the time of the Final Redemption (Isaiah 49:3)].
כ The form of His head is like that of the very finest gold [Illumination from Chochmah (Zohar Va'etchanan 66)] and (that is why He) carved on his [the High Priest's] forehead is His glorious, Sacred Name [יהוה].

Songs

לָחֵן lechen וּלְכָבוֹד ulchavod צְבִי tzevi תִּפְאָרָה tifara.

אֻמָּתוֹ umato לוֹ lo עֲטָרָה itra עֲטָרָה atara.

מַחְלְפוֹת machlefot רֹאשׁוֹ rosho כְּבִימֵי kevimei בְּחוּרוֹת vechurot.

קְוֻצּוֹתָיו kevutzotav תַּלְתַּלִּים taltalim שְׁחוֹרוֹת shechorot.

נְוֵה neve הַצֶּדֶק hatzedek צְבִי tzevi תִּפְאַרְתּוֹ tifarto.

יַעֲלֶה ya'ale נָא na עַל al רֹאשׁ rosh שִׂמְחָתוֹ simchato.

סְגֻלָּתוֹ segulato תְּהִי tehi נָא na בְּיָדוֹ veyado עֲטֶרֶת ateret.

וּצְנִיף utznif מְלוּכָה melucha צְבִי tzevi תִּפְאֶרֶת tiferet.

עֲמוּסִים amusim נְשָׂאָם nesa'am עֲטֶרֶת ateret עֲנָדָם indam.

מֵאֲשֶׁר me'asher יָקְרוּ yakru בְּעֵינָיו ve'enav כִּבְּדָם kibdam.

פְּאֵרוֹ pe'ero עָלַי alai וּפְאֵרִי uferi עָלָיו alav.

וְקָרוֹב vekarov אֵלַי elai בְּקָרְאִי bekari אֵלָיו elav.

צַח tzach וְאָדוֹם ve'adom לִלְבוּשׁוֹ lilvusho אָדוֹם adom.

פּוּרָה pura בְּדָרְכוֹ bedarcho בְּבוֹאוֹ bevo'o מֵאֱדוֹם me'edom.

קֶשֶׁר kesher תְּפִלִּין tefilin הֶרְאָה hera לֶעָנָו le'anav.

תְּמוּנַת temunat ה' Hashem לְנֶגֶד leneged עֵינָיו enav.

לֹ For grace and glory of His Beautiful splendor; His nation crowns Him with a Tiara [the angel that is in charge on the prayers takes them and makes of them tiaras over the Creator's head (Midrash Shemot Rabba 21:4)].
מֹ The tresses of His head are like His youthful days, His locks are jet black ringlets [see above].
נֹ The Abode of righteousness [Jerusalem (Metzudat David on Jeremiah 31:22)] is the Beauty of His splendor; may He elevate it [Jerusalem (Zohar Chadash, Balak 8)] to His foremost joy [based on Psalms 137:6].
סֹ May His peculiar possession [the Unification of the Three Columns—Chesed, Gevurah, and Tiferet (Zohar Bamidbar 52)] be in His hand like a crown [when the Shechinah (the Crown) illuminates upon Them, being their fourth (Zohar Terumah 576)], and like a royal diadem [the Shechinah is] the beauty of His splendor.
עֹ From infancy [out of Egypt] He bore them [the Israelites] and affixed them with a crown [on Mount Sinai], (only) because they are precious in His eyes He honored them [based on Isaiah 43:4, also see Zohar Acharei Mot 115].
פֹ His splendor [as we have learned that the Holy One blessed Be He (Zeir Anpin), put on Tefilin—the Supernal Crowns—the Mochin of Chochmah, Binah, and Chesed And Gevurah of Da'at (Zohar Vayetze 6)] is upon me and my splendor is upon Him, and He is near to me when I call upon Him [based on Deuteronomy 4:7].
צֹ He is radiant [Attribute of Mercy] and ruddy [Attribute of Judgment—the secret of joining Judgment with Mercy (Zohar Toldot 47-57)]; (but) His garment will be crimson (only Judgment in the time of the Final Redemption), when He tramples as in a press on His coming from Edom [see Zohar Vayishlach 177].
קֹ He showed the Tefilin-knot to the humble [Moses (see Babylonian Talmud, Tractate Berachot 7:1 and Zohar Pinchas 754)], the resemblance of the Lord before his eyes ["the prophecy that descends from the shining mirror—the Internal aspect of Sefirat Tiferet." (Zohar Vayechi 1-4)]

Songs

רוֹצֶה rotze בְּעַמּוֹ be'amo עֲנָוִים anavim יְפָאֵר yefaer.
יוֹשֵׁב yoshev תְּהִלּוֹת tehilot בָּם bam לְהִתְפָּאֵר lehitpa'er.
רֹאשׁ rosh דְּבָרְךָ devarcha אֱמֶת emet קוֹרֵא kore מֵרֹאשׁ merosh.
דּוֹר dor וָדוֹר vador עַם am דּוֹרְשֶׁיךָ doreshcha דְּרוֹשׁ derosh.
שִׁית shit הֲמוֹן hamon שִׁירַי shirai נָא na עָלֶיךָ alecha.
וְרִנָּתִי verinati תִּקְרַב tikrav אֵלֶיךָ elecha.
תְּהִלָּתִי tehilati תְּהִי tehi נָא na לְרֹאשְׁךָ leroshcha עֲטֶרֶת ateret.
וּתְפִלָּתִי utfilati תִּכּוֹן tikon קְטֹרֶת ketoret.
תִּיקַר tikar שִׁירַת shirat רָשׁ rash בְּעֵינֶיךָ be'enecha.
כַּשִּׁיר kashir יוּשַׁר yushar עַל al קָרְבָּנֶךָ karbanecha.
בִּרְכָתִי birchati תַּעֲלֶה ta'ale לְרֹאשׁ lerosh מַשְׁבִּיר mashbir.
מְחוֹלֵל mecholel וּמוֹלִיד umolid צַדִּיק tzadik כַּבִּיר kabir.
וּבְבִרְכָתִי uvevirchati תְּנַעֲנַע tena'ana לִי li רֹאשׁ rosh.
וְאוֹתָהּ ve'ota קַח kach לְךָ lecha כִּבְשָׂמִים kivsamim רֹאשׁ rosh.
יֶעֱרַב ye'erav נָא na שִׂיחִי sichi עָלֶיךָ alecha.
כִּי ki נַפְשִׁי nafshi תַעֲרֹג ta'arog אֵלֶיךָ elecha.
לְךָ) lecha ה' Hashem הַגְּדֻלָּה hagedula וְהַגְּבוּרָה vehagevura וְהַתִּפְאֶרֶת vehatiferet
וְהַנֵּצַח vehanetzach וְהַהוֹד vehahod. כִּי ki כֹל chol בַּשָּׁמַיִם bashamayim וּבָאָרֶץ uva'aretz.
לְךָ lecha ה' Hashem הַמַּמְלָכָה hamamlacha וְהַמִּתְנַשֵּׂא vehamitnaseh לְכֹל lechol לְרֹאשׁ (lerosh).
מִי mi יְמַלֵּל yemalel גְּבוּרוֹת gevurot ה' Hashem.
יַשְׁמִיעַ yashmia כָּל kol תְּהִלָּתוֹ tehilatv.

ר He takes delight in His people, He will adorn the humble (with salvation) *(based on Psalms 149:4)*, enthroned upon (their) praises, He glories with them *(see Midrash Shemot Rabba 21:4)*.
ר The very essence of Your word [Malchut] is truth [Zeir Anpin. And when They are united it is called devar emet or "word of truth," (Zohar Chadash Chukat 91)] the One who is summoning each and every generation; seek the people and their leaders (of each generation) *(see Zohar Lech Lecha 331)*.
ש Please, place the yearning of my songs before You; and my prayer bring before You.
ת May my praise be a crown for Your head, and may my prayer be set (before You) like incense. May the song of the poor be cherished in Your eyes, like the song that is sung over Your offerings. May my blessing rise up upon the head of the Provider, Originator, Deliverer, Mighty and Righteous One. And to my blessing, nod Your head to me [based on the story of Rav Yishmael the High Priest *(Babylonian Talmud, Tractate Berachot 7:1)*], and take it to Yourself like the principal spices [the Illumination of Chochmah from the Three Upper Sefirot that are awakened after midnight *(Zohar Chadash Acharei Mot 53)*]. May my meditation be pleasing to You *(based on Psalms 104:34)*, for my soul shall yearn for You. ("Yours, Lord, is the greatness, the power, the glory, the victory, and the splendor. Everything in the Heavens and Earth is Yours. Yours, Lord, is the kingship; You are over all those who ascend to lead." *(I Chronicles 29:9)*) "Who can proclaim the glorious acts of the Lord? Who can declare his Praise? *(Psalms 106:2)*

Songs

YAH ECHSOF (YAH, HOW I YEARN FOR THE BLISS OF SHABBAT)

Written by Kabbalist Rav Aharon of Karlin (18th century, student of the Magid of Mezeritch). One *Shabbat*, while sitting with his students, the Magid shared that when Rav Aharon started singing *Shir Hashirim* (the Song of Songs) on Friday night all the angels in the Upper World stopped working and listen to his singing. Then he pointed to Rav Aharon and asked him if he could create a song for them for the Holy *Shabbat*. This song is based on the saying from the *Zohar* (Zohar Acharei Mot 299): "We learned there are three levels intertwined with each other, meaning the Holy One Blessed Be He, the Torah and Israel." as a representation of this special connection "A cord of three strands is not quickly broken." (Ecclesiastes 4:12) And therefore, the first letter of the three words of each verse of this song creates the words:

(*Neshamah*-soul) נשמה (*Aharon*) אהרן (the Tetragrammaton Name) יהוה

Yah יָהּ echsof אֶכְסֹף no'am נֹעַם Shabbat שַׁבָּת.
hamat'emet הַמִּתְאַמֶּת umit'achedet וּמִתְאַחֶדֶת bisgulatecha בִּסְגֻלָּתֶךָ.
meshoch מְשֹׁךְ no'am נֹעַם yir'atcha יִרְאָתְךָ. le'am לְעַם mevakshei מְבַקְשֵׁי
retzonecha רְצוֹנֶךָ. kadeshem קַדְּשֵׁם bikdushat בִּקְדֻשַּׁת haShabbat הַשַּׁבָּת.
hamit'achedet הַמִּתְאַחֶדֶת betoratecha בְּתוֹרָתֶךָ. petach פְּתַח lahem לָהֶם
no'am נֹעַם veratzon וְרָצוֹן liftoach לִפְתּוֹחַ sha'arei שַׁעֲרֵי retzonecha רְצוֹנֶךָ.
Yah יָהּ echsof אֶכְסֹף no'am נֹעַם Shabbat שַׁבָּת.
hamat'emet הַמִּתְאַמֶּת umit'achedet וּמִתְאַחֶדֶת bisgulatecha בִּסְגֻלָּתֶךָ.
haya הָיָה hoveh הֹוֶה. shemor שָׁמוֹר shomrei שׁוֹמְרֵי umtzapim וּמְצַפִּים
Shabbat שַׁבָּת kodshecha קָדְשֶׁךָ. ke'ayal כְּאַיָּל ta'arog תַּעֲרֹג
al עַל afikei אֲפִיקֵי mayim מָיִם. ken כֵּן nafsham נַפְשָׁם
ta'arog תַּעֲרֹג lekabel לְקַבֵּל no'am נֹעַם. no'am נֹעַם Shabbat שַׁבָּת.
hamit'achedet הַמִּתְאַחֶדֶת beshem בְּשֵׁם kodshecha קָדְשֶׁךָ.

YAH ECHSOF (YAH, HOW I YEARN FOR THE BLISS OF SHABBAT)

Yah [the Holy Name Yah—יָהּ represents the Three Upper Sefirot: Keter (620 Columns of Light), Chochmah (32 Paths) and Binah (50 Gates) that come together to 702, the same numerical value of Shabbat (see Zohar Pinchas 854)], how I yearn for the bliss of Shabbat, as She is united and She is the mate [as Rav Shimon states (Midrash Beresheet Raba 11:40)] of your peculiar treasure [Am Segulah – Exodus 19:5. See Zohar Pinchas 452 in the Sulam commentary; and also see the Writings of the Ari, the Gate of the Teaching of Rashbi, p.144] Extend the pleasure of Your awe [the Supernal Yirah] to the people who seek Your passionate wish. Sanctify them with the Holiness of Shabbat as She is united (also) with Your Torah. Open for them desire (pleasure) and will [so they can awaken from below (Itaruta Diletata. see Zohar Lech Lecha 209)] so they can open [only on Shabbat (Zohar Noach 364)] the gates for Your desire. (Yah, how I yearn...) The One Who was [the Left Column] and is [the Right Column], protect those who guard the Shabbat and anticipate it (based on Babylonian Talmud, Tractate Shabbat 118). "As the hart is longing after the water brooks," (Psalms 42:2) so their soul [Nefesh from Malchut] longs to receive the bliss of Shabbat [as the Light of Ima (ס"ג) illuminates in Nukva on Shabbat and is called noam—bliss (166=ס"ג ריבוע)], as She is united with Your Holy Name (Tana Devei Eliyahu 26).

hatzel הַצֵּל	me'acharei מֵאַחֲרֵי	lifrosh לִפְרֹשׁ	min מִן	haShabbat הַשַׁבָּת.
levilti לְבִלְתִּי	tihye תִּהְיֶה	sagur סָגוּר	mehem מֵהֶם	shisha שִׁשָּׁה	yamim יָמִים.
hamekablim הַמְקַבְּלִים	kedusha קְדֻשָׁה	miShabbat מִשַׁבַּת	kodshecha קָדְשֶׁךָ.
vetaher וְטַהֵר	libam לִבָּם	be'emet בֶּאֱמֶת	uve'emuna וּבֶאֱמוּנָה	le'avdecha לְעָבְדֶךָ.
Yah יָהּ	echsof אֶכְסֹף	no'am נֹעַם	Shabbat שַׁבָּת.
hamat'emet הַמִּתְאַמֶּת	umit'achedet וּמִתְאַחֶדֶת	bisgulatecha בִּסְגֻלָּתֶךָ.
veyihyu וְיִהְיוּ	rachamecha רַחֲמֶיךָ	mitgolelim מִתְגּוֹלְלִים	al עַל	am עַם
kodshecha קָדְשֶׁךָ.	veyihyu וְיִהְיוּ	rachamecha רַחֲמֶיךָ	mitgolelim מִתְגּוֹלְלִים
al עַל	am עַם	kodshecha קָדְשֶׁךָ.	veyihyu וְיִהְיוּ	rachamecha רַחֲמֶיךָ
mitgolelim מִתְגּוֹלְלִים	al עַל	am עַם	kodshecha קָדְשֶׁךָ.	lehashkot לְהַשְׁקוֹת
tzeme'ei צְמֵאֵי	chasdecha וְסַדְּךָ.	minahar מִנָּהָר
hayotze הַיּוֹצֵא	me'eden מֵעֵדֶן	le'ater לְעַטֵּר	et אֶת	Yisrael יִשְׂרָאֵל
betiferet בְּתִפְאֶרֶת.	hamfa'arim הַמְפָאֲרִים	otcha אוֹתָךְ	al עַל	yedei יְדֵי
Shabbat שַׁבַּת	kodshecha קָדְשֶׁךָ.	kol כָּל	shisha שִׁשָּׁה	yamim יָמִים.
lehanchilam לְהַנְחִילָם	nachalat נַחֲלַת	Ya'akov יַעֲקֹב	bechirecha בְּחִירֶךָ.
Yah יָהּ	echsof אֶכְסֹף	no'am נֹעַם	Shabbat שַׁבָּת.
hamat'emet הַמִּתְאַמֶּת	umit'achedet וּמִתְאַחֶדֶת	bisgulatecha בִּסְגֻלָּתֶךָ.
haShabbat הַשַׁבָּת	no'am נֹעַם	haneshamot הַנְּשָׁמוֹת.	vehasehvi'i וְהַשְּׁבִיעִי
oneg עֹנֶג	haruchot הָרוּחוֹת.	ve'eden וְעֶדֶן	hanefashot הַנְּפָשׁוֹת.

Spare the ones who wait leave taking from Shabbat (and by that drawing Her Holiness for the rest of the week) so it will not be sealed from them during the (next) six days ["This gate is not opened during the six ordinary days because during these days, the lower world, where the klipot and the external forces reside, is nourished... But on Shabbat and the new moon, the klipot are all removed from this world and do not rule it. When the gate is opened, the world is happy and receives nourishment from it, and the world is not under the influence of another power." (Zohar Noach 363-364)] As they (the six days) absorb their holiness from Your Holy Shabbat (Zohar Beshalach 412). And purify their heart with truth [Zeir Anpin] and faith [Malchut (see Zohar Balak 260)] to serve You. (Yah, how I yearn...) May Your mercy [the attributes of Arich Anpin] overpower your [attributes of Zeir Anpin], (so You can treat Your) holy people (with mercy): (A.) to water those who are thirsty for Your mercy that comes from the river [Binah] flowing forth from Eden [Chochmah of Arich Anpin (Zohar Yitro 485)]; (B.) to crown Israel [Zeir Anpin, when He has the Three Upper Sefirot (Zohar Shmini 12)] with splendor [Tiferet of Ima] those who praise You by (guarding) Your Holy Shabbat; (C. and) during the six days [of the week—the secret of Zeir Anpin with Six Edges (Zohar Beresheet A 341)] grant them "the portion of Jacob" [(Isaiah 58:14) the Mochin of Supernal Abba and Ima (Zohar Vayetze 232)] Your chosen one (Midrash Beresheet Raba 76:1). (Yah, how I yearn...) The Shabbat [Binah] is the bliss [166=ג"ס רִיבּוּעַ] of the Higher Souls [Neshamah] and the Seventh [Zeir Anpin] is the delight for the Spirits [Ru'ach] and the Heaven [Malchut of Atzilut] for the Lower Souls [Nefesh];

Songs

lehit'aden לְהִתְעַדֵּן	be'ahavatcha בְּאַהֲבָתְךָ	veyir'atecha וְיִרְאָתֶךָ•	
Shabbat שַׁבַּת	kodesh קוֹדֶשׁ	Shabbat שַׁבַּת	kodesh קוֹדֶשׁ
nafshi נַפְשִׁי	cholat וְחוֹלַת	ahavatecha אַהֲבָתֶךָ•	Shabbat שַׁבַּת
kodesh קוֹדֶשׁ	nafshot נַפְשׁוֹת	Yisrael יִשְׂרָאֵל	betzel בְּצֵל	kenafecha כְּנָפֶיךָ
yechesayun יֶחֱסָיוּן	yirveyun יִרְוְיֻן	mideshen מִדֶּשֶׁן	betecha בֵּיתֶךָ•
Yah יָהּ	echsof אֶכְסֹף	no'am נֹעַם	Shabbat שַׁבַּת•
hamat'emet הַמִּתְאַמֵּת	umit'achedet וּמִתְאַחֶדֶת	bisgulatecha בִּסְגֻלָּתֶךָ•

AVINU AV HARACHAMAN (OUR FATHER, MERCIFUL FATHER)
An excerpt from the Morning prayers that helps us to open our heart so we can have a real connection with the spiritual teaching of the Torah.

avinu אָבִינוּ	av אָב	harachaman הָרַחֲמָן•	hamerachem הַמְרַחֵם	rachem רַחֵם
na נָא	alenu עָלֵינוּ	veten וְתֵן	belibenu בְּלִבֵּנוּ	vina בִּינָה	lehavin לְהָבִין•
lehaskil לְהַשְׂכִּיל•	lishmo'a לִשְׁמֹעַ•	lilmod לִלְמֹד	ulelamed וּלְלַמֵּד•
lishmor לִשְׁמֹר	vela'asot וְלַעֲשׂוֹת	ulkayem וּלְקַיֵּם	et אֶת	kol כָּל
divrei דִּבְרֵי	talmud תַּלְמוּד	toratecha תוֹרָתֶךָ	be'ahava בְּאַהֲבָה•

AVINU MALKENU (OUR FATHER, OUR KING)
An excerpt from *Rosh Hashanah* prayers that helps us to open the Gates of Heaven to our prayers.

avinu אָבִינוּ	malkenu מַלְכֵּנוּ,		
petach פְּתַח	sha'arei שַׁעֲרֵי	shamayim שָׁמַיִם	litfilatenu לִתְפִלָּתֵנוּ•

So they (our Nefesh, Ru'ach and Neshamah) will be blissful [also can be translated: bonded (see Rashi on Job 38:31)] with Your love [Rechimu] and awe [Dechilu]. Holy Shabbat, my soul is languishing from love (Song of Songs 2:5) to you. Holy Shabbat, the souls of Israel "take refuge in the Shadow of your wings" (Psalms 36:8) [as on Shabbat the world is under Supernal protection (Zohar Beresheet B 193)] "and they will be saturated from the fatness of your house." (Psalms 36:9) (Yah, how I yearn...)

AVINU AV HARACHAMAN (OUR FATHER, MERCIFUL FATHER)
Our Father, merciful Father, merciful One be merciful to us, and place understanding in our hearts so we may understand, discern, hear, study, teach, keep, do, and fulfill all the words of the teachings of Your Torah in love.

AVINU MALKENU (OUR FATHER, OUR KING)
Our Father, Our King open the Gates of Heaven for our prayers.

Songs

Adir Hu (Mighty is He)

This song was composed in Israel in the 5th century and was based on texts from the ancient kabbalistic book "The Great Chambers" (Hechalot Rabati 23:2) from the Tana, Rav Yishmael the High Priest, and it was sung especially at the end of the night of Pesach, during the *Seder*. It follows the *Talmudic* discussion about the idea that the sacrifices should not contain any *chametz*, which represents the ego, as it is *Pesach* and then describes God as Mighty (*adir*) during the time of the Final Redemption (the time the ego will be removed) and the rebuilding of the Temple in Jerusalem (Babylonian Talmud, Tractate Menachot 53:1.)

bimehera בִּמְהֵרָה bekarov בְּקָרוֹב veto בֵּיתוֹ yivne יִבְנֶה hu הוּא adir אַדִיר

bene בְּנֵה, El אֵל bekarov בְּקָרוֹב beyamenu בְּיָמֵינוּ bimehera בִּמְהֵרָה

bekarov בְּקָרוֹב. betcha בֵּיתְךָ bene בְּנֵה, bene בְּנֵה El אֵל

Aderaba (On the Contrary)

Written by Kabbalist Rav Elimelech of Lizansk (Poland, 18th century), this song helps us to overcome our judgmental nature, and open our hearts to see the good in others and make a real and genuine connection with our friends and our spiritual community.

kol כָּל shenir'e שֶׁנִּרְאֶה belibenu בְּלִבֵּנוּ ten תֵּן, aderaba אַדְרַבָּה

chesronam וְחֶסְרוֹנָם, velo וְלֹא chaverenu חֲבֵרֵינוּ ma'alat מַעֲלַת echad אֶחָד

chavero וַחֲבֵרוֹ et אֶת echad אֶחָד kol כָּל veshendaber וְשֶׁנְּדַבֵּר

ve'al וְאַל, lefanecha לְפָנֶיךָ veharatzuy וְהָרָצוּי hayashar הַיָּשָׁר baderech בַּדֶּרֶךְ

al עַל me'echad מֵאֶחָד sine'a שִׂנְאָה shum שׁוּם belibenu בְּלִבֵּנוּ ya'ale יַעֲלֶה

hitkashrutenu הִתְקַשְּׁרוּתֵנוּ utchazek וּתְחַזֵּק. chalila וְחָלִילָה chavero חֲבֵרוֹ

veyadu'a וְיָדוּעַ galuy גָּלוּי ka'asher כַּאֲשֶׁר, elecha אֵלֶיךָ be'ahava בְּאַהֲבָה

elecha אֵלֶיךָ. rua'ch רוּחַ nachat נַחַת hakol הַכֹּל sheyhe שֶׁיְּהֵא. lefanecha לְפָנֶיךָ

Ahavat Olam (Everlasting Love)

The *Zohar* states (Zohar Vaetchanan 70): "Everlasting love is the secret of the Lower World (*Malchut*) to which the love of the Holy One, Blessed Be He, is attached… love surpasses every kind of worship in the world." There is a discussion in the Talmud (Babylonian Talmud, Tractate Shabbat 55:1) about how long the merit of the patriarchs (*zechut avot*) can last and protect us, and it is concluded by saying "*Zchut avot* ended."

Adir hu (Mighty is He)
Mighty is He, May He soon rebuild His house speedily, speedily and in our days, soon. God, rebuild. God, rebuild. Rebuild Your house soon!

Aderaba (On the Contrary)
On the contrary, place in our hearts the ability to see only the good in our friends and not their shortcomings. May we speak to each other in a way that is straight and desirable before You. May there be no hatred between friends in our heart, Heaven forbid. And may You Strengthen our connection with love to You, as it is revealed and known to You (that we strive) to give You only satisfaction and pleasure.

Songs

Kabbalist Rabbenu Tam (France, 12th century) added: "*Zechut avot* ended but *brit avot* (the covenant of the patriarchs) never ends and still protects us." In this song we ask the Creator to reveal His everlasting love to us and to remember the covenant of the patriarchs and protect us.

ahavat אַהֲבַת   olam עוֹלָם   tavi תָּבִיא   lahem לָהֶם.

uvrit וּבְרִית   avot אָבוֹת   labanim לְבָנִים   tizkor תִּזְכּוֹר:

Or Zaru'a Latzadik (Light is Sown for the Righteous)

This verse was written by King David and is recited during *Kol Nidrei* on *Yom Kippur*. This song helps us connect to the power of the Righteous—*Tzadik* inside us.

or אוֹר   zarua זָרוּעַ   latzadik לַצַּדִּיק   ulyishrei וּלְיִשְׁרֵי   lev לֵב   simcha שִׂמְחָה.

En Aroch Lecha (There is No Comparison to You)

An excerpt from *Shabbat* Morning prayers that helps us to connect to the true spiritual reality.

en אֵין   aroch עֲרוֹךְ   lecha לְךָ,   Hashem ה',   Elohenu אֱלֹהֵינוּ,

baolam בָּעוֹלָם   hazeh הַזֶּה. ve'en וְאֵין   zulatcha זוּלָתְךָ,   malkenu מַלְכֵּנוּ,

lechayei לְחַיֵּי   ha'olam הָעוֹלָם   haba הַבָּא. efes אֶפֶס   biltecha בִּלְתְּךָ,

go'alenu גּוֹאֲלֵנוּ,   limot לִימוֹת   hamashi'ach הַמָּשִׁיחַ. umi וּמִי   domeh דּוֹמֶה

lecha לָךְ,   moshi'enu מוֹשִׁיעֵנוּ,   litchiyat לִתְחִיַּת   hametim הַמֵּתִים.

El Na (Please God)

This verse was said by Moses as a prayer to heal his sister Miriam the Prophetess. The *Zohar* (Zohar Chadash, Acharei Mot 84) teaches us that this verse contains 11 letters and has the power to call upon the Archangel Raphael and his Light and healing power.

El אֵל   יא"י   (מילוי)   דס"ג   na נָא   refa רְפָא   na נָא   la לָהּ:

Ahavat Olam (Everlasting Love)
Bring to them everlasting love, and remember the Covenant of the Fathers for the children. (Musaf of Rosh Chodesh)

Or Zaru'a Latzadik (Light is Sown for the Righteous)
"Light is sown for the righteous, and gladness for the upright in heart." (Psalms 97:11)

En Aroch Lecha (There is No Comparison to You)
There is no comparison to You, Lord, our God, in this world and there will be nothing except for You, our King, in the life of the World to Come. There will be nothing without You, our Redeemer in the days of the Messiah. And who will be like You, our Savior, at the Resurrection of the Dead? (Shabbat Morning Connection)

El Na (Please God)
"Please, God, heal her, please" (Numbers 12:13)

Songs

AL TIRA (DO NOT BE AFRAID)

Our teacher, Karen Berg, teaches that there are people who are extremely wealthy but are still unhappy. In fact, they seem almost to be cursed by their material wealth. Korach was such an individual because despite having everything he still wanted more. His desire for more blinded him to what was really important; consequently, the earth opened up and swallowed him and his followers. They lost everything. Most of us behave like Korach. We carry with us a sense of entitlement. These words from Psalms 49 were written by Korach's sons, and can help us maintain focus on the right priorities in our life so that we do not fall into the same trap that Korach did.

אַל al תִּירָא tira כְּבוֹד kevod בֵּיתוֹ beto: כִּי ki יַעֲשִׁר ya'ashir אִישׁ ish כִּי ki יִרְבֶּה yirbe יְקָר yikach בְּמוֹתוֹ bemoto לֹא lo כִּי ki הַכֹּל hakol לֹא lo יֵרֵד yered אַחֲרָיו acharav כְּבוֹדוֹ kevodo.

AL TIRA—UTZU ETZA (DO NOT BE AFRAID—DEVISE A PLAN)

Our teacher, Karen Berg, says that our thoughts create our reality. When we think negative thoughts, we express doubt in the Creator. This creates an empty space in the cosmic realm—and that empty space is filled with negativity. These words to remove doubt and fear were written by King Solomon and the prophet Isaiah, and were used by Mordechai to defeat Haman and eventually to bring redemption for the Judeans in Persia.

אַל al תִּירָא tira מִפַּחַד mipachad פִּתְאֹם pit'om וּמִשֹּׁאַת umisho'at רְשָׁעִים resha'im כִּי ki תָבֹא tavo: עֻצוּ utzu עֵצָה etza וְתֻפָר vetufar, דַּבְּרוּ daberu דָבָר davar וְלֹא lvelo יָקוּם yakum, כִּי ki עִמָּנוּ imanu אֵל El:

ELECHA (TO YOU)

This song is made up of two verses from Psalms 30, written by King David, who through his prophecy speaks about Queen Esther and Mordechai in Persia and their salvation (see Midrash Esther Rabba 10:5). When we sing it, we are awakening the assistance and support of the Creator in times of distress.

אֵלֶיךָ elecha ה' Hashem אֶקְרָא ekra וְאֶל ve'el ה' Hashem אֶתְחַנָּן etchanan: שְׁמַע shema ה' Hashem וְחָנֵּנִי vechoneni ה' Hashem הֱיֵה heye עֹזֵר ozer לִי li:

AL TIRA (DO NOT BE AFRAID)
"Do not be afraid when a man becomes rich, when the glory of his house increases. For when he dies he will carry nothing away; His glory will not descend after him." (Psalms 49:17-18)

AL TIRA—UTZU ETZA (DO NOT BE AFRAID—DEVISE A PLAN)
"Do not be afraid of sudden fear Nor of the onslaught of the wicked when it comes." (Proverbs 3:25)
"Devise a plan, but it will be thwarted; State a proposal, but it will not stand, for God is with us." (Isaiah 8:10)

ELECHA (TO YOU)
"It is to You, Lord, that I call, and to the Lord that I plead." (Psalms 30:9)
"Lord, hear me and be gracious to me. Lord, be my helper." (Psalms 30:11)

Songs

Im Eshkachech (If I Forget You)

This song is a section from Psalms 137, and is recited during the *Tikkun Chazot* connection. The *Zohar* states (Zohar Chadash, Balak 7-9): "And the voice is awakened from the middle of the Firmament, and is heard in 390 Firmaments, as there is no joy and happiness before the Holy One, Blessed Be He, but during this time (after midnight) while He stands with the righteous there (in the Garden of Eden), and therefore He swears and says: 'If I forget you, Jerusalem… if I do not exalt Jerusalem above my chief joy.' Any time there is joy before the Holy One, Blessed Be He; this voice is awakened and is heard."

tishkach תִּשְׁכָּחֵוּ	,Yerushalayim יְרוּשָׁלַיִם	eshkachech אֶשְׁכָּחֵךְ	im אִם
lechiki לְוֹחִכִּי	leshoni לְשׁוֹנִי	tidbak תִּדְבַּק	.yemini יְמִינִי
a'aleh אַעֲלֶה	lo לֹא	im אִם	,ezkerechial אֶזְכְּרֵכִי	lo לֹא	im אִם
:simchati שִׂמְחָתִי	rosh רֹאשׁ	al עַל	Yerushalayim יְרוּשָׁלַיִם	et אֶת

Amar Rabbi Akiva (Rav Akiva Says)

Rav Akiva explains that the verse "Love your neighbor as yourself" is the great principle of the Torah. Our teacher, Karen Berg, explains that when the *Zohar* discusses the eleven fabrics that were used as the walls of the Tabernacle, it is talking about a protective covering that chaos cannot penetrate. We all have such a protective shield. The only way forms of negativity enter into our lives is when we become vulnerable and permit Satan to enter through this protective barrier. But we do not have to experience chaos. By fortifying ourselves and taking care to keep our protective shield intact, we can get rid of Satan before he has a chance to enter. It is when we behave towards others with anything less than tolerance and human dignity that we puncture holes in our protective shield. This is why "love your neighbor as yourself" is not just a moral way to live, but also a smart way to live.

lere'acha לְרֵעֲךָ	ve'ahavta וְאָהַבְתָּ	Akiva עֲקִיבָא	Rabbi רַבִּי	amar אָמַר
:batorah בַּתּוֹרָה	gadol גָּדוֹל	kelal כְּלָל	ze זֶה	,kamocha כָּמוֹךָ

Ana Hashem (Please Lord)

This section of Psalms 116 helps us to diminish our ego and become like a servant to the Creator. The *Zohar* (Zohar Balak 203-204) says: "It is certain that the prayers of this man (who put himself as a servant of the king) will never be returned empty."

ani אֲנִי	avdecha עַבְדְּךָ	ani אֲנִי	ki כִּי	,Hashem ה'	ana אָנָּה
:lemoserai לְמוֹסֵרָי	pitachta פִּתַּחְתָּ	amatecha אֲמָתֶךָ	ben בֶּן	avdecha עַבְדְּךָ

Im Eshkachech (If I Forget You)
"If I forget you, Jerusalem, let my right hand forget her cunning. Let my tongue cleave to the roof of my mouth, if I do not remember you, if I do not exalt Jerusalem above my chief joy." (Psalms 137:5-6)

Amar Rabbi Akiva (Rav Akiva Says)
Rav Akiva says: "Love your neighbor as yourself" (Leviticus 19:18)
is the great principle of the Torah. (Jerusalem Talmud, Nedarim, 30:2)

Ana Hashem (Please Lord)
"Please, Lord, I am Your servant.
I am Your servant, then a son of Your handmaid. You have untied my bonds." (Psalms 116:15)

Songs

Ani Ma'amin (I Believe)

This verse is based on the teaching of the Rav Moshe ben Maimon (Maimonides, 12th century) and helps us to have certainty in the coming of the Messiah and the Final Redemption.

אֲנִי ani מַאֲמִין ma'amin בֶּאֱמוּנָה be'emuna שְׁלֵמָה shelema בְּבִיאַת beviat הַמָשִׁיחַ hamashiach, וְאַף ve'af עַל al פִּי pi שֶׁיִּתְמַהְמֵהַּ sheyitmahmeha, עִם im כָּל kol זֶה ze אֲחַכֶּה achake לוֹ lo בְּכָל bechol יוֹם yom שֶׁיָּבוֹא sheyavo.

Orech Yamim (With Long Life)

Orech Yamim, a verse from Psalms 91:16, was Rav Yehuda Ashlag's final words before his passing and elevation from this physical world on *Yom Kippur*. Singing this verse helps us to connect to our teachers, the lineage, and their effort to bring the Final Redemption and the end of death, pain, and suffering.

אֹרֶךְ orech יָמִים yamim אַשְׂבִּיעֵהוּ asbi'ehu וְאַרְאֵהוּ ve'arehu בִּישׁוּעָתִי bishu'ati:

Ashirah Lashem (I Shall Sing to the Lord)

Psalms 104:34-35 can awaken real happiness for the ultimate removal of the forces of darkness and negativity from the world and supports our transformation. Beruria (the wife of the Tana Rav Meir, 2nd century) teaches that King David actually says here: 'Let negative deeds (*chata'im*—which is similar to the Hebrew word for negative people—*chot'im*) be vanished from the earth' and then 'there will be no wicked people anymore,' meaning it is about transformation not the elimination of negative people.

אָשִׁירָה ashira לַה' lashem בְּחַיָּי bechayai אֲזַמְּרָה azamera
לֵאלֹהַי lelohai בְּעוֹדִי be'odi: יֶעֱרַב ye'erav עָלָיו alav שִׂיחִי sichi
אָנֹכִי anochi אֶשְׂמַח esmach בַּה': bahashem יִתַּמּוּ yitamu חַטָּאִים chata'im
מִן min הָאָרֶץ ha'aretz וּרְשָׁעִים ursha'im עוֹד od אֵינָם enam
בָּרְכִי barchi נַפְשִׁי nafshi אֶת et ה' Hashem הַלְלוּיָהּ haleluya:

Ani Ma'amin (I Believe)
I believe with complete faith in the coming of the Messiah and although he may tarry, nevertheless, I wait every day for him to come (Based on the Thirteen Principles of Faith by the Rambam)

Orech Yamim (With Long Life)
"With long life I will satiate him and I will show him My salvation." (Psalms 91:16)

Ashirah Lashem (I Shall Sing to the Lord)
"I shall sing to the Lord as long as I live and play melodies to my God as long as I exist. May my utterances be sweet to Him, and let me rejoice in the Lord. Let negative deeds be vanished from the earth and then there will be no wicked people anymore. Bless the Lord, my soul. Praise the Lord." (Psalms 104:34-35)

Songs

Asher Bara (Who Created Joy)

These words of the *Zohar* (Zohar Terumah 798) help us to bring down all the blessings and thereby create more Light and joy in the Worlds, as it is stated: "The seventh blessing establishes them all, and all are blessed from that seventh one, which is *Binah*."

chatan וְחָתָן	vesimcha וְשִׂמְחָה	sason שָׂשׂוֹן	bara בָּרָא	asher אֲשֶׁר
vechedva וְחֶדְוָה,	ditza דִּיצָה	rina רִנָּה	gila גִּילָה	vechala וְכַלָּה,
vere'ut וְרֵעוּת.	veshalom וְשָׁלוֹם	ve'achva וְאַחֲוָה	ahava אַהֲבָה

Atah Takum (You Shall Rise)

This verse from Psalms 102:14 helps us shorten the process and bring the end to pain and suffering sooner. Kabbalist Rav Tzvi Elimelech of Dinov (the Benei Yisachar, 18th century) explains: Whatever delays the arrival of the Final Redemption should be removed; if the prevention comes from the Creator, King David says "*Atah takum*" (meaning You—the Creator shall rise); if the hindrance is because of us he says "*Tziyon*" and if the reason for the delay is because the time is not right he says "*ki va mo'ed*—it is the appointed time."

Tziyon צִיּוֹן	terachem תְּרַחֵם	takum תָּקוּם	Ata אַתָּה
mo'ed מוֹעֵד.	va בָא	ki כִּי	lechenena לְחֶנְנָהּ	et עֵת	ki כִּי

Biglal Avot (For the Sake of the Ancestors)

This song is part of a poem called *Yom leyabasha*, written by Kabbalist Rav Yehuda Halevi (Spain, 12th Century) for *Shabbat Shirah* (*Shabbat Beshalach*; portion of the Splitting of the Red Sea). It helps us to arouse the power of miracles and mind over matter, not because of our merit but for the sake of the merit of the Patriarchs.

banim בָּנִים,	toshi'a תּוֹשִׁיעַ	avot אָבוֹת	biglal בִּגְלַל
venehem בְּנֵיהֶם.	livnei לִבְנֵי	ge'ula גְּאוּלָה	vetavi וְתָבִיא

Bilvavi (In My Heart)

When Betzalel [Lit. "in the Shadow of God" (*Zohar* Pekudei 56-59)] was about to build the Tabernacle, he went to God and asked: "Who am I to be part of the building of Your house? Why have You chosen me?" Our teacher, Karen Berg, explains that the reason he was chosen and the entire construction of the Tabernacle assigned to him was because of his willingness to the do the work of the Creator. He said to God: "I am your shadow, these are my hands, use them to do Your work."

Asher Bara (Who Created Joy)
"Who created joy and happiness, groom and bride, gladness, cheer, delight and rejoicing, love and harmony, and peace, and companionship." (Zohar Teruma 788)

Atah Takum (You Shall Rise)
"You shall rise and be merciful to Zion, for the time for favor has come and it is the appointed time." (Psalms 102:14)

Biglal Avot (For the Sake of the Ancestors)
For the sake of the ancestors, save the children, and bring redemption to their children's children.

SONGS

Bilvavi was written by Kabbalist Rav Eliezer Azikri (Safed, Israel, 16th Century) to help us to transform our heart and soul and make them a resting place for the Light of the Creator.

kevodo כְּבוֹדוֹ,	lehadar לְהַדֵּר	evne אֶבְנֶה	mishkan מִשְׁכָּן	bilvavi בִּלְבָבִי
hodo הוֹדוֹ,	lekarnei לְקַרְנֵי	akim אָקִים	mizbe'ach מִזְבֵּחַ	uvamishkan וּבַמִּשְׁכָּן
ha'akeda הָעֲקֵדָה,	esh אֵשׁ	et אֶת	li לִי	ekach אֶקַּח	tamid תָּמִיד	ulner וּלְנֵר
hayechida הַיְּחִידָה.	nafshi נַפְשִׁי	et אֶת	lo לוֹ	akriv אַקְרִיב	ulkorban וּלְקָרְבָּן

BECHA BATCHU (IN YOU THEY TRUST)

Psalms 22:5-6 speaks about certainty in the Creator, the certainty Esther and Mordechai had (see Midrash Tehilim Rabba 22), which saved their generation from annihilation. Kabbalist Rav Moshe Chaim Lutzatto (Acre, 18th century) says that when we have certainty and trust in the Creator during the time of exile, this removes Bread of Shame and will bring about the Final Redemption even if we do not deserve it.

batchu בָּטְחוּ	avotenu אֲבֹתֵינוּ	batchu בָּטְחוּ	becha בְּךָ
venimlatu וְנִמְלָטוּ	za'aku זָעֲקוּ	elecha אֵלֶיךָ	vatefaltemo וַתְּפַלְּטֵמוֹ.
voshu בוֹשׁוּ.	velo וְלֹא	batchu בָּטְחוּ	becha בְּךָ

BESHEM HASHEM (IN THE NAME OF THE LORD)

The *Zohar* says (Zohar Bo 200-213): "...before all of this (coming to this world) four angels descended with him... if he has ancestral merit then (he will be surrounded by) Michael from the Right (Abraham), Gabriel from the Left (Isaac), Nuriel (or Uriel) from the Centre (Jacob) and Raphael beneath (Adam)... and at that time the Tetragrammaton Name rules over him... But if he has no merit, then the four angels of destruction accompany him." This song invites the protective energy of the Archangels to come and surround us.

Yisrael יִשְׂרָאֵל,	Elohei אֱלֹהֵי	Hashem ה'	beshem בְּשֵׁם
Gavri'el גַּבְרִיאֵל,	umismoli וּמִשְּׂמֹאלִי	Michael מִיכָאֵל	mimini מִימִינִי
Refa'el רְפָאֵל,	ume'achorai וּמֵאֲחוֹרַי	Uri'el אוּרִיאֵל	umilfanai וּמִלְּפָנַי
El אֵל.	shechinat שְׁכִינַת	roshi רֹאשִׁי	ve'al וְעַל

BILVAVI (IN MY HEART)
I will build a Tabernacle (place of rest) in my heart to glorify His honor. And I will place an alter in the Tabernacle dedicated to His rays of splendor. And for the eternal flame I will take upon myself the fire that fueled the Binding [of Isaac]. And as a sacrifice I will offer Him my unique soul.

BECHA BATCHU (IN YOU THEY TRUST)
"In You our ancestors put their trust (certainty); they trusted and You delivered them. They cried out to You and were saved. They trusted in You and were never disgraced." (Psalms 22:5-6)

BESHEM HASHEM (IN THE NAME OF THE LORD)
In the Name of the Lord, the God of Israel, may Michael be at my right hand; Gabriel at my left; before me, Uriel; behind me, Raphael; and above my head the Divine Presence of God [the Shechinah].

Songs

Gam Ki Elech (Though I walk)

Psalms 23:4 gives us support and certainty in difficult times, as well as protection from the evil spirit called "*Ra*" (see Zohar Beresheet B, 398.) The *Zohar* states (Zohar Vayeshev 205): "wherever the righteous go the Holy One, Blessed Be He, protects them and never abandons them."

צַלְמָוֶת, tzalmavet   בְּגֵיא bege   אֵלֵךְ elech   כִּי ki   גַּם gam

עִמָּדִי. imadi   אַתָּה ata   כִּי ki   רָע, ra   אִירָא ira   לֹא lo

David Melech Israel (David, King of Israel)

This is a verse from the blessing of the moon connection and composed by the Tana Rav Yehuda Hanasi (a direct descendent of King David. Israel, 2nd Century). The moon and King David represent the world of *Malchut*—our physical illusionary world. This song helps us to remove the illusion and limited aspects from our lives and bring blessings, flow and continuation.

וְקַיָם. vekayam   וְחַי chai   יִשְׂרָאֵל Yisrael   מֶלֶךְ melech   דָּוִד David

והו   טוֹב tov   וּבְמַזָּל uvemazal   והו   טוֹב tov   בְּסִימָן besiman   יְהֵא yehe

יִשְׂרָאֵל: Yisrael   יה אדני   וּלְכָל ulchol   אהיה, אלהים, אדני   לָנוּ lanu

Hashem Melech (The Lord is King)

An excerpt from the morning connection that helps us to overcome the limitation and the illusion of the physical world. Our teacher, the Rav, quoting Rav Isaac Luria (the Ari), says that the words *melech* ("reign" present), *malach* ("reigned" past) and *yimloch* ("shall reign" future) together add up to the same numerical value of the five Final Letters of the Hebrew Alphabet (280=מנצפך), thereby helping us to remove the limitation of time, space, and motion that exists in the physical reality.

מָלַךְ, malach   ה' Hashem   מֶלֶךְ, melech   ה' Hashem

וָעֶד: va'ed   לְעֹלָם le'olam   יִמְלֹךְ yimloch   ה' Hashem

---

Gam Ki Elech (Though I walk)
"Though I walk in the valley overshadowed by death, I will fear no evil for You are with me." (Psalms 23:4)

David Melech Israel (David, King of Israel)
"David, King of Israel lives forever." (Babylonian Talmud, Tractate Rosh Hashana 25a)
May there be a good sign and a good fortune for us and for all Israel.

Hashem Melech (The Lord is King)
The Lord is King, the Lord has reigned, the Lord shall reign forever and for eternity.

Hashem, Lo Gava Libi (Lord, My Heart is Not Proud)

Psalms 131:1-2, written by King David, teaches us a lesson in humility and appreciation. (Zohar Mishpatim 143-144)

ה' Hashem לֹא lo גָבַהּ gava לִבִּי libi וְלֹא velo רָמוּ ramu עֵינָי enai
וְלֹא velo הִלַּכְתִּי hilachti בִּגְדֹלוֹת bigdolot וּבְנִפְלָאוֹת uvnifla'ot מִמֶּנִּי mimeni.
אִם im לֹא lo שִׁוִּיתִי shiviti וְדוֹמַמְתִּי vedomamti נַפְשִׁי nafshi
כְּגָמֻל kegamul עֲלֵי alei אִמּוֹ imo כַּגָּמֻל kagamul עָלַי alai נַפְשִׁי nafshi.

Hashem Oz Le'amo Yiten (The Lord Gives Might to His People)

Singing Psalms 29:11 helps us receive strength in times of weakness.

ה' Hashem עֹז oz לְעַמּוֹ le'amo יִתֵּן yiten
ה' Hashem יְבָרֵךְ yevarech אֶת et עַמּוֹ amo בַשָּׁלוֹם vashalom:

Hoshi'a et Amecha (Redeem Your Nation)

It says in the *Midrash* (Yalkut Shimoni, Deuteronomy 33:951): that "All of his life, Moses asked to bless the Israelites but the Angel of Death never let him do so. What did Moses do? He took the Angel of Death, tied him and put him underneath his feet and then (without any interruption) blessed the Israelites." Psalms 28:9 is the verse that Moses recited to bless the Israelites.

הוֹשִׁיעָה hoshi'a אֶת et עַמֶּךָ amecha וּבָרֵךְ uvarech אֶת et
נַחֲלָתֶךָ nachalatecha וּרְעֵם ur'em וְנַשְּׂאֵם venas'em עַד ad הָעוֹלָם ha'olam.

Hatov (The Good One)

An excerpt from the *Amidah* connection that helps us to appreciate the endless mercy and support of the Creator.

הַטּוֹב hotov כִּי ki לֹא lo כָלוּ kalu רַחֲמֶיךָ rachamecha
וְהַמְרַחֵם vehamerachem כִּי ki לֹא lo תַמּוּ tamu וְחֲסָדֶיךָ chasadecha
כִּי ki מֵעוֹלָם me'olam קִוִּינוּ kivinu לָךְ lach.

Hashem, Lo Gava Libi (Lord, My Heart is Not Proud)
"Lord, My heart is not proud, my eyes are not haughty; I do not concern myself with great matters or things too wonderful for me [the secret of the Three Upper Sefirot – Chochmah, Binah and Da'at]. But I have calmed and quieted myself, I am like a weaned child with its mother; like a weaned child I am content." (Psalms 131:1-2)

Hashem Oz Le'amo Yiten (The Lord Gives Might to His People)
"The Lord gives might to His people. The Lord will bless His people with peace." (Psalms 29:11)

Hoshi'a et Amecha (Redeem Your Nation)
"Redeem Your Nation and bless Your inheritance, provide for them and uplift them forever." (Psalms 28:9)

Hatov (The Good One)
You are the good One, for Your compassion has never ceased. You are the compassionate One, for Your kindness has never ended, for we have always placed our hope in You.

Songs

Hineh Ma Tov (Behold, How Good)

King David, the Psalmist, is the chariot for *Malchut*. In Psalms 133:2 King David expresses his longing for the original state when *Malchut* was a sister to *Zeir Anpin*, meaning that on one hand, *Malchut* and *Zeir Anpin* are equal but on the other hand, *Malchut* is in darkness and cannot illuminate the Lower Worlds. The secondary state, which we are now in, is when *Zeir Anpin* is above *Malchut*, and although They are not Equal, They are able to bring Light and joy to the Lower Worlds. Kind David asks that *Malchut* and *Zeir Anpin* be together (*yachad*) so that *Malchut* will have both advantages (equal and illuminating) and exist in its original state, which is face-to-face with the Holy One, Blessed Be He, and the Lower Worlds will be illuminated and rejoice. (See Sulam commentary on Zohar Vayikra 100)

na'im נָעִים uma וּמַה tov טוֹב ma מַה hineh הִנֵּה

♦yachad יַחַד gam גַּם achim אַחִים shevet שֶׁבֶת

Hineh Yamim Ba'im (Behold, the Days Come)

Amos 8:11 is discussed in the *Talmud* (Babylonian Talmud, Tractate Shabbat 138:2) as a prophecy that reveals that in the period before the Final Redemption, the Torah is destined to be forgotten in Israel. This discussion is concluded with the following words of Rav Shimon: "Heaven forbid that the Torah be forgotten in Israel, for it is said, 'for it shall not be forgotten out of the mouths of their seed.'" The last letters of these words creates the name "Yochai—יוֹחַאי—זַרְעוֹ מִפִּי תִשָּׁכַח לֹא כִּי)." The kabbalists explain that despite Amos' prophecy, the Torah will never be forgotten as long as we connect to the teachings of Rav Shimon bar Yochai, to the *Zohar*.

Hashem ה׳ ne'um נְאֻם ba'im בָּאִים yamim יָמִים hineh הִנֵּה

ra'av רָעָב lo לֹא ba'aretz, בָּאָרֶץ ra'av רָעָב vehishlachti וְהִשְׁלַחְתִּי

lamayim, לַמַּיִם tzama צָמָא velo וְלֹא lalechem לַלֶּחֶם

♦Hashem ה׳ divrei דִּבְרֵי et אֵת lishmo'a לִשְׁמֹעַ im אִם ki כִּי

Harachaman (The Compassionate One)

An excerpt from *Birkat Hamazon* that connects us to the days of the Messiah and the Final Redemption.

vichayenu וִיחַיֵּינוּ yezakenu יְזַכֵּנוּ hu הוּא harachaman הָרַחֲמָן

ulvinyan וּלְבִנְיַן hamashiach, הַמָּשִׁיחַ limot לִימוֹת vikarvenu וִיקָרְבֵנוּ

♦haba הַבָּא haolam הָעוֹלָם ulchayei וּלְחַיֵּי hamikdash, הַמִּקְדָּשׁ bet בֵּית

Hineh Ma Tov (Behold, How Good)
"Behold, how good and how pleasant it is for brothers to dwell together in unity." *(Psalms 133:2)*

Hineh Yamim Ba'im (Behold, the Days Come)
"Behold, the days come, said the Lord (God); That I will send a famine in the land, not a famine of bread, nor a thirst for water, but of hearing the words of the Lord." *(Amos 8:11)*

Harachaman (The Compassionate One)
The Compassionate One. May He make us worthy, grant us with life and bring us closer to the days of Messiah, the rebuilding of the Temple, and the life of the World to Come.

SONGS

HASHIVENU (BRING US BACK TO YOU)

There is a discussion in the *Midrash* (Midrash Eichah Rabba 5:21) about whether the process of change and transformation that is required to bring the Final Redemption will begin by the Creator or by us. Generally, to awaken and activate any Supernal Force requires an action from Below, from us first. However in this song, written by the prophet Jeremiah, we receive the gift, despite the fact that we will not be able to awaken the Redemption from Below, the Creator will awaken it from Above and this will cause the awakening from Below.

הָשִׁיבֵנוּ hashivenu ה' Hashem אֵלֶיךָ elecha וְנָשׁוּבָה venashuva, חַדֵּשׁ chadesh יָמֵינוּ yamenu כְּקֶדֶם kekedem.

UVA'U HA'OVDIM (THEY WHO LOSE SHALL COME BACK)

The *Zohar* (Zohar Va'etchanan 129) asks about this verse: "it should have said 'they who were lost' or 'they who are lost' (*ne'evdu*). What is meant by 'they who lose' (*ovdim*)?" and the *Zohar* answers: "It speaks about those who lost their faith." It is about those people who have lost their conscious connection to the Light of the Creator, and not people who have lost their way in a physical sense. *Uva'u Ha'ovdim* is written by the prophet Isaiah and with it we are given the opportunity to reconnect to all the lost aspects in our life.

וּבָאוּ uva'u הָאֹבְדִים ha'ovdim בְּאֶרֶץ be'eretz אַשּׁוּר Ashur וְהַנִּדָּחִים vehanidachim בְּאֶרֶץ be'eretz מִצְרַיִם Mitzrayim וְהִשְׁתַּחֲווּ vehishtachavu לַה' lashem בְּהַר behar הַקֹּדֶשׁ hakodesh בִּירוּשָׁלָיִם birushala'im.

VEHA'ER ENENU (ENLIGHTEN OUR EYES)

Veha'er Enenu is an excerpt from the morning connection where we ask the Creator to help us not feel ashamed or humiliated so as not to fall, which is opposite to the natural order of things. Generally, we fall spiritually and then become ashamed. Kabbalist Rav Moshe Kordovero (Safed, Israel, 16th century) explains (see Siddur 'Tefilah Lemoshe' regarding this verse), that here we ask the Creator to help purify us from the *klipa* because the shame that we feel from the *klipa* is the reason we fall.

וְהָאֵר veha'er עֵינֵינוּ enenu בְּתוֹרָתֶךָ betoratecha, וְדַבֵּק vedabek לִבֵּנוּ libenu בְּמִצְוֹתֶיךָ vemitzvotecha, וְיַחֵד veyached לְבָבֵנוּ levavenu לְאַהֲבָה le'ahava וּלְיִרְאָה ulyir'a אֶת et שְׁמֶךָ shemecha, וְלֹא velo נֵבוֹשׁ nevosh וְלֹא velo נִכָּלֵם nikalem וְלֹא velo נִכָּשֵׁל nikashel לְעוֹלָם le'olam וָעֶד va'ed.

HASHIVENU (BRING US BACK TO YOU)
"Bring us back to You, Lord, and we shall return, renew our days as of old." (Lamentations 5:21)

UVA'U HA'OVDIM (THEY WHO LOSE SHALL COME BACK)
"And they who lose in the land of Assyria and the ones sent away to the land of Egypt shall come to prostrate before the Lord at His Holy Mountain, in Jerusalem" (Isaiah 27 13)

VEHA'ER ENENU (ENLIGHTEN OUR EYES)
Enlighten our eyes with Your Torah. Bond our hearts with Your commandments. Unify our hearts to love and fear Your Name; then we shall be neither ashamed nor humiliated; nor shall we fail ever, and for all eternity.

Songs

Vehi She'amda (It is This That Has Stood)

An excerpt from *The Haggadah of Pesach* that speaks about the battle between us and the negative forces, and the constant protection and salvation of the Light.

וְהִיא vehi שֶׁעָמְדָה she'amda לַאֲבוֹתֵינוּ la'avotenu וְלָנוּ, velanu שֶׁלֹא shelo
אֶחָד echad בִּלְבַד bilvad עָמַד amad עָלֵינוּ alenu לְכַלוֹתֵנוּ, lechalotenu
וְהַקָדוֹשׁ vehakadosh בָּרוּךְ baruch הוּא hu מַצִילֵנוּ matzilenu מִיָדָם miyadam.

Vehar'enu (And Show Us)

An excerpt from *retza vehachalitzenu*, the additional *Shabbat* connection in *Birkat Hamazon* that helps us to connect to the big picture. When a person experiences the loss of a loved one, we usually offer comfort, condolences, and consolation (*nechamah*). From a kabbalistic point of view, real *nechamah* comes from being able to see the big picture, realize that no loss has occurred and instead become aware that there is real salvation (*yeshua'ah*).

וְהַרְאֵנוּ vehar'enu ה' Hashem אֱלֹהֵינוּ Elokenu בְּנֶחָמַת benechamat
צִיוֹן Tziyon עִירֶךָ irecha וּבְבִנְיַן uvevinyan יְרוּשָלַיִם Yerushalayim
עִיר ir קָדְשֶׁךָ, kodshecha כִּי ki אַתָּה Ata הוּא hu
בַּעַל ba'al הַיְשׁוּעוֹת hayeshu'ot וּבַעַל uva'al הַנֶחָמוֹת hanechamot.

Vetaher Libenu (And Purify Our Hearts)

A pure heart is a prerequisite to a true connection with the Light of the Creator. This verse helps us yearn for a pure heart.

וְטַהֵר vetaher לִבֵּנוּ libenu לְעָבְדְךָ le'avdecha בֶּאֱמֶת ve'emet.

Velirushalayim (And to Jerusalem)

It says in the *Midrash* (Midrash Shemuel Rabba 13:5) in the name of Rav Shimon Bar Yochai, that in the future we will lose our faith in the ruling of the Creator, the rebuilding of Jerusalem and the Temple and in the coming of the Messiah descended from King David, and because of this we might lose all the blessings. Reciting these excerpts from the *Amidah* connection helps us keep the blessings in our life.

Vehi She'amda (It is This That Has Stood)
It is this that has stood by our fathers and us. For not only has one risen against us to annihilate us, but in every generation they rise against us to annihilate us; and the Holy One, Blessed Be He, redeems us from their hands.

Vehar'enu (And Show Us)
And show us, Lord, our God, the consolation of Zion, Your city, and the rebuilding of Jerusalem, city of Your Holiness, for You are the Master of salvation and Master of consolations.

Vetaher Libenu (And Purify Our Hearts)
And purify our hearts to serve You sincerely.

berachamim בְּרַחֲמִים	ircha עִירְךָ	velirushalayim וְלִירוּשָׁלַיִם	
ka'asher כַּאֲשֶׁר	betocha בְּתוֹכָהּ	vetishkon וְתִשְׁכּוֹן	◆tashuv תָּשׁוּב
bekarov בְּקָרוֹב	ota אוֹתָהּ	uvne וּבְנֵה	◆dibarta דִּבַּרְתָּ
vechise וְכִסֵּא	◆olam עוֹלָם	binyan בִּנְיַן	beyamenu בְּיָמֵינוּ
◆tachin תָּכִין	letocha לְתוֹכָהּ	mehera מְהֵרָה	avdecha עַבְדְּךָ David דָּוִד

UMACHA (AND THE LORD WILL WIPE AWAY)

Rav Ashlag explains (Sulam commentary on Zohar Prologue 125) that the time of the revelation on Mount Sinai and the receiving of the Torah is equal to the time of the *Gemar Hatikkun* or the Final Correction, and brought with it freedom from the Angel of Death. This verse, from the prophet Isaiah, helps us to accelerate the process of the removal of pain, suffering, and death from the world.

◆panim פָּנִים	kol כָּל	me'al מֵעַל	dima'a דִּמְעָה	Hashem ה' umacha וּמָחָה

VENISGAV (AND THE LORD WILL BE EXALTED)

The *Midrash* (Midrash Beresheet Rabba, Vayishlach 77:1) compares Jacob/Israel to the Creator using the word *levado* (alone), which appeared in each of these two verses. Israel is a level that each of us can reach when we do our spiritual work and become like the Creator.

◆hahu הַהוּא	bayom בַּיּוֹם	levado לְבַדּוֹ	Hashem ה' venisgav וְנִשְׂגַּב
vaye'avek וַיֵּאָבֵק	,levado לְבַדּוֹ	ya'akov יַעֲקֹב	vayivater וַיִּוָּתֵר
◆hashachar הַשָּׁחַר	alot עֲלוֹת	ad עַד	imo עִמּוֹ ish אִישׁ

VE'ATA BANIM (AND NOW, SONS)

An excerpt from a poem, written by one of the earliest kabbalists, Rav Shimon ben Isaac (Germany, 10th century) for *Shavuot*. These two verses speak about the difference between the son and the servant, which we all have inside us. The *Zohar* states (Zohar Behar 75-85): "there are two grades Above in which man should be adorned; they are the secret of the Faith, and they are one. The first is the secret of the servant (*Malchut*) and the other is the secret of the son (*Zeir Anpin*)." It says in the *Talmud* (Babylonian Talmud, Tractate Chulin 91:2) that we are loved by the Creator more than the angels and that the angels await our singing and prayers before they start. Here we can connect to the highest level of "son," which is even above the angels.

VELIRUSHALAYIM (AND TO JERUSALEM)
And to Jerusalem, Your city, return in mercy, and dwell therein as You had spoken; Rebuild it soon in our days as an everlasting building, and speedily set up therein the throne of David Your servant.

UMACHA (AND THE LORD WILL WIPE AWAY)
"And the Lord God will wipe away tears from all faces" (Isaiah 25:8)

VENISGAV (AND THE LORD WILL BE EXALTED)
"And the Lord alone will be exalted in that day." (Isaiah 2:11)
"Then Jacob was left alone, and a man wrestled with him until the dawn began to break." (Genesis 32:25)

Songs

ve'ata וְעַתָּה	banim בָּנִים	shiru שִׁירוּ	lamelech לַמֶּלֶךְ
betiferet בְּתִפְאָרֶת	mefoar מְפוֹאָר.		ve'ashrei וְאַשְׁרֵי
avadav עֲבָדָיו	hamashmi'im הַמַּשְׁמִיעִים	bekol בְּקוֹל	shivcho שִׁבְחוֹ.

Ufduye (And the Redeemed)

The *Zohar* says (Zohar Yitro 503): "The joy in Zion (at the Final Redemption) will surpass them all (all the other kinds of joy). This verse, Isaiah 51:11, speaks of four kinds of joy, which correspond to the four exiles."

| ufduyei וּפְדוּיֵי | Hashem ה' | yeshuvun יְשֻׁבוּן | uvau וּבָאוּ | tziyon צִיּוֹן | berina בְּרִנָּה. |

Ufros (And Spread)

Our teacher, the Rav, teaches us that the *Sukkah* is the Surrounding Light that both protects us and also creates pressure for spiritual transformation. In this song we ask that the *Sukkah* be with us constantly with mercy, life, and peace.

| ufros וּפְרוֹשׂ | sukat סֻכַּת | alenu עָלֵינוּ | sukat סֻכַּת | shelomecha שְׁלוֹמֶךָ |
| sukat סֻכַּת | rachamim רַחֲמִים | vechayim וְחַיִּים | veshalom וְשָׁלוֹם: |

Vekarev Pezurenu (Draw Near Our Scattered)

This verse, translated literally, speaks about the physical gathering of all humanity, from all parts of the world into one place. But, in essence, it is about gathering all the sparks that had been lost. The *Talmud* (Babylonian Talmud, Tractate Pesachim 87:2) says that the reason for the exiles, as painful they are, is to draw near and bring back all of the lost souls.

| vekarev וְקָרֵב | pezurenu פְּזוּרֵינוּ | miben מִבֵּין | hagoyim הַגּוֹיִם. |
| unfutzotenu וּנְפוּצוֹתֵינוּ | kanes כַּנֵּס | miyarketei מִיַּרְכְּתֵי | aretz אָרֶץ. |

Vesamachta Bechagecha (And You Shall Rejoice in Your Feast)

This verse can help to awaken real happiness during spiritual cosmic time zones but especially during *Sukkot*.

| vesamachta וְשָׂמַחְתָּ | bechagecha בְּחַגֶּךָ. | vehayita וְהָיִיתָ | ach אַךְ | same'ach שָׂמֵחַ. |

Ve'ata Banim (And Now, Sons)
And now, sons sing to the King as He magnificent (in His) glory.
And happy are His servants, who raise their voices in His praise.

Ufduye (And the Redeemed)
"Therefore the redeemed of the Lord shall return, and come with singing into Zion" (Isaiah 51:11)

Ufros (And Spread)
And spread over us shelter of Your peace, a shelter of mercy and life and peace.

Vekarev Pezurenu (Draw Near Our Scattered)
Draw near our scattered from among the nations, and gather our dispersed from the ends of the earth.

Vesamachta Bechagecha (And You Shall Rejoice in your Feast)
"And you shall rejoice in your feast… and your joy will be complete" (Deuteronomy 16:14-15)

Veten Banu (Give Us a Virtuous Desire)

A verse from the connection of *Ribon Kol HaOlamim* on *erev Shabbat* that gives us the ability to have a pure desire for a true connection to the Light.

| veten וְתֵן | banu בָּנוּ | yetzer יֵצֶר | tov טוֹב, |
| le'avdecha לְעָבְדְּךָ | be'emet בֶּאֱמֶת | uvyira וּבְיִרְאָה | uvahava וּבְאַהֲבָה: |

Chemdat Yamim (Most Coveted of Days)

An excerpt from the *Amidah* connection of *Shabbat* that helps us to have a greater appreciation for *Shabbat*.

| chemdat וְחֶמְדַּת | yamim יָמִים | oto אוֹתוֹ | karata קָרָאתָ. |
| zecher זֵכֶר | lema'aseh לְמַעֲשֵׂה | beresheet בְּרֵאשִׁית: | | |

Chasdei Hashem (The Mercy of the Lord)

The *Zohar* asks (Zohar Chadash, Balak 58): "It should have said 'it is of the Lord's mercy that is not consumed (finished),' so why does it say: 'we are not finished'?" And the *Zohar* answers that it speaks about the complete and ultimate protection shield of the Creator over us, and that all the enemies who would like to destroy us will never succeed because the Creator protects us.

| chasdei וְחַסְדֵי | Hashem ה' | ki כִּי | lo לֹא | tamnu תָמְנוּ, |
| ki כִּי | lo לֹא | chalu כָלוּ | rachamav רַחֲמָיו: | |

Tov Lehodot (It is Good to Say Thanks)

The *Zohar* (Zohar, Beresheet B, 345) shares with us the story about Adam to help us understand the origin of Psalms 92:2-3. "Adam asked his son Cain: 'What was done with your sentence?' Cain replied: 'I was forgiven.' Adam then asked: 'How did you merit that?' and Cain answered: 'Because I did *teshuvah* (repentance).' Adam said: 'I did not know that the strength of *teshuvah* is so great.' Adam then began to praise his Master and recite this verse."

tov טוֹב	lehodot לְהֹדוֹת	lashem לַה'	ulzamer וּלְזַמֵּר
leshimcha לְשִׁמְךָ	elyon עֶלְיוֹן:	lehagid לְהַגִּיד	baboker בַּבֹּקֶר
chasdecha חַסְדֶּךָ	ve'emunat'cha וֶאֱמוּנָתְךָ		balelot בַּלֵּילוֹת:

Veten Banu (Give Us a Virtuous Desire)
Give us a virtuous desire to serve You with truth, with awe, and with love.

Chemdat Yamim (Most Coveted of Days)
Most coveted of days, You have called it, a remembrance of the works of Creation.

Chasdei Hashem (The Mercy of the Lord)
"It is of the Lord's mercies that we are not consumed, for His mercies never end" (Lamentations 3:22)

Tov Lehodot (It is Good to Say Thanks)
"It is good to say thanks to You, the Lord, and to sing Your Name, Exalted One. To relate Your kindness in the morning and Your faithfulness in the evenings." (Psalms 92:2-3)

Songs

Yibane Hamikdash (May the Temple be Rebuilt)

An excerpt from the ancient song *Tzur Mishelo* that speaks about the joy we will have in the End of Days.

יִבָּנֶה yibane הַמִּקְדָּשׁ hamikdash, עִיר ir צִיּוֹן Tziyon תְּמַלֵּא temale,
וְשָׁם vesham נָשִׁיר nashir שִׁיר shir וְחָדָשׁ chadash, וּבִרְנָנָה uvirnana נַעֲלֶה na'ale:

Yehi Shalom (May There be Peace)

The *Zohar* (Zohar Chadash, Yitro 259) says that in the future all the questions and the doubts will disappear and we will have only peace and serenity. Also says the *Zohar* (Zohar Bamidbar 20): "When this Light of blessings and life awakens, all is joined. Everything is with love, perfection and is peaceful, Above and Below. This is the meaning of this verse."

יְהִי yehi שָׁלוֹם shalom בְּחֵילֵךְ bechelech
שַׁלְוָה shalva בְּאַרְמְנוֹתָיִךְ be'armenotayich:

Yachad (Together)

An excerpt from the *Kedusha* connection that helps us to create unity. The verse can be read as "together they are all holy" instead of "together, they will all recite the holiness," meaning only when we are together are we connected to holiness.

יַחַד yachad (כֻּלָּם kulam) קְדֻשָּׁה kedusha לְךָ lecha יְשַׁלֵּשׁוּ yeshaleshu:)

Yamim (Days)

Written by King David in appreciation for the 70 years of life (number of years of a generation) he received from Adam. When we sing this song we meditate to extend the life of our spiritual teachers.

יָמִים yamim עַל al יְמֵי yemei מֶלֶךְ melech תּוֹסִיף tosif
שְׁנוֹתָיו shenotav כְּמוֹ kemo דֹר dor וָדֹר vador.

Yibane Hamikdash (May the Temple be Rebuilt)
May the Temple be rebuilt; May You fill the city of Zion,
and there we shall sing a new song, and there go up with joyous song.

Yehi Shalom (May There be Peace)
"May there be peace within your walls and serenity within your palaces." (Psalms 122:8)

Yachad (Together)
Together (they will all recite the holiness three times.)

Yamim (Days)
"Add many years to the life of the king. May his years span the generations." (Psalms 61:7)

YIFRACH BEYAMAV TZADIK (IN HIS DAYS MAY THE RIGHTEOUS FLOURISH)

Based on a story in the *Talmud* (Babylonian Talmud, Tractate Chulin 60:2) about the sun and the moon, our teacher, Karen Berg, shares that on the fourth day of Creation it was decided that until the time of the Messiah the sun, which is *Zeir Anpin* or masculine energy, would rule over the moon, which is *Malchut* or feminine energy. From this we can better understand why throughout history the female has been oppressed. Within the context of the Bible, we see that the struggle of women throughout the generations existed only because it was not yet time for the Lightforce of the female to shine equal to the Light of her male counterpart. But now, during the Age of Aquarius—a time of serious depletion of spiritual energy—the female is rising to the occasion, and the sun and the moon will soon have equal Light.

The *Midrash* adds (Yalkut Shimoni, Psalms 806): "'No more moon' means that in the future the Light of the righteous (*tzadik*) will illuminate the world like the light of the sun and the moon does today."

יִפְרַח yifrach בְּיָמָיו beyamav צַדִּיק tzadik וְרֹב verov שָׁלוֹם shalom
עַד ad בְּלִי beli יָרֵחַ yare'ach: וְיֵרְד veyerd מַיִם miyam עַד ad יָם yam
וּמִנָּהָר uminahar עַד ad אַפְסֵי afsei אָרֶץ aretz: לְפָנָיו lefanav
יִכְרְעוּ yichre'u צִיִּים tziyim וְאֹיְבָיו ve'oyvav עָפָר afar יְלַחֵכוּ yelachechu:

YERUSHALYIM ORO SHEL OLAM (JERUSALEM IS THE LIGHT OF THE WORLD)

The *Midrash* (Midrash Beresheet Rabba 59:8) emphasizes the ability and power of Jerusalem as the energy center of the world and the channel for Lightforce of the Creator for all of humanity.

יְרוּשָׁלַיִם Yerushalayim אוֹרוֹ oro שֶׁל shel עוֹלָם olam.
וּמִי umi הוּא hu אוֹרָהּ ora שֶׁל shel יְרוּשָׁלַיִם Yerushalayim?
הַקָּדוֹשׁ hakadosh בָּרוּךְ baruch הוּא hu.

YASIS (YOUR GOD WILL REJOICE)

An excerpt from *Lecha Dodi*, written by Kabbalist Rav Shlomo Elkabetz (Safed, Israel, 16th Century) to increase happiness.

יָשִׂישׂ yasis עָלַיִךְ alayich אֱלֹהָיִךְ Elohayich,
כִּמְשׂוֹשׂ kimsos וְחָתָן chatan עַל al כַּלָּה kala:

YIFRACH BEYAMAV TZADIK (IN HIS DAYS MAY THE RIGHTEOUS FLOURISH)
"In his (Messiah) days may the righteous [Yesod] flourish, And abundance of peace till the moon [Malchut] is no more. May he rule from sea to sea and from the river to the ends of the Earth. Desert nomads will bow before him; his enemies will fall before him in the dust." (Psalms 72:7-9)

YERUSHALYIM ORO SHEL OLAM (JERUSALEM IS THE LIGHT OF THE WORLD)
"Jerusalem is the Light of the World. And who is the Light of Jerusalem? The Holy One, Blessed Be He."

YASIS (YOUR GOD WILL REJOICE)
Your God will rejoice over you as a groom rejoices over a bride.

Songs

Yisrael Betach Bashem (Israel, Trust in the Lord)

The *Midrash* (Midrash Tehilim Rabba, 31) says that having certainty and trust in the Creator brings protection and salvation.

Yisrael יִשְׂרָאֵל betach בְּטַח bashem בַּה׳, ezram עֶזְרָם umaginam וּמָגִנָּם hu הוּא.

anachnu אֲנַחְנוּ ma'aminim מַאֲמִינִים benei בְּנֵי ma'aminim מַאֲמִינִים,

ve'en וְאֵין lanu לָנוּ al עַל mi מִי lehishaen לְהִשָּׁעֵן,

ela אֶלָּא al עַל avinu אָבִינוּ shebashamayim שֶׁבַּשָּׁמַיִם.

Yitbarech Shimcha (May Your Name be Blessed)

An excerpt from *Birkat Hamazon* that helps to awaken appreciation for the Creator and bless his Name in any occasion and situation.

yitbarech יִתְבָּרַךְ shimcha שִׁמְךָ befi בְּפִי kol כָּל chai וָזִי tamid תָּמִיד le'olam לְעוֹלָם va'ed וָעֶד.

Ke'ayal Ta'arog (As the Hart is Longing)

An excerpt from Psalms 42:2-3 to help to awaken within us a desire and yearning for the Light. The *Zohar* says (Zohar Acharei Mot 208): "'As the hart' refers to the Congregation of Israel, namely *Malchut*. The words, "Longing after the water brooks," means to be watered by the water of the spring, referring to *Binah*, through the aid of the Righteous, namely *Yesod*. "So my soul longs for You, God," means to be watered by God in this world and in the World to Come.

ke'ayal כְּאַיָּל ta'arog תַּעֲרֹג al עַל afikei אֲפִיקֵי mayim מָיִם,

ken כֵּן nafshi נַפְשִׁי ta'arog תַּעֲרֹג elecha אֵלֶיךָ Elokim אֱלֹהִים.

tzam'a צָמְאָה nafshi נַפְשִׁי lelokim לֵאלֹהִים leEl לְאֵל chai חָי,

matai מָתַי avo אָבוֹא ve'erae וְאֵרָאֶה penei פְּנֵי Elokim אֱלֹהִים.

Yisrael Betach Bahashem (Israel, Trust in the Lord)
"Israel, trust in the Lord! He is their help and shield." (Psalms 115:9)
As we (Israel) are believers the descendants of believers and upon whom is it for us to rely? Upon our Father Who is in Heaven. (based on Babylonian Talmud, Tractate Shabbat 97:1 and tractate Sotah 49:1)

Yitbarech Shimcha (May Your Name be Blessed)
May Your Name be blessed by the mouth of all the living, continuously for all eternity.

Ke'ayal Ta'arog (As the Hart is Longing)
"As the hart is longing after the water brooks, so my soul longs for you, God My soul thirsts for God, for the living God When may I come and appear in God's presence?" (Psalms 42:2-3)

Ki Besimcha Tetze'u (For You Shall Go Out with Joy)

The *Zohar* (Zohar Bamidbar 26) says that Isaiah 55:12 speaks about the Final Redemption and the rejoicing at the time of going out from exile. As long as we are in exile we cannot call anything we experience as true happiness. When "the Holy One, Blessed Be He, comes and raises Her (*Kneset Israel*—the Congregation of Israel) from the dust... and They will join together, this will be the time called rejoicing. This will be happiness for everyone and certainly, 'you shall go out with joy.' Then many legions will go out to greet and receive the Matron to the joyous festivity of the King, as it is written: 'The Mountains and the hills shall break forth."

כִּי ki בְשִׂמְחָה vesimcha תֵצֵאוּ tetze'u וּבְשָׁלוֹם uvshalom תּוּבָלוּן tuvalun,
הֶהָרִים heharim וְהַגְּבָעוֹת vehagvaot יִפְצְחוּ yiftzechu לִפְנֵיכֶם lifnechem
רִנָּה rina, וְכָל vechol עֲצֵי atzei הַשָּׂדֶה hasade יִמְחֲאוּ yimchau כָף chaf.

Ki Hirbeta (Since You Have Given Much)

Excerpts from a poem *Shir Hayichud* that was written by Kabbalist Rav Shemuel son of Kelonimus the Elder (Germany, 12th century,) to help to remove our attribute of entitlement.

כִּי ki הִרְבֵּיתָ hirbeta טוֹבוֹת tovot אֵלַי elai, כִּי ki הִגְדַּלְתָּ higdalta
וְחַסְדְּךָ chasdecha עָלַי alai. וּמָה uma אָשִׁיב ashiv לָךְ lach,
וְהַכֹּל vehakol שֶׁלָּךְ shelach, לְךָ lecha שָׁמַיִם shamayim
אַף af אֶרֶץ eretz לָךְ lach. וַאֲנוּנוּ va'anachnu עַמָּךְ amcha וְצֹאנֶךָ vetzonecha,
וְחָפֵצִים vachafetzim לַעֲשׂוֹת la'asot רְצוֹנֶךָ retzonecha.

Ki Lishu'atcha (Because it is For Your Salvation)

The *Talmud* (Babylonian Talmud, Tractate Shabbat 31:1) says that one of the questions one is asked after leaving this world is if he or she has watched and waited for salvation. What is so special about watching and waiting for the salvation? Is salvation not something we are all watching and waiting for? The *Zohar* (Zohar Beshalach 249) says that one who watches and waits is what brings the salvation. These excerpts from the *Amidah* connection help us to maintain our certainty in the coming of the Messiah and the Final Redemption.

Ki Besimcha Tetze'u (For You Shall Go Out with Joy)

"For you shall go out with joy and be led forth in peace; the mountains and the hills shall break forth before you into singing and all the trees of the field shall clap their hands." (Isaiah 55:12)

Ki Hirbeta (Since You Have Given Much)

Since You have given much of Your goodness to me, since You have increased Your kindness upon me. What can I give back to you as all is (already) Yours; Yours is the Heavens also the Earth is yours. And we are Your nation and Your sheep, and we yearn to do your will.

Songs

hayom הַיּוֹם   kol כָּל־   kivinu קִוִּינוּ   lishu'atcha לִישׁוּעָתְךָ   ki כִּי

lishu'a לִישׁוּעָה: umetzapim וּמְצַפִּים

Kol Ha'olam Kulo (The Whole World)

This verse was written by Kabbalist Rav Nachman of Breslev (Ukraine, 18th Century) and helps us to overcome the fears that originate from the illusionary reality of this physical world.

me'od מְאֹד,   tzar צַר   gesher גֶּשֶׁר   kulo כֻּלּוֹ   haolam הָעוֹלָם   kol כָּל

kelal כְּלָל.   lefached לְפַחֵד   lo לֹא   veha'ikar וְהָעִקָּר

Kol Zeman (As Long)

During the 1960s, our teacher, the Rav, studied and communicated with his teacher, Kabbalist Rav Yehuda Tzvi Brandwein, through letters (as well as travelling to Israel to meet with him). In one of these letters the Rav made a commitment to his teacher with these words, which can help us connect to the Rav, and also assist us in having the ability to go the extra mile in our spiritual work.

ko'ach כּוֹחַ   yiten יִתֵּן   sheHashem שֶׁה'   zeman זְמַן   kol כָּל

nefesh נֶפֶשׁ:   uvimsirat וּבִמְסִירַת   kochi כֹּחִי   bechol בְּכָל   e'evod אֶעֱבוֹד

Lo Yisa (Nation Shall not Lift Up)

These words of the prophet Isaiah help us to remove hatred and war from the world and bring peace.

cherev וְרֶב   goy גּוֹי   el אֶל   goy גּוֹי   yisa יִשָּׂא   lo לֹא

milchama מִלְחָמָה: od עוֹד   yilmedu יִלְמְדוּ   velo וְלֹא

Lulei Toratcha (Unless Your Torah)

The *Zohar* discusses this verse (Zohar Acharei Mot 206-207): "All those who delight in the Torah need not fear anything." Then the *Zohar* asks: "What are my delights?" and answers: "The Torah, as the Torah is called delights… all those that toil in the Torah will merit to find delight in the righteous who drink of the stream, meaning *Binah*."

Ki Lishu'atcha (Because it is For Your Salvation)
Because it is for Your salvation that we have watched all day long.
Kol Ha'olam Kulo (The Whole World)
The whole world is a very narrow bridge, but the principle is not to fear at all.
Kol Zeman (As Long)
As long as the Creator gives forte I will work with all of my strength (even) by giving up of my soul.
Lo Yisa (Nation Shall not Lift Up)
"Nation shall not lift up sword against nation; neither shall they learn war anymore." (Isaiah 2:4)

לוּלֵי lulei תוֹרָתְךָ toratcha שַׁעֲשֻׁעָי sha'ashuai

אָז az אָבַדְתִּי avadti בְעָנְיִי ve'anyi.

LEMA'AN ACHAY VERE'AY (BECAUSE OF MY BROTHERS AND FRIENDS)

Regarding this verse, Rav Shimon explains that because of the affection the *chaverim* or "friends," have for each other and their desire to not be apart from one another, the Holy One, Blessed Be He, rejoices with them and will call peace upon them. And for their merit, peace will prevail in the world. (Zohar Acharei Mot 66)

לְמַעַן lema'an אַחַי achai וְרֵעָי vere'ai,

אֲדַבְּרָה adbara נָּא na שָׁלוֹם shalom בָּךְ bach. לְמַעַן lema'an בֵּית bet

ה' Hashem אֱלֹהֵינוּ Elokenu, אֲבַקְשָׁה avaksha טוֹב tov לָךְ lach.

LESHANAH HABA'AH (NEXT YEAR)

This verse is sung at the end of the *Seder* on the night of *Pesach,* as part of creating the certainty in the rebuilding of Jerusalem and the coming of the Messiah.

לְשָׁנָה leshana הַבָּאָה haba'a בִּירוּשָׁלַיִם birushalayim הַבְּנוּיָה habenuya:

MI HA'ISH (WHO IS THE MAN)

The *Midrash* (Midrash Vayikra Rabba 16:2) tells a story: There was a peddler who went from town to town calling out, "Who wants to buy the potion of life? When he arrived to the city of Tzipori, people started to gather around, and the Tana, Rav Yanai, among them. He thought, *let's see who is this forgery.* When Rav Yanai asked him to sell him the potion, the peddler said: "it is not for you or people in your level." When Rav Yanai urged him, he eventually opened the *Book of Psalms* and read: "Who is the man that desires life? ... Keep your tongue from evil, and your lips from speaking guile. Depart from evil, and do good; seek peace, and pursue it." When he finished, Rav Yanai said: "I have read these verses so many times, yet I never fully understood them until this peddler revealed their true meaning."

LULEI TORATCHA (UNLESS YOUR TORAH)
"Unless Your Torah had been my delights, I should have perished in my affliction." (Psalms 119:92)

LEMA'AN ACHAY VERE'AY (BECAUSE OF MY BROTHERS AND FRIENDS)
"Because of my brothers and friends, Because of my sisters and friends please let me ask please let me speak peace to you. For this is the House of the Lord (Hashem), I wish the best for you." (Psalms 122:8-9)

LESHANAH HABA'AH (NEXT YEAR)
Next year in rebuilt Jerusalem.

Songs

mi מִי ha'ish הָאִישׁ hechafetz הֶחָפֵץ chayim חַיִּים ohev אֹהֵב yamim יָמִים
lir'ot לִרְאוֹת tov טוֹב: netzor נְצֹר leshonech לְשׁוֹנְךָ mera מֵרָע
usfatecha וּשְׂפָתֶיךָ midaber מִדַּבֵּר mirma מִרְמָה sur סוּר mera מֵרָע
va'ase וַעֲשֵׂה tov טוֹב bakesh בַּקֵּשׁ shalom שָׁלוֹם verodfehu וְרָדְפֵהוּ:

Mi Shema'amin (He Who Believes)

Kabbalist Rav Aharon of Karlin (student of the Magid of Mezerich, Belarus, 18th Century) says that the meaning of Job 19:26, "in my flesh (as the word *mibesari*—in my flesh—מִבְּשָׂרִי is the abbreviations of "from the teaching of Rav Shimon bar Yochai—מִבִּתוֹרַת רַבִּי שִׁמְעוֹן בַּר יוֹחַאי") I shall see God," is that he who believes in Rav Shimon will be reinforced by Rav Shimon Bar Yochai, and as the Creator is God for everyone, so too, is Rav Shimon for everyone (Bet Aharon pg. 106-107).

mi מִי shema'amin שֶׁמַּאֲמִין berabi בְּרַבִּי Shimon שִׁמְעוֹן bar בַּר Yochai יוֹחַאי.
yesh יֵשׁ lo לוֹ chizuk וְחִזּוּק merabi מֵרַבִּי Shimon שִׁמְעוֹן bar בַּר Yochai יוֹחַאי.
keshem כְּשֵׁם shaHakadosh שֶׁהַקָּדוֹשׁ Baruch בָּרוּךְ Hu הוּא lakol לַכֹּל.
kach כָּךְ rabi רַ' Shimon שִׁמְעוֹן bar בַּר Yochai יוֹחַאי lakol לַכֹּל.
miMeron מִמֵּירוֹן im עִם rabi רַ' Shimon שִׁמְעוֹן
adonenu אֲדוֹנֵנוּ bar בַּר Yochai יוֹחַאי.

Melech Rachman (Compassionate King)

This verse is recited during the *Musaf* connection of *Pesach, Shavuot* and *Sukkot,* and also during *Tikkun Chatzot*. It helps us to awken mercy in the world.

melech מֶלֶךְ rachaman רַחֲמָן rachem רַחֵם alenu עָלֵינוּ.
tov טוֹב umetiv וּמֵטִיב hidaresh הִדָּרֶשׁ lanu לָנוּ.
shuva שׁוּבָה alenu עָלֵינוּ bahamon בַּהֲמוֹן rachamecha רַחֲמֶיךָ.

Mi Ha'ish (Who is the Man)

"Who is the man that desires life, and loves days, that he may see good therein? Keep your tongue from evil, and your lips from speaking guile. Depart from evil, and do good; seek peace, and pursue it." (Psalms 34:13-15)

Mi Shema'amin (He Who Believes)

He who believes in Rav Shimon Bar Yochai will be reinforced by Rav Shimon Bar Yochai. As the Holy One, Blessed Be He, is God to everyone so too is Rav Shimon Bar Yochai is for everyone. From Meron with Rav Shimon, (he is) our master, the son of Yocahi.

Melech Rachman (Compassionate King)

Compassionate King, have mercy upon us. Good and kind, seek us. Return for us with Your mass compassion.

MIMEKOMCHA (FROM YOUR PLACE)

Excerpts from the *Kedusha* of *Shabbat* connect us to the Final Redemption and the coming of the Messiah.

מִמְּקוֹמְךָ mimekomcha מַלְכֵּנוּ malkenu תּוֹפִיעַ tofi'a, וְתִמְלוֹךְ vetimloch
עָלֵינוּ alenu כִּי ki מְחַכִּים mechakim אֲנַחְנוּ anachnu לָךְ lach.
מָתַי matai תִּמְלוֹךְ timloch בְּצִיּוֹן beTziyon, בְּקָרוֹב bekarov בְּיָמֵינוּ beyamenu
לְעוֹלָם le'olam וָעֶד va'ed תִּשְׁכּוֹן tishkon. תִּתְגַּדֵּל titgadel וְתִתְקַדֵּשׁ vetitkadesh
בְּתוֹךְ betoch יְרוּשָׁלַיִם Yerushalayim עִירְךָ ircha, לְדוֹר ledor וָדוֹר vador
וּלְנֵצַח ulnetzach נְצָחִים netzachim. וְעֵינֵינוּ ve'enenu תִרְאֶינָה tir'ena
מַלְכוּתֶךָ malchutecha, כַּדָּבָר kadavar הָאָמוּר ha'amur בְּשִׁירֵי beshirei
עֻזֶּךָ uzecha, עַל al יְדֵי yedei דָוִד David מְשִׁיחַ meshi'ach צִדְקֶךָ tzidkecha:

MIN HAMETZAR (OUT OF MY DISTRESS)

Psalms 118:5 is recited before the blowing of the *Shofar* on *Rosh Hashanah*. The *Zohar* says (Zohar Beshalach 337): "Also, that prayer and that spirit should ascend and exit from the narrow strait in a straight path towards Jerusalem. For it is necessary to have a place that is narrow and tight to cast into it that spirit, so that it should not turn to the Right or to Left. Similar to this is the sound of the *Shofar* that is projected outward in a smooth, straight way from a narrow place, and it goes and splits Firmaments and ascends upwards to stimulate the spirit of Above."

מִן min הַמֵּצַר hametzar קָרָאתִי karati יָהּ Yah
עָנָנִי anani בַמֶּרְחָב vamerchav יָהּ Yah.

MOSHE EMET (MOSES IS TRUE)

The *Talmud* (Babylonian Talmud, Tractate Baba Batra 74:1) tells us that even though Korach and his followers were against Moses, claiming that Moses was a liar and his Torah a fabrication, when the land opened itself and swallowed them, they all regretted what they had done and repented. While they were descending into the earth, they recited this verse. Singing this verse gives us the power to admit our mistakes and correct them.

מֹשֶׁה Moshe אֱמֶת emet וְתוֹרָתוֹ vetorato אֱמֶת emet:

MIMEKOMCHA (FROM YOUR PLACE)
From Your place, our King, You will appear and reign over us, for we await You. When will You reign in Zion? Soon, in our days forever and ever, may You dwell there. May You be exalted and sanctified within Jerusalem Your city, from generation to generation and for all eternity. May our eyes see Your kingdom as it is said in the songs of Your might, written by David, Your righteous anointed.

MIN HAMETZAR (OUT OF MY DISTRESS)
"Out of my distress I called upon Yah. Patient Yah answered me in His expansiveness." (Psalms 118:5)

MOSHE EMET (MOSES IS TRUE)
Moses is true and his Torah is true.

Songs

NA'ALE (WE SHALL GO UP)

The *Zohar* (Zohar Vayikra 113-115) expresses the importance of singing (*renana*) in happiness: "Man should not stand before his Master in sadness but with gladness (*simcha*) and singing (*renana*)... for gladness is in the heart and singing in the mouth, and there is more perfection in the mouth (*renana*). The perfection of *Malchut* (the Illumination of *Chochmah* is revealed in Her in both stages: *simcha* and *renena*) is when this gladness is revealed and it is known. Such is the service of the Holy One, Blessed Be He."

נַעֲלֶה na'ale לְבֵית levet הַמִּקְדָּשׁ hamikdash,
בִּרְנָּה birnana נַעֲלֶה na'ale בִּרְנָּה birnana נִשְׁתַּחֲוֶה nishtachave.

OD YISHAMA (MAY THERE EVER BE HEARD)

Regarding this verse from the prophet Jeremiah, the *Talmud* says (Babylonian Talmud, Tractate Berachot 6:2): "He who does gladden a bride and a groom it is as if he restored (rebuilt) one of the ruins of Jerusalem," which represents the removal of the negative forces of destruction and helps to bring back the ruling of the positive forces of construction.

עוֹד od יִשָּׁמַע yishama בְּעָרֵי be'arei יְהוּדָה Yehuda
וּבְחֻצוֹת uvchutzot יְרוּשָׁלַיִם Yerushalayim, קוֹל kol שָׂשׂוֹן sason
וְקוֹל vekol שִׂמְחָה simcha קוֹל kol וְחָתָן vechatan וְקוֹל vekol כַּלָּה kala.

PITCHU LI (OPEN TO ME)

Rav Ashlag says (the Sulam commentary on Zohar Beresheet B, 340): Righteousness (*tzedek*) is *Malchut* and the Gates of Righteousness are the Judgments that prevent us from coming closer to Her (*Malchut*), unless we convert and transform them into "*sha'ar lahashem* or Gate for the Lord—שַׁעַר לַיהוה" (as יהוה is mercy and not Judgment) with actions of righteousness (and only then can we gain access through the Gate of the Lord (see also the Sulam commentary on Zohar, Prologue 120-124 and the Sulam commentary on Zohar Va'etchanan 72-77).

פִּתְחוּ pitchu לִי li שַׁעֲרֵי sha'arei צֶדֶק tzedek אָבֹא avo בָם vam אוֹדֶה odeh
יָהּ Yah: זֶה ze הַשַּׁעַר hasha'ar לַה' lahashem צַדִּיקִים tzadikim יָבֹאוּ yavo'u בוֹ vo.

NA'ALE (WE SHALL GO UP)
We shall go up to the Temple. With singing we shall go up, with singing we shall bow (before You).

OD YISHAMA (MAY THERE EVER BE HEARD)
"May there ever be heard in the cities of Judah and in the streets of Jerusalem voices of joy and gladness, voices of groom and bride." (Jeremiah 33:11)

PITCHU LI (OPEN TO ME)
"Open to me the Gates of Righteousness; I will go through them and give thanks to Yah. This is the Gate of the Lord; the righteous may go through it." (Psalms 118:19-20)

Songs

SHABECHI YERUSHALIM (PRAISE THE LORD, JERUSALEM)

According to the *Zohar* (Zohar Vayeshev 147), Jerusalem and Zion are not just physical places but actually code names for spiritual forces: "Here is the secret of the faith; for Zion constructs and beautifies the world, and the world is nourished by Zion from its two aspects, namely *Chochmah* and *Chasadim*. This is similar to the two grades that are one, namely Zion and Jerusalem; the former of Judgment and the latter of Mercy, and both are one. Judgment is issued from one, and Mercy is issued from the other." Rav Ashlag adds, "The Judgments go away because of the ruling of the Central Column and the *Mochin* illuminate in paths of Mercy and Judgment, which are in *Yesod* of *Nukva*; in the paths of Mercy, which is in Zion, *Chochmah* illuminates, and in the paths of Judgment, which is in Jerusalem, *Chasadim* illuminate."

These verses help balance the forces of Judgment and Mercy in our life. Moreover, it opens us to the Light so we can be worthy of Mercy, rather than Judgment, when the time comes for them to appear in our lives.

שַׁבְּחִי shabechi יְרוּשָׁלַם Yerushala'im אֶת et הֹ Hashem, הַלְלִי haleli
אֱלֹהַיִךְ Elokayich צִיּוֹן Tziyon: כִּי ki וְחִזַּק chizak בְּרִיחֵי berichei
שְׁעָרָיִךְ she'arayich, בֵּרַךְ berach בָּנָיִךְ banayich בְּקִרְבֵּךְ bekirbech:

SHOMER ISRAEL (GUARDIAN OF ISRAEL)

An excerpt from the *Slichot* connection activates the power of protection of the Creator. We are meant to fall and make mistakes, but when we are in the process of transformation and spiritual growth, we will not suffer from our mistakes.

שׁוֹמֵר shomer יִשְׂרָאֵל Israel שְׁמֹר shmor שְׁאֵרִית she'erit יִשְׂרָאֵל Israel,
וְאַל ve'al יֹאבַד yovad יִשְׂרָאֵל Israel הָאוֹמְרִים ha'omrim:
שְׁמַע shema יִשְׂרָאֵל Israel:

SHOMRIM (WATCHMEN)

An excerpt from one of the most ancient poems that was composed by Rav Yeni (Israel, 6th Century). *Vayehi bachatzi halayla* which is sang on the night of *Pesach* at the end of the *Seder*. This verse speaks about the protection of the Creator, during the day and specifically at night (time of darkness).

שׁוֹמְרִים shomrim הַפְקֵד hafked לְעִירְךָ le'ircha
כָּל kol הַיּוֹם hayom וְכָל vechol הַלַּיְלָה halayla.

SHABECHI YERUSHALIM (PRAISE THE LORD, JERUSALEM)
"Praise the Lord, Jerusalem, and laud your God, Zion,
for He has strengthened the bolts of your Gates and blessed your children within." (Psalms 147:12-13)

SHOMER ISRAEL (GUARDIAN OF ISRAEL)
Guardian of Israel: guard the remnant of Israel, don't let Israel be destroyed, those who say every day: 'Hear Israel.'

SHOMRIM (WATCHMEN)
Watchmen shall stand guard over your city all day and all night.

Songs

Shir Lama'alot (A Song of Ascents)

Rav Isaac Luria (the Ari) says (Pri Etz Chaim B, Gate of Shabbat 19): In this Psalms the word *shomer* or "protect" (or derivatives of it) appears six times and gives us protection in the physical world in all six directions: North, South, East, West, Up and Down.

shir שִׁיר lama'alot לַמַּעֲלוֹת esa אֶשָּׂא enai עֵינַי el אֶל heharim הֶהָרִים me'ayin מֵאַיִן yavo יָבֹא ezri עֶזְרִי: ezri עֶזְרִי me'im מֵעִם Hashem 'ה ose עֹשֵׂה shamayim שָׁמַיִם va'aretz וָאָרֶץ: al אַל yiten יִתֵּן lamot לַמּוֹט raglecha רַגְלְךָ al אַל yanum יָנוּם shomrecha שֹׁמְרֶךָ: hineh הִנֵּה lo לֹא yanum יָנוּם velo וְלֹא yishan יִישָׁן shomer שׁוֹמֵר Yisrael יִשְׂרָאֵל: Hashem 'ה shomrecha שֹׁמְרֶךָ Hashem 'ה tzilcha צִלְּךָ al עַל yad יָד yeminecha יְמִינֶךָ: yomam יוֹמָם hashemesh הַשֶּׁמֶשׁ lo לֹא yakeka יַכֶּכָּה veyare'ach וְיָרֵחַ balayla בַּלָּיְלָה: Hashem 'ה yishmorcha יִשְׁמָרְךָ mikol מִכָּל ra רָע yishmor יִשְׁמֹר et אֶת nafshecha נַפְשֶׁךָ: Hashem 'ה yishmor יִשְׁמֹר tzetcha צֵאתְךָ uvo'echa וּבוֹאֶךָ me'ata מֵעַתָּה ve'ad וְעַד olam עוֹלָם:

Simcha Le'artzecha (Gladness to Your Land)

An excerpt from the *Amidah* connection of *Rosh Hashanah* and *Yom Kippur* that awakens happiness and gladness in the world as it will be in the time of the coming of the Messiah.

simcha שִׂמְחָה le'artzecha לְאַרְצֶךָ, vesason וְשָׂשׂוֹן le'irecha לְעִירֶךָ, utzmichat וּצְמִיחַת keren קֶרֶן leDavid לְדָוִד avdecha עַבְדֶּךָ, va'arichat וַעֲרִיכַת ner נֵר leven לְבֶן Yishai יִשַׁי meshichecha מְשִׁיחֶךָ.

Shifchi (Pour Out)

The *Midrash* asks (Midrash Beresheet Rabba 2:4): "In the merit of what will 'the spirit of God' (the Messiah) eventually come?" And answers: "For the sake of that which 'hovered over the face of the waters,' meaning in the merit of *teshuvah* or "repentance," which is likened to water, as it is written: 'Pour out your heart like water'." These words of Jeremiah help us clear our heart of all negativity like pouring water from a bucket.

Shir Lama'alot (A Song of Ascents)

"A Song of Ascents: I lift up my eyes to the mountains; from where will my help come? My help is from the Lord, Creator of the Heavens and the Earth. He will not allow your legs to falter. Your Guardian shall not sleep. Behold: the Guardian of Israel shall neither slumber nor sleep. The Lord is your Guardian. The Lord is your protective shade at your right hand. During the day, the sun shall not harm you, nor shall the moon, at night. The Lord shall protect you from all evil; He will guard your soul. He shall guard you when you leave and when you come, from now and for eternity." (Psalms 121)

Simcha Le'artzecha (Gladness to Your Land)

Gladness to Your land and joy to Your city and flourishing of pride to David, Your servant, and preparation of a lamp for the son of Ishai, Your anointed.

shifchi שִׁפְכִי kamayim כַמַיִם libech לִבֵּךְ nochach נֹכַח penei פְּנֵי Hashem ה':

Tehe Hasha'a Hazot (May This Time Be)

An excerpt from the *Avinu Malkenu* connection recited during the time from *Rosh Hashanah* to *Yom Kippur*. The *Zohar* says (Zohar Terumah 546-547): "Here is the secret of the union... It is the place that is called Redemption, which is *Malchut* when joined with *Yesod*... When one brings together the blessing of *ge'ula* (Redemption) to the *Amidah* prayer, then it is a time of goodwill—עת רצון. A time of goodwill is also... the secret of the favor that becomes revealed from *Keter*, and they are combined together to become one... for when there is unity, Judgment joins and combines with Mercy and everything is sweetened, as it is written: 'A time of goodwill.' 'A time of goodwill' shows that everything, Judgment and Mercy, is combined together, that Judgment is sweetened at that time, and there is joy in everything."

tehe תְּהֵא hasha'a הַשָּׁעָה hazot הַזֹּאת she'at שְׁעַת rachamim רַחֲמִים ve'et וְעֵת ratzon רָצוֹן milfanecha מִלְּפָנֶיךָ.

Tefilah Le'ani (A Prayer of the Poor)

The *Zohar* says (Zohar Balak 187-192): "There are three that are considered a prayer: A prayer of Moses, a prayer of David, and a prayer of the poor. Which is the most important? One says, a prayer of the poor as this prayer takes priority over Moses' prayer, and is before David's prayer, and preempts all other prayers of the world." The *Zohar* asks: "What is the reason?" And replies: "Because the poor man is brokenhearted and it is written: 'The Lord is near to them who are of a broken heart.' As soon as the poor man says his prayer, the Holy One, Blessed Be He, opens all the windows of the Firmament, and all the rest of the prayers rising Above get pushed away by that destitute, broken-hearted man. There exists no other prayer in the world to which the Holy One, blessed be He, will give His immediate attention as [He does] to the poor man's prayer... Therefore, if a person makes himself poor and desires constantly to be poor, his prayer ascends and meets up with the poor's prayers. It joins up with them and rises together with them, and enters in combination with theirs. And it is received with willingness before the Holy King."

tefila תְּפִלָּה le'ani לְעָנִי chi כִי ya'atof יַעֲטֹף velifnei וְלִפְנֵי
Hashem ה' yishpoch יִשְׁפֹּךְ sicho שִׂיחוֹ: Hashem ה' shim'a שִׁמְעָה
tefilati תְּפִלָּתִי veshav'ati וְשַׁוְעָתִי elecha אֵלֶיךָ tavo תָבֹא:
al אַל taster תַּסְתֵּר panecha פָּנֶיךָ mimeni מִמֶּנִּי beyom בְּיוֹם tzar צַר li לִי:

Shifchi (Pour Out)
"Pour out your heart like water before the face of the Lord." (Lamentations 2:19)
Tehe Hasha'a Hazot (May This Time Be)
May this time be an hour of mercy and a time of acceptance before You.
Tefilah Le'ani (A Prayer of the Poor)
"A prayer of the poor; when he faints, and pours out his complaint before the Lord. Lord, Hear my prayer, and let my cry for help come to You." (Psalms 102:1-3)

Songs

HINENI BEYADECHA (I AM IN YOUR HANDS)

An excerpt from a prayer composed by Kabbalist Rav Meir Halevi (Oaptow Poland, 18th Century), as the opening to his book *Or Lashamyim* (Light to the Heavens). Kabbalist Rav Shlomo Hakohen (also known as the Tiferet Shlomo, Radomsko Poland, 19th Century) recited *Hineni Beyadecha* twice a day, and said that reciting it on a daily basis could bring success and sustenance. Singing *Hineni Beyadecha* strengths our clarity and certainty in understanding that our success is only because of the assistance and support of the Light of the Creator.

רִבּוֹן ribon הָעוֹלָמִים ha'olamim יָדַעְתִּי yada'ati
כִּי ki הִנְנִי hineni בְּיָדְךָ beyadecha לְבַד levad
כַּחוֹמֶר kachomer בְּיַד beyad הַיּוֹצֵר hayotzer.
וְאִם ve'im גַּם gam אֶתְאַמֵּץ et'ametz
בְּעֵצוֹת be'etzot וְתַחְבּוּלוֹת vetachbulot
וְכָל vechol יוֹשְׁבֵי yoshvei תֵבֵל tevel
יַעַמְדוּ ya'amdu לְהוֹשִׁיעֵנִי lehoshi'eni לִימִינִי limini
וְכִלְתְּמוֹךְ velitmoch נַפְשִׁי nafshi,
מִבַּלְעֲדֵי mibal'adei עֻזְּךָ uzecha וְעֶזְרָתְךָ ve'ezratcha,
אֵין en עֶזְרָה ezra וִישׁוּעָה vishu'a.

AHALELA (I SHALL PRAISE)

An excerpt from one of the more ancient songs of Simchat Torah that is sung while dancing with the Torah scrolls. Ahalela expresses our trust and certainty in the Creator.

אֲהַלְלָה ahalela אֱלֹהַי Elohai וְאֶשְׂמְחָה ve'esmecha בּוֹ vo,
וְאָשִׂימָה ve'asima תִקְוָתִי tikvati בּוֹ bo:
אֲהוֹדֶנּוּ ahodenu בְּסוֹד besod עַם am קְרוֹבוֹ kerovo,
אֱלֹהֵי Elohei צוּרִי tzuri אֱוֹסֶה echese בּוֹ bo:

HINENI BEYADECHA (I AM IN YOUR HANDS)
Master of the Universe, I know that I am solely in Your hands, like clay in the hands of the potter. And even if I will have all the advice and strategies, and all the people of the world will stand by my right side to save me, without Your power and help there is no support and salvation.

AHALELA (I SHALL PRAISE)
*I shall praise my God and be glad with Him, and place my hope in Him.
I shall thank Him in the counsel of His intimate people. My God, my Rock, in Him I will put my trust.*

Songs

KANFEI RU'ACH (WINGS OF SPIRIT)

The Zohar teaches (Prologue 216-217): "As a person labors in the study of the Torah, he is endowed with an additional holy soul.... If a person does not delve in the study of the Torah, he does not receive this holy soul, and the holiness of Above does not rest upon him. However, when he does study the Torah, he merits that living soul by his mouthing of the words of the Torah. Hence he becomes like the angels of Above. As it is written, 'Bless the Lord, you angels of His.' (Psalms 103:20) This refers to those who study the Torah and are called 'His angels' on Earth... And as far as the other world is concerned, we have learned that the Holy One, blessed be He, will provide them with '*wings like those of the eagles*' to allow them to meander around in all the worlds. As is written, 'But they that wait upon the Lord shall renew their strength; they shall mount up with wings as eagles.' (Isaiah 40:31)" Rav Ashlag explains (Zohar, Prologue 217) that "the Holy One, blessed be He, will provide them with wings like those of the eagles to allow them to meander around in all the worlds" means that they are meandering with their *thoughts* in all the Worlds and can see how the Creator, blessed Be He, rules the Worlds, which by doing so, not only are they protected from the negative side but they also receive more power to strengthen their certainty. The following words are an excerpt from Orot Hakodesh – the Holy Lights, part A, article 64 written by Kabbalist Rav Abraham Isaac Hakohen Kook (Jerusalem, 20th Century), and is based on the above mentioned verses from the Zohar. In this article Rav Kook, encouraged humankind to look at reality with spiritual eyes and see the beauty of Creation, since only then could humankind recognize their real powers (wings of powerful eagles) and rise upward in times of difficulty.

בֶּן ben אָדָם adam, עֲלֵה aleh לְמַעְלָה lema'ala עֲלֵה aleh.

כִּי ki כּוֹחַ ko'ach עָז az לְךָ lecha,

יֵשׁ yesh לְךָ lecha כַּנְפֵי kanfei רוּחַ ru'ach,

כַּנְפֵי kanfei נְשָׁרִים nesharim אַבִּירִים abirim,

אַל al תְּכַחֵשׁ tekachesh בָּם bam, פֶּן pen יְכַחֲשׁוּ yechachashu לְךָ lecha,

דְּרוֹשׁ derosh אוֹתָם otam דְּרוֹשׁ derosh בֶּן ben אָדָם adam,

וְיִמָּצְאוּ veyimatze'u לְךָ lecha מִיָּד miyad.

LEMA'ANCHA (FOR YOUR SAKE)

An excerpt from the Slichot connection of Arvit of Yom Kippur, which expresses the fact that the mercy the Creator bestows on us is beyond what we deserve, and awakens within us gratitude.

לְמַעַנְךָ lema'ancha אֱלֹקֵינוּ Elokenu עֲשֵׂה aseh וְלֹא velo לָנוּ lanu,

רְאֵה re'eh עֲמִידָתֵנוּ amidatenu, דַּלִּים dalim וְרֵקִים verekim.

KANFEI RU'ACH (WINGS OF SPIRIT)
Man, rise up, rise. For you have the strength to do so. You have wings of spirit, wings of powerful eagles. Do not deny them or they will deny you. Seek them and you will find them instantly.

LEMA'ANCHA (FOR YOUR SAKE)
For Your sake, our God, act, and not for ours, behold our [spiritual] position, pour and empty.

Songs

הַנְּשָׁמָה haneshamah לָךְ lach וְהַגּוּף vehaguf פָּעֳלָךְ pa'olach,
וְחוּסָה chusa עַל al עֲמָלָךְ amalach.

OCHILA LAEL (I SHALL PUT MY HOPE IN GOD)

An ancient poem recited by the prayer leader before he begins the main part of the Musaf prayer of Rosh Hashanah (the blowing of the *Shofar*) and Yom Kippur (the Work of the High Priest). This poem expresses the enormous spiritual responsibility of the prayer leader, who, therefore, asks for support and assistance not to fail with his words. Singing *Ochila LaEl* gives us similar assistance in our prayers.

אוֹחִילָה ochila לָאֵל laEl אֲחַלֶּה achale פָּנָיו panav.
אֶשְׁאֲלָה esh'ala מִמֶּנּוּ mimenu מַעֲנֵה ma'ne לָשׁוֹן lashon:
אֲשֶׁר asher בִּקְהַל bikehal עָם am אָשִׁירָה ashira עֻזּוֹ uzo.
אַבִּיעָה abi'ah רְנָנוֹת renanot בְּעַד be'ad מִפְעָלָיו mif'alav:
לְאָדָם le'adam מַעַרְכֵי ma'archei לֵב lev.
וּמֵהַשֵּׁם umeHashem מַעֲנֵה ma'ane לָשׁוֹן lashon:
הַשֵּׁם Hashem שְׂפָתַי sefatai תִּפְתָּח tiftach
וּפִי ufi יַגִּיד yagid תְּהִלָּתֶךָ tehilatecha:

ATITI LECHANENACH (I HAVE COME TO PLEAD BEFORE YOU)

An excerpt from an ancient poem written by Kabbalist Rav Shimon the Great (Germany, 10th century) that is said by the prayer leader before the repetition of Musaf of Rosh Hashanah that express the concept of approaching our prayers as a poor person with no sense of entitlement.

אָתִיתִי atiti לְחַנְנֶךָ lechanenach בְּלֵב belev קָרוּעַ karu'a וּמוּרְתָח umurtach,
בַּקֵּשׁ bakesh רַחֲמִים rachamim כְּעָנִי ke'ani בַּפֶּתַח bapetach
(גַּלְגֵּל galgel רַחֲמֶיךָ rachamecha וְדִין vedin אַל al תִּמְתַּח timtach).

The soul is Yours, and the body is Your handiwork, take pity on Your labor.
OCHILA LAEL (I SHALL PUT MY HOPE IN GOD)
I shall put my hope in God, I shall beseech His Presence;
I shall request of Him proper expression. So that, in the congregation of people,
I shall sing of His strength, that I can express joyous songs for the sake of His works.
It is for people to arrange their feelings, but from the Lord comes proper expression.
Lord open my lips and my mouth shall recite your praise.
ATITI LECHANENACH (I HAVE COME TO PLEAD BEFORE YOU)
I have come to plead before You, With a torn and burning heart
Pleading for mercy, like a poor man at the door. (Reveal Your Mercy, and do not mete out harsh Judgment.)

Mikolot Mayim Rabim (Mightier Than the Noise of Many Waters)

Zohar Chadash, (Bereesheet 509-512) explains that when God created the worlds, the waters were rushing about in all directions and were rising, They took the earth that was gathered within them and covered it. He told them, "This should not be so, gather to one place and let the dry land appear." Yet the waters rose and fell, sounding their voices to the end of the Heavens until God rebuked them and drove them into the deep. To this day their voice is not silent, and when they try to rise there, their strength fails them and they drop and do not leave because of their fear of the Lord's might. King David wrote, "The Lord on high is mightier than the noise of many waters, than the mighty waves of the sea. Your testimonies are very sure: holiness becomes Your house, Lord, for endless days."(Psalm 93:4-5) Rav Yitzchak explains, "David said, 'Master of the Universe, It is You who made the whole world. You made the water, and the waters were covering the whole world because of their massive magnitude. You arranged it so that they shrink and gather into one place. May it please You that Your *Shechinah* (holiness), which fills the entire universe, be constricted to fit into Your house, for endless days (and not for a limited time).'" Singing *Mikolot Mayim Rabim* brings serenity to the judgments in the world and awakens real longing for the *Shechinah* and the rebuilding of the Temple.

מִקֹּלוֹת | mikolot מַיִם mayim רַבִּים rabim
אַדִּירִים adirim מִשְׁבְּרֵי mishberei יָם yam
אַדִּיר adir בַּמָּרוֹם bamarom הַשֵּׁם Hashem:

Hashmi'ini et Kolech (Let Me Hear Your Voice)

In the Zohar (Pinchas 3-4) in the name of Rav Shimon: "This verse has in it the secret of wisdom. 'You that dwell in the gardens' refers to the Congregation of Israel that is Malchut, which is with Israel in exile and accompanies them in their troubles. '…the companions hearken for your voice…' refers to the camps of the higher Heavenly angels, all of whom listen to your voice, the voice of your praises in exile. Rav Shimon says, "'…let me hear your voice' refers to the voice of the friends who engage in Torah, for the Holy One, Blessed be He has only praise for those who engage in Torah…' It is as if all those who are privileged to engage in Torah at midnight and as the day begins to dawn, come with the Queen to welcome the King, grow stronger and take possession of the Shechinah. Moreover, a thread of grace hangs over such a one, as the sages have explained. Singing these words awakens and draws mercy to the world."

(יוֹנָתִי בְּחַגְוֵי הַסֶּלַע בְּסֵתֶר הַמַּדְרֵגָה הַרְאִינִי אֶת־מַרְאַיִךְ)
הַשְׁמִיעִנִי hashmi'ini אֶת־ et קוֹלֵךְ kolech
כִּי ki קוֹלֵךְ kolech עָרֵב arev וּמַרְאֵיךְ umar'ech נָאוֶה naveh:

Mikolot Mayim Rabim (Mightier Than the Noise of Many Waters)
"The Lord on high is mightier than the noise of many waters,
than the mighty waves of the sea." (Psalms 93:4)

Hashmi'ini et Kolech (Let Me Hear Your Voice)
(My dove in the clefts of the rock, in the hiding places on the mountainside, show me your face,)
let me hear your voice; for your voice is sweet, and your face is lovely. (Song of Songs 2:14)

Songs

Ve'afilu Behastara (Even in a Concealment)

It is written in the Torah (Deuteronomy 31:18): "And I will certainly hide my face in that day." Concerning this, Kabbalist Rav Nachman (Breslev 18th century) says (Likutei Moharan 56:3) "...even in a Concealment inside a Concealment, it is certain that the Lord, Blessed Be He is enclosed." Rav Ashlag elaborates (in his book "And You Shall Choose Life") that humankind experiences, perceives, and relates to the power of the Creator in this world in four stages, and the lower stage is called Double Concealment. In One Concealment, the second stage, we experience life with challenges and difficulties but with knowing that the Creator is there, somewhere. In Double Concealment, we experience all life as random, which can cause us to lose hope. In the third phase—One Revealment—we experience the good outcome of positive actions and the damaging outcome of negative actions. All these three levels are inevitable and are to prepare us to the fourth stage—Double Revealment, which is to achieve the complete, true, and Eternal Providence. Thus the purpose of Concealment is to give us space to toil and engage in the spiritual work out of free will. Every person must go through this transition, and complete it to be deserving of the Light of the Face of the King of Life. After a person has gained the Illumination of the Face, they become glad about all their prior experiences of bitter sufferings and troubles they have endured while experiencing Concealment because this Concealment has caused the Illumination of the Face of the Creator. All the sorrow and strife that caused them to lose self-control and fail—either by committing various errors in the aspect of the One Concealment or by committing intentional malicious actions in the aspect of the Double Concealment—are now transformed, and become a platform preparing them for doing the spiritual work and receiving a great and wonderful reward for all eternity. All past agony now becomes great joy, and all past evil is transformed into wonderful beneficence. Rav Ashlag says that this concept is analogous to a story concerning a trusted worker of a certain master, whom the master loved as himself. It happened once, that the master was travelling and appointed a deputy to handle his business. This person hated the trusted worker, and took him and thrashed him five times in public for all to see, to deeply humiliate him. The trusted worker went home crying and in pain, telling his wife all that had happened. When the master returned, the trusted worker told him all that had transpired. The master became very angry, and he called his deputy and commanded him to immediately hand out one thousand golden coins to the trusted worker for each time that he had struck him. The trusted worker returned home weeping again, and when his wife asked what had happened, he told her everything. She then asked, "So why are you weeping?" He answered, "I am crying because he only struck me five times. I wish he would have struck me at least ten times because then I would have gained ten thousand golden coins!" This song helps us to connect to true and eternal Providence in time of Concealment.

hahastara הַהַסְתָּרָה	shebetoch שֶׁבְּתוֹךְ	behastara בְּהַסְתָּרָה	ve'afilu וַאֲפִילוּ	
yitbarech יִתְבָּרֵךְ	Hashem הַשֵּׁם	nimtza נִמְצָא	sham שָׁם	gam גַּם	bevadai בְּוַדַּאי
hakashim הַקָּשִׁים	hadevarim הַדְּבָרִים	me'achorei מֵאֲחוֹרֵי	gam גַּם	
omed עוֹמֵד.	ani אֲנִי	alecha עָלֶיךָ	ha'ovrim הָעוֹבְרִים	

Hazor'im Bedim'ah (Those Who Sow With Tears)

Ve'afilu Behastara (Even in a Concealment)

Even in a concealment inside a concealment,
it is certain that even there the Blessed Be He, the Lord, is also found there.
Even through the hard times that befall you I stand (with you).

Psalms 126:5, written by King David expresses the concept that real reward comes through the challenges. This relates to a story in the Babylonian Talmud (Ta'anit 5a) that says, "In that year, although Adar (Pisces) had passed, no rain had fallen. It was not until the first of Nissan (Aries) that the first rain came down. Joel, the son of Pethuel, the prophet said to them, 'Go and sow.' They replied, 'If a man has a small measure of wheat or barley, should he eat them and keep himself alive or sow them and die?' He answered: "Despite this, go and sow.' Trusting the prophet they went and sowed. A miracle happened for them: "…the second rain came down on the fifth of Nissan (Aries); and on the sixteenth of Nissan (Aries) they offered the Omer. Thus came about that the grain that should have taken six months to ripen, ripened in eleven days. To this generation was applied the verse: "Those who sow with tears will reap with songs of joy."'" Singing this verse strengths our certainty in the Light of the Creator.

הַזֹּרְעִים hazor'im בְּדִמְעָה bedim'ah בְּרִנָּה berina יִקְצֹרוּ yiktzoru:

SHOSHANAT YAACOV (LILY OF JACOB)

An excerpt from a very ancient poem (from the era of the Men of the Great Assembly – 400 B.C.). It is recited right after the reading of the scroll of Esther in Purim. The kabbalists ask why the poet praises the pale blue color of Mordechai's clothing, and why seeing it arouse happiness? The Babylonian Talmud (Tractate Chulin, 89:1) says, "…pale blue similar to the sky, that is similar to the Throne of Honor—this similarity can awaken awe." The Zohar, Prologue 189 teaches that fear (Heb *Yir'ah*) motivates people to do good deeds in this world and there are three kinds of fear: fear of the negative consequences in the physical world; fear of the negative consequences in the spiritual realm. And fear that arouse admiration and inspiration of the Creator and His Creation. The pale blue represents the third type of fear. When it says that they saw the pale blue of Mordechai's clothing, this means they were influenced by it. And when people connect to the Creator from the right fear – *Yir'at Ha'oromemut*, which is the gate for all the good in the world (see Zohar, Prologue 123), it increases the happiness in all the Worlds.

שׁוֹשַׁנַּת shoshanat — יַעֲקֹב Yaacov — צָהֲלָה tzahala — וְשָׂמֵחָה vesamecha,

בִּרְאוֹתָם bir'otam — יַחַד yachad — תְּכֵלֶת techelet — מָרְדֳּכָי Mordechai.

תְּשׁוּעָתָם teshu'atam — הָיִיתָ hayita — לָנֶצַח lanetzach,

וְתִקְוָתָם vetivatam — בְּכָל bechol — דּוֹר dor — וָדוֹר vador:

בָּרוּךְ baruch — מָרְדֳּכַי Mordechai — הַיְּהוּדִי hayehudi:

ISH YEHUDI (A MAN FROM THE TRIBE OF YEHUDA)

HAZOR'IM BEDIM'AH (THOSE WHO TEARFULLY SOW)
Those who sow with tears will reap with songs of joy. (Psalms 126)
SHOSHANAT YAACOV (THE LILY OF JACOB)
Lily of Jacob thrilled with joy and exulted when they beheld Mordechai's pail blue.
You have always been their salvation, and their hope in every generation,
blessed be Mordechai the Judean.

Songs

A verse from the scroll of Esther. In the Writings of the Ari, (Gate of Meditations B, first article of Purim), Rav Isaac Luria (the Ari) says that the name Mordechai, is not only a name of a person who lived in Persia 2,500 years ago, it is also an expression for very special and unique Light, which is based on the Babylonian Talmud (Tractate Megilah 10:2). The Ari explains that the name Mordechai means "pure Light," which express the powerful Light the kabbalists call: Yesod of Abba. Mordechai is Light that has the power to eradicate the power of Amalek—the power of doubt—from the world. Singing this verse increases our certainty and removes doubts from our life.

ish אִישׁ yehudi יְהוּדִי haya הָיָה beShushan בְּשׁוּשַׁן habira הַבִּירָה
ushmo וּשְׁמוֹ Mordechai מָרְדֳּכַי ben בֶּן Ya'ir יָאִיר
ben בֶּן Shimi'i שִׁמְעִי ben בֶּן Kish קִישׁ ish אִישׁ Yemini יְמִינִי׃

ISH YEHUDI (A MAN FROM THE TRIBE OF YEHUDA)

A men from the Tribe of Juda was in Shushan the capital, whose name was Mordecai, the son of Jair, the son of Shimei, the son of Kish, a Benjamite.